Ocean Ships

Ocean Ships

David Hornsby

Ian Allan
PUBLISHING

Contents

First published 1964
This Edition 2004

ISBN 0 7110 3039 1

Published by Ian Allan Publishing

an imprint of Ian Allan Publishing Ltd, Hersham, Surrey KT12 4RG.
Printed by Ian Allan Printing Ltd, Hersham, Surrey KT12 4RG.

Code: 0405/C

Front cover: **Carnival Corp. (Cunard).** QUEEN MARY 2. *Cunard Line*

Back cover, top: **OMI Marine Services.** AMAZON. *Hans Kraijenbosch*

Back cover, bottom: **Vroon BV.** COLUMBIAN EXPRESS. *Hans Kraijenbosch*

Half-title page: **Knutsen OAS Shipping.** ANNA KNUTSEN. *Hans Kraijenbosch*

Title page: **Malaysian International Shipping.** BUNGA PELANGI. *Hans Kraijenbosch*

Below: **Saudi Arabian Oil.** LIBRA STAR. *Hans Kraijenbosch*

Preface

It is four years since the previous edition of *Ocean Ships* was published, during which time many changes have taken place in the shipping industry and many notable new vessels have been delivered. This new edition records over 250 passenger ships operating world-wide and over 5,000 cargo vessels (aggregating nearly 320 million tonnes deadweight) in service with companies based or operating deep-sea routes to the UK and northern Europe.

The delivery of *Queen Mary 2*, the first genuine 'liner' for a generation, set many new records, but an even larger cruise-ship has since been ordered and others are in the pipe-line. The take-over of P&O-Princess by Carnival (now selling under 12 'brands'), together with the continuing delivery of so many enormous vessels to the main cruise companies seems to be having a polarising effect on the cruise market. New cruising areas and markets are opening-up, but pressure is mounting on medium-sized companies, such as Festival and Royal Olympic, and many older vessels have disappeared to the breakers yards.

Massive growth continues in container shipping, not only in the size of new vessels, including orders for the first over 10,000 TEU (20-foot equivalent unit) capacity, but also the large numbers of 'post-panamax' vessels too long and too wide to transit the Panama Canal. An increasing trend has been for many shipping companies to charter newbuildings directly from management companies or German KG investment funds and in many cases these ships are now listed under the owners, rather than operators.

The decline in the number of tween-deck and part-container dry cargo ships owned or operated by the major companies has continued, the traditional 'reefer' market is still under pressure from even greater refrigerated capacity on container ships, but the bulk carrier and tanker sectors have remained stable.

As the result of the aftermath of 11 September, an increasingly litigious society and Health & Safety regulation, it is now increasingly difficult for enthusiasts to gain access to many UK ports, but in most locations there are still opportunities to see and photograph shipping, even if at a greater distance.

The greater availability of information on the internet has been a mixed blessing in the production of this new edition. Many previously used publications are now either a shadow of their former use or are web-based on subscription only to 'commercial' users at a cost which is uneconomic for enthusiasts. As for shipping company web-sites, don't believe everything you read, some are up to date and user-friendly, others not so, some provide great detail, others little of use. Wherever possible information is cross-checked against several sources, as there are instances where competing companies both claim to have the same vessel on charter, or 'pool' partners list different vessels being operated!

I again express my very grateful thanks to those who have provided their excellent photographs and to many friends, acquaintances and correspondents for their interest, comments and information. Finally, a great 'thank you' to my wife, who after seven editions of *Ocean Ships* and *Coastal Ships & Ferries* is now resigned to the chaos and stress as each new edition reaches 'copy' deadline!

David Hornsby
Southampton, England
March 2004

Disclaimer

The publishers, the shipping companies and the Author accept no liability for any loss or damage caused by error or inaccuracy in the information published in this edition of *Ocean Ships*.

Glossary

The companies in each section are listed in alphabetical order under the main company name, followed by the country of origin. Individual 'one-ship' owning companies are not given, but in some cases subsidiary fleets are separately listed. Other variations in ownership, joint ownership, management or charter are generally covered by footnotes. Funnel and hull colours are those normally used by the companies, although these may vary when a vessel is operating on a particular service, or on charter to another operator.

Name   registered name

all vessels are diesel motorships with a single screw; unless indicated as having more than one screw or other types of main propulsive machinery as follows

as	auxiliary sail
me	diesel with electric drive
gm	combined gas turbine and diesel with electric drive
gt	gas turbine with electric drive
st	steam turbine
swath	twin hull vessel with small waterplane area

Flag

Ant	Netherlands Antilles	Deu	Germany	Kwt	Kuwait	Qat	Qatar
Are	United Arab Emirates	Dis	Danish International	Lbr	Liberia	Rom	Romania
Atf	Kerguelen Islands	Ecu	Ecuador	Lka	Sri Lanka	Rus	Russia
Atg	Antigua and Barbuda	Egy	Egypt	Ltu	Lithuania	Sau	Saudi Arabia
Aus	Australia	Est	Estonia	Lux	Luxembourg	Sdn	Sudan
Bel	Belgium	Eth	Ethiopia	Lva	Latvia	Sgp	Singapore
Bgr	Bulgaria	Fin	Finland	Mex	Mexico	Swe	Sweden
Bhr	Bahrain	Fra	France	Mhl	Marshall Islands	Tha	Thailand
Bhs	Bahamas	Gbr	United Kingdom	Mlt	Malta	Tur	Turkey
Blz	Belize	Gib	Gibralter	Mmr	Myanmar (Burma)	Tuv	Tuvalu
Bmu	Bermuda	Grc	Greece	Mus	Mauritius	Twn	Taiwan
Bra	Brazil	Hkg	Hong Kong (China)	Mys	Malaysia	Ukr	Ukraine
Brb	Barbados	Hrv	Croatia	Nis	Norwegian International	Usa	United States of America
Brn	Brunei	Ind	India	Nld	Netherlands		
Can	Canada	Iom	Isle of Man (British)	Nor	Norway	Vct	St. Vincent and Grenadines
Che	Switzerland	Irl	Ireland	Pak	Pakistan		
Chl	Chile	Irn	Iran	Pan	Panama	Ven	Venezuela
Chn	China	Isr	Israel	Phl	Philippines	Vgb	British Virgin Islands
Cub	Cuba	Ita	Italy	Pmd	Madeira	Vut	Vanuatu
Cym	Cayman Islands	Jpn	Japan	Pol	Poland	Wlf	Wallis & Futura
Cyp	Cyprus	Kor	South Korea			Zaf	South Africa

Year	year of completion — not necessarily of launching or commissioning.
GRT	gross registered tonnage — not weight, but volume of hull and enclosed space — one gross ton equals 100 cu. ft.
DWT	deadweight tonnes — maximum weight of cargo, stores, fuel etc — one tonne (1000 kg) equals 0.984 ton (British)
LOA	overall length (metres); (- -) length between perpendiculars
Bm	overall breadth of hull (metres) - some vessels have greater width to superstructure/bridge etc.
Kts	service speed in normal weather and at normal service draught — one knot equals 6,050ft per hour or 1.146 mph.
Type	general description of type of vessel

B	bulk carrier	hl	heavy-lift vessel	R	refrigerated cargo
BC	bulk/container carrier	hls	heavy-lift / semi-submersible	RO	roll-on, roll-off
BO	bulk/oil carrier	L	livestock carrier	ROI	roll-on, roll-off/icebreaker
Bu	bulk carrier - self discharging	LC	lighter/containers	Rr	refrigerated with roll-on, roll-off
Bv	bulk/vehicle carrier	Lgc	liquefied gas carrier	T	tanker
Bw	bulk woodchip carrier	Lng	liquefied natural gas carrier	Tfj	tanker-fruit juice
C	general cargo	Lpg	liquefied petroleum gas carrier	Ts	storage tanker
Ca	cable layer	O	ore carrier	V	vehicle carrier
CC	cellular container	Obo	ore/bulk/oil carrier		
Co	cargo/part container	OO	ore/oil carrier		

Pass	maximum number of passengers in lower and upper berths or (—) in lower berths only
Remarks:	

ex:	previous names followed by year of change to subsequent name	len	date hull lengthened
		short	date hull shortened
l/a	name at launch or 'float-out'	wid	date hull widened
l/dn	name allocated when laid-down at commencement of construction.	NE	date re-engined
		teu	twenty-foot equivalent unit (one teu equals about 14 tonnes deadweight)
pt:	part of ship		

PART ONE

Passenger Liners and Cruise Ships

Name	Eng	Flag	Year	GRT	Loa	Bm	Kts	Pass	Former names

Arcalia Shipping Co. Ltd.

Portugal

Funnel: Yellow with light blue band, black top
Hull: White with blue band, blue boot-topping.

Name	Eng	Flag	Year	GRT	Loa	Bm	Kts	Pass	Former names
Arion	(m2)	Pmd	1965	5,888	117	17	18	312	ex Nautilus 2000-99, Astra I-99, Astra-96, Istra-91
Funchal	(m2)	Pmd	1961	9,563	153	19	14	442	
Princess Danae	(m2)	Pan	1955	9,783	162	21	17	497	ex Baltica-96, Starlight Princess-94, Anar-92, Danae-92, Therisos Express-74, Port Melbourne-72

Marketed under subsidiary Classic International Cruises or chartered out to other operators.

Carnival Corporation

USA

Carnival Cruise Line Inc.

Funnel: Red forward, blue aft, separated by white curved vertical band.
Hull: White with narrow red band, blue boot-topping.

Name	Eng	Flag	Year	GRT	Loa	Bm	Kts	Pass	Former names
Carnival Conquest	(me2)	Pan	2002	110,239	290	36	21	3,700	
Carnival Destiny	(me2)	Bhs	1996	101,353	272	36	21	3,336	
Carnival Glory	(me2)	Pan	2003	110,239	290	36	22	3,700	
Carnival Legend	(me2)	Pan	2002	85,942	293	32	22	2,680	
Carnival Miracle	(me2)	Pan	2004	85,600	293	32	22	(2,124)	
Carnival Pride	(me2)	Pan	2001	85,920	293	32	22	2,680	
Carnival Spirit	(me2)	Pan	2001	85,920	293	32	22	2,680	
Carnival Triumph	(me2)	Bhs	1999	101,509	273	36	21	3,470	
Carnival Victory	(me2)	Pan	2000	101,509	272	36	22	3,470	
Celebration	(2)	Pan	1987	47,262	223	28	19	1,896	
Ecstasy	(me2)	Bhs	1991	70,367	262	32	18	2,634	
Elation	(me2)	Pan	1998	70,390	262	32	20	2,634	
Fantasy	(me2)	Pan	1990	70,367	261	32	18	2,634	
Fascination	(me2)	Bhs	1994	70,367	262	32	18	2,624	
Holiday	(2)	Bhs	1985	46,052	222	28	22	1,794	
Imagination	(me2)	Bhs	1995	70,367	262	32	18	2,624	
Inspiration	(me2)	Bhs	1996	70,367	262	32	18	2,634	
Jubilee *	(2)	Bhs	1986	47,262	225	28	19	1,800	
Paradise	(me2)	Pan	1998	70,390	262	32	21	2,634	
Sensation	(me2)	Bhs	1993	70,367	262	32	20	2,634	
newbuildings									
Carnival Valor		Pan	2004	110,000	-	-	-	(3,000)	
Carnival Liberty		Pan	2005	110,000	-	-	-	(2,974)	

* to be transferred to subsidiary P&O Australia in 2004/5 and renamed Pacific Sun.

Costa Crociere SpA/Italy

Funnel: Yellow with blue 'C' and narrow black top.
Hull: White with blue line and blue boot-topping.

Name	Eng	Flag	Year	GRT	Loa	Bm	Kts	Pass	Former names
Costa Allegre	(2)	Ita	1969	28,430	188	26	20	924	ex Alexandra-90, Regent Moon-88, Annie Johnson-86
Costa Atlantica	(me2)	Ita	2000	85,619	292	32	22	2,680	
Costa Classica	(2)	Ita	1991	52,926	221	31	19	1,905	
Costa Europa	(2)	Ita	1986	53,872	243	30	19	1,773	ex Westerdam-02, Homeric-88
Costa Fortuna	??	Ita	2003	101,350	272	38		3,470	
Costa Marina	(2)	Ita	1969	25,558	174	26	20	1,025	ex Italia-90, Regent Sun-86, Axel Johnson-86
Costa Mediterranea	(me2)	Ita	2003	85,700	292	32	24	2,680	
Costa Romantica	(2)	Ita	1993	53,049	221	31	19	1,782	
Costa Tropicale	(2)	Ita	1981	33,250	205	26	19	1,411	ex Tropicale-01
Costa Victoria	(me2)	Ita	1996	75,166	253	32	23	2,200	
newbuilding									
Costa Magica		Ita	2004	101,350	272	38	-	3,470	
Un-named		Ita	2006	112,000	290	-	-	3,800	

Holland-America Line

Funnel: White with black/white ship symbol within double black ring, narrow black top or vents.
Hull: Black with red boot-topping.

Name	Eng	Flag	Year	GRT	Loa	Bm	Kts	Pass	Former names
Amsterdam	(me2)	Nld	2000	60,874	237	32	21	1,380	
Maasdam	(me2)	Nld	1993	55,451	219	31	20	1,629	
Noordam **	(2)	Nld	1984	33,933	215	27	21	1,340	

Arcalia Shipping. FUNCHAL. *F. de Vries*

Carnival Corp. (Carnival Cruise Line). CARNIVAL LEGEND. *Oliver Sesemann*

Carnival Corp. (Costa Crociere S.p.A.). COSTA ATLANTICA. *Hans Kraijenbosch*

Name	Eng	Flag	Year	GRT	Loa	Bm	Kts	Pass	Former names
Oosterdam	(gm2)	Nld	2003	85,920	292	32	24	2,272	
Prinsendam	(2)	Nld	1988	37,845	204	29	21	837	ex Seabourn Sun-02, Royal Viking Sun-99
Rotterdam	(me2)	Nld	1997	59,652	238	32	22	1,620	
Ryndam	(me2)	Nld	1994	55,451	219	31	20	1,629	
Spirit *	(2)	Bhs	1983	33,930	215	27	21	1,374	ex Nieuw Amsterdam-02, Patriot-02, Nieuw Amsterdam-00
Statendam	(me2)	Nld	1993	55,451	219	31	20	1,629	
Veendam	(me2)	Bhs	1996	55,451	219	31	20	1,629	
Volendam	(me2)	Nld	1999	60,906	237	32	22	1,824	
Zaandam	(me2)	Nld	2000	60,906	237	32	22	2,272	
newbuildings									
Westerdam	(gm2)	Bhs	2004	84,000	290	32	24	1,800	
Noordam	(gm2)	Bhs	2006	86,000	290	32	24	1,800	

* on10-year charter to Louis Cruise Lines and sub-chartered until 2006 to Thomson Holidays q.v.

** to be withdrawn November 2004 and to be renamed Thomson Celebration in 2005.

Windstar Cruises Ltd.

Funnel: White with turquoise symbol.
Hull: White with turquoise band and blue boot-topping.

Name	Eng	Flag	Year	GRT	Loa	Bm	Kts	Pass	Former names
Wind Spirit	(as/me)	Bhs	1988	5,736	134	16	11	150	
Wind Star	(as/me)	Bhs	1986	5,307	134	16	11	150	
Wind Surf	(as/me2)	Bhs	1989	14,745	187	20	15	453	ex Club Med 1-97, l/a La Fayette

Cunard Line Ltd./UK

Funnel: Red with two narrow black rings and black top.
Hull: Black with white band above red boot-topping.

Name	Eng	Flag	Year	GRT	Loa	Bm	Kts	Pass	Former names
Caronia *	(2)	Gbr	1973	24,492	191	25	21	670	ex Vistafjord-99
Queen Elizabeth 2	(me2)	Gbr	1969	70,327	294	32	28	1,850	
Queen Mary 2	(gm4)	Gbr	2003	148,528	345	41	28	2,800	
newbuilding									
Queen Victoria	(gm3)	Gbr	2007	85,000	290	32	24	1,850	

* sold to Saga Holidays Ltd. for delivery in 2005, new name not yet announced.

Seabourn Cruises Inc./USA

Funnel: White with three narrow white lines forming 'S' on blue shield and blue top.
Hull: White with pale blue band and blue boot-topping.

Name	Eng	Flag	Year	GRT	Loa	Bm	Kts	Pass	Former names
Seabourn Legend	(2)	Bhs	1992	9,961	135	19	16	212	ex Queen Odyssey-96, Royal Viking Queen-94, l/dn Seabourn Legend
Seabourn Pride	(2)	Bhs	1988	9,975	134	19	16	212	
Seabourn Spirit	(2)	Bhs	1989	9,975	134	19	16	212	

Operates as subsidiary of Cunard Line.

P&O Cruises Ltd./UK

Funnel: Yellow.
Hull: White with red boot-topping.

Name	Eng	Flag	Year	GRT	Loa	Bm	Kts	Pass	Former names
Adonia*	(me2)	Lbr	1998	77,499	261	32	19	2,342	ex Sea Princess-03
Artemis		See Royal Princess (Princes Cruises)							
Aurora	(me2)	Gbr	2000	76,152	270	32	24	1,878	
Oceana	(me2)	Gbr	1999	77,499	261	32	21	2,272	ex Ocean Princess-02
Oriana	(2)	Gbr	1995	69,153	260	32	24	2,108	
newbuilding									
Arcadia	(gm3)	Gbr	2005	85,000	290	32	24	1,968	l/dn Queen Victoria

* to be transferred to Princess Cruises in May 2005 and renamed Sea Princess

Ocean Village/UK

Funnel: Pink with multi-coloured 'ocean' on large white oval disc.
Hull: White with multi-coloured half rings above waterline

Name	Eng	Flag	Year	GRT	Loa	Bm	Kts	Pass	Former names
Ocean Village	(me2)	Gbr	1989	63,524	246	32	19	1,692	ex Arcadia-03, Star Princess-97, Sitmar Fairmajesty-89

Carnival Corp. (Holland-America Line). OOSTERDAM. *G. J. de Boer*

Carnival Corp. (Windstar). WIND SURF. *Hans Kraijenbosch*

Name		Eng	Flag	Year	GRT	Loa	Bm	Kts	Pass	Former names

P&O Cruises Australia Ltd./Australia

Funnel: Blue with small white 'Pacific' and large yellow 'Sky'.
Hull: White with broad blue above narrow yellow bands.

Pacific Sky	(st2)	Gbr	1984	46,087	240	28	21	1,600	ex Sky Princess-00, Fairsky-88

Jubilee to be transferred from Carnival Cruise Line 2004/5 and to be renamed Pacific Sun

Swan Hellenic/UK

Funnel: Dark blue with yellow swan symbol.
Hull: Dark blue with white band above red boot-topping.

Minerva II	(me2)	Mhl	2001	30,277	181	25	18	777	ex R Eight-03

On 3-year charter from CruiseInvest LLC, France (managed by Martinoli S.A.M., Monaco)

Princess Cruises Inc./USA

Funnel: White funnel with blue 'Princess' insignia with flowing hair, dark green top.
Hull: White.

Coral Princess	(gm2)	Bmu	2002	91,627	294	36	-	1,950	
Dawn Princess	(me2)	Gbr	1997	77,441	261	32	21	1,950	
Diamond Princess	(me2)	Lbr	2004	108,806	290	36	22	3,300	I/dn Sapphire Princess
Golden Princess	(me2)	Bmu	2001	108,865	290	36	22	3,209	
Grand Princess	(me2)	Bmu	1998	108,806	290	36	22	3,209	
Island Princess	(gt2)	Bmu	2003	91,627	294	36	-	2,590	
Pacific Princess	(me2)	Gib	1999	30,277	181	25	18	688	ex R Three-02
Regal Princess *	(me2)	Gbr	1991	70,285	245	32	19	1,900	
Royal Princess **	(2)	Gbr	1984	44,588	231	29	21	1,260	
Sea Princess		see Adonia (P&O Cruises)							
Star Princess	(me2)	Bmu	2002	108,977	290	36	22	3,211	
Sun Princess	(me2)	Gbr	1995	77,441	261	32	21	2,342	
Tahitian Princess	(me2)	Gib	1999	30,277	181	25	18	688	ex R Four-02
newbuildings									
Sapphire Princess	(me2)	Lbr	2004	108,800	290	36	22	3,300	I/dn Diamond Princess
Caribbean Princess		Bmu	2004	116,000				(3,100)	I/dn Crown Princess
Un-named			2006	116,000				(3,100)	

* To be transferred to Seetours late 2004.
** To be transferred to P&O Cruises in May 2005 and renamed Artemsis.

Seetours International/Germany

Funnel: White with 'AIDA' (letters in blue, red, yellow and green respectively).
Hull: White with colourful 'eye' graphics and blue wave symbols.

AIDAaura	(me2)	Gbr	2003	42,289	203	28	19	1,687	
AIDAblu	(me2)	Gbr	1990	70,285	245	32	19	1,900	ex A'Rosa Blu-04, Crown Princess-02
AIDAcara	(2)	Gbr	1996	38,531	193	28	18	1,186	ex Aida-01
AIDAvita	(me2)	Gbr	2002	42,289	202	28	19	1,582	

Subsidiary of Princess Cruises.
See also Transocean Tours

Peter Deilmann Reederei   Germany

Funnel: White with red 'D' outline containing insignia.
Hull: White with red band.

Berlin	(2)	Deu	1980	9,570	139	18	17	470	ex Princess Mahsuri-85, Berlin-82
Deutschland	(2)	Deu	1998	22,496	175	23	20	600	
Lili Marleen *	(as)	Deu	1994	704	76	10	8	54	

* operated by subsidiary Tall Ship Cruising.

Disney Cruise Vacations   USA

Funnel: Red with white 'Mickey Mouse' symbol over three black waves, black top.
Hull: Black with white band above red boot-topping

Disney Magic	(me2)	Bhs	1998	83,338	294	32	21	2,500	
Disney Wonder	(me2)	Bhs	1999	83,308	294	32	21	2,500	

Carnival Corp. (Princess Cruises). GOLDEN PRINCESS. *Phil Kempsey*

Carnival Corp (Seetours International). AIDACARA. *M. D. J. Lennon*

Name	Eng	Flag	Year	GRT	Loa	Bm	Kts	Pass	Former names

Festival Cruises

Greece

Funnel: *Blue with three reducing horizontal bands forming 'F' inside yellow ring.*
Hull: *White with narrow yellow above blue bands, blue boot-topping.*

Name	Eng	Flag	Year	GRT	Loa	Bm	Kts	Pass	Former names
Bolero *	(2)	Pan	1968	15,781	160	23	20	928	ex Starward-95
European Stars	(me2)	Fra	2002	58,625	251	29	21	1,566	laid down as European Dream
European Vision +	(me2)	Ita	2001	58,714	251	29	21	1,566	
Mistral	(me2)	Fra	1999	47,276	216	29	19	1,667	
The Azur *	(2)	Pan	1971	9,159	142	22	18	1,334	ex Azur 87, Eagle-75
Valtur Prima **	(2)	Ita	1948	16,144	160	21	18	566	ex Italia Prima-00, Italia I-93, Fridtjof Nansen-93, Volker-86, Volkerfreundschaft-85, Stockholm-60

*Company under pressure from mortgagors and * handed back to banks for disposal and + reported sold to Mediterranean Shipping Cruises.*
*** on 3-year charter from Compagnia di Navigazione N.I.N.A. SpA, Italy and operating as* **Caribe**

Hapag-Lloyd Cruises

Germany

Funnel: *Orange with blue 'HL'*
Hull: *White with orange/blue band, red boot-topping*

Name	Eng	Flag	Year	GRT	Loa	Bm	Kts	Pass	Former names
Bremen †	(2)	Bhs	1990	6,752	112	17	16	184	ex Frontier Spirit-93
C. Columbus **	(2)	Bhs	1997	15,067	145	22	18	423	
Europa	(me2)	Bhs	1999	28,437	199	24	21	408	
Hanseatic *	(2)	Bhs	1991	8,378	123	18	14	188	ex Society Adventurer-92
Sea Cloud ‡	(as2)	Mlt	1931	2,532	110	15	-	68	ex Sea Cloud of Grand Cayman-87, Sea Cloud-80, Antarna-79, Patria-64, Angelita-61, Sea Cloud-52, Hussar-35
Sea Cloud II ‡	(as2)	Mlt	2000	3,849	117	16	14	96	

* chartered from Hanseatic Cruises GmbH until 2008 and ** chartered from NSB Niederelbe Schiffahrts. GmbH & Co. KG.
‡ operated for Sea Cloud Cruises (managed by Hansa Shipmanagement GmbH or † operated by Radisson Seven Seas Cruises q.v.

Hoteles Marinos SA

Spain

Funnel: *White with horizontal red above blue narrow striped disc above blue base.*
Hull: *White with yellow band.*

Name	Eng	Flag	Year	GRT	Loa	Bm	Kts	Pass	Former names
Vistamar	(2)	Spn	1989	7,478	117	17	17	350	

operated by Plantours & Partner GmbH, Germany.

Louis Cruise Lines Ltd.

Cyprus

Funnel: *White with red sun/wave symbol above blue 'L', black top*
Hull: *White with blue band and red boot-topping.*

Name	Eng	Flag	Year	GRT	Loa	Bm	Kts	Pass	Former names
Ausonia *	(st2)	Cyp	1957	12,609	159	21	20	755	
Calypso	(2)	Bhs	1967	11,162	135	19	16	509	ex Regent Jewel-94, Sun Fiesta-93, Ionian Harmony-90, Durr-89, Canguro Verde-81
Princesa Cypria *	(2)	Cyp	1968	9,984	125	19	18	633	ex Asia Angel-88, Lu Jiang-88, Prinsesse Margrethe-85
Princesa Marissa	(2)	Cyp	1966	10,487	134	20	18	884	ex Prinsessan-87, Finnhansa-77
Princesa Victoria *	(2)	Cyp	1936	14,583	174	22	16	831	ex The Victoria-92, Victoria-77, Dunnottar Castle-58
Sapphire	(2)	Cyp	1967	12,263	149	21	16	562	ex Princesa Oceanica-96, Sea Prince V-95, Sea Prince-95, Ocean Princess-93, Italia-83
Serenade	(2)	Bhs	1957	14,173	162	20	16	757	ex Mermoz-99, Jean Mermoz-70
The Emerald **	(st2)	Grc	1958	23,428	178	26	20	960	ex Regent Rainbow-96, Diamond Island-92, Santa Rosa-90

* currently laid up or ** on charter to Thomson Cruises.
See also My Travel (Sun Cruises), Holland America (under Carnival Corp.) and Thomson Cruises.

Royal Olympic Cruises Ltd./Greece

Funnel: *Blue or white with yellow 'Byzantine' cross on blue diamond at centre of four narrow white rings.*
Hull: *White or light stone with blue or red boot-topping or blue with red boot-topping.*

Name	Eng	Flag	Year	GRT	Loa	Bm	Kts	Pass	Former names
Iason	(2)	Pan	1965	4,561	97	16	15	325	ex Jason-95, Eros-66
Odysseus	(2)	Grc	1962	9,821	146	19	16	486	ex Aquamarine-88, Marco Polo-78, Princesa Isabel-69
Olympia Explorer	(2)	Gib	2001	24,500	178	26	27	836	l/a Olympic Explorer

Festival Cruises. EUROPEAN STARS. *M. D. J. Lennon*

Hapag-Lloyd Cruises. EUROPA. *M. D. J. Lennon*

Louis Cruise Lines. CALYPSO. *G. J. de Boer*

Name	Eng	Flag	Year	GRT	Loa	Bm	Kts	Pass	Former names
Olympia Voyager	(2)	Grc	2000	24,391	180	26	28	836	ex Olympic Voyager-01
Triton	(2)	Grc	1971	13,995	148	22	24	912	ex Sunward II-91, Cunard Adventurer-77
World Renaisance	(2)	Grc	1966	11,429	150	21	18	536	ex Awani Dream-98, World Renaissance-95, Homeric Renaissance-78, Renaissance-77

Jointly owned by Louis Cruise Lines Ltd. and Potomianos family and all vessels under arrest or laid-up.

Mediterranean Shipping Cruises Italy

Funnel: *White with 'M' over 'SC'.*
Hull: *White with narrow blue band, blue boot-topping.*

Melody	(2)	Pan	1982	35,143	205	27	23	1,292	ex Starship Atlantic-97, Atlantic-88
Monterey	(st)	Pan	1952	20,046	172	23	16	661	ex Free State Mariner-56
MSC Lirica	(me2)	Pan	2003	59,058	251	29	-	2,200	
Rhapsody	(2)	Ita	1977	17,095	164	23	18	947	ex Cunard Princess-95, I/a Cunard Conquest
newbuilding									
MSC Opera	(me2)	Pan	2004	59,000	251	29	-	2,200	
Cruise ships (2)		Pan	2006/7	95,000	294	32	-	3,000	

Mitsui-OSK Lines KK Japan

Funnel: *Light red.*
Hull: *White.*

Fuji Maru	(2)	Jpn	1989	23,235	167	27	20	603	
Nippon Maru	(2)	Jpn	1990	21,903	167	24	18	607	

My Travel UK
Sun Cruises

Funnel: *Blue forward with white 'MY' symbol, separated by curved narrow white band from stern orange panel.*
Hull: *White with orange band and oval blue/orange 'My Travel' symbol, blue boot-topping.*

Carousel	(2)	Bhs	1971	23,149	194	24	21	1,194	ex Nordic Prince-95
Seawing *	(2)	Bhs	1971	16,710	163	23	21	750	ex Southward-95
Sunbird+	(2)	Bhs	1982	37,773	215	28	20	1,595	ex Song of America-99
Sundream **	(2)	Bhs	1970	22,945	194	24	20	1,196	ex Song of Norway-97

** chartered from Royal Olympic Cruises until 2006 (summer only) and ** being withdrawn from service September 2004.*
Vessels sold April 2004 for 2005 delivery to Louis Cruise Lines; +to be chartered to Thomson Cruises and renamed Thomson Destiny.

Nippon Yusen Kaisha Japan
Crystal Cruises Inc./USA

Funnel: *Black, large white side panels with blue symbol.*
Hull: *White with narrow blue band.*

Crystal Harmony	(me2)	Bhs	1990	48,621	241	30	22	960	
Crystal Serenity	(me2)	Bhs	2003	68,000	250	34	23	1080	
Crystal Symphony	(me2)	Bhs	1995	51,044	238	31	21	975	

Yusen Cruise/Japan

Funnel: *White with two red bands and black top.*
Hull: *White with blue boot-topping.*

Asuka	(2)	Jpn	1991	28,856	190	25	21	604	

Jointly owned by Asuka Ship Co., Japan

Oceania Cruises Monaco

Funnel: *White with 'O' symbol.*
Hull: *Dark blue.*

Insignia	(me2)	Mhl	1998	30,277	181	25	18	702	ex R One -03
Regatta	(me2)	Mhl	1998	30,277	181	25	18	684	ex Insignia-03, R Two-03

On charter from CruiseInvest LLC (Credit Agricole), France

Mediterranean Shipping Cruises. MSC LIRICA. *M. D. J. Lennon*

Oceania Cruises. REGATTA. *F. de Vries*

Name	Eng	Flag	Year	GRT	Loa	Bm	Kts	Pass	Former names

Fred Olsen & Co. — Norway

Funnel: White with red oval and white/blue houseflag.
Hull: White with green boot-topping.

Name	Eng	Flag	Year	GRT	Loa	Bm	Kts	Pass	Former names
Black Prince	(2)	Bhs	1966	11,209	142	20	18	451	ex Black Prince/Venus-87
Black Watch	(2)	Bhs	1972	28,670	205	25	18	902	ex Star Odyssey-96, Westward-94, Royal Viking Star-91
Braemar	(2)	Pan	1993	19,089	164	23	18	916	ex Crown Dynasty-01, Norwegian Dynasty-99, Crown Majesty-97, Crown Dynasty-97, Cunard Dynasty-97, Crown Dynasty-95

Pullmantur Cruises — Spain

Funnel: Blue or white with three red stripes on white disc.
Hull: White or very dark blue with red or white 'Pullmantur Cruises', red boot-topping.

Name	Eng	Flag	Year	GRT	Loa	Bm	Kts	Pass	Former names
Oceanic	(st2)	Bhs	1965	38,772	238	29	20	1,562	ex Starship Oceanic-98, Royale Oceanic-85, Oceanic-85
Pacific **	(2)	Bhs	1970	20,186	169	25	19	723	ex Pacific Princess-02, Sea Venture-75
R Five (Blue Dream) *	(me2)	Mhl	2000	30,277	181	25	18	777	
R Six (Blue Star) *	(me2)	Mhl	2000	30,277	181	25	18	777	
SuperStar Aries †	(2)	Bhs	1981	37,012	200	29	21	758	ex SuperStar Europe-99, Europa-99

* on short-term charter from CruiseInvest LLC, France (managed by Martinoli S.A.M., Monaco)
** chartered from Seahawk North America Inc., USA.
† newly purchased and to be renamed.

Radisson Seven Seas Cruises — USA

Funnel: White with blue 'harp' symbol or with brown curved symbols (Radisson Diamond)
Hull: White with blue band and blue waterline above red boot-topping.

Name	Eng	Flag	Year	GRT	Loa	Bm	Kts	Pass	Former names
Paul Gauguin **	(me2)	Fra	1997	19,170	156	22	18	320	
Radisson Diamond	(swath-2)	Bhs	1992	20,295	131	32	12	354	
Seven Sea Mariner	(me2)	Wlf	2001	48,075	216	29	19	769	
Seven Seas Navigator	(2)	Bhs	1999	28,550	171	24	17	550	l/dn Akademik Nikolay Pilyugin (1991)
Seven Seas Voyager	(me2)	Bhs	2003	41,500	200	29	19	769	

Formed with Radisson Hotel Corp., Mitsui O.S.K. Lines and others,
See also chartered vessels under Hapag-Lloyd AG, Germany and Societe Services et Transports (Club Mediterranee), France.
** operated by Compagnie Maritime de Croisieres (Societe Services et Transports), France.

Royal Caribbean International — Norway

Funnel: White with blue crown and anchor symbol.
Hull: White with blue band and blue boot-topping.

Name	Eng	Flag	Year	GRT	Loa	Bm	Kts	Pass	Former names
Adventure of the Seas	(me3)	Lbr	2001	137,276	311	39	22	3,840	
Brilliance of the Seas	(gt2)	Bhs	2002	90,090	294	32	24	2,500	
Empress of the Seas	(2)	Lbr	1990	48,563	211	31	19	2,284	ex Nordic Empress-04
Enchantment of the Seas	(me2)	Nis	1997	74,136	280	32	22	2,430	
Explorer of the Seas	(me3)	Lbr	2000	137,308	311	39	23	3,840	
Grandeur of the Seas	(me2)	Lbr	1996	73,817	279	32	22	2,440	
Legend of the Seas	(me2)	Lbr	1995	69,490	264	32	24	2,060	
Majesty of the Seas	(2)	Nis	1992	73,937	268	32	20	2,766	
Mariner of the Seas	(me3)	Bhs	2004	138,279	311	39	22	3,840	
Monarch of the Seas	(2)	Nis	1991	73,937	268	32	20	2,764	
Navigator of the Seas	(me3)	Bhs	2003	138,279	311	39	22	3,840	
Radiance of the Seas	(gt2)	Lbr	2001	90,090	293	32	24	2,500	
Rhapsody of the Seas	(me2)	Nis	1997	78,491	279	32	22	2,416	
Serenade of the Seas	(gt2)	Bhs	2003	90,090	293	32	24	2,501	
Sovereign of the Seas	(2)	Nis	1987	73,192	268	32	21	2,600	
Splendour of the Seas	(me2)	Nis	1996	69,130	264	32	24	2,066	
Vision of the Seas	(me2)	Bhs	1998	78,340	279	32	22	2,416	
Voyager of the Seas	(me3)	Bhs	1999	137,276	311	39	22	3,840	
newbuildings.									
Jewel of the Seas	(gt2)	Lbr	2004	90,090	293	32	24	(2,500)	

Olsen. BRAEMAR. *Hans Kraijenbosch*

Pullmantur Cruises. R SIX (BLUE STAR). *M. D. J. Lennon*

Radisson Seven Seas Cruises. SEVEN SEAS NAVIGATOR. *Hans Kraijenbosch*

Name	Eng	Flag	Year	GRT	Loa	Bm	Kts	Pass	Former names
Un-named		Bhs	2006	160,000	339	39	22	(3,600)	

Controlled by Anders Wilhelmsen & Co. AS q.v.

Celebrity Cruises/Greece

Funnel: *Black or black/white horizontal striped with large white diagonal cross (edged yellow on later vessels)*
Hull: *White with broad black band and black or blue boot-topping or dark blue with black boot-topping.*

Name	Eng	Flag	Year	GRT	Loa	Bm	Kts	Pass	Former names
Celebrity Xpedition		Ecu	2001	2,842	89	14	13	96	ex Sun Bay-04
Century	(2)	Lbr	1995	70,606	243	32	21	1,778	
Constellation	(gt2)	Bhs	2002	90,280	294	32	24	2,449	
Galaxy	(2)	Lbr	1996	76,522	260	32	21	1,896	
Horizon	(2)	Lbr	1990	46,811	208	29	19	1,798	
Infinity	(gt2)	Lbr	2001	90,228	294	32	24	2,449	
Mercury	(2)	Pan	1997	76,522	243	32	21	1,896	
Millennium	(gt2)	Lbr	2000	90,228	294	32	24	2,449	
Summit	(gt2)	Lbr	2001	90,280	294	32	24	2,449	
Zenith	(2)	Bhs	1992	47,255	208	29	21	1,774	

Island Cruises/UK

Funnel: *White with green, red and yellow 'palm tree' symbol.*
Hull: *White with 'palm tree' symbol on five coloured squares (three shades of blue and yellow)*

Name	Eng	Flag	Year	GRT	Loa	Bm	Kts	Pass	Former names
Island Escape	(2)	Bhs	1982	40,132	185	27	18	1,863	ex Viking Serenade-02, Stardancer-90, Scandinavia-85

Joint venture between RCCL and First Choice

Saga Holidays Ltd.   UK

Funnel: *Yellow with narrow white band below narrow dark blue top.*
Hull: *Dark blue with red boot-topping.*

Name	Eng	Flag	Year	GRT	Loa	Bm	Kts	Pass	Former names
Caronia				*acquired and chartered back to Cunard Line Ltd. until delivery in 2005, new name not yet reported.*					
Saga Pearl *	(2)	Bhs	1996	12,331	133	20	16	428	ex Minerva-02, I/a Okean
Saga Rose	(2)	Bhs	1965	24,528	189	24	20	587	ex Gripsholm-97, Sagafjord-96

managed by Columbia Shipmanagement Ltd., Cyprus
* on summer charter from Vlasov Group (V.Ships) until 2008 (remainder of year as Explorer II on charter to Abercrombie & Kent.)

Silversea Cruises Ltd.   Italy

Funnel: *White with plain and striped blue flags.*
Hull: *White.*

Name	Eng	Flag	Year	GRT	Loa	Bm	Kts	Pass	Former names
Silver Cloud	(2)	Bhs	1994	16,927	156	21	17	314	
Silver Shadow	(2)	Bhs	2000	28,258	182	25	21	388	
Silver Whisper	(2)	Bhs	2001	28,258	182	25	21	388	I/dn Silver Mirage
Silver Wind	(2)	Bhs	1995	16,927	156	21	17	296	

managed by V. Ships (Vlasov Group) q.v.

Sovcomflot AKP   Russia

Funnel: *White with blue band interupted with white 'F' partly edged red.*
Hull: *White with blue band, blue or red boot-topping.*

Name	Eng	Flag	Year	GRT	Loa	Bm	Kts	Pass	Former names
Maxim Gorkiy	(st2)	Bhs	1969	24,220	195	27	23	600	ex Maksim Gorkiy-92, Hanseatic-74, Hamburg-73

managed by Unicom Management Services (Cyprus) Ltd. and operated by Phoenix Seereisen GmbH, Germany.
See also Transocean Tours, Germany.

Star Clippers Ltd.   Monaco

Hull: *White*

Name	Eng	Flag	Year	GRT	Loa	Bm	Kts	Pass	Former names
Royal Clipper	(as)	Lux	2000	4,425	133	16	13	224	I/a Gwarek
Star Clipper	(as)	Lux	1992	2,298	112	15	12	194	
Star Flyer	(as)	Lux	1991	2,298	112	15	12	194	I/a Star Clipper

Royal Caribbean International. EXPLORER OF THE SEAS. *Phil Kempsey*

Royal Caribbean (Celebrity). CENTURY. *Hans Kraijenbosch*

Royal Caribbean (Island Cruises). ISLAND ESCAPE. *M. D. J. Lennon*

Name	Eng	Flag	Year	GRT	Loa	Bm	Kts	Pass	Former names

Star Cruise AS Sendirian Berhad — Singapore

Funnel: Dark blue with yellow eight-pointed star on broad red band.
Hull: White with red band and blue boot-topping.

Name	Eng	Flag	Year	GRT	Loa	Bm	Kts	Pass	Former names
MegaStar Aries	(2)	Pan	1991	3,264	82	14	16	82	ex Aurora II-94, l/a Lady Sarah
MegaStar Taurus	(2)	Pan	1991	3,264	82	14	16	82	ex Aurora I-94, Lady D-91, l/a Lady Diana
Star Pisces	(2)	Pan	1990	40,053	177	30	22	2,165	ex Kalypso-93
SuperStar Capricorn †	(2)	Pan	1973	28,288	205	25	18	1,022	ex Hyundai Kumgang-01, SuperStar Capricorn-98, Golden Princess-96, Sunward-93, Birka Queen-92, Sunward-92, Royal Viking Sky-91
SuperStar Gemini *	(2)	Pan	1992	19,093	164	23	19	916	ex Crown Jewel-95
SuperStar Leo **	(me2)	Pan	1998	75,338	269	32	24	(1,966)	
SuperStar Virgo	(me2)	Pan	1999	75,338	269	32	24	(1,960)	

* chartered from Neptun Maritime (51% controlled by Sea Containers group) and ** to be transferred to Norwegian Cruise Line subsidiary.
† reported sold to Viajes Iberojet SA, Spain.

Norwegian Cruise Line/Norway

Funnel: Dark blue with gold 'NCL' within gold square outline.
Hull: White with red stripe (Norwegian Dawn with multi-coloured artwork), or dark blue, blue boot-topping.

Name	Eng	Flag	Year	GRT	Loa	Bm	Kts	Pass	Former names
Independence	(st2)	Usa	1950	20,221	208	27	22	1,077	ex Oceanic Independence-82, Independence-74
Norway **	(st2)	Bhs	1961	76,049	316	34	18	2,565	ex France-79
Norwegian Crown	(2)	Bhs	1988	34,242	188	28	22	1,209	ex Crown Odyssey-03, Norwegian Crown-00, Crown Odyssey-96
Norwegian Dawn	(me2)	Bhs	2002	92,250	292	32	25	2,500	l/dn SuperStar Sagittarius
Norwegian Dream	(2)	Bhs	1992	50,764	230	29	18	2,100	ex Dreamward-98
Norwegian Majesty	(2)	Bhs	1992	40,876	207	28	19	1,800	ex Royal Majesty-97 (len-99)
Norwegian Sea	(2)	Bhs	1988	42,276	216	32	20	1,798	ex Seaward-97
Norwegian Star	(me2)	Bhs	2001	91,740	294	32	24	2,500	l/dn SuperStar Libra
Norwegian Sun	(me2)	Bhs	2001	78,309	258	32	20	2,359	
Norwegian Wind	(2)	Bhs	1993	50,760	230	29	21	2,100	ex Windward-98 (len-98)
Pride of Aloha	(me2)	Usa	1999	77,104	260	32	20	2,450	ex Norwegian Sky-04, l/a Costa Olympia
United States *	(st4)	Usa	1952	38,216	302	31	30	1,930	
newbuildings									
Pride of America	(me2)	Usa	2004	72,000	256	32	22	2,200	
Un-named	(me2)	Bhs	2005	93,000	292	32	24	2,400	
Un-named	(me2)	Bhs	2006	93,000	292	32	24	2,400	

* laid up pending rebuilding or ** pending machinery repairs.

Orient Lines/UK

Funnel: White with broad blue band above narrow white and red bands, black top.
Hull: Black with red boot-topping.

Name	Eng	Flag	Year	GRT	Loa	Bm	Kts	Pass	Former names
Marco Polo	(2)	Bhs	1965	22,080	176	24	20	850	ex Aleksandr Pushkin-91

Thomson Cruises — UK

Funnel: Pale blue with red logo.
Hull: White with blue over yellow over red bands, blue or red boot-topping.

Name									
The Emerald	*see under Louis Cruise Lines Ltd.*
Thomson Celebration	*see Noordam under Holland America Line.*
Thomson Destiny	*see Sunbird under My Travel (Sun Cruises)*
Thomson Spirit	*see under Carnival Corp. (Holland America) and on sub-charter from Louis Cruise Lines Ltd.*

Transocean Tours — Germany

Funnel: White with blue 't' symbol inside blue ring (*interupting pale blue over blue narrow bands).
Hull: White with pale blue over blue bands, red boot-topping.

Name	Eng	Flag	Year	GRT	Loa	Bm	Kts	Pass	Former names
Astor *	(2)	Bhs	1987	20,606	176	23	18	650	ex Fedor Dostoevskiy-95, Astor-88
Astoria **	(2)	Bhs	1981	18,591	164	23	18	540	ex Arkona-02, Astor-85

managed by Passat Shipmanagement Ltd., Cyprus
* chartered from Sovcomflot AKP, Russia to 2007 and ** from Seetours International, Germany (Carnival Corp-Princess Cruises) to 2010

Saga Holidays. SAGA PEARL. *M. D. J. Lennon*

Silversea Cruises. SILVER WHISPER. *M. D. J. Lennon*

Star Cruise (Norwegian Cruise). NORWEGIAN CROWN (in Orient Lines colours). *Hans Kraijenbosch*

Other Passenger Cruise Ships

Abercrombie & Kent

Name	Eng	Flag	Year	GRT	Loa	Bm	Kts	Pass	Former names
Explorer *		Lbr	1969	2,398	73	14	14	102	ex Society Explorer-92, Lindblad Explorer-85
Explorer II		*Seasonal charter - see Saga Pearl under Saga Holidays Ltd.*							

Owned by Explorer Shipping Corp., US and managed by V. Ships Inc., Monte Carlo.

Actinor Shipping ASA, Norway

Omar III	(2)	Pan	1972	18,455	172	24	21	882	ex Pongnae-03, Hyundai Pongnae-03, SuperStar Sagittarius-98, Sun Viking-98

Antarktika Joint Stock Co., Ukraine

Odessa	(2)	Vct	1974	11,889	136	22	16	482	ex Odessa I-01, Odessa-99, Copenhagen-75

China Sea Cruises, China

China Sea Discovery	(st2)	Lbr	1956	24,799	185	24	19	906	ex Fair Princess-00, Fairsea-88, Fairland-71, Carinthia-68

Clipper Cruise Line, USA

Clipper Adventurer *	(2)	Bhs	1975	4,376	100	16	17	116	ex Alla Tarasova-97
Clipper Odyssey	(2)	Bhs	1989	5,218	103	15	18	128	ex Oceanic Odyssey-98, Oceanic Grace-97
Yorktown Clipper **	(2)	Usa	1988	2,354	78	13	-	149	

** operated for part of year by Swiss-owned Kuoni Group and ** owned by New World Shipmanagement.*

Club Cruise, Netherlands

Albatros **	(2)	Bhs	1973	29,518	205	25	18	812	ex Crown-04, Norwegian Star I-02, Norwegian Star-01, Royal Odyssey-97, Royal Viking Sea-91 (len-83)
Van Gogh *	(2)	Vct	1975	15,402	156	22	22	640	ex Club Cruise I-99, Odessa Sky-98, Gruziya-95

** on charter to Travelscope or ** to Phoenix Seereisen, Germany.*

Compagnie des Isles, France

Le Diamant *	(2)	Fra	1974	8,282	124	16	16	265	ex Song of Flower-04, Explorer Starship-89, Begonia-87, Fernhill-74
Le Levant	(2)	Wlf	1990	3,504	100	14	16	95	

Also operates sail-cruise vessels La France and Le Ponant. * jointly operated with Tapis Rouge.

Conning Shipping Ltd., Hong Kong (China)

Columbus Caravelle	(2)	Bhs	1990	7,560	116	17	17	330	ex Sally Caravelle-91, Delfin Caravelle-91

Croatia Cruise Lines, Croatia

Dalmacija	(2)	Hrv	1964	5,619	117	17	17	312	

Cruise West, USA

Spirit of Oceanus	(2)	Bhs	1991	4,200	90	15	16	114	ex MegaStar Sagittarius-01, Sun Viva-00, Renaissance Five-97, Hanseatic Renaissance-92, Renaissance Five-91

Delphin Seereisen GmbH, Germany

Delphin *	(2)	Mlt	1975	16,214	156	22	21	554	ex Kazakhstan II-96, Byelorussiya-93
Delphin Renaissance †	(me2)	Mhl	2000	30,277	181	25	18	702	ex R Seven-03

* managed by Marine Trade Consulting GmbH, Germany.
† chartered from CruiseInvest LLC, France (managed by Martinoli S.A.M., Monaco)

Compagnie des Isles. LE DIAMANT. *M. D. J. Lennon*

Delphin Seereisen. DELPHIN RENAISSANCE. *J. M. Kakebeeke*

Name	Eng	Flag	Year	GRT	Loa	Bm	Kts	Pass	Former names

Di-Maio & Partners, Italy

Name	Eng	Flag	Year	GRT	Loa	Bm	Kts	Pass	Former names
Paloma I	(2)	Vct	1980	12,586	134	21	20	376	ex Dmitriy Shostakovich-00

on charter to Hansa Touristik and managed by PSM Shipmanagement, both Germany

Discoverer Reederei GmbH, Germany

Name	Eng	Flag	Year	GRT	Loa	Bm	Kts	Pass	Former names
World Discoverer	(2)	Gbr	1969	6,072	108	16	15	299	ex Dream 21-01, Delfin Star-97, Baltic Clipper-92, Sally Clipper-92, Delfin Clipper-90

EasyCruise Ltd., UK

Name	Eng	Flag	Year	GRT	Loa	Bm	Kts	Pass	Former names
Renaissance Two	(2)	-	1990	4,077	88	16	15	100	ex The Neptune-04, Renaissance Two-98

To be rebuilt 2004/5 to accommodate 180 'budget' passengers.

Elysian Cruises, USA

Name	Eng	Flag	Year	GRT	Loa	Bm	Kts	Pass	Former names
Elysian Flamenco	(2)	Bhs	1972	17,042	163	25	25	700	ex Flamenco-04, Southern Cross-97, Starship Majestic-95, Sun Princess-89, Spirit of London-74

Enchanted Islands Corp., Bahamas

Name	Eng	Flag	Year	GRT	Loa	Bm	Kts	Pass	Former names
Galapagos Explorer II	(2)	Lbr	1990	4,077	88	16	15	100	ex Renaissance Three-97

Operated by Canodros SA, Ecuador

Eurasia International, China

Name	Eng	Flag	Year	GRT	Loa	Bm	Kts	Pass	Former names
Golden Princess	(2)	Bhs	1967	12,704	158	20	22	725	ex Joy Wave-00, Oriental Pearl-99, Costa Playa-98, Pearl of Scandinavia-88, Innstar-82, Finlandia-78

Golden Sea Cruises, Greece.

Name	Eng	Flag	Year	GRT	Loa	Bm	Kts	Pass	Former names
Clelia II	(2)	Bhs	1990	4,077	88	15	15	84	ex Renaissance Four-96

Chartered by Classical Cruises.

Golden Star Cruises, Greece

Name	Eng	Flag	Year	GRT	Loa	Bm	Kts	Pass	Former names
Aegean 1	(2)	Grc	1973	11,563	141	21	-	650	ex Aegean Dolphin-96, Dolphin-90, Aegean Dolphin-89, Alkyon-86, Narcis-85

Goliat Shipping A/S, Norway

Name	Eng	Flag	Year	GRT	Loa	Bm	Kts	Pass	Former names
Island Sky	(2)	Lbr	1992	4,200	90	15	15	114	ex Renai II-03, Renaissance Eight-01
Island Sun	(2)	Lbr	1991	4,200	91	15	15	114	ex Renai I-03, Renaissance Seven-01, Regina Renaissance-98, Renaissance Seven-92

Operating as Maritius Island Cruises, Norway

Gute Bucher Fur Alle E.V. ("Good Books for All")/Germany

Name	Eng	Flag	Year	GRT	Loa	Bm	Kts	Pass	Former names
Doulos		Mlt	1914	6,804	130	17	13	-	ex Franca C-78, Roma-52, Medina-49
Logos II *	(2)	Mlt	1968	4,804	110	16	10	129	ex Argo-88, Antonio Lazaro-88

* owned by Educational Book Exhibits Ltd., UK.

Hebridean Island Cruises Ltd., UK

Name	Eng	Flag	Year	GRT	Loa	Bm	Kts	Pass	Former names
Hebridean Princess	(2)	Gbr	1964	2,112	72	14	14	49	ex Columba-89
Hebridean Spirit	(2)	Gbr	1991	4,200	91	15	15	79	ex Capri-01, MegaStar Capricorn-01, Sun Viva 2-00, Renaissance Six-98

Helios Shipping, Greece

Name	Eng	Flag	Year	GRT	Loa	Bm	Kts	Pass	Former names
Constellation		Vct	2002	2,842	89	14	13	96	ex Corinthian-04, Sun Bay II-03

Imperial Majesty Cruises, USA

Name	Eng	Flag	Year	GRT	Loa	Bm	Kts	Pass	Former names
Regal Empress	(2)	Bhs	1953	21,909	186	24	18	1,160	ex Caribe 1-93, Caribe-82, Olympia-82

International Shipping Partners Inc., USA

Name	Eng	Flag	Year	GRT	Loa	Bm	Kts	Pass	Former names
Big Red Boat II	(st2)	Bhs	1966	32,753	217	29	21	996	ex Edinburgh Castle-00, Eugenio Costa-97, Eugenio C-87
Enchanted Capri	(2)	Bhs	1975	15,410	156	22	21	650	ex Island Holiday-98, Arkadiya-97, Azerbaydzhan-96

Gute Bucher fur Alle. LOGOS II. *J. M. Kakebeeke*

Kristina Cruises. KRISTINA REGINA. *Hans Kraijenbosch*

Name	Eng	Flag	Year	GRT	Loa	Bm	Kts	Pass	Former names
Rembrandt *	(st2)	Bhs	1959	39,674	228	29	21	1,114	ex Rotterdam-97

* laid up and reported to move to Rotterdam in 2005 to be preserved as static hotel/exhibition centre under original name.

Japan Cruise Line, Japan

Name	Eng	Flag	Year	GRT	Loa	Bm	Kts	Pass	Former names
Orient Venus	(2)	Jpn	1990	21,884	174	24	21	626	
Pacific Venus	(2)	Jpn	1998	26,518	183	25	20	720	

Kristina Cruises Ltd., Finland

Name	Eng	Flag	Year	GRT	Loa	Bm	Kts	Pass	Former names
Kristina Regina		Fin	1960	4,295	100	15	-	353	ex Borea-87, Bore-77

Kyma Ship Management, USA

Name	Eng	Flag	Year	GRT	Loa	Bm	Kts	Pass	Former names
Mona Lisa *	(2)	Gbr	1966	28,891	210	27	21	720	ex Victoria-03, Sea Princess-95, Kungsholm-79
The Topaz **	(st2)	Pan	1956	32,327	195	26	20	1,050	ex Olympic-98, FiestaMarina-94, Carnivale-93, Queen Anna Maria-75, Empress of Britain-64

* On charter to Holiday Kreuzfahrten, Germany until 2007 and ** to Japanese operators as 'The Peace Boat'.

Lindblad Special Expeditions, USA

Name	Eng	Flag	Year	GRT	Loa	Bm	Kts	Pass	Former names
Endeavour		Bhs	1966	3,132	89	14	15	110	ex Caledonian Star-01, North Star-89, Lindmar-83, Marburg-82
Polaris	(2)	Ecu	1960	2,138	72	13	14	82	ex Lindblad Polaris-87, Oresund-81

Martinoli S.A.M., Monaco

Name	Eng	Flag	Year	GRT	Loa	Bm	Kts	Pass	Former names
Adriana	(2)	Vct	1972	4,490	104	14	16	312	ex Aquarius-87

see also vessels managed for CruiseInvest LLC, France chartered to Oceania Cruises, P&O/Swan Hellenic, Pulmantur and Transocean

Majestic International Cruises

Name	Eng	Flag	Year	GRT	Loa	Bm	Kts	Pass	Former names
Ocean Countess	(2)	Grc	1976	16,795	164	23	18	950	ex Olympia Countess-04, Olympic Countess-01, Awani Dream 2-98, Cunard Countess-96
Ocean Majesty *	(2)	Grc	1966	10,417	131	19	20	613	ex Homeric-95, Ocean Majesty-95, Olympic-95, Ocean Majesty-94, Kypros Star-89, Sol Christiana-86, Juan March-85
Ocean Monarch*	(2)	Pan	1955	15,833	162	21	17	500	ex Ocean Odyssey-02, Switzerland-02, Daphne-96, Akrotiri Express-74, Port Sydney-72
Ocean Explorer I	(st2)	Pan	1944	20,071	190	23	12	1,069	ex Sapphire Seas-98, Terrifica-92, Funtastica-92, Emerald Seas-92, Atlantis-72, President Roosevelt-70, Leilani-61, Laguardia-56, General W. P. Richardson-49

* on charter to Page & Moy Holidays, UK.

Med Queen Lines, Cyprus

Name	Eng	Flag	Year	GRT	Loa	Bm	Kts	Pass	Former names
Atalante	(2)	Cyp	1953	13,562	167	21	16	549	ex Homericus-91, Atalante-91, Tahitien-72

Operated by New Paradise Cruises, Cyprus.

Mercy Ships International

Name	Eng	Flag	Year	GRT	Loa	Bm	Kts	Pass	Former names
Africa Mercy		Mlt	1960	16,071	152	23	17	-	ex Ingrid-00, Dronning Ingrid-99
Anastasis	(2)	Mlt	1953	11,701	159	21	13	-	ex Victoria-78
Caribbean Mercy		Pan	1952	2,125	80	12	13	172	ex Polarlys-94

New Century Cruise Lines, Singapore

Name	Eng	Flag	Year	GRT	Loa	Bm	Kts	Pass	Former names
Leisure World	(2)	Bhs	1969	15,653	160	23	-	920	ex Continental World-93, Fantasy World-93, Asian World-92, Shangri La World-92, Skyward-91

NCV Expedition Cruises, Norway

Name	Eng	Flag	Year	GRT	Loa	Bm	Kts	Pass	Former names
Lofoten		Nor	1964	2,621	87	13	16	223	
Nordstjernen		Nor	1956	2,568	81	13	15	179	

Perosea Shipping Co., Greece

Name	Eng	Flag	Year	GRT	Loa	Bm	Kts	Pass	Former names
Sea Harmony	(2)	Bhs	1957	24,254	196	25	-	850	ex Regent Star-96, Rhapsody-86, Statendam-82

Reported sold for demolition.

Majestic International Cruises. OCEAN MAJESTY. *Tom Walker*

Mercy Ships International. ANASTASIS. *J. M. Kakebeeke*

ResidenSea. THE WORLD. *Hans Kraijenbosch*

Name	Eng	Flag	Year	GRT	Loa	Bm	Kts	Pass	Former names

ResidenSea Ltd., Norway

Name	Eng	Flag	Year	GRT	Loa	Bm	Kts	Pass	Former names
The World	(2)	Bhs	2002	43,188	196	29	18	656	

operated by Silversea Cruises Ltd and with accommodation comprising110 privately owned apartments and 88 guest suites

Salamis Lines (Hellas) Ltd., Cyprus

Name	Eng	Flag	Year	GRT	Loa	Bm	Kts	Pass	Former names
Salamis Glory	(2)	Cyp	1962	10,392	150	20	17	480	ex Regent Spirit-96, Morning Star-92, Constellation-92, Danaos-78, Anna Nery-78

SeaDream Yacht Club, Norway

Name	Eng	Flag	Year	GRT	Loa	Bm	Kts	Pass	Former names
SeaDream I	(2)	Bhs	1984	4,253	105	15	17	116	ex Seabourn Goddess I-01, Sea Goddess I-00
SeaDream II	(2)	Bhs	1985	4,260	105	15	17	116	ex Seabourn Goddess II-01, Sea Goddess II-00

Investment group formed by Atlye Brynestead, founder of Seabourn Cruises.

Shipping & General (UK) Ltd, UK

Name	Eng	Flag	Year	GRT	Loa	Bm	Kts	Pass	Former names
Discovery	(2)	Bmu	1972	20,216	169	25	18	689	ex Platinium-02, Hyundai Pungak-01, Island Princess-99, Island Venture-72

Chartered to UK-based Voyages of Discovery (summer) and Discovery Cruises (winter) until 2007.

Societe Services et Transports, France

Name	Eng	Flag	Year	GRT	Loa	Bm	Kts	Pass	Former names
Club Med 2	(as/me2)	Fra	1992	14,983	187	20	15	441	

Operated by Club Mediterranee; see also Radisson Seven Seas Cruises.

StarLine Cruises Ltd., Switzerland

Name	Eng	Flag	Year	GRT	Loa	Bm	Kts	Pass	Former names
Royal Star	(2)	Bhs	1956	5,067	112	16	15	276	ex Ocean Islander-90, City of Andros-84, San Giorgio-76

operated by Africa Safari Club

Tapias Naviera, Spain

Name	Eng	Flag	Year	GRT	Loa	Bm	Kts	Pass	Former names
Riviera I	(2)	Pan	1967	9,805	131	19	21	486	ex D. Juan-00, Crown del Mar-94, Las Palmas de Gran Canaria-88

On charter to Riviera Holiday Cruises, Mexico.

Unknown owner, Hong Kong

Name	Eng	Flag	Year	GRT	Loa	Bm	Kts	Pass	Former names
Macau Success		Bhs	1974	9,848	130	19	21	509	ex Omar II-04, Astra II-00, Golden Odyssey-94

Viking Cruises SA, Luxembourg

Name	Eng	Flag	Year	GRT	Loa	Bm	Kts	Pass	Former names
Viking Bordeaux	(2)	Pan	1960	3,008	88	14	18	180	ex Stella Maris II-98, Bremerhaven-65

World Explorer Cruises, USA

Name	Eng	Flag	Year	GRT	Loa	Bm	Kts	Pass	Former names
Lyubov Orlova *	(2)	Mlt	1976	4,251	100	16	17	206	operates as 'Marine Discovery'
Universe Explorer	(st2)	Pan	1958	22,162	188	26	23	715	ex Enchanted Seas-96, Queen of Bermuda-90, Canada Star-88, Liberte-87, Island Sun-85, Volendam-84, Monarch Sun-78, Volendam-75, Brasil-72

* chartered by Marine Expeditions

PART TWO

Cargo Vessels and Tankers

Name		Eng	Flag	Year	GRT	DWT	Loa	Bm	Kts	Type	Former names

Abu Dhabi National Tanker Co.

United Arab Emirates

Funnel: Black with yellow 'eagle' symbol on white square, narrow blue over white over red bands beneath narrow black top.
Hull: Black with grey boot-topping

Name	Eng	Flag	Year	GRT	DWT	Loa	Bm	Kts	Type	Former names
Al Dhabiyyah		Are	1983	19,245	32,055	178	28	15	T	
Al Dhibyaniyyah		Are	1984	34,240	57,211	232	32	14	T	
Arzanah		Are	1983	19,245	32,027	178	28	15	T	
Baynunah		Are	1983	34,240	57,211	232	32	14	T	
Diyyinah		Are	1983	24,699	38,602	193	30	16	T	
Umm Al Lulu		Are	1983	22,126	35,225	193	30	16	T	
Yamilah		Are	1983	19,245	32,042	178	28	15	T	

Owned by Abu Dhabi National Oil Co., which also controls National Gas Shipping Co. with 8 large Lng tankers

Aboitiz Jebsen Bulk Transport Corp.

Philippines

Funnel: Light blue with blue wavy line on broad white band.
Hull: Dark grey with red boot-topping

Name		Eng	Flag	Year	GRT	DWT	Loa	Bm	Kts	Type	Former names
General Delgado			Phl	1985	19,510	28,936	175	28	14	Co	ex Frederike Oldendorff-02, General Delgado-00, Lanka Aruna-92, General Delgado-89, Jebsen Napier-88
General Villa			Cyp	1985	19,510	29,152	175	28	14	Co	ex Lanka Asitha-91, General Villa-89, Jebsen Timaru-88
Rocknes *			Atg	2001	17,765	28,100	166	25	14	Bu	ex Kvitnes-03
Splittnes **	(2)		Pan	1994	9,855	16,073	148	21	14	B	ex Kari Arnhild-02
Sharpnes			Pan	1985	18,993	29,402	170	28	14	B	
Stones **			Atg	2001	17,357	28,115	166	25	14	Bu	
Surenes			Hkg	1985	18,977	29,319	170	28	14	B	ex Hawk-99, Western Hawk-99, Surenes-95
Trimnes *			Pan	1990	14,145	17,309	150	24	13	Bu	ex Express-96

Associated WG & A Philippines Inc., Philippines.
* operated by Beltships (Jebsens Management), including ** owned by Reederei Frank Dahl, Germany.

Christian F. Ahrenkiel GmbH & Co.

Germany

Funnel: Buff or buff with houseflag on blue band, or charterers colours.
Hull: Black, dark blue, green or grey with red boot-topping.

Name	Eng	Flag	Year	GRT	DWT	Loa	Bm	Kts	Type	Former names
Alicantia		Lbr	2000	26,047	30,850	196	30	20	CC	ex Commander-03, Jaguar Max-02
Amalia del Bene		Pan	1989	34,838	64,221	225	32	14	B	
Andalusia		Lbr	2001	26,047	30,703	196	30	20	CC	ex Centurion-03, Puma Max-02
Aquitania		Lbr	2000	26,044	31,000	196	30	21	CC	ex Maersk Aquitania-03, Corrado-03, Lion Max-02
Asturia		Lbr	2000	26,047	28,337	195	30	21	CC	ex Comanche-03, Ocelot Max-02
Bahamian Express		Mhl	2000	17,167	21,150	169	27	20	CC	
Carinthia		Lbr	2003	27,779	40,878	222	30	22	CC	
Cimbria		Lbr	2002	27,779	39,358	222	30	22	CC	
CMA CGM Greece		Lbr	2003	27,779	39,421	222	30	22	CC	ex Carpathia-04
CMA CGM Puma		Lbr	2000	19,131	24,973	189	27	22	CC	ex Scandia-03, P&O Nedlloyd Scandia-02, Scandia-02
CMA CGM Ukraine		Lbr	2003	27,779	39,418	222	30	22	CC	ex Cardonia-03
Columbus Australia		Lbr	1999	26,047	31,000	196	30	21	CC	ex Cherokee-03, Panthermax-02, CanMar Supreme-02, Panther Max-01
Cordelia		Lbr	2003	27,779	38,200	222	30	22	CC	
Franconia †		Lbr	1979	16,198	18,821	177	27	18	CC	ex Eagle Integrity-95, Sea Breeze-92, CMB Motion-91, European Senator-90, Franklin 1-87, TFL Franklin 86, Seatrain Bennington-80
Kersaint *		Lux	2001	23,232	37,263	183	27	14	T	
Magpie		Lbr	1999	23,843	35,930	183	27	14	T	
Masovia †		Lbr	1995	17,285	22,148	175	29	20	CC	
Melide		Lbr	1999	23,843	35,841	183	27	14	T	
Montania †		Deu	1996	17,287	22,148	175	29	20	CC	
Montreux		Lbr	1999	23,843	35,953	183	27	14	T	
Nordscot		Lbr	2001	23,740	35,770	183	27	14	T	
P&O Nedlloyd San Francisco		Lbr	1999	19,131	25,414	189	27	20	CC	ex Saxonia-99
Robin		Lbr	1999	23,843	35,966	183	27	14	T	
Samaria		Lbr	2000	19,131	25,360	189	27	20	CC	ex P&O Nedlloyd Samaria-03, Samaria-00
Scotia		Lbr	2000	19,131	25,414	189	27	20	CC	ex P&O Nedlloyd Scotia-02, Scotia-01

Aboitiz Jebsen Bulk Transport. SHARPNES. *J. M. Kakebeeke.*

Christian F. Ahrenkiel GmbH. ROBIN. *Hans Kraijenbosch.*

Christian F. Ahrenkiel GmbH. ST. KATHARINEN. *Hans Kraijenbosch.*

Name	Eng	Flag	Year	GRT	DWT	Loa	Bm	Kts	Type	Former names
Silvia		Lbr	2000	23,842	35,000	183	27	14	T	
St. Katharinen		Lbr	1999	25,202	43,760	182	30	14	T	
Tasman Trader		Tuv	1990	17,331	22,568	177	27	18	Co	ex El Dorado-01

newbuildings - four 25,000 grt 38,200 dwt (2,600 teu) container ships due for 2005/6 delivery from South Korean builder.
* managed by C.F.Ahrenkiel Shipmanagement (Rotterdam) BV and † owned by Constantia Schiffahrts GmbH, Germany

Alpha Ship GmbH Germany

Funnel: Green with wide light green and narrow light blue 'darts' on broad cream band or charterers colours
Hull: Green or brown with red boot-topping.

Name	Eng	Flag	Year	GRT	DWT	Loa	Bm	Kts	Type	Former names
Astor		Ant	1995	14,241	18,395	159	24	18	CC	ex APL Caracus-01, Astor-00, Infanta-97, I/a Astor
Cap Vincent		Ant	1998	23,722	29,240	194	28	21	CC	ex Neptun-02, Kota Perdana-00, Neptun-99
Castor		Ant	1997	14,241	18,445	159	24	19	CC	ex TMM Guadalajara-99, Castor-97
Columbus Waikato		Ant	1998	23,722	29,240	194	28	21	CC	ex Taurus-02, Kota Perabu-01, Taurus-99
Condor		Ant	1995	14,241	18,395	159	24	18	CC	ex TMM Chiapas-01, Condor-99, Recife-97, Condor-95
Maersk Hong Kong		Ant	1997	21,199	25,039	178	28	21	CC	ex Nadir-98
Maersk Itajai		Ant	2000	23,722	29,240	194	28	21	CC	ex Aries-01
Maersk Valparaiso		Ant	2000	23,722	29,240	194	28	21	CC	ex Maersk Wellington-01, Maersk Itajai-01, Vega-00
Mars		Ant	1996	14,241	18,449	159	24	19	CC	ex Sea Viking-99, CMBT Mars-97, CGM La Bourdonnais-97, Mars-96
Merkur		Ant	1996	14,241	18,447	159	24	19	CC	ex Sea Valiant-99, Merkur-97, CMBT Endeavour-97, Merkur-96
Orion		Ant	1997	21,199	25,107	178	28	21	CC	ex Maersk Lima-99, Orion-98, TNX Mercury-98, I/a Orion
Pegasus		Ant	1997	23,722	29,229	194	28	21	CC	
Pluto		Ant	1999	23,722	29,210	194	28	21	CC	
Pollux		Ant	1997	14,241	18,400	159	24	18	CC	
Safmarine Amazon		Ant	1998	21,199	24,049	178	28	21	CC	ex Maersk Wellington-01, Zenit-98
Safmarine Memling		Ant	1999	23,722	29,240	194	28	21	CC	ex SCL Memling-02, Poseidon-99
Saturn		Ant	1996	14,241	18,400	159	24	18	CC	ex TMM Leon-01, CMB Endurance-97, Saturn-96
Sirius		Ant	1998	21,199	25,107	183	28	21	CC	
Uranus		Ant	1999	23,722	29,240	194	28	21	CC	
Venus		Ant	1996	14,241	18,400	159	24	19	CC	ex CMBT Encounter-97, Venus-96

Angelicoussis Group Greece

Anangel Shipping Enterprises SA/Greece

Funnel: White with green 'trefilli' between two narrow red bands beneath black top.
Hull: Light grey, dark grey or blue with red boot-topping.

Name	Eng	Flag	Year	GRT	DWT	Loa	Bm	Kts	Type	Former names
Alpha Action *		Grc	1994	77,211	150,790	274	45	14	B	ex Action-02, World Action-02
Alpha Afovos *		Grc	2001	39,941	74,428	225	32	15	B	ex Anangel Afovos-01
Alpha Century *		Grc	2000	87,407	170,415	289	45	14	B	ex Anangel Century-02
Alpha Effort *		Grc	1999	38,564	72,844	225	32	15	B	
Alpha Era *		Grc	2000	87,407	170,387	289	45	14	B	ex Mineral Sakura-02
Alpha Flame		Grc	1999	38,852	74,545	225	32	14	B	ex United Support-04
Alpha Friendship *		Grc	1996	81,140	161,524	280	45	14	B	ex Anangel Friendship-02
Alpha Future *		Grc	1999	38,564	72,893	225	32	15	B	
Alpha Gemini *		Grc	1985	34,541	65,298	222	32	14	B	ex Ios-97
Alpha Happiness *		Pan	1999	38,564	72,800	225	32	15	B	
Alpha Harmony *		Grc	2001	39,941	74,492	225	32	14	B	ex Alpha Harmony I-02, Alpha Harmony-01
Alpha Melody		Grc	2002	39,941	74,374	225	32	15	B	I/a Anangel Melody
Alpha Millennium *		Grc	2000	87,407	170,415	280	45	15	B	ex Anangel Millennium-02
Anangel Ambition		Grc	1994	81,120	161,587	280	44	13	B	
Anangel Argonaut		Grc	1981	36,782	65,668	223	32	14	B	ex Thorsdrake-82
Anangel Bravery		Grc	1985	14,283	23,278	164	23	14	BC	ex Alpha Bravery-01, Anangel Leader-91
Anangel Dawn		Grc	1994	75,871	149,321	270	43	14	B	ex Stellar Era-01
Anangel Destiny		Grc	1999	87,523	171,997	289	45	15	B	
Anangel Dignity		Grc	1984	24,643	41,479	183	31	14	B	ex Sun Ray-86, Sanko Antares-86
Anangel Dynasty		Grc	1999	86,600	171,101	289	45	14	B	ex Yangtze Ore-02
Anangel Eagle		Grc	1983	20,432	34,070	178	27	14	B	ex Libexport-86
Anangel Enosis		Grc	1995	38,859	75,464	225	32	14	B	
Anangel Eternity		Grc	1999	86,600	171,176	289	45	14	B	ex Virginie Venture-02

Alpha Ship GmbH. ASTOR. *Hans Kraijenbosch.*

Angelicoussis Group (Anangel Shipping). ANANGEL ETERNITY. *N. Kemps.*

Name	Eng	Flag	Year	GRT	DWT	Loa	Bm	Kts	Type	Former names
Anangel Express		Grc	1982	34,407	61,537	223	32	14	B	ex Oak Sun-87
Anangel Galini		Grc	2002	39,941	74,374	225	32	15	B	
Anangel Innovation		Grc	2004	85,600	173,000	289	45	15	B	
Anangel Jupiter		Grc	1985	14,337	23,278	164	24	15	B	ex Alpha Jupiter-01
Anangel Legend		Grc	1996	81,151	161,059	280	45	14	B	ex Bavang-03
Anangel Loyalty		Grc	1995	38,131	71,550	224	32	14	B	ex Panagiotis A-02
Anangel Omonia		Grc	1996	38,859	73,519	225	32	14	B	
Anangel Power		Grc	1982	20,432	34,170	178	27	14	B	ex Libexpress-86
Anangel Pride		Grc	1993	81,569	161,643	280	45	13	B	
Anangel Progress		Grc	1989	36,781	69,406	225	32	13	B	ex Channel Express-89
Anangel Solidarity		Grc	1993	81,569	161,545	280	44	13	B	
Anangel Splendour		Grc	1993	81,120	161,643	280	45	13	B	
Anangel Success		Grc	1984	24,643	41,502	183	31	13	B	ex Sun Crest-86, Sanko Deneb-86
Anangel Venture		Grc	1989	36,781	69,406	225	32	13	B	ex Channel Enterprise-89
Anna L *		Grc	1984	22,215	38,213	188	28	14	B	ex Frangiscos C.K.-03
Annoula *		Grc	1997	36,559	70,281	225	32	14	B	
Antonis I. Angelicoussis		Grc	1989	36,986	69,346	225	32	13	B	ex Channel Endeavour-89
Maria A. Angelicoussi *		Grc	2001	86,201	169,163	289	45	15	B	I/a Fabulous
Sky L **		Grc	1979	10,274	17,199	146	21	14	C	ex Anangel Sky-02, Suncaribe-82, Anangel Sky-79
Victory L **		Grc	1979	10,274	17,188	146	21	14	B	ex Anangel Victory-02, Sunguajira-84, Anangel Victory-79, I/a Anangel Sky

newbuildings - 85,600 grt 173,000 dwt bulk carrier due for 2006 delivery from South Korean builder.
* owned by subsidiary Alpha Tankers & Freighters International Ltd and ** managed by Lomar Shipping & Management Inc., Greece.

Kristen Navigation Inc./Greece

Funnel: *Dark blue with dark blue disc on broad light blue band.*
Hull: *Black with red boot-topping.*

Name	Eng	Flag	Year	GRT	DWT	Loa	Bm	Kts	Type	Former names
Alpha Intelligence		Grc	1982	29,149	53,524	177	32	14	T	ex Anangel Intelligence-91, Award-86, Crown Award-84
Antonis I. Angelicoussis		Bhs	2000	156,758	306,085	332	58	15	T	
Astro Altair		Grc	1997	53,074	98,805	248	43	15	T	
Astro Antares		Grc	1996	53,074	98,876	248	43	15	T	
Astro Arcturus		Grc	1997	53,074	98,805	248	43	15	T	
Astro Callisto		Grc	1999	157,833	299,167	332	58	15	T	ex Picardie-03
Astro Canopus		Grc	1998	79,714	159,899	274	48	15	T	
Astro Capella		Grc	1998	79,714	147,998	275	48	15	T	
Astro Carina		Grc	2003	153,911	306,314	332	58	-	T	
Astro Cassiopeia		Grc	2003	83,000	159,000	274	48	15	T	
Astro Castor		Grc	2001	153,911	306,344	332	58	16	T	
Astro Centaurus		Grc	1995	156,565	300,294	332	58	15	T	ex Mindoro-00
Astro Challenge		Pan	2002	157,878	299,222	332	58	15	T	ex Maia-04, I/a Uvas
Astro Chorus		Grc	2001	159,016	305,704	332	58	16	T	ex Zeeland-03
Astro Corona		Grc	2003	153,911	305,870	332	58	-	T	
Astro Cygnus		Grc	2001	153,911	306,317	332	58	16	T	
Astro Leon		Grc	1992	153,427	285,771	328	57	15	T	ex Ambon-00
Astro Libra		Grc	1992	153,437	286,006	328	57	15	T	ex Irian-00
Astro Luna		Grc	1995	147,007	264,340	322	58	15	T	ex Tango-02, Diamond Iris-01
Astro Lupus		Grc	1989	137,893	257,589	321	57	15	T	ex Navix Seibu-00
Astro Lynx		Grc	1992	137,501	243,870	324	58	15	T	ex Cosmo Pleiades-00
Astro Lyra		Grc	1995	153,429	284,410	328	57	15	T	ex Flores-00
Astro Perseus		Grc	2004	80,620	158,982	274	48	15	T	
Astro Polaris		Grc	2004	85,000	159,460	274	48	15	T	
Astro Phoenix		Grc	2004	85,000	159,000	274	48	15	T	
Astro Saturn		Grc	2003	57,022	105,167	248	43	-	T	
Astro Sculptor		Grc	2003	57,022	105,108	248	43	-	T	
Astro Sirius		Grc	1996	53,074	98,805	248	43	15	T	
Elizabeth I. Angelicoussis		Grc	2004	83,000	159,000	274	48	15	T	
Front Vanadis *		Sgp	1990	153,413	285,872	327	57	14	T	ex Vanadis-00

newbuildings - three 159,000 dwt and three 306,000 dwt tankers on order for 2005/6 delivery, also two 95,000 grt Lng tankers.
* managed by Wallem Shipmanagement Ltd., Hong Kong.

Name	Eng	Flag	Year	GRT	DWT	Loa	Bm	Kts	Type	Former names

Atlanship SA   Netherlands

Funnel: *White with narrow red diagonal line aft of blue triagle.*
Hull: *Stone or white with red boot-topping.*

Name	Eng	Flag	Year	GRT	DWT	Loa	Bm	Kts	Type	Former names
Orange Blossom	Lbr	1985	9,984	15,108	145	22	-	Tj	
Orange Sky	Lbr	2002	22,063	26,863	172	27	14	Tj	l/a May Oldendorff
Orange Star	Lbr	1975	9,981	12,320	156	21	24	Tj	ex Fife-86, Andalucia Star-84
Orange Wave	Lbr	1993	13,444	16,700	157	26	18	Tj	

Seereederei Baco-Liner GmbH   Germany

Funnel: *Black with yellow/black 'bl' symbol on broad white band.*
Hull: *Blue with white 'BACO-LINER', red boot-topping.*

Name	Eng	Flag	Year	GRT	DWT	Loa	Bm	Kts	Type	Former names
Baco-Liner 1	Lbr	1979	22,345	21,801	204	29	15	LC	
Baco-Liner 2	Lbr	1980	22,345	21,801	201	29	14	LC	
Baco-Liner 3	Lbr	1984	22,528	21,771	204	29	14	LC	

Belships ASA   Norway

Funnel: *Blue with blue 'S' inside 'C' above blue anchor within narrow blue ring on white disc.*
Hull: *Blue or dark grey with red boot-topping.*

Name	Eng	Flag	Year	GRT	DWT	Loa	Bm	Kts	Type	Former names
Belgrace	Nis	1984	25,457	40,890	186	30	14	T	ex Nortank Baltic-93, Baltic Current-90, Tenryo Maru-87
Belgreeting *	Lbr	1987	25,865	43,549	197	30	14	Obo	ex Western Greeting-96, l/a Pacific Greeting
Belguardian *	Lbr	1987	25,865	43,434	197	30	14	Obo	ex Western Guardian-96, l/a Pacific Guardian
Belnor	Nis	1996	26,449	47,369	190	31	14	B	
Siri Phatra *	Tha	1985	25,865	43,467	186	30	14	Obo	ex Belgallantry-02, Western Gallantry-96, l/a Pacific Gallantary
Stove Campbell	Nis	1999	26,966	46,223	186	31	14	Co	ex Western Onyx-01
Stove Trader	Nis	1999	26,966	46,223	186	31	14	Co	ex Western Obelisk-01
Stove Tradition	Nis	1998	26,966	46,223	186	31	14	C	ex Western Opal-01
Stove Transport	Nis	1998	26,966	46,223	186	31	16	C	ex Western Olivin-01
Super Adventure	Pan	1996	17,977	28,630	172	27	14	B	ex IVS Super Adventure-03, Super Adventure-01
Super Challenge	Pan	1996	17,977	28,581	172	27	14	B	ex IVS Super Challenge-03, Super Challenge-02
Western Ondina	Pan	1996	26,449	47,639	190	31	14	B	

*Managed by Belships Management Singapore Pte. Ltd., Singapore or * by Chemikalien Seetransport GmbH, Germany.*

Western Bulk Shipping ASA

Funnel: *Dark blue with red 'WB' above red 'C' on broad white band, narrow black top.*
Hull: *Black or grey with white 'WESTERN BULK' red boot-topping.*

Name	Eng	Flag	Year	GRT	DWT	Loa	Bm	Kts	Type	Former names
Western Iris	Nis	1998	24,954	39,200	182	31	14	B	
Western Island	Nis	1998	24,954	42,527	182	31	14	B	
Western Muse	Pan	2001	28,097	48,913	190	32	14	B	ex Muse Venture-01
Western Tide	Pan	1995	25,968	45,406	186	30	14	B	ex Western Island-03, Western Tide-03
Western Trader ‡	Phl	2001	38,928	74,000	225	32	15	B	

Owned by Sjoinvest (40%) and Kistefos International (39%)
managed by Belships Management Singapore or ‡ time-chartered to Western Bulk Carriers Pool.

Beluga Shipping   Germany
Beluga GenChart/Netherlands

Funnel: *Buff with dark green 'G'.*
Hull: *Dark green with white 'GREENFLEET', red boot-topping.*

Name	Eng	Flag	Year	GRT	DWT	Loa	Bm	Kts	Type	Former names
Magdelena Green *	Nld	2001	11,894	17,520	141	22	15	Co	
Makiri Green *	Nld	1999	11,894	17,539	143	22	16	Co	
Margaretha Green	Gib	1999	11,894	17,539	143	22	16	Co	ex Nirint Voyager-02, Coral Green-01, Margaretha Green-00
Maria Green	Gib	1998	11,894	17,539	143	22	16	Co	
Marinus Green *	Nld	2000	11,894	16,000	143	22	16	Co	
Marion Green	Gib	1999	11,894	17,539	143	22	16	Co	

Name	Eng	Flag	Year	GRT	DWT	Loa	Bm	Kts	Type	Former names
Marissa Green *		Nld	2000	11,894	16,000	143	22	16	Co	
Marlene Green		Nld	2001	11,894	17,500	143	22	16	Co	

* managed by Clipper Elite Carriers (Clipper Group) q.v.

Bergshav Management AS   Norway

Funnel: Red with white 'B' and narrow white band beneath black top.
Hull: Brown with red or grey boot-topping.

Name	Eng	Flag	Year	GRT	DWT	Loa	Bm	Kts	Type	Former names
Berana		Pan	1985	43,733	83,890	229	32	14	T	ex Danita-00
Bergina		Pan	1982	77,704	134,089	265	49	14	T	ex Jarena-91
Bergitta		Nis	1999	56,207	105,641	239	42	14	T	
Berthea		Nis	1981	37,904	59,999	213	32	15	T	ex Polysunrise-90
Bertina		Nis	1982	39,673	65,979	236	32	14	T	ex Petrobulk Saturn-89, Kohyoh Maru-88
Bertora		Bhs	2001	55,796	100,257	238	42	14	T	
Bregen	(2)	Nis	1994	10,012	13,941	150	21	13	T	

Bibby Line Ltd.   UK

Funnel: Pink with black top or 'Stolt' colours.
Hull: Black or red with red or green boot-topping.

Name	Eng	Flag	Year	GRT	DWT	Loa	Bm	Kts	Type	Former names
Cheshire		Iom	1989	19,719	29,171	166	27	16	Lpg	
Lancashire		Iom	2002	22,902	26,616	174	28	16	Lpg	
Oxfordshire		Iom	1997	22,289	26,943	170	27	16	Lpg	
Stolt Dorset		Pan	1997	12,140	19,299	148	23	14	T	ex Botany Triumph-02
Stolt Kent		Iom	1998	12,141	19,125	148	23	15	T	

managed by Bibby-Harrison Management Services Ltd.

Blystad Shipping (USA) Inc.   USA

Funnel: Yellow with red 'B' on broad white band edged with narrow blue bands, narrow black top.
Hull: Black or red wih red boot-toping.

Name	Eng	Flag	Year	GRT	DWT	Loa	Bm	Kts	Type	Former names
Anella		Pan	1995	79,694	149,735	270	44	15	B	ex CIC Hope-03, Farenco-00
Anette		Lbr	1989	38,878	62,326	225	32	14	T	ex Annette-00, Nichian-00, World S-95,
										World Shanghai-95, I/a Cabo de Homos
Anja		Pan	1993	77,090	149,394	270	43	13	B	ex Chou Shan-03
Team Actinia *		Cyp	1993	22,633	40,296	176	32	14	T	ex Actinia-00
Team Anemonia *		Cyp	1995	22,633	40,296	176	32	14	T	ex Anemonia-00
Team Aniara		Lbr	1985	25,362	40,738	178	32	14	T	ex Aniara-03, Levant-89, Avanti-88
Team Anmaj		Lbr	1988	27,736	44,773	178	30	14	T	ex Anmaj-03, Galahad-97
Team Jupiter **		Nis	2000	27,185	48,338	182	32	14	T	
Team Mars		Nis	1982	21,057	42,010	184	30	14	T	ex Team Troma-98, Troma-82
Team Merkur		Nis	1981	24,330	41,985	184	30	14	T	ex Team Frosta-98, Frosta-82
Team Neptun **		Nis	2000	27,185	48,309	182	32	14	T	
Team Saturn		Nis	1987	24,653	45,831	186	30	14	T	ex Team Hada-98

newbuildings : Four 46,000 dwt tankers on order for 2004-6 delivery.
Norwegian subsidiary Team Tankers AS (acquired 9/2001) normally has 10-15 additional chartered vessels in operating pool.
** owned by Consultores de Navegacion SA, Spain or ** by Chemikalien Seetransport GmbH, Germany.*

Aug. Bolten Wm. Miller's Nachfolger GmbH & Co.   Germany

Funnel: Black with black 'B' over red diagonal crosses on white houseflag or * black 'L' on blue-edged white disc at centre of blue diagonal crossed and edged
          houseflag on broad white band.
Hull: Black with red boot-topping.

Name	Eng	Flag	Year	GRT	DWT	Loa	Bm	Kts	Type	Former names
Andros		Cyp	1996	14,599	24,279	157	26	-	B	ex Sea Wisdom-03
Delos *		Cyp	1997	15,888	24,000	160	26	16	B	ex Sea Master-01
Dorothea		Cyp	1984	13,021	22,025	155	23	14	B	ex Garnet Star-94
Elisabeth Bolten		Lbr	2001	10,132	13,275	127	21	14	Co	
Evelyn		Cyp	1983	12,866	21,373	153	24	13	B	ex Oriental Angel-93
Marielle Bolten		Lbr	1997	19,354	29,538	181	26	14	Co	
Milos *		Cyp	1997	14,397	24,045	154	26	13	B	ex Pacific Trader-03
Natalie Bolten		Lbr	2001	10,132	13,275	127	21	14	Co	
Paros *		Cyp	1997	14,397	23,984	154	26	14	B	ex Pacific Bridge-03

Atlanship SA. ORANGE WAVE. *G. J. de Boer.*

Beluga Shipping. MARION GREEN. *F. de Vries.*

Bibby Line Ltd. STOLT KENT. *Hans Kraijenbosch.*

Name	Eng	Flag	Year	GRT	DWT	Loa	Bm	Kts	Type	Former names
Santorin II *		Cyp	1984	14,147	23,899	160	24	14	B	ex Cynthia No. 5-93, Jovian Lark-90, Sanko Melody-85
Sigrun Bolten		Lbr	1997	19,354	29,538	181	26	14	Co	ex Cielo di Savona-01. Sigrun Bolten-97
Tinos *		Cyp	1995	14,431	23,725	151	26	13	B	ex Bright Nextage-03
William		Cyp	1995	15,164	23,829	153	26	14	B	ex Pacific Rainbow II-01

* owned by subsidiary Lydia Shipping Co. S.A., Greece.

A/S Borgestad ASA

Norway

Funnel: Dark blue with dark blue 'B' on white shield overlapping white band or * white with red 'W' symbol.
Hull: Grey, orange or * green with red boot-topping.

Name	Eng	Flag	Year	GRT	DWT	Loa	Bm	Kts	Type	Former names
Breeze Arrow		Nis	1992	29,369	46,908	199	31	15	BC	ex Westwood Breeze-03, Saga Breeze-98
Westwood Anette *		Bhs	1987	28,805	45,252	200	31	15	BC	
Westwood Borg		Nis	1992	29,369	46,998	199	31	15	BC	ex Spero-98, Saga Ocean-95
Westwood Bridge		Nis	1992	29,369	46,956	199	31	15	BC	ex Saga River-03, Sea River-92
Westwood Cascade *		Bhs	2004	32,500	45,000	200	31	17	BC	
Westwood Columbia *		Bhs	2002	32,551	45,000	200	31	17	BC	
Westwood Fraser *		Bhs	2004	32,500	45,000	200	31	17	BC	
Westwood Marianne *		Bhs	1986	28,805	45,252	200	31	15	BC	
Westwood Olympia *		Bhs	2004	32,500	45,000	200	31	17	BC	
Westwood Robson *		Bhs	2004	32,500	45,000	200	31	17	BC	
Westwood Rainier *		Bhs	2002	32,551	45,000	200	31	17	BC	
Westwood Victoria *		Bhs	2003	31,772	45,851	200	31	17	BC	

* managed for Westwood Shipping Lines Inc.(Weyerhaeuser Corp.), USA.

BP Amoco Plc

UK

Funnel: Red with green band on broad white band beneath black top.
Hull: Black with red boot-topping.

Name	Eng	Flag	Year	GRT	DWT	Loa	Bm	Kts	Type	Former names
Alaskan Frontier †		Usa	2004	95,000	185,000	287	50	15	T	
Baltic Challenger §		Iom	2003	23,240	37,330	183	27	14	T	
Baltic Champion §		Iom	2003	23,240	37,333	183	27	14	T	
Baltic Commodore §		Iom	2003	23,240	37,343	183	27	14	T	
British Adventure		Bmu	1990	23,983	41,035	176	31	14	T	ex BP Adventure-94
British Beech		Iom	2003	58,200	106,138	241	42	15	T	
British Curlew		Iom	2004	63,661	114,760	250	44	-	T	
British Endeavour		Gbr	2002	23,235	37,224	183	27	15	T	
British Endurance		Gbr	2002	23,235	37,296	183	27	14	T	
British Energy		Gbr	2001	23,682	35,970	183	27	14	T	
British Enterprise		Gbr	2001	23,682	35,858	183	27	14	T	
British Esteem		Gbr	2003	23,235	37,220	183	27	15	T	
British Explorer		Gbr	2003	23,235	37,321	183	27	15	T	
British Harrier *		Iom	1997	80,187	151,459	274	46	14	T	
British Hawk *		Iom	1997	80,187	151,400	274	46	14	T	
British Hawthorn		Gbr	2003	57,567	81,697	241	42	15	T	
British Hazel		Iom	2004	58,070	106,085	241	42	15	T	
British Hunter *		Iom	1997	80,100	151,400	274	46	14	T	
British Innovator		Iom	2002	92,900	67,850	279	43	19	Lng	
British Laurel		Iom	2002	57,567	106,500	241	42	15	T	
British Loyalty		Iom	2004	28,000	46,080	183	32	14	T	
British Merchant	(st)	Iom	2003	93,498	67,850	279	43	-	Lng	
British Merlin		Iom	2003	63,661	114,761	250	44	-	T	
British Oak		Iom	2003	57,567	106,500	241	42	15	T	
British Osprey		Iom	2003	63,661	101,760	250	44	-	T	
British Pioneer **		Iom	1999	160,216	306,397	334	58	15	T	
British Pride **		Iom	2000	160,216	305,994	334	58	15	T	
British Progress **		Iom	2000	160,216	306,497	334	58	15	T	
British Purpose **		Iom	2000	160,216	306,307	334	58	15	T	
British Security		Iom	2004	28,000	46,080	183	32	14	T	
British Swift		Iom	2003	63,661	114,809	250	44	-	T	
British Tenacity		Iom	2004	28,000	46,080	183	32	14	T	
British Trader		Iom	2003	93,498	75,109	279	43	19	Lng	
British Unity		Iom	2004	28,000	46,080	183	32	14	T	

Blystad Shipping (USA) Inc. TEAM SATURN. *Hans Kraijenbosch.*

BP Amoco. BRITISH ESTEEM. *Hans Kraijenbosch.*

BP Amoco. BRITISH MERLIN. *Hans Kraijenbosch.*

Name	Eng	Flag	Year	GRT	DWT	Loa	Bm	Kts	Type	Former names
British Vine		Iom	2004	58,200	106,000	241	42	15	T	
British Willow		Iom	2003	57,500	106,000	241	42	15	T	

newbuildings - eight further 28,000 grt 46,000 dwt (British's Courtesy, Chivalry, Fidelity, Harmony, Integrity, Liberty, Serenity, Tranquility), three 45,000 grt 54,500 dwt and nine 63,500 grt 114,780 dwt tankers for 2004-7 delivery from South Korean and Japanese builders.

† owned by BP Oil Shipping Co, USA (3 sister-ships on order and owns three 11,300 grt tankers managed by Keystone Services Inc., USA)

§ on charter from Interorient Navigation, * from Nordic American Tanker Shipping (managed by Scandic American Shipping, Bermuda - see Ugland Nordic Shipping ASA under Teekay) or ** from Cambridge Oil Transportation (Frontline) q.v.

Brostrom Van Ommeren Shipping AB   Sweden

Brostrom Tankers SA/France

Funnel: Blue with broad white band having Brostrom houseflag (above) partly overlapping green rectangle. Previous colours still in use include black with two narrow white bands on broad green band (VO), yellow with blue 'U' above yellow 'T' on blue square (United Tankers) or (†) black with red hexagonal outline interrupting three narrow red bands on broad white band.

Hull: Blue or grey with red boot-topping.

Name	Flag	Year	GRT	DWT	Loa	Bm	Kts	Type	Former names
Bro Albert	Atf	1995	28,226	46,768	183	32	14	T	ex Port Albert-00
Bro Alexandre	Atf	1995	28,226	46,738	183	32	14	T	ex Port Alexandre-00
Bro Anton *	Swe	1999	11,375	16,376	144	23	15	T	ex United Anton-00
Bro Arthur	Atf	1995	28,226	46,802	183	32	14	T	ex Port Arthur-00
Bro Atland *	Swe	1999	11,377	16,326	144	23	15	T	ex United Atland-00, United Albert-99
Bro Axel *	Swe	1998	11,324	16,389	144	23	13	T	ex United Axel-00
Bro Bara	Atf	1982	18,999	29,992	173	28	15	T	ex Port Bara-00
Bro Caroline	Atf	1995	29,083	45,014	183	32	14	T	ex Port Caroline-00
Bro Catherine	Atf	1997	29,083	44,922	180	32	14	T	ex Port Catherine-00
Bro Cecile	Atf	1997	29,083	44,936	180	32	14	T	ex Port Cecile-00
Bro Charlotte	Atf	1997	29,083	44,970	181	32	14	T	ex Port Charlotte-00
Bro Edward	Atf	2004	25,000	37,300	184	30	14	T	
Bro Elizabeth	Atf	2001	24,099	37,026	184	30	15	T	
Bro Ellen	Atf	2002	24,100	37,000	184	30	15	T	
Bro Etienne	Atf	2004	25,000	37,300	184	30	14	T	
Bro Selma *	Nis	1987	45,140	81,351	229	32	13	T	ex United Selma-00, OT Selma-92, Osco Bellona-89
Bro Sincero ‡	Swe	2002	11,855	16,008	146	22	14	T	
Bro Stella *	Nis	1995	40,958	70,260	213	36	14	T	ex United Stella-01
Bro Tina *	Swe	1987	16,555	27,821	155	27	14	T	ex United Tina-00, Okarina-95, Staland-90
Cilaos †	Atf	1996	29,083	44,885	180	32	14	T	ex Port Christine-98

newbuildings: further 25,000 grt 37,300 dwt tanker (BRO ELLIOT) due for 2005 delivery from Chinese builder.

Formed jointly by Brostrom and Royal Vopak Group (Van Ommeren Tankers and Soflumar), France q.v.

* owned by Brostrom Tankers AB (managed by Brostrom Ship Management AB).

† jointly owned with Societe d'Armement et de Transport (SOCATRA), France and ‡ owned by Rederi Donsotank A/B, Sweden.

Iver Ships/Norway

Funnel: As above, except red-edged white houseflag with blue 'V' overlapping green rectangle.

Name	Flag	Year	GRT	DWT	Loa	Bm	Kts	Type	Former names
Iver Exact	Nld	1999	29,289	45,790	183	32	15	T	
Iver Example	Nld	1999	29,289	45,790	183	32	15	T	
Iver Excel	Nld	1997	29,289	45,750	183	32	14	T	
Iver Experience	Nld	2000	29,289	45,500	183	32	15	T	
Iver Expert	Nld	1997	29,289	45,750	183	32	14	T	
Iver Explorer	Mhl	1991	22,733	40,077	176	32	14	T	
Iver Exporter	Lbr	2000	29,289	45,500	183	32	15	T	
Iver Express	Mhl	1990	22,733	40,041	176	32	14	T	ex Product Express-90
Iver Libra *	Cyp	1994	21,142	28,840	179	25	14	T	
Iver Pride	Nld	1996	21,145	28,840	179	25	14	T	
Iver Progress	Mhl	2001	21,517	31,265	177	28	14	T	
Iver Prosperity	Pan	2001	21,517	31,265	177	28	14	T	
Iver Spirit **	Pan	2001	15,016	22,820	153	25	13	T	
Iver Spring **	Pan	2001	15,042	22,780	153	25	14	T	

50% owned subsidiary with vessels owned by Vroon B.V., Netherlands q.v., except * by Prisco, Singapore (subsidiary of Primorsk Shipping Corp., Russia) or ** by Fleet Management Ltd., Hong Kong (China)

Brostrom Tankers SA. BRO ATLAND. *F. de Vries.*

Brostrom Tankers SA. BRO ELLEN. *Hans Kraijenbosch.*

Name	Eng	Flag	Year	GRT	DWT	Loa	Bm	Kts	Type	Former names

Hermann Buss GmbH

Germany

Funnel: Charterers colours.
Hull: Various.

Name	Eng	Flag	Year	GRT	DWT	Loa	Bm	Kts	Type	Former names
Alemania Express		Atg	2000	25,535	33,917	200	30	21	CC	ex Sea Cheetah-02, I/a Ems Trader
Baltrum Trader		Atg	1999	25,361	34,017	207	30	21	CC	ex P&O Nedlloyd Fremantle-01, Baltrum Trader-99
Calaparati		Atg	1996	16,165	22,250	168	27	19	CC	ex Atlantic Trader-04, CSAV Rauten-98, Sea Vista-97, Atlantic Trader -96
Cap Castillo		Atg	2000	25,535	33,934	200	30	22	CC	I/a Leda Trader
Cielo del Canada		Deu	1998	25,361	34,041	207	30	20	CC	ex Juist Trader-99
CMA CGM Kiwi		Atg	1998	16,800	22,900	185	25	19	CC	ex Maruba Trader-04, I/a Szczecin Trader
CMA CGM Springbok		Atg	1996	16,165	22,250	168	27	21	CC	ex Warnow Trader-04, Libra Valencia-99, Warnow Trader-96
CMA CGM Tucano		Atg	1998	23,792	30,340	207	30	21	CC	ex Arkona Trader-03, Cielo d'Italia-02, Arkona Trader-99
CSAV Hamburgo		Atg	1998	25,361	33,976	207	30	21	CC	ex Brasil Star-99, Borkum Trader-98
CSAV New York		Atg	1998	25,361	33,919	207	30	21	CC	ex Lykes Osprey-03, ECL Rotterdam-02, Maersk Sao Paulo-99, Helgoland Trader-99
CSAV Yokohama		Atg	1994	15,922	22,525	168	27	21	CC	ex Trave Trader-04, Zim Montevideo-98, Trave Trader-96
Jade Trader		Atg	1995	11,987	14,700	157	24	20	CC	ex OOCL Accord-98, Jade Trader-96
Dollart Trader		Atg	1997	15,929	22,250	168	27	21	CC	ex Libra Genova-00, Repubblica de la Boca-99, Dollart Trader-97
Melfi Canada		Atg	1995	11,987	14,717	157	24	22	CC	ex Maersk La Guaira-03, Weser Trader-97, CTE Algeciras-96, Weser Trader-95
Monteverde		Deu	1998	25,355	33,987	207	30	21	CC	I/a Juemme Trader
Ocean Trader		Atg	1996	16,165	22,250	168	27	19	CC	ex Calapadria-03, Zim Brasil I-01, Atlantico-98, Ocean Trader-96
Oder Trader		Atg	1998	23,809	30,360	188	30	21	CC	ex Zim Lisbon I-03, Oder Trader-03, Cielo d'America-02, Maersk Rio Grande-99, Oder Trader-98
Pacific Trader		Atg	1996	16,165	22,525	168	27	19	CC	ex CSAV Recife-98, Maersk Sao Paulo-97, Pacific Trader-96
Zim Argentina III		Atg	1994	15,895	22,525	168	27	21	CC	ex CSAV Rauli-98, Elbe Trader-95

newbuildings - five 12,500 dwt container ships due for 2005/6 delivery from Chinese builder.

Carl Buttner GmbH & Co.

Germany

Funnel: Yellow with white 'CB' on red houseflag, narrow black top.
Hull: Black with red boot-topping.

Name	Eng	Flag	Year	GRT	DWT	Loa	Bm	Kts	Type	Former names
Admiral		Gib	2002	16,914	23,998	168	26	15	T	
Apollo		Gib	2003	16,914	24,028	169	26	15	T	
Dorsch		Deu	1991	14,332	23,400	170	25	14	T	
Seabass *		Deu	2001	21,353	32,480	178	28	14	T	
Seadevil *		Deu	1996	21,367	32,250	178	28	14	T	
Seahake *		Deu	2003	21,329	32,480	178	28	16	T	
Sealing *		Deu	2003	21,356	32,480	178	28	16	T	
Seamullet *		Deu	2001	21,353	32,230	178	28	15	T	
Searay *		Deu	2004	21,353	32,230	178	28	16	T	
Seaturbot *		Deu	2000	21,353	32,230	178	28	14	T	
Wels *		Deu	1992	14,332	23,400	170	25	14	T	

newbuildings - three 21,300 grt and two 17,300 grt tankers for 2004/5 delivery from German and Croatian builders respectively.
*Managed by Buttner Shipmanagement, Germany, except * owned by Emil Hartmann and managed by German Tanker Shipping GmbH.*

Carisbrooke Shipping PLC

UK

Funnel: Buff with buff 'CS' on blue rectangle.
Hull: Light grey with green waterline over red boot-topping

Name	Eng	Flag	Year	GRT	DWT	Loa	Bm	Kts	Type	Former names
Greta-C		Gbr	2002	14,159	19,150	156	24	14	Co	I/a Dina-C
Innogy Sprite		Gbr	2003	14,357	19,460	160	24	14	Co	ex Dina-C-03

Carl Buttner GmbH. DORSCH. *F. de Vries.*

Ceres Hellenic Shipping. FERTILITY L. *F. de Vries.*

Name	Eng	Flag	Year	GRT	DWT	Loa	Bm	Kts	Type	Former names

Ceres Hellenic Shipping Enterprises Ltd.   Greece

Funnel: Blue with three white bands, middle band interupted by white diamond.
Hull: Black with red boot-topping.

Name	Eng	Flag	Year	GRT	DWT	Loa	Bm	Kts	Type	Former names
Bulk Africa		Lbr	2002	87,590	170,578	289	45	14	B	
Bulk Australia		Lbr	2002	87,590	170,578	289	45	14	B	
Cap Diamant		Grc	2001	94,729	160,044	-	53	-	T	
Cap Georges		Grc	1998	81,148	147,443	274	48	14	T	
Cap Jean		Grc	1998	81,148	146,439	274	48	14	T	
Cap Laurent		Grc	1998	81,148	147,436	274	48	14	T	
Cap Pierre		Grc	2004	81,500	159,060	-	-	-	T	
Cap Romuald		Grc	1998	81,148	146,639	274	48	14	T	
Captain Vangelis L		Mlt	1992	78,504	145,856	278	43	14	B	ex Captain Vangelis-03, Bulktirreno-03, Maria Rebecca-96
Fantasy		Grc	2002	357,000	106,560	241	42	-	T	
Fertility L		Grc	1987	27,963	39,611	177	32	14	T	
Fidelity		Grc	2002	57,683	106,548	241	42	-	T	
Filikon		Grc	2002	78,845	150,709	274	48	-	T	ex Paros-04
Fraternity L		Grc	1987	27,262	45,593	177	32	14	T	
Kyla		Lbr	1982	70,517	134,806	270	42	16	B	ex Bulktiger-03, Gallant Teger-96, Juanita II-88, Onstad Trader-85
Maasslot L		Grc	1982	24,794	38,039	172	32	15	T	ex Maasslot-93
Maasstad L		Grc	1983	24,794	38,039	172	32	15	T	ex Maasstad-94
Maasstroom L		Grc	1983	24,794	38,039	172	32	15	T	ex Maasstroom-93
Nike		Lbr	1995	77,135	151,688	270	43	15	B	ex China Transport-97
Red Cedar		Gbr	1998	38,995	73,322	225	32	14	B	
Red Fern		Gbr	1998	38,995	73,326	225	32	14	B	l/a Halla Pride

Also owns 17 chemical tankers operating in 'Seachem' Pool, see under Odfjell ASA.

Coeclerici Armatori SpA/Italy

Funnel: Blue with black top.
Hull: Black with red boot-topping.

Name	Eng	Flag	Year	GRT	DWT	Loa	Bm	Kts	Type	Former names
Bulk Asia		Lbr	2001	87,590	170,578	289	45	14	B	
Bulk Atlanta		Lbr	1990	77,096	149,495	270	43	13	B	ex Cape Asia-00
Bulk Europe		Lbr	2001	87,590	169,770	289	45	14	B	
Bulk Ispat Leher		Lbr	1992	77,273	149,532	270	43	13	B	ex Aberous-99
Bulkazores		Mlt	1977	34,705	61,131	225	32	15	B	ex NL Trader-94, Bergitta-91, Continental Trader-89
Capo Noli		Pmd	1981	14,454	23,683	160	25	17	Bu	ex Timpe-95, Cynthia No.4-88, Great Tempo-86, World Tempo-85
Porto Cervo		Mlt	1983	46,518	87,659	259	32	15	B	ex Cetra Lyra-95, Hunga-87, Louis L.D.-84, l/a Richfield
Prosperous		Pan	1990	77,273	149,498	270	43	13	B	ex Bulkprosperous-03, Prosperous-97

newbuildings - 14 large bulk carriers on order for 7-10 year Time Charter from various owners.
Owns controlling interest (65%) in jointly owned Coeclerici Ceres Bulk carriers NV

ChevronTexaco Corporation   USA

Funnel: White with black 'Chevron' above blue and red chevrons, narrow black top.
Hull: Black with red boot-topping.

Name	Eng	Flag	Year	GRT	DWT	Loa	Bm	Kts	Type	Former names
Aberdeen		Bhs	1996	47,274	87,055	222	37	14	T	
Altair Voyager *		Bhs	1993	80,914	135,829	259	48	15	T	ex Condoleezza Rice-01
Antares Voyager **		Bhs	1998	160,036	309,995	333	58	16	T	ex Frank A. Shrontz-03
Bellatrix Voyager		Bhs	1972	52,459	96,711	268	39	16	Ts	ex Chevron Zenith-02, Afran Zenith-89, La Nina-79
Arizona Voyager	(gt)	Usa	1977	22,664	39,836	199	29	16	T	ex Chevron Arizona-02
Capella Voyager		Bhs	1993	80,914	136,055	275	48	15	T	ex George Shultz-01
Colorado Voyager	(gt)	Usa	1976	22,735	39,842	199	29	15	T	ex Chevron Colorado-03
Cygnus Voyager *		Bhs	1993	88,919	156,835	275	50	15	T	ex Samuel Ginn-03
Dynamic Energy		Bhs	2002	46,506	53,556	227	36	17	Lpg	
Dynamic Vision		Bhs	2001	46,506	53,503	227	36	17	Lpg	
Gemini Voyager		Bhs	1999	160,036	310,138	330	58	16	T	ex Richard H. Matzke-03
Maria A. Angelicoussis		Bhs	2000	156,505	300,000	332	58	15	T	
Neptune Voyager		Bhs	2003	58,156	104,875	244	42	-	T	
Orion Voyager		Bhs	1994	88,919	156,447	275	50	15	T	ex Chevron Employee Pride-02, Chevron Africa-94
Phoenix Voyager **		Bhs	1999	160,036	310,137	331	58	16	T	ex J. Bennet Johnston-03

Name	Eng	Flag	Year	GRT	DWT	Loa	Bm	Kts	Type	Former names
Regulus Voyager		Bhs	2000	160,036	310,138	331	58	16	T	ex Chang-Lin Tien-03
Sirius Voyager *		Bhs	1994	88,919	156,382	275	50	15	T	ex Chevron Mariner-02
Star Ohio †		Bhs	1992	80,569	143,750	274	49	14	T	ex Citadelle-92
Stellar Voyager		Bhs	2003	58,088	104,801	244	42	-	T	ex Stella Voyager-03
Sun Voyager		Bhs	1992	80,914	135,915	259	48	15	T	ex James N. Sullivan-02
Vega Voyager		Bhs	2003	58,088	104,864	244	42	-	T	
Virgo Voyager *		Bhs	1992	88,946	155,127	275	50	15	T	ex William E. Crain-02
Washington Voyager	(gt)	Usa	1976	22,761	39,795	199	29	15	T	ex Chevron Washington-03

*owned by Frontline Ltd q.v.or ** Cambridge Petroleum Transport Corp. and managed by ChevronTexaco Shipping Co., USA.
† owned by Texaco Panana Inc (Texaco Marine Services Inc.) managed by Northern Marine Management, UK*

China Ocean Shipping (Group) Co. (COSCO)   China

Funnel: Blue with white vertical line through white ring above white 'COSCO', broad yellow base and narrow black top.
Hull: Grey or black with blue 'COSCO', green or red boot-topping.

Cosco Container Lines

Name		Flag	Year	GRT	DWT	Loa	Bm	Kts	Type	Former names
An Ting		Chn	1970	9,992	14,517	152	21	18	C	ex Kunlunshan-71
Beauty River		Pan	1990	22,712	33,667	188	28	18	BC	ex Belstar-90
Bing He		Chn	1985	23,542	33,389	201	28	15	CC	
Chao He		Chn	1985	19,835	25,955	170	28	17	CC	
Chuan He·		Chn	1997	65,140	69,285	280	40	24	CC	
Chun He		Chn	1984	19,835	25,955	170	28	17	CC	
Buyihe		Pan	1997	36,772	44,911	243	32	21	CC	
Cosco Antwerp		Hkg	2001	65,500	68,910	280	40	25	CC	
Cosco Felixstowe		Bhs	2002	65,532	69,107	280	40	24	CC	
Cosco Hamburg		Hkg	2001	65,531	69,193	280	40	24	CC	
Cosco Hong Kong		Bhs	2002	65,531	69,207	280	40	24	CC	
Cosco Qingdao		Pan	1997	65,140	69,285	280	40	24	CC	ex Yun He-01
Cosco Rotterdam		Bhs	2002	65,531	69,224	280	40	25	CC	
Cosco Shanghai		Hkg	2001	65,531	69,192	280	40	25	CC	
Cosco Singapore		Hkg	2001	65,531	69,196	280	40	25	CC	
Da He		Chn	1994	49,375	51,950	275	32	25	CC	
Dainty River		Pan	1993	22,746	33,650	188	28	18	CC	
Dong He		Chn	1990	37,143	47,625	236	32	19	CC	
Empress Dragon		Pan	1994	46,734	46,103	276	32	24	CC	
Empress Phoenix		Pan	1994	46,734	46,125	276	32	24	CC	
Empress Sea		Pan	1994	46,734	46,074	276	32	24	CC	
Fei He		Chn	1994	48,311	51,280	275	32	24	CC	
Fei Yun He		Chn	2000	20,569	25,723	180	28	20	CC	
Feng Yun He		Pan	1998	16,737	24,251	183	28	19	CC	
Gao He		Chn	1990	37,143	47,625	236	32	19	CC	
Hanihe		Pan	1997	36,772	44,911	243	32	21	CC	
Hong Yun He		Chn	1999	20,624	26,027	180	28	20	CC	
Honor River		Pan	1990	22,712	33,161	188	28	16	CC	ex Canstar-90, Belhaven-90
Hua Tai He		Chn	1981	21,758	22,623	198	29	21	CC	ex Pacific Sunrise-88, Khyber-88, Pacific Sunrise-87
Hua Yun He		Chn	2000	20,624	25,850	180	28	20	CC	
Hui He		Chn	1968	21,551	25,007	197	30	22	CC	ex Chastine Maersk-88
Jin He		Pan	1997	65,140	69,285	280	40	24	CC	
Liao He		Chn	1983	19,915	26,025	170	28	17	CC	
Ling Yun He		Chn	2000	20,569	25,723	180	28	20	CC	
Lu He		Pan	1997	65,140	69,285	280	40	24	CC	
Luan He		Chn	1978	18,503	25,550	169	26	15	Co	ex Victoria Bay-83, Columbia-81, Arabian Strength-79, l/a Columbia
Luo Ba He		Pan	1998	36,772	44,700	243	32	21	CC	
Luo He		Chn	1983	19,915	26,025	170	28	17	CC	
Min He		Chn	1989	37,143	47,625	236	32	19	CC	
Naxihe		Pan	1997	36,772	44,911	243	32	21	CC	
Pretty River		Pan	1993	22,746	33,650	188	28	18	CC	
Pu He		Chn	1990	35,963	46,136	236	32	19	CC	
Qing Yun He		Chn	2000	20,624	21,200	180	28	20	CC	
Qiu He		Chn	1984	19,732	25,808	171	29	15	CC	
River Elegance		Pan	1994	48,161	49,945	277	32	24	CC	
River Wisdom		Pan	1994	48,161	49,955	277	32	24	CC	
Sha He		Chn	1983	19,915	26,025	171	28	17	CC	
Shan He		Chn	1994	49,375	51,985	275	32	24	CC	

Name	Eng	Flag	Year	GRT	DWT	Loa	Bm	Kts	Type	Former names
Shun He		Chn	1968	21,349	25,007	197	30	22	CC	ex Christian Maersk-88
Song He		Chn	1986	24,438	33,265	199	29	16	CC	
Song Yun He		Pan	1998	16,737	23,831	183	28	19	CC	
Tai He		Chn	1989	35,963	45,987	236	32	19	CC	
Teng He		Chn	1994	48,311	51,280	275	32	24	CC	
Wei He		Chn	1979	18,503	25,550	169	26	15	Co	ex Nedlloyd Caledonia-83, Caledonia-81
Xiang He		Chn	1985	24,043	30,939	200	28	17	CC	
Xibohe		Pan	1997	36,772	44,911	243	32	21	CC	
Xing Hai He		Chn	1972	15,189	11,151	171	25	20	CC	ex Ngan Chau-89, Main Express-81, Oriental Importer-76, Main Express-73
Xing He		Chn	1985	19,237	25,925	170	28	15	CC	
Yi He		Chn	1968	21,609	25,078	197	30	22	CC	ex TFL Adams-86, Clara Maersk-84
Yin He		Chn	1984	19,237	25,925	172	29	17	CC	
Yu He		Chn	1986	24,043	30,940	200	29	17	CC	
Yuan He		Chn	1994	48,311	51,280	275	32	24	CC	
Yue He		Pan	1997	65,140	69,285	280	40	24	CC	
Yuguhe		Pan	1997	65,140	69,285	280	40	24	CC	
Zhen He		Chn	1993	49,375	51,985	275	32	24	CC	
Zhong He		Chn	1993	48,311	51,280	264	32	23	CC	
Zhuang He		Chn	1985	24,438	33,240	199	29	17	CC	

newbuildings - about 36 on order including eight 66,300 grt 100,000 dwt container ships for 2005 delivery from Japanese builder.

Cosco (H.K.) Shipping Co. Ltd./Hong Kong (China)

Funnel: Buff with black top or * yellow with red band beneath black top.
Hull: Grey with green boot-topping.

Name	Eng	Flag	Year	GRT	DWT	Loa	Bm	Kts	Type	Former names
Aleslevada		Pan	1990	36,544	70,231	225	32	13	B	ex Channel Victory-90
Beatanavis		Hkg	1985	24,950	39,924	184	31	14	B	
Bright City		Hkg	1988	36,120	68,200	224	32	14	B	ex Bright Field-98, Oceanus-90
Bright Days		Hkg	1989	36,120	68,676	224	32	14	B	ex Garnet-91
Bright State		Hkg	1989	36,120	68,676	224	32	14	B	ex Belore-90
Cos Angel *		Sgp	1983	32,649	65,029	228	32	14	B	ex Sunny Glorious-96, Sunrise Glory-85, Ocean Prosper-84
Cos Bonny *		Sgp	1996	26,759	46,840	187	32	14	B	
Cos Cherry *		Sgp	1996	26,759	46,840	187	32	14	B	
Cos Fair *		Pan	1999	26,829	46,689	187	32	14	B	
Cos Glory *		Pan	1999	26,829	46,680	187	32	14	B	
Cos Hero *		Pan	1998	25,982	45,574	186	30	14	B	
Cos Intrepid *		Hkg	2001	39,795	74,119	225	32	14	B	
Cos Joy *		Hkg	2001	39,795	74,119	225	32	14	B	
Cos Knight *		Pan	2002	30,053	52,323	190	32	-	B	
Cos Lucky *		Pan	2003	30,100	52,270	190	32	-	B	
Festivity		Pan	1982	27,423	45,548	193	32	14	B	
Full Beauty		Hkg	1994	36,586	70,198	225	32	14	B	
Full City		Pan	1995	15,873	26,758	167	26	14	B	
Full Comfort		Hkg	1994	36,586	70,181	225	32	14	B	
Full Sources		Hkg	1994	36,639	69,573	225	32	14	B	
Full Spring		Hkg	1994	36,639	69,587	225	32	14	B	
Full Strong		Hkg	1994	36,586	70,171	225	32	14	B	
Full Wealth		Hkg	1995	24,055	43,217	185	31	14	B	
Grand View		Hkg	1994	26,818	43,980	190	31	14	B	
Grand Way		Hkg	1994	26,818	44,006	190	31	14	B	
Joviality		Hkg	1982	28,224	45,564	193	32	14	B	
Joyous Age		Hkg	1994	35,879	69,271	225	32	14	B	
Joyous Land		Hkg	1994	35,879	69,283	225	32	15	B	
Joyous Society		Hkg	1994	35,879	69,274	225	32	15	B	
Joyous World		Hkg	1995	35,879	69,286	225	32	15	B	
Jurong Sea *		Sgp	1983	38,107	69,203	235	32	13	B	ex Eaton Breeze-95, Donpafu-93
Mass Enterprise		Pan	1993	36,560	69,555	225	32	13	B	
Mass Glory		Pan	1993	36,560	69,555	225	32	13	B	
Mass Prosperity		Pan	1993	36,560	69,555	225	32	13	B	
Mass Success		Pan	1987	36,987	69,347	225	32	16	B	ex Channel Fortune-92
Salusnavis		Hkg	1985	24,950	39,940	185	31	14	B	
Sea Crane *		Sgp	1985	26,951	46,040	190	32	13	B	ex New League-94
Sea Gloria		Pan	1994	80,203	157,600	280	43	14	B	ex Sea Glory I-94
Sea Grace		Pan	1994	80,203	157,600	280	43	14	B	

China Ocean Shipping. COSCO FELIXSTOWE. *Hans Kraijenbosch.*

China Shipping. XIN PU DONG. *Hans Kraijenbosch.*

Clipper Group. CLIPPER EAGLE. *F. de Vries.*

Name	Eng	Flag	Year	GRT	DWT	Loa	Bm	Kts	Type	Former names
Searadiance		Hkg	1977	38,412	71,733	228	32	15	B	ex Orient City-78
Weddell Sea		Pan	1978	19,911	33,789	182	27	16	B	

owned by Cosco (Singapore) Pte. Ltd., Singapore.
COSCO is the world's largest shipping group with over 600 vessels (23.5 million tonnes deadweight).
The above list is a cross section from over 80 bulk carriers between 22,000 dwt and 72,000 dwt
See Chinese-Polish Joint Stock Co. (Chinsko-Polskie Towarzystwo Okretowe SA) under Polish Ocean Line.

China Shipping (Group) Co.   China

China Shipping Container Lines Co. Ltd.

Funnel: Blue with blue 'CIS' on broad white/yellow band.
Hull: Green with white 'China Shipping Line', red boot-topping

Name	Eng	Flag	Year	GRT	DWT	Loa	Bm	Kts	Type	Former names
CSCL Chiwan *		Cyp	2001	39,941	50,488	260	32	24	CC	
CSCL Dalian *		Cyp	2002	39,941	50,871	260	32	24	CC	
CSCL Felixstowe *		Cyp	2002	39,941	50,500	260	32	24	CC	
CSCL Hamburg *		Cyp	2001	39,941	50,500	260	32	24	CC	
CSCL Ningbo *		Cyp	2002	39,941	50,500	260	32	24	CC	
Xin Chong Quig		Chn	2003	43,800	50,500	263	32	-	CC	
Xin Da Lian		Chn	2003	66,433	68,000	280	40	-	CC	
Xin Lian Yun Gang		Chn	2003	66,433	69,023	280	40	-	CC	
Xin Nanjing		Chn	2004	40,000	52,000	263	32	-	CC	
Xin Ning Bo		Chn	2003	66,433	69,303	280	40	-	CC	
Xin Pu Dong		Chn	2003	66,433	68,000	280	40	-	CC	
Xin She Kou		Chn	1983	33.267	34,477	216	32	-	CC	ex River Crystal-02, Providence Bay-93
Xin Qing Bao		Chn	2003	66,433	68,000	280	40	-	CC	
Xin Tian Jin		Chn	2003	66,433	68,000	280	40	-	CC	
Xin Yan Tian		Chn	2004	66,433	68,023	280	40	-	CC	

newbuildings : nearly 40 on order including fourteen container ships between 40,000-110,000 dwt for 2004 /5 delivery.
* Chartered from Seaspan Container Lines Ltd., Cyprus (Seaspan International, Canada).
See other vessels with CSCL prefix in index.

Chiquita Brands Inc.   USA

Great White Fleet Ltd./Belgium

Funnel: Buff with white diamond on red band beneath black top.
Hull: White with white 'Chiquita' on blue oval, red boot-topping.

Name	Eng	Flag	Year	GRT	DWT	Loa	Bm	Kts	Type	Former names
Chiquita Belgie *		Bhs	1992	13,049	13,930	158	24	22	R	
Chiquita Bremen		Bmu	1992	10,842	12,890	157	23	21	R	
Chiquita Deutschland *		Bhs	1991	13,049	13,930	158	24	22	R	
Chiquita Italia *		Bhs	1992	13,049	13,930	158	24	22	R	
Chiquita Nederland *		Bhs	1991	13,049	13,930	158	24	21	R	
Chiquita Rostock		Bmu	1993	10,842	12,850	157	24	21	R	
Chiquita Scandinavia *		Bhs	1992	13,049	13,930	159	24	21	R	
Chiquita Schweiz *		Bhs	1992	13,049	13,930	158	24	22	R	
Courtney L		Bmu	1992	19,595	15,672	203	27	21	CC	ex Martha L-92
Edyth L		Bhs	1990	19,595	15,672	203	27	21	CC	
Frances L		Bhs	1991	19,595	15,646	203	27	21	CC	
Puritan		Bmu	1983	13,998	9,649	148	26	17	CC	ex Eagle Prestige-96, Puritan-93

* owned by K/S Difko companies,

Clipper Group Ltd.   Bahamas

Funnel: Black with white 'C' symbol.
Hull: Black with white 'CLIPPER', red boot-topping.

Name	Eng	Flag	Year	GRT	DWT	Loa	Bm	Kts	Type	Former names
Clipper Eagle *		Bhs	1994	11,542	16,906	149	23	14	B	
Clipper Falcon *		Bhs	1995	11,542	16,900	149	23	14	B	
Clipper Flamingo		Bhs	1997	19,354	29,516	181	26	14	Co	ex VOC Flamingo-04, Cielo di Calgary-01, Clipper Flamingo-00, Chuqui-00, Clipper Flamingo-97
Clipper Frontier		Bhs	1997	19,354	28,106	181	26	14	Co	ex VOC Frontier-04, Clipper Frontier-00, Pudahuel-99, Clipper Frontier-97
Clipper Melody		Bhs	1997	16,405	25,069	172	25	14	B	ex Jan Zizka-99

Name	Eng	Flag	Year	GRT	DWT	Loa	Bm	Kts	Type	Former names
Clipper Ranger		Bhs	2002	12,578	20,200	155	24	16	B	I/a Clipper Reunion
Clipper Regal		Bhs	2002	12,578	20,035	155	24	16	B	ex VOC Regal-03
Clipper Reunion		Bhs	2002	12,578	20,001	155	24	16	B	ex VOC Reunion-03

newbuildings: two 27,000 dwt, eight 30,000 dwt and one 34,300 dwt bulk carriers for 2004/5 delivery from Chinese builder.
Management by Dockendale Shipping Co. Ltd., Bahamas or * by Polish Steamship Co. and reported sold 3/2004.

Dockendale Shipping Co. Ltd./Bahamas

Funnel: White with red 'D' and 'S' above points of black anchor.
Hull: Black with white 'DOCKENDALE' or 'DOCKSHIP' red boot-topping.

Name	Eng	Flag	Year	GRT	DWT	Loa	Bm	Kts	Type	Former names
African Eagle		Bhs	2003	17,944	27,102	178	26	14	B	ex DS Mascot-03
African Falcon		Bhs	2003	17,944	27,101	178	26	14	B	ex Clipper Majestic-03
Austyn Oldendorff		Bhs	2002	22,072	34,656	179	28	-	B	ex IVS Valiant-03
Barachois		Atf	1998	18,597	29,538	181	26	14	Co	
Clipper Faith		Bhs	1998	19,354	28,106	181	26	14	Co	ex Cielo di Victoria-01, Clipper Faith-00
Clipper Ipanema		Bhs	1981	15,992	22,882	166	27	15	C	ex Concord Daisen-98, Brave Spirit-86, Eternal Fuji-83
Clipper Mermaid		Bhs	2001	17,944	27,105	178	26	14	B	
Clipper Morning		Bhs	2002	17,944	27,141	178	26	14	B	
Dolisle		Atf	1998	18,597	29,538	181	26	14	Co	
DS Attica		Bhs	1984	13,911	20,412	154	23	15	Co	ex Albert Oldendorff-01, Attica-99, Vaimama-96, Attica-96, Ushuaia-95, Mostween 8-92, Silver Gulf-89
DS Fantasy		Bhs	1996	19,354	29,538	181	26	14	Co	ex Cielo di Spagna-01, Clipper Fantasy-00, Paipote-98, Clipper Fantasy-97, Paipote-97, Clipper Fantasy-96
DS Fiesta		Bhs	1997	19,354	29,516	181	26	14	Co	ex Clipper Fiesta-01
DS Garnet		Bhs	2003	30,928	51,195	190	32	14	B	
DS Manatee		Bhs	2002	17,944	27,128	178	26	14	B	
DS Mirage		Bhs	1997	16,405	25,096	172	25	14	B	ex Clipper Mirage-03, Prokop Holy-99
DS Montrose		Bhs	2001	17,944	27,028	178	26	14	B	
DS Regent		Bhs	2003	12,578	20,001	155	24	-	B	
DS Splendour		Bhs	1999	14,118	20,742	158	23	15	Co	ex Splendour-02
DS Vanguard		Bhs	2004	22,072	34,300	179	28	-	B	
IVS Viking		Bhs	2003	22,072	34,682	179	28	-	B	
IVS Viscount		Lbr	2003	22,072	34,699	179	28	-	B	
Leopold Oldendorff		Bhs	2002	22,072	34,656	179	28	-	B	ex IVS Victory-03

Clipper Bulk (Portland) Inc./USA

Name	Eng	Flag	Year	GRT	DWT	Loa	Bm	Kts	Type	Former names
Clipper Harvest		Bhs	2004	19,730	32,040	168	29	14	B	
Clipper Horizon		Bhs	2004	19,900	32,040	168	29	14	B	
Clipper Lagoon		Bhs	2004	16,954	28,200	169	27	-	B	
Clipper Lasco		Bhs	2004	16,954	28,200	169	27	-	B	
Grand Iris		Bhs	1995	26,062	45,712	186	30	14	B	
Grand Orchid		Bhs	1996	27,610	45,513	190	31	14	B	
Pacdream		Lbr	1985	14,868	25,759	159	26	13	B	ex Bright Ocean-94
Paclogger		Lbr	1996	17,209	28,249	170	27	14	B	ex Sea Dream-99
Pacocean		Lbr	1986	22,064	38,870	180	31	16	B	ex Dianthus-89, I/a Sanko Dianthus
Pacrose		Bhs	1996	16,041	27,609	169	26	14	B	
Pacsea		Lbr	1986	17,126	26,966	174	28	13	B	ex Sunny Mermaid-89, Summer Breeze-87
Pacstar		Lbr	1986	17,275	26,863	174	28	12	B	ex Sun Light-89
Pacsun		Lbr	1986	17,142	26,943	174	28	12	B	ex Port Star-89, Pacific Stream-87, Hope River-87, River Star-86
Pactimber		Bhs	1998	17,784	28,215	169	27	14	B	
Pactrader		Lbr	1997	16,794	28,426	169	27	14	B	ex Sea Winner-99

newbuildings: two 17,050 grt and two 19,800 grt bulk carriers due for 2004 delivery from Japanese builders.
Formerly Lasco Shipping Co., USA and acquired by Clipper Group December 2003.

Van Ommeren Clipper Shipholding

Funnel: Black with white 'V' inside white 'O'.
Hull: Grey or red with red boot-topping.

Name	Eng	Flag	Year	GRT	DWT	Loa	Bm	Kts	Type	Former names
Papendrecht **		Bhs	1989	26,128	40,908	196	28	13	B	ex Kosice-97
Pendrecht **		Bhs	1989	26,128	40,908	196	28	13	B	ex Vitkovice-97
VOC Endeavour		Bhs	2004	30,400	52,270	190	32	14	B	I/a Clipper Endeavour
VOC Gallant		Bhs	2002	30,928	51,215	190	32	14	B	ex DS Gallant-04

Name	Eng	Flag	Year	GRT	DWT	Loa	Bm	Kts	Type	Former names
VOC Sterling *		Bhs	1999	14,118	20,730	158	23	15	Co	ex Clipper Sterling-00

newbuildings : two 30,400 grt 52,300 dwt bulk carriers due 2004 from Japanese builder.
* owned by Van Ommeren Clipper Shipping BV, Netherlands or ** by Van Ommeren Clipper Bulk Shipping (USA) Inc.
Clipper Group took complete control of previously joint venture in December 2003.

CMA CGM Holding France

Funnel: *White with blue oval outline interupted by red 'CMA' and blue 'CGM', narrow blue top.*
Hull: *Blue with white 'CMA CGM', red boot-topping.*

Name		Eng	Flag	Year	GRT	DWT	Loa	Bm	Kts	Type	Former names
ANL Explorer			Bhs	1985	35,739	34,194	218	30	20	CC	ex CMA CGM Enterprise-02, Australian Enterprise-01, Asia Venus-97, California Venus-95, Med Kobe-95, California Venus-94
CMA CGM Arno	(2)		Pan	1979	32,428	30,998	210	32	22	CC	ex Fort Royal-03
CMA CGM Bellini			Bhs	2004	69,022	72,500	277	40	24	CC	
CMA CGM Berlioz			Atf	2001	73,157	80,250	300	40	25	CC	
CMA CGM Bizet			Atf	2001	73,157	77,200	300	40	25	CC	
CMA CGM Chopin			Bhs	2004	69,022	72,500	277	40	24	CC	
CMA CGM Debussy			Atf	2001	73,157	80,251	300	40	26	CC	
CMA CGM Eiffel			Bhs	2002	49,855	58,344	282	32	26	CC	
CMA CGM Fort Saint Louis			Fra	2003	26,210	30,804	198	30	21	CC	
CMA CGM Fort St. Georges			Fra	2003	26,047	30,450	198	30	21	CC	
CMA CGM Fort St. Marie			Fra	2003	26,210	30,450	198	30	21	CC	
CMA CGM Fort Ste. Pierre			Atf	2003	26,047	30,450	198	30	21	CC	
CMA CGM Hudson	(2)		Pan	1980	32,428	30,998	210	32	22	CC	ex Fort Fleur d' Epee-03
CMA CGM La Tour			Bhs	2001	26,050	30,500	196	30	22	CC	
CMA CGM Manet			Bhs	2001	26,050	30,442	196	30	21	CC	
CMA CGM Makassar ‡			Grc	1990	37,193	44,044	243	32	21	CC	ex Hanjin Felixstowe-03
CMA CGM Matisse			Atf	1999	25,777	32,274	196	30	21	CC	
CMA CGM Mozart			Bhs	2004	69,022	72,500	277	40	24	CC	
CMA CGM Potomac			Pan	1980	31,154	28,955	215	31	21	CC	ex Douce France-03, Fort Saint Charles-95
CMA CGM Puccini			Bhs	2004	69,022	72,500	277	40	24	CC	
CMA CGM Puget			Bhs	2002	50,561	58,548	282	32	24	CC	
CMA CGM Ravel			Atf	2001	73,059	79,465	300	40	25	CC	
CMA CGM Rossini			Bhs	2004	73,059	72,500	277	40	24	CC	
CMA CGM Seine ‡			Grc	1990	37,193	43,940	243	32	21	CC	ex Hanjin Hamburg-03, I/a Hanjin Vancouver
CMA CGM Straus			Bhs	2004	69,022	72,500	277	40	24	CC	
CMA CGM Tage			Pan	1980	31,154	28,955	215	31	21	CC	ex Fort Desaix-03
CMA CGM Utrillo			Atf	1999	25,777	32,274	196	30	21	CC	
CMA CGM Vega †			Bhs	2001	39,812	51,020	258	32	24	CC	
CMA CGM Verdi			Bhs	2004	69,022	72,500	277	40	24	CC	
CMA CGM Vivaldi			Pan	2004	69,022	72,500	277	40	24	CC	
CMA CGM Wagner			Bhs	2004	69,022	72,500	277	40	24	CC	
Ville de Mars			Pan	1990	37,235	43,714	242	32	22	CC	ex Australian Endurance-00, Lykes Challenger-99, CGM Pasteur-98, Nedlloyd Pasteur-98, CGM Pasteur-95, Ville de Virgo-91, CGM Pasteur-90

newbuildings : nine 89,800 grt 100,000 dwt container ships (334 x 43m.) for 2004-6 delivery from South Korean builders.
† on charter from Reimarus Schiffahrtskantor GmbH & Co KG, Germany or ‡ from Cardiff Marine SA (Drytank SA), Greece.
See other vessels in index with 'CMA CGM', 'ANL' or 'Ville de' prefixes.

N.V. CMB S.A. Belgium
Bocimar N.V./Belgium

Funnel: *Blue with blue 'B' on broad cream band*
Hull: *Black or orange with blue or red boot-topping.*

Name	Eng	Flag	Year	GRT	DWT	Loa	Bm	Kts	Type	Former names
Alpha Cosmos		Grc	2001	87,378	169,770	289	45	15	B	ex Mineral York-02, Mineral Trader-01
Channel Poterne		Lbr	1997	87,368	172,091	289	45	14	B	
Mineral Antwerpen ‡		Pan	2003	87,495	172,150	289	45	15	B	
Mineral Beijing		Bel	2004	88,500	176,000	-	-	-	B	
Mineral Dragon		Lbr	1994	79,694	149,782	270	44	-	B	
Mineral Kiwi		Lbr	2004	87,179	172,000	289	45	15	B	
Mineral Oak ‡		Pan	1996	85,721	165,693	288	44	13	B	
Mineral Ordaz		Lbr	1997	90,392	172,632	296	46	13	B	
Mineral Sines ‡		Pan	2002	87,495	172,319	289	45	15	B	

CMA CGM Holding. CMA CGM FORT ST. GEORGES. *Hans Kraijenbosch.*

CMA CGM Holding. CMA CGM PUGET. *Phil Kempsey.*

CMA CGM Holding. CMA CGM RAVEL. *C. J. Dornom.*

Name	Eng	Flag	Year	GRT	DWT	Loa	Bm	Kts	Type	Former names
Mineral Venture †		Hkg	1996	77,255	150,393	273	43	14	B	
Mineral Viking		Lbr	2001	87,363	172,964	289	45	15	B	ex Bagru-04
United Talent		Pan	2001	30,053	46,719	190	32	14	B	

newbuildings : three 176,000 dwt, one 172,000 dwt and four 74,500 dwt bulk carriers due 2004/5 from South Korean and Chinese builders.
Partner in Cape International pool formed jointly with ABC/Zodiac, Belships, Moller, Torvald Klaveness and Overseas Shipholding Corp.
Managed by subsidiary Tecto Cyprus † owned by Wah Kwong Shipping Agency Co. Ltd., Hong Kong (27.1% owned by CMB) or ‡ by Oak Maritime (Canada) Ltd., Canada.

Euronav Luxembourg SA/Luxembourg

Funnel: *Black with white flag containing narrow red horizontal cross on broad white horizontal cross on blue disc.*
Hull: *Black with red boot-topping.*

Name	Eng	Flag	Year	GRT	DWT	Loa	Bm	Kts	Type	Former names
Algarve		Atf	1999	157,833	298,969	332	58	15	T	
Artois		Atf	2001	159,456	298,330	334	60	16	T	
Bourgogne *		Lux	1996	161,287	296,230	333	58	13	T	
Famenne		Atf	2001	159,456	298,412	333	60	15	T	
Flandre		Lux	2004	150,000	300,000	-	-	-	T	
Luxembourg		Atf	1999	157,833	298,997	332	58	15	T	
Namur		Bel	2000	159,397	298,628	333	60	15	T	ex Ichiban-03, Berge Ichiban-02
Provence		Atf	1994	153,778	284,912	327	57	15	T	ex Provence I-94
Savoie *		Nis	1993	160,214	306,430	331	58	16	T	ex Berge Sigval-04

* operated by subsidiary G-Tec Shipmanagement GmbH, Germany.

Exmar NV/Belgium

Funnel: *Blue with red 'E' on broad white band.*
Hull: *Red with dark red boot-topping*

Name	Eng	Flag	Year	GRT	DWT	Loa	Bm	Kts	Type	Former names
Brugge Venture ‡		Hkg	1997	22,352	26,777	170	27	17	Lpg	
Carli Bay		Lux	1998	17,527	20,613	155	26	17	Lpg	
Chaconia		Lux	1990	19,643	29,271	166	27	16	Lpg	
Courcheville		Lux	1989	19,719	29,171	166	27	16	Lpg	ex Nyhall-96
Donau		Lux	1985	23,508	32,339	183	30	15	Lpg	ex Gaz Nordsee-96, Donau-91
Eeklo †		Lux	1995	23,519	28,993	179	27	16	Lpg	
Elversele §		Lux	1996	23,519	28,993	179	27	18	Lpg	
Eupen §		Lux	1999	23,952	29,121	180	27	16	Lpg	
Flanders Harmony		Lux	1992	47,597	64,220	228	36	-	Lpg	
Flanders Tenacity		Bel	1996	47,027	54,155	230	36	19	Lpg	
Gent		Lux	1985	18,155	26,820	155	27	16	Lpg	
Kemira Gas		Bel	1995	10,018	13,289	143	21	16	Lpg	
Libin		Bel	1982	29,240	30,466	192	31	15	Lpg	ex Nichizan Maru-98
Reggane *		Lbr	1999	47,174	54,592	230	36	16	Lpg	
Touraine †		Hkg	1996	25,337	30,309	196	29	19	Lpg	ex Antwerpen Venture-97

newbuildings: five 38000 cubic metre Lpg tankers from Daewoo for 2005/6 delivery to Exmar Pool (Bergesen (2), Moller (2) and Exmar (1))
Partly demerged from CMB Group (6/2003).
Also operates four Lng tankers - Excalibur, Excel, Fuwairit and Methania and various Lpg tankers chartered from Moller, Bibby and Bergesen.
Managed by subsidiary Tecto Belgium NV, * for Sonatrach Petroleum Corp., UK or † for Gaz Atlantique, France
‡ owned by Wah Kwong Shipping Agency Co. Ltd., Hong Kong (China) or § by Dr. Peters KG fund, Germany

Cobelfret N.V.   Belgium

Funnel: *Yellow.*
Hull: *Black or grey with green boot-topping.*

Name	Eng	Flag	Year	GRT	DWT	Loa	Bm	Kts	Type	Former names
Lowlands Rose		Pan	1996	83,658	171,039	278	45	14	B	
Lowlands Saguenay		Pan	1985	37,721	66,995	228	32	16	B	ex Northern Enterprise-01
Lowlands Yarra		Pan	1985	78,625	148,140	284	47	14	B	ex Iron Newcastle-99
Samarinda *		Pan	1994	79,694	149,647	270	44	13	B	

newbuildings - 76,600 dwt bulk carrier on order from Japanese builder for 2004 delivery.
managed by subsidiary EuroShip Services Ltd., UK and * jointly owned by Walleniusrederierna

Compania Chilena de Navegacion Interoceanica SA (CCNI)   Chile

Funnel: *Red with white band beneath blue top.*
Hull: *Blue with red boot-topping, or owners colours.*

Name	Eng	Flag	Year	GRT	DWT	Loa	Bm	Kts	Type	Former names
Alicahue		Lbr	1998	25,537	46,570	183	31	14	B	
Allipen		Lbr	1998	25,537	46,570	183	31	14	B	

Name	Eng	Flag	Year	GRT	DWT	Loa	Bm	Kts	Type	Former names
Andino		Chl	1993	17,738	22,257	177	27	18	CC	ex CCNI Andino-00
Antuco		Lbr	1998	25,537	46,570	183	31	14	B	
Spring Hawk		Lbr	1998	25,537	46,570	183	31	14	B	ex Antillanca-03

Controlled by Navieros Group with minority interests owned by P Dohle (13%) and by CSAV (27%) q.v.
See other chartered ships with 'CCNI' prefix under various owners.

Compania SudAmericana de Vapores SA (CSAV) — Chile

Funnel: Red with deep black top.
Hull: Grey or white with red or green boot-topping.

Name	Eng	Flag	Year	GRT	DWT	Loa	Bm	Kts	Type	Former names
Braztrans I *		Bra	1980	22,011	38,186	194	28	15	B	ex Docemarte-99
Grand Lebanon		Lbr	1977	38,754	18,099	199	30	20	V	ex Pacific Runner-03, American Highway-92
Libra Albacora *		Bra	1977	69,780	132,007	273	45	16	OO	ex Jurua-97
Mapocho		Chl	1999	16,986	21,182	168	27	20	CC	ex Kribi-02, ANL Okapi-02, Fesco Endeavor-01, Kribi-00
Pacific Explorer		Mhl	1978	38,970	18,069	199	30	20	V	ex Asian Highway-93
Pacific Winner		Mhl	1987	48,688	18,845	213	30	18	Ro	ex Republica di Pisa-03
Rio Blanco **		Chl	1981	41,208	18,142	199	30	17	V	ex Fuji Ace-98
Rio Bueno		Pan	1980	25,984	11,076	161	27	16	V	ex Pacific Winner-94, Subaru Maru-92
Rio Enco		Chl	1978	19,867	7,426	139	26	18	V	ex Bright Ace-94, Singa Satu-83
Tolten		Bhs	1999	36,008	51,459	200	32	15	BC	

newbuildings : three 70,000 dwt, three 80,250 dwt, four 67,970 dwt and 12 other container ships over 40,000 dwt for 2004-7 delivery.
*managed by Southern Shipmanagement (Chile) Ltd. and * owned by subsidiary Cia. Libra de Navegacao or ** jointly with Mitsui OSK Lines q.v.*
see chartered ships with 'CSAV' prefix in index and jointly owned vessels under Kristian Gerhard Jebsen and Odfjell ASA.

Norasia Services SA/Switzerland

Name	Eng	Flag	Year	GRT	DWT	Loa	Bm	Kts	Type	Former names
Conti Shanghai		Deu	1996	42,323	41,460	242	32	22	CC	ex Norasia Shanghai-02
MSC Boston		Mlt	1993	42,323	41,570	242	32	22	CC	ex Norasia Fribourg-97
MSC New York		Lbr	1994	42,323	41,570	242	32	22	CC	ex Norasia Kiel-97

Wholly owned by CSAV with vessels operated by subsidiary Ganymed Shipping GmbH, Germany, see vessels with 'Norasia' prefix in index.

Conoco Inc. — USA

Funnel: Red with white 'globe' device
Hull: Black with red boot-topping.

Name	Eng	Flag	Year	GRT	DWT	Loa	Bm	Kts	Type	Former names
Constitution		Mhl	1999	58,242	104,700	244	42	-	T	
Continental		Lbr	1993	53,848	96,683	243	42	14	T	
Guardian		Lbr	1992	53,772	96,920	243	42	14	T	
Patriot		Lbr	1992	53,772	96,920	248	42	14	T	
Pioneer		Lbr	1993	53,858	96,724	248	42	14	T	
Randgrid	(me2)	Nor	1995	75,273	122,535	266	46	15	T	ex Heidrun-96
Sentinel		Pan	1999	58,242	104,700	244	42	-	T	

newbuildings - 55,000 grt 103,000 dwt tanker on order from South Korean builder.
Owned by E. I. Du-Pont de Nemours & Co. Inc., USA.

Costamare Shipping Co. SA — Greece

Funnel: Blue with black top or charterers colours
Hull: Grey or black with red boot-topping.

Name	Eng	Flag	Year	GRT	DWT	Loa	Bm	Kts	Type	Former names
Kuala Lumpur Express		Grc	2000	54,437	66,781	294	32	24	CC	
Liguria		Grc	1978	14,050	15,451	157	25	18	CC	ex MSC Liguria-03, Romania-02, MSC Busan-99, Captain George-97, Eagle Nova-96, ACX Orchid-95, Ratana Thevi-91, Pylos-91, Leon-91, Freedom-91, Zim Venezia-91, JSS Los Angeles-88, British Senator-88, Freedom-87, TFL Freedom-86
Maersk Bilbao		Grc	1976	34,382	37,852	223	31	21	CC	ex MSC Antwerp-03, Vancouver-98, Maersk Vancouver-98, Alva Maersk-95
Maersk Kalamata		Grc	2003	74,656	81,094	304	40	25	CC	
Maersk Kolkata		Grc	2003	74,656	81,577	304	40	25	CC	
Maersk Toba		Dis	1982	43,325	53,690	270	32	24	CC	ex Leda Maersk-98
Maersk Tokyo		Pan	1981	43,325	53,540	270	32	23	CC	ex Lexa Maersk-97
Maersk Trondheim		Grc	1984	43,332	53,325	270	32	22	CC	ex Lars Maersk-99

Name	Eng	Flag	Year	GRT	DWT	Loa	Bm	Kts	Type	Former names
MSC Alabama		Grc	1996	37,518	42,966	243	32	23	CC	ex APL Italy-01,Chetumal-00, TMM Chetumal-97
MSC Attica		Grc	1984	40,238	48,600	256	32	24	CC	ex safmarine Victory-02, Maersk Toyama-01, Laust Maersk-98
MSC Austria		Lbr	1977	38,991	40,624	241	32	21	CC	ex Houston Express-03, Rotterdam Express-00, Duesseldorf Express-97
MSC Japan		Grc	1996	37,518	42,938	243	32	23	CC	ex APL Panama-01, Manzanillo-00, TMM Manzanillo-97, Manzanillo-96, Carmen-96
MSC Korea		Grc	1996	37,518	42,938	243	32	23	CC	ex APL Spain-01, Sinaloa-00, TMM Sinaloa-97, Sinaloa-96
MSC Mexico		Lbr	1978	38,991	40,849	241	32	22	CC	ex Koeln Express-03, Koln Atlantic-93, Koln Express-87
MSC Namibia		Grc	1977	27,754	27,893	204	31	20	CC	ex Namibia-04, MSC Namibia-03, Cap Vilano-00, Laser Stream-96, Advisor-93, CGM Provence-90, Advisor-85, Asia Winds-84, Advisor-83
MSC Sicily		Grc	1978	20,676	24,382	186	28	20	CC	ex Carmen-01, MSC China-00, Prestige-98, California Express-93, Carmen-92, Asian Pearl-91
MSC Sudan		Grc	1976	27,971	27,795	204	31	21	CC	ex Caribia Express-03, Woermann Ulanga-91, ScanDutch Ledra-90, Caribia Express-87
MSC Tuscany		Grc	1978	20,676	24,383	186	24	14	CC	ex Mumbai-01, Indamex Mumbai-01, MSC Singapore-00, Nedlloyd Java-98, Asian Jade-91
MSC Yokohama		Grc	1979	30,249	27,738	203	31	21	CC	ex Romanos-97, Hyundai Vancouver-97, Gulf Speed-94, OOCL Brilliance-93, Gulf Speed-91, Incotrans Speed-86, China Winds-84, Incotrans Speed-83
Navarino		Grc	1986	39,678	37,915	233	32	21	CC	ex Zim Shenzhen-02, California Zeus-98, Hidaka Maru-88
New York Express		Grc	2000	54,437	66,818	294	32	24	CC	
Safmarine Antwerp		Grc	2003	74,661	81,183	304	40	25	CC	ex Maersk Kobe-03
Safmarine Himalaya		Grc	2000	74,661	81,584	304	40	25	CC	ex Sealand Virginia-04
Safmarine Igoli		Grc	1987	42,304	39,579	250	32	22	CC	ex APL Costa Rica-03, APL Pacific-01, MSC Pacific-01, Houston Express-99, Saturn-98, California Saturn-97
Sealand Illinois		Grc	2000	74,661	81,584	304	40	25	CC	
Sealand Michigan		Grc	2000	74,661	81,584	304	40	25	CC	
Sealand New York		Grc	2000	74,661	81,584	304	40	25	CC	
Sealand Washington		Grc	2000	74,661	81,584	304	40	25	CC	
Sierra Express		Grc	1977	27,970	23,020	204	31	20	CC	ex Cordillera Epress-83
Singapore Express		Grc	2000	54,415	66,793	294	32	24	CC	
Sophia Britannia		Grc	1993	50,501	59,567	292	32	23	CC	ex Kirishima-99
Zim New York		Grc	2002	53,453	62,740	294	32	24	CC	
Zim Shanghai		Mlt	2002	53,453	66,597	294	32	24	CC	

newbuildings - five 88,000 grt 83,500 dwt (8500 teu) container ships due 2006 from South Korean builder for charter to COSCO.

CP Ships Inc.   Canada

Canada Maritime Services Ltd./UK

Funnel: White with red flag.
Hull: Red with red boot-topping.

Name	Eng	Flag	Year	GRT	DWT	Loa	Bm	Kts	Type	Former names
APL Honduras		Gbr	2003	39,941	50,790	260	32	-	CC	
CanMar Bravery		Bmu	1978	26,383	33,869	219	31	23	CC	ex Cast Privilege-01, CanMar Bravery—99, OOCL Bravery-98, Canadian Explorer-90, Dart Canada-81
CanMar Dynasty *		Gbr	1994	23,540	30,621	187	30	19	CC	ex TMM Guadalajara-03, P&O Nedlloyd Melbourne-01, Coral Seatel-89, Contship Sydney-98, Coral Seatel-94
CanMar Endurance *		Bmu	1983	32,152	32,424	222	32	22	CC	ex Cast Performance-03, Contship Endeavour-99, CanMar Endeavour-98, Alligator Joy-95, Tokyo Maru-90
CanMar Glory		Bmu	1979	16,145	18,964	177	27	22	CC	ex Sea Falcon-94, CMB Monarch-91, CMB Mover-90, Asian Senator-90, Jefferson-88, TFL Jefferson-86, Seatrain Saratoga-80
CanMar Honour *		Bmu	1998	39,174	40,120	245	32	21	CC	
CanMar Pride *		Bmu	1998	39,174	40,881	245	32	21	CC	
CanMar Spirit *		Bmu	2003	55,994	62,300	294	32	-	CC	

CSAV (Norasia Services). CONTI SHANGHAI. *Hans Kraijenbosch.*

Costamare Shipping. NEW YORK EXPRESS. *Hans Kraijenbosch.*

CP Ships (Contship). CONTSHIP AUCKLAND. *J. M. Kakebeeke.*

Name	Eng	Flag	Year	GRT	DWT	Loa	Bm	Kts	Type	Former names
CanMar Triumph		Bmu	1978	16,289	18,606	177	27	19	CC	ex CMB Marque-90, American Senator-89, Dart Americana-87, Seapac Independence-81, Seatrain Independence-81
CanMar Valour		Bmu	1979	15,145	18,800	177	27	18	CC	ex OOCL Assurance-97, Taiwan Senator-90, Dart Britain-87, Seapac Oriskany-81, Seatrain Oriskany-81
CanMar Venture *		Gbr	2003	55,994	62,300	294	32	-	CC	
CanMar Victory		Bmu	1979	16,289	18,381	177	27	18	CC	ex American Senator-90, Singapore Senator-89, Dart Atlantica-87, Seapac Chesapeake-81, Seatrain Chesapeake-81

newbuildings: nine 39,900 grt 50,500 dwt container ships for 2005-7 delivery from South Korean builder.
* managed by Anglo-Eastern Ship Management Ltd., Hong Kong (China)

Cast (1983) Ltd.

Funnel: Blue with white 'cast'.
Hull: Blue with red boot-topping.

Name	Eng	Flag	Year	GRT	DWT	Loa	Bm	Kts	Type	Former names
Cast Premier		Bmu	1996	33,663	33,659	216	32	20	CC	ex OOCL Canada-03
Cast Prominence		Bmu	1996	33,735	34,330	216	32	20	CC	ex CanMar Courage-03
Cast Prospect		Bmu	1996	33,735	34,330	216	32	20	CC	ex CanMar Fortune-03

managed by Anglo-Eastern Ship Management Ltd., Hong Kong (China)

Contship Containerlines Ltd./UK

Funnel: Blue with white linked 'CS' between two narrow red bands.
Hull: Black or dark blue with white 'CONTSHIP', red boot-topping

Name	Eng	Flag	Year	GRT	DWT	Loa	Bm	Kts	Type	Former names
Contship Auckland **		Lbr	1998	26,131	30,781	196	30	19	CC	I/a Patricia Rickmers
Contship Aurora		Gbr	2002	46,009	54,156	281	32	25	CC	
Contship Australis		Gbr	2002	46,009	54,157	281	32	25	CC	
Contship Borealis †		Gbr	2003	46,009	54,220	281	32	25	CC	
Contship Champion *		Deu	1994	35,595	42,085	240	32	22	CC	ex Northern Relianace-02, Ville de Vela-02
Contship Indigo		Gbr	2003	39,941	50,900	260	32	-	CC	ex APL Panama-04
Contship Innovator *		Deu	1994	35,595	42,673	240	32	22	CC	ex Northern Faith-02, Ville de Libra-02
Contship London **		Lbr	1997	26,131	30,781	195	30	20	CC	ex Alexandra Rickmers-97
Contship Rome **		Deu	1998	26,131	30,781	196	30	19	CC	I/a Aenne Rickmers

* owned or managed by Norddeutsche or ** Reederei Bertram Rickmers GmbH q.v.
† managed by Anglo-Eastern Ship Management Ltd., Hong Kong (China)

Lykes Bros. Steamship Co. Inc./USA

Funnel: White with white 'L' on blue diamond beneath deep black top or light grey with 'L' and blue diamond on the bridge side.
Hull: Black with white 'LYKES LINES', red boot-topping.

Name	Eng	Flag	Year	GRT	DWT	Loa	Bm	Kts	Type	Former names
Lykes Achiever		Gbr	1987	40,439	40,870	270	32	20	CC	ex Ming Pleasure-01
Lykes Ambassador		Gbr	1987	40,436	40,845	270	32	20	CC	ex Ming Plenty-01
Lykes Challenger		Gbr	1986	40,464	40,744	270	32	20	CC	ex Ming Peace-01
Lykes Deliverer		Gbr	2003	39,800	50,500	260	32	-	CC	
Lykes Discoverer		Usa	1987	39,132	44,966	259	32	21	CC	ex Margaret Lykes-97, President Harding-96, I/a James Lykes
Lykes Eagle		Gbr	2000	23,652	29,841	188	30	20	CC	ex Clivia-00
Lykes Energiser *		Cyp	1992	16,075	17,510	174	23	18	Ro	ex Thorsriver-00, ex Elan Vital-97, Kovrov-97
Lykes Explorer		Usa	1987	39,132	44,966	259	32	21	CC	ex Genevieve Lykes-98, President Arthur-96, I/a Doctor Lykes
Lykes Flyer		Gbr	2003	40,146	40,478	243	32	22	CC	
Lykes Hero		Bmu	1986	41,023	40,009	243	32	22	CC	ex Cast Progress-03, Alligator Reliance-01, Astro Prosperity-96
Lykes Inspirer *		Cyp	1990	16,075	17,565	174	23	17	Ro	ex Thorslake-00, Res Cogitans-99, Elena K-98, Krasnodon-96
Lykes Liberator		Usa	1987	39,132	44,966	259	32	21	CC	ex Stella Lykes-97, President Garfield-96, Tillie Lykes-87
Lykes Motivator		Usa	1991	37,474	43,084	242	32	21	CC	ex Jupiter-01, Ville de Jupiter-01, CGM Pascal-00 Nedlloyd Pascal-98, CGM Pascal-95
Lykes Navigator		Usa	1987	39,132	44,966	259	32	21	CC	ex Almeria Lykes-98, President Buchanan-96, I/a Almeria Lykes
Lykes Provider		Gbr	2003	39,941	50,500	260	32	-	CC	
Lykes Raider *		Mlt	1990	16,075	17,420	173	23	17	Co	ex Global Brazil-01, Nota Libre-00, Seaboard Venezuela-00, Nordana Successor-99, Bremer Voyager-98, Barbara L-97, Kislovodsk-96

Name	Eng	Flag	Year	GRT	DWT	Loa	Bm	Kts	Type	Former names
Lykes Ranger		Gbr	2002	40,146	36,644	243	32	20	CC	
Lykes Runner *		Mlt	1992	16,077	17,420	174	24	18	Ro	ex Nordana Surveyor-01, Nordana Kigoma-99, Nordana Kitale-98, Beloostrov-98, I/a Krasnograd
Lykes Voyager		Iom	1995	23,540	30,645	187	30	19	CC	ex P&O Nedlloyd Bandar Abbas-01, P&O Nedlloyd Yafo-99, Pax-98, CMBT Melbourne-97, Contship Melbourne-97, I/a Pax
Lykes Winner *		Cyp	1990	16,075	17,565	173	23	17	Ro	ex Thorshope-00, Cobra-99, Nordana Kampala-99, Global Hawk-98, Alioth Star-97, Marcela R-96, Yevgeniy Mravinskiy-96

* chartered from Oceanbulk Maritime SA, Greece. Also see other chartered vessels in index with 'Lykes' prefix.

ANZDL Ltd./Hong Kong (China)
See chartered-in vessels with 'Direct' prefix in index.

TMM Lines/Mexico
Name	Eng	Flag	Year	GRT	DWT	Loa	Bm	Kts	Type	Former names
Monte Alban		Lbr	1987	23,127	37,583	175	30	15	T	ex Al Salam-94, Atlantic Concord-90
TMM Campeche		Gbr	1989	35,958	42,976	240	32	21	CC	ex Choyang Park-01
TMM Colima		Iom	2002	40,146	40,478	243	32	21	CC	ex Contship Tenacity-02
TMM Guanajuato		Iom	2002	40,146	35,200	244	32	22	CC	
TMM Hermosillo		Gbr	1986	40,447	40,744	270	32	20	CC	ex Ming Propitious-01
TMM Jalisco		Bmu	1988	40,436	40,845	270	32	20	CC	ex Ming Progress-01
TMM Sinaloa		Gbr	1987	40,439	40,744	270	32	20	CC	ex Ming Promotion-01
TMM Tabasco		Gbr	2001	23,652	29,894	188	30	21	CC	ex Silvia-01
TMM Yucatan		Gbr	2003	40,146	40,478	243	32	22	CC	
Veracruz I		Pan	1977	30,259	10,535	180	28	18	V	ex Veracruz-02, Guanajuato-01, President-86

Danaos Shipping Co. Ltd.   Greece

Funnel: Blue or charterers colours.
Hull: Black with red boot-topping.

Name	Eng	Flag	Year	GRT	DWT	Loa	Bm	Kts	Type	Former names
Achilleas		Pan	1994	35,879	69,180	225	32	14	B	ex Milky Ace-02, Milky Star-02
Alexandra I		Pan	1994	35,886	69,090	225	32	14	B	ex Ocean Cherry-02
ANL Hamburg		Cyp	1989	46,697	44,851	275	32	22	CC	ex Norasia Hamburg-03, Cosco Bremerhaven-01, Honour-00, OOCL Honour-00, APL Arabia-97, OOCL Honour-96
APL Belgium		Sgp	2002	65,792	67,500	277	40	24	CC	
APL England		Sgp	2001	65,792	67,967	277	40	24	CC	
APL Guatemala		Pan	1986	41,280	38,717	245	32	22	CC	ex Zim Xingang-01, Cape Henry-99
APL Holland		Sgp	2001	65,792	67,500	277	40	24	CC	
APL Scotland		Sgp	2001	65,792	67,500	277	40	24	CC	
CMA CGM Elbe		Grc	1991	37,134	44,008	243	32	22	CC	ex Hanjin Bremen-03
CMA CGM Komodo		Grc	1991	37,134	43,966	243	32	22	CC	ex Hanjin Elizabeth-03
CMA CGM Kalamata		Grc	1991	37,134	43,967	243	32	22	CC	ex Hanjin Singapore-03
Dimitris C		Pan	1994	26,824	43,815	190	31	14	B	ex Aditya Gopal-02, Skausund-94
Eagle Express		Bhs	1978	28,078	23,047	204	31	21	CC	ex MSC Izmir-01, Eagle Quest-97, OOCL Beacon-95, Eagle Express-94, America Express-93
Fareast Sunny		Hkg	1989	23,270	42,248	180	31	14	B	ex Amalia-03, Golden Pegasus-02, Golden Wing-97
Fivos		Pan	1994	36,561	69,659	225	32	14	B	ex Global Ace-02, Global Star-02
Hyundai Commodore		Grc	1992	51,836	61,152	275	37	25	CC	
Hyundai Duke		Grc	1992	51,836	61,152	275	37	26	CC	
Independence		Pan	1986	41,413	38,624	248	32	22	CC	ex MOL Independence-03, Alligator Independence-01
Maria C		Pan	1994	26,093	45,205	188	31	14	B	ex May Star-02
MSC Noa		Pan	1986	35,953	43,270	241	32	20	CC	ex Hanjin Newyork-02
P&O Nedlloyd Caracas		Cyp	2004	39,941	32,000	-	-	-	CC	
P&O Nedlloyd Caribbean		Cyp	2004	39,941	32,000	-	-	-	CC	
Pacific Bridge		Cyp	1984	30,500	35,472	240	30	20	CC	ex MSC Fremantle-02, Pacific Bridge-98, Zim Mumbai-98, Hyundai Seattle-96, Pacific Bridge-94, Makalu-89, Pacific Bridge-86 (len-89)
Roberto C		Pan	1994	26,057	45,210	188	31	14	B	ex Azusa-02
Victory I		Pan	1988	42,809	40,638	253	32	22	CC	ex MOL Victory-03, Alligator Victory-01

Name	Eng	Flag	Year	GRT	DWT	Loa	Bm	Kts	Type	Former names
YM Milano		Grc	1988	41,786	45,036	248	32	21	CC	ex MSC Pegasus-03, Pegasus-02, Maersk Livorno-99, Pegasus-98, California Pegasus-98, Yamaaki Maru-92
YM Yantian		Cyp	1989	46,697	45,570	276	32	22	CC	ex Hope-03, OOCL Hope-00

Herm Dauelsberg GmbH & Co.   Germany

Funnel: White with black 'D' on cream band between narrow blue bands, or charterers colours.
Hull: Black or grey with red boot-topping.

Name	Eng	Flag	Year	GRT	DWT	Loa	Bm	Kts	Type	Former names
Lindavia		Lbr	1996	23,825	30,615	188	30	20	CC	ex Maersk Sydney-00, Lindavia-98, Sea Lindavia-98, Lindavia-96
Lobivia		Lbr	2001	23,652	30,375	188	30	21	CC	
Magnavia		Lbr	1996	23,825	30,743	188	30	20	CC	ex MOL Waratah-02, Alligator Unity-01, Maersk Oceania-00, Magnavia-97
Marivia		Lbr	2001	23,652	30,375	188	30	21	CC	
Novia		Lbr	1995	14,968	20,176	167	25	19	CC	ex Sea Novia-97, Novia-95
Safmarine Maluti		Lbr	1995	23,691	30,615	188	30	21	CC	ex Maersk Algeciras-01, Contship Auckland-97, Bonavia-95
Safmarine Tugela		Lbr	1995	23,691	30,743	188	30	21	CC	ex Altavia-03, Safmarine Tugela-03, Maersk Nagoya-01, Maersk Santos-99, Choyang Fortune-97, Altavia-95

newbuildings - two 60,000 grt 67,170 dwt container ships on order from South Korean builder for 2005 delivery.

Del Monte Fresh Fruit International Inc.   Bermuda

Funnel: Dark green with white 'Del Monte' on yellow edged red fruit symbol.
Hull: White with green boot-topping.

Name	Eng	Flag	Year	GRT	DWT	Loa	Bm	Kts	Type	Former names
Alcazar Carrier **		Bhs	1979	15,834	15,200	169	26	22	R	ex Winter Moon-99, Zenit Moon-87, Winter Moon-85
Algeciras Carrier *		Bhs	1979	15,834	15,200	169	26	22	R	ex Winter Sun-00, Zenit Sun-87, Winter Sun-84
Alicante Carrier **		Bhs	1979	15,834	15,200	169	26	22	R	ex Winter Star-99, Zenit Star-87, Winter Star-85
Cadiz Carrier **		Bhs	1979	15,833	15,100	169	26	22	R	ex Winter Water-99, Zenit Water-87, Winter Water-85
Malaga Carrier **		Bhs	1979	15,834	15,100	169	26	22	R	ex Winter Wave-99, Zenit Wave-87, Winter Wave-85
Planter		Lbr	1989	8,945	9,867	141	22	20	R	ex Del Monte Planter-00
Segovia Carrier **		Bhs	1980	15,834	15,200	169	26	22	R	ex Winter Sea-99, Zenit Sea-87, Winter Sea-85
Transporter *		Lbr	1990	8,945	9,867	141	22	20	R	ex Del Monte Transporter-00
Valencia Carrier		Bhs	1984	12,340	10,126	148	24	19	R	ex Spring Bride-02

** owned by subsidiary Network Shipping Ltd., USA (managed by Norbulk Shipping UK Ltd.) or ** managed by DFM Ltd., Poland.*

Horn-Linie OHG/Germany

Funnel: Grey with white 'H' on blue above red bands
Hull: White with red boot-topping.

Name	Eng	Flag	Year	GRT	DWT	Loa	Bm	Kts	Type	Former names
Hornbay		Lbr	1990	12,887	9,069	154	23	20	RR	
Horncap		Lbr	1991	12,887	9,069	154	23	20	RR	
Horncliff		Lbr	1992	12,877	9,069	154	23	20	RR	

Delmas Armement   France

Funnel: Blue with white ships wheel or buff (Elder Dempster service vessels).
Hull: Black with white 'DELMAS' or white with black lettering, white line above red boot-topping.

Name	Eng	Flag	Year	GRT	DWT	Loa	Bm	Kts	Type	Former names
Adeline Delmas		Atf	1985	23,275	33,520	176	30	14	BC	
Blandine Delmas		Atf	1986	23,275	33,611	176	30	14	BC	
Caroline Delmas		Atf	1986	23,275	33,611	176	30	14	BC	
Delmas Jacaranda ‡		Pan	1978	18,792	22,500	173	27	17	Co	ex Pathfinder-01, Lykes Pathfinder-00, Charles Lykes-98, Nedlloyd Bahrain-93
Delmas Surcouf †		Bhs	1983	17,280	22,312	170	27	17	Co	ex DSR Qingdao-95, Delmas Surcouf-94, C.R.Libreville-91
Delphine Delmas		Atf	1986	23,275	33,520	176	30	14	BC	
Flora Delmas		Hkg	2002	16,916	21,420	169	27	20	CC	
Gaby Delmas		Hkg	2002	16,916	20,944	169	27	20	CC	
Julie Delmas		Bhs	2002	26,047	30,453	196	30	21	CC	

Delmas Armement. ROSA DELMAS. *Hans Kraijenbosch.*

Peter Dohle Schiffs. ALTONIA. *Hans Kraijenbosch.*

Dole Food Company. DOLE ASIA. *Hans Kraijenbosch.*

Name	Eng	Flag	Year	GRT	DWT	Loa	Bm	Kts	Type	Former names
Kamina *		Bhs	1982	20,829	26,288	177	28	18	CC	ex Renee Delmas-00, CGM Mascareignes-96, Renee Delmas-95, Nedlloyd Bordeaux-92, Ville de Rouen-91, Ibn Zaidoun-91, Ville de Rouen-90, Renee Delmas-87
Karib *		Bhs	1982	20,424	26,287	177	28	18	CC	ex Kariba-03, Nordana Benefactor-00, Nathalie Delmas-99, MSC Jessica-99, Nathalie Delmas-97
Laura Delmas **		Hkg	1979	35,748	22,564	197	32	20	Ro	ex Kintampo-02, Towada-98, Kintampo-97, Nedlloyd Rochester-96, Rochester-88, Nedlloyd Rochester-86
Lucie Delmas **		Hkg	1979	35,748	22,564	197	32	19	Ro	ex Kagoro-03, Nedlloyd Rotterdam-96, Rotterdam-88, Nedlloyd Rotterdam-86
Marie Delmas		Bhs	2001	26,061	30,450	196	30	21	CC	
MOL Horizon **		Bhs	1982	20,829	26,287	177	28	17	CC	ex Suzanne Delmas-03, Suzanne-99, Marfret Caraibes-98, Suzanne Delmas-97, Ville de Marseille-89, Suzanne Delmas-87
MOL Rainbow		Bhs	2003	26,047	30,450	196	30	21	CC	ex Louis Delmas-03
MSC Ipanema		Bhs	1984	30,750	32,709	189	32	18	CC	ex Ursula Delmas-03, Sherbro-94, Nedlloyd Zaandam-91, Ursula Delmas-90, Etienne Denis-89
Nicolas Delmas		Bhs	2002	26,061	30,450	196	31	21	CC	
Patricia Delmas **		Bhs	1982	20,424	26,287	177	28	18	CC	ex Patricia D-98, Patricia-98, Patricia Delmas-97
Rokia Delmas		Lbr	1985	32,924	27,601	185	32	16	Ro	ex Rosa Blanca-98
Roland Delmas		Bhs	1980	30,774	24,223	187	32	17	Ro	ex Grand Bereby-94, Saint Roparzh-92, Hoegh Banniere-91, Woermann Banniere-90, Hoegh Banniere-89
Romain Delmas		Bhs	1981	31,007	24,260	187	32	17	Ro	ex Saint Romain-94, Hoegh Biscay-84
Rosa Delmas		Lbr	1985	32,951	25,577	185	32	16	Ro	ex Rosa Tucano-98, Calapoggio-95, Rosa Tucano-93
Roxane Delmas		Bhs	1979	32,875	27,980	188	32	17	Ro	ex Robert-95, Grand Bassam-95, Saint Roland-92, Bullaren-84, Tarifa-83, Vindafjord-81, Bullaren-81
Saint Roch		Bhs	1980	16,744	24,260	187	32	18	Ro	ex Hoegh Belle-81
Veronique Delmas		Bhs	1984	30,750	31,983	189	32	18	CC	
WAL Ubangi		Bhs	2002	26,047	30,450	196	30	21	CC	ex Catherine Delmas-03

* owned by Otal Invstments Ltd. (OT Africa Line) and ** managed by V. Ships UK
† chartered from Enterprises Shipping & Trading SA. (Restis Group, Greece) or ‡ from Cyprus Maritime Co. Ltd., Greece.

Dockwise NV   Netherlands

Funnel: Dark blue with black 'D' on white disc on light blue square on white band.
Hull: Black, orange or green with 'DOCKWISE', red boot-topping.

Name	Eng	Flag	Year	GRT	DWT	Loa	Bm	Kts	Type	Former names
Dock Express 10	(2)	Ant	1979	13,110	12,928	154	27	16	HLS	ex Dock Express France-94, Dock Express 10-87
Dock Express 11	(2)	Ant	1979	13,110	12,928	154	27	16	HLS	
Dock Express 12	(2)	Ant	1979	13,110	12,928	154	27	16	HLS	
Dock Express 20	(2)	Ant	1983	14,413	7,900	164	26	15	Ca	
Mighty Servant 1	(me2)	Ant	1983	19,954	23,473	160	40	14	HLS	(len/wid-98)
Mighty Servant 3	(me2)	Ant	1984	22,391	27,720	181	40	14	HLS	
Super Servant 3	(2)	Ant	1982	10,224	14,138	140	32	13	HLS	
Super Servant 4	(2)	Ant	1982	12,642	17,600	140	32	13	HLS	
Swan *		Ant	1981	22,788	30,060	181	32	16	HLS	ex Sea Swan-96, Swan H.L.-89, Dyvi Swan-88
Swift *		Ant	1983	22,835	32,187	183	32	15	HLS	ex Sea Swift-96, Swift H.L.-89, Dyvi Swift-88
Teal		Ant	1984	22,835	32,101	181	32	15	HLS	ex Sea Teal-96, Teal H.L.-89, Dyvi Teal-88
Tern		Ant	1982	22,788	30,060	181	32	16	HLS	ex Sea Tern-96, Tern H.L.-89, Dyvi Tern-88

Company owned by Heerema BV, Netherlands (70%) and van Ommeren (30%) and * managed by V. Ships (UK) Ltd.

Peter Dohle Schiffahrts-KG   Germany

Funnel: Black, black 'PD' on white diamond on broad red band bordered by narrow white bands, black with yellow 'ICL' above yellow wave inside yellow rectangular outline (Independent) or charterers colours.
Hull: Dark grey or black with red boot-topping.

Name	Eng	Flag	Year	GRT	DWT	Loa	Bm	Kts	Type	Former names
Adonia		Lbr	2004	51,350	58,341	286	32	-	CC	
Alabama		Lbr	1998	38,440	74,002	225	32	14	B	ex Belgrano-03, Golden Disa-99
Alaska *		Iom	1997	37,808	71,694	224	32	14	B	ex Oinoussian Leader-00
Alba *		Iom	1997	38.520	73,049	225	32	14	B	ex Hawthorn-01, NOL Sirius-00
Alberta		Cyp	1992	21,053	30,007	182	29	18	CC	ex Fesco Enterprise-00, Nedlloyd Singapore-99, Santa Victoria-96, MSC Victoria-95, Muscat Bay-94, Santa Victoria-92

Name	Eng	Flag	Year	GRT	DWT	Loa	Bm	Kts	Type	Former names
Altonia		Atg	2000	16,803	22,968	184	25	20	CC	ex Safmarine Buffalo-03, Maersk Felixstowe-01, CSAV Marsella-00
Amanda		Atg	2000	16,803	22,967	184	25	19	CC	ex Libra Livorno-03, I/a Amanda
APL Jakarta		Lbr	2003	35,645	41,850	220	32	22	CC	ex Julia-03, Alessa-03, I/a Carmen
APL Mexico		Atg	2001	35,645	42,089	220	32	22	CC	I/a Katjana
APL Portugal		Atg	2002	35,645	42,200	220	32	22	CC	I/a Antonia
APL Shanghai		Lbr	2003	35,645	42,062	220	32	22	CC	ex Azalea-03, I/a Clarissa
Atlantica		Mhl	1995	39,017	72,506	219	32	14	B	ex Atlantic Crown-00, Atlantic Rose-95
Attila *		Sgp	1997	38,520	73,049	225	32	14	B	ex Aspen-02, NOL Pollux-00
Cap Norte		Cyp	1997	25,608	34,015	208	30	21	CC	ex Santos Express-03, Sea Ocelot-02, Transroll Argentina-99, Cap Norte-99, Impala-98, Brasil Star-98, Impala-97
Columbus Chile		Cyp	1998	25,608	34,015	208	30	21	CC	ex Alianca Rotterdam-02, Lykes Traveler-01, CMA CGM Gaugain-01, CGM Gaugin-00, Charlotta-98
CSAV Chicago		Cyp	1997	25,608	34,015	208	30	21	CC	ex Maersk Freeport-99, Liberta-99, Montebello-99, I/a Liberta
DAL East London		Cyp	1994	30,526	34,079	205	32	19	CC	ex Ajama-02, Sea Star-99, Choyang Grace-97, Delaware Bay-95, Sea Musketeer-94, Ajama-94, I/a Charles de Foucauld
Independent Action		Lbr	1992	14,867	20,140	167	25	17	CC	ex Cielo di Colombia-99, Annabella D-98, CSAV Rupanco-97, Augusta-97, Brasil Express-94, Annabella D-92, I/a Auriga
Independent Endeavor		Lbr	1995	14,923	20,406	167	25	19	CC	ex Astoria D-00, Libra New York-99, Libra Valencia-97, I/a Astoria
Independent Spirit		Cyp	1991	12,997	17,610	152	25	17	CC	ex Erika E-97, Nuova Asia-97, Alabama-96, Atlantic Express-93, Donata Schulte-91
Independent Trader		Cyp	1991	12,997	17,610	150	25	17	CC	ex Carola E-97, Caroline-96, America-96, Carolina-91
Independent Venture		Lbr	1993	14,849	20,540	167	25	19	CC	ex Sea Voyager-99, Nautique-98
Latona		Lbr	1996	38,639	73,301	225	32	14	B	ex Atalanta-01, Anaisai-98
Libra Rio		Atg	2003	35,645	41,850	221	32	22	CC	I/a Katharina
Libra Santos		Lbr	2003	34,300	41,850	220	32	22	CC	ex Patricia-04, Amasia-03, I/a Cyrill
Marie Schulte		Atg	2001	16,803	22,900	185	25	20	CC	
Norasia Ayla		Lbr	2004	35,881	41,748	220	32	22	CC	ex Azulea-04
Norasia Enterprise		Deu	2003	51,350	58,341	286	32	-	CC	ex Amaranta-03

newbuildings : one further 51,350 grt 57,000 dwt, seven further 34,300 grt 41,800 dwt and two 58,340 dwt container ships on order from Polish builder for 2004-6 delivery, also four 40,300 grt 52,450 dwt and two 88,600 grt 97,470 dwt container ships from South Korean builder (2005/6).
* managed by Dohle IOM Ltd

Dole Food Company

Costa Rica

Funnel: Dark blue with with red 'Dole' symbol on white band or charterers colours.
Hull: White or cream with red 'Dole' symbol above blue line, blue boot-topping.

Name		Flag	Year	GRT	DWT	Loa	Bm	Kts	Type	Former names
Dole Africa		Lbr	1994	10,584	10,288	150	23	21	R	
Dole America		Lbr	1994	10,584	10,288	150	23	21	R	
Dole Asia		Lbr	1994	10,584	10,288	150	23	21	R	
Dole California *		Lbr	1989	16,488	11,800	179	27	20	CC	
Dole Chile		Lbr	1999	34,840	30,145	205	32	21	CC	
Dole Colombia		Lbr	1999	34,840	30,145	205	32	21	CC	
Dole Costarica *		Ita	1991	16,488	11,800	179	27	20	CC	
Dole Ecuador *		Lbr	1989	16,488	11,800	179	27	20	CC	
Dole Europa		Lbr	1994	10,584	10,288	150	23	21	R	
Dole Honduras *		Ita	1991	16,488	11,800	179	27	20	CC	
Tropical Land		Mlt	1972	9,932	10,973	156	21	21	R	ex Rio Guayas-97, Tropical Land-86, Brunsland-78, Maranga-76
Tropical Mist		Lbr	1986	9,749	11,998	149	22	20	R	
Tropical Morn		Lbr	1986	9,749	11,998	149	22	20	R	
Tropical Sky		Lbr	1986	9,749	11,998	149	22	20	R	
Tropical Star		Lbr	1986	9,749	11,998	149	22	20	R	

*Managed by subsidiary Reefership Marine Services Ltd including * on behalf of Tropical Shipping Italiana SpA., Italy.*

Name	Eng	Flag	Year	GRT	DWT	Loa	Bm	Kts	Type	Former names

Jan-Erik Dyvi

Norway

Funnel: Black with blue 'D' between two narrow blue bands on broad white band.
Hull: Grey with blue boot-topping or ** dark blue with light blue diagonal stripes.

Name	Eng	Flag	Year	GRT	DWT	Loa	Bm	Kts	Type	Former names
Black Marlin *		Ant	2000	37,938	57,021	218	42	14	HLS	
Blue Marlin *		Pan	2000	37,838	78,000	218	63	14	HLS	(wid-03)
Dyvi Adriatic		Lbr	1988	39,187	9,772	183	30	18	V	ex Wolfsburg-04
Dyvi Antwerpen		Nis	1973	25,615	9,652	188	23	18	V	ex Dyvi Kattegat-03
Dyvi Baltic		Hkg	1989	39,043	9,772	183	30	17	V	ex Hannover-02
Dyvi Pamplona		Nis	1999	37,237	12,778	180	31	19	V	
Dyvi Puebla		Nis	1999	37,237	12,780	180	31	19	V	
Kassel **		Pan	1999	51,204	17,297	180	32	19	V	

* managed for Offshore Heavy Transport ASA, Norway (35% owned by Wilh. Wilhelmsen and 13% by Dyvi) and ** on charter to NYK

The Egyptian Navigation Co.

Egypt

Funnel: Pale blue with crest on white disc, narrow black top or * pale green with black ship crest and 'MSC' on white disc.
Hull: Grey with green boot-topping or * pale green with white 'MISR SHIPPING LINE', dark green boot-topping.

Name	Eng	Flag	Year	GRT	DWT	Loa	Bm	Kts	Type	Former names
Abu Egila		Egy	1984	10,022	12,750	133	21	16	Ro	
Abu Zenima *		Egy	1983	10,022	12,402	133	21	16	Ro	
Aburdees *		Egy	1983	10,022	12,600	133	21	16	Ro	
Al Minufiyah		Egy	1991	10,022	12,802	130	21	16	Ro	
Alexandria		Egy	1991	10,022	12,802	130	21	16	Ro	
Domiat		Egy	1985	24,105	38,391	200	27	15	B	ex Al Sedik-85
Ebn Al Waleed		Egy	1987	10,022	12,800	133	21	14	Ro	
Edfu *		Egy	1997	38,464	71,572	224	32	14	B	
Esna *		Egy	1998	37,794	71,598	224	32	14	B	
Qena		Egy	1986	24,105	38,391	200	27	15	BC	

* owned by 40% owned associated company Misr Shipping Co., Egypt.

John T. Essberger GmbH & Co.

Germany

DAL Deutsche Afrika-Linien GmbH & Co.

Funnel: Buff, narrow red band on black-edged broad white band and black top or buff with broad green band.
Hull: Light grey or black with red boot-topping

Name	Eng	Flag	Year	GRT	DWT	Loa	Bm	Kts	Type	Former names
DAL Kalahari *	(2)	Lbr	1978	52,682	50,313	259	32	22	CC	ex Maersk Hamburg-95, Aberdeen Bay-93, Ortelius-92, London Express-92, Ortelius-91, London Express-90, Nuptse-88, Ortelius 86
DAL Reunion *		Lbr	1983	20,345	28,422	174	28	18	CC	ex Delmas Mascareignes-02, SEAL Ubena-00, Sea Merchant-97, Hongkong Senator-88, Ubena-87
Helvetia		Pan	1980	16,235	24,000	185	23	15	Ce	
Invicta		Pan	1983	9,948	16,730	145	22	15	Ce	
Karonga		Lbr	1991	14,793	17,328	159	24	16	C	ex Nordana Advisor-99, Karonga-98, Prosperity-96
MSC Agata		Pan	1982	20,345	28,422	174	28	18	CC	ex DAL Madagascar-03, SEAL Usaramo-00, Sea Trade-97, Usaramo-87
Sanaga		Lbr	1998	17,784	28,215	169	27	14	B	ex Paclogger-98
Sankuru		Lbr	2000	17,784	28,075	169	27	14	B	
Selinda		Lbr	2001	17,784	28,107	169	27	14	B	
Swakop		Lbr	2001	17,784	28,083	169	27	14	B	

newbuildings - 50,700 grt container ship from Danish builder (2005) and two 62,300 grt tankers South Korean builder (2006/7)
*managed by associated Transocean Shipmanagement GmbH, Germany and * on charter from Ciel Shipmanagement, Greece.*

Evergreen Marine Corp. (Taiwan) Ltd.

Taiwan

Funnel: Black with green eight-pointed star above 'EVERGREEN' within brown globe outline on broad white band.
Hull: Black or dark green with red or green boot-topping.

Name	Eng	Flag	Year	GRT	DWT	Loa	Bm	Kts	Type	Former names
Ever Able		Pan	1996	14,807	15,605	165	27	18	CC	
Ever Ally		Pan	1996	14,807	15,605	165	27	18	CC	
Ever Apex		Pan	1997	14,807	15,605	165	27	18	CC	
Ever Dainty		Pan	1997	52,700	55,604	294	32	25	CC	
Ever Decent		Pan	1997	52,090	55,604	294	32	25	CC	
Ever Delight		Pan	1998	52,090	55,515	294	32	25	CC	

Evergreen Marine Corp. EVER DELUXE. *M. D. J. Lennon.*

Evergreen Marine Corp. EVER GOVERN. *M. D. J. Lennon.*

Name	Eng	Flag	Year	GRT	DWT	Loa	Bm	Kts	Type	Former names
Ever Deluxe		Pan	1998	52,090	54,300	294	32	25	CC	
Ever Develop		Pan	1998	52,090	55,515	294	32	25	CC	
Ever Devote		Pan	1998	52,090	55,604	294	32	25	CC	
Ever Diadem		Pan	1998	52,090	55,604	294	32	25	CC	
Ever Diamond		Pan	1998	52,090	55,515	294	32	25	CC	
Ever Divine		Pan	1998	52,090	55,604	294	32	25	CC	
Ever Dynamic		Pan	1998	52,090	55,515	294	32	25	CC	
Ever Gaining		Pan	1987	46,410	53,240	270	32	20	CC	
Ever Garden		Twn	1984	37,023	43,401	231	32	20	CC	
Ever Gather		Pan	1984	37,023	43,401	231	32	20	CC	ex LT Gather-04, Ever Gather-02, Cosco Durban-01, Ever Gather-00
Ever General		Pan	1987	46,410	53,240	270	32	20	CC	
Ever Genius		Twn	1984	37,023	43,401	231	32	20	CC	
Ever Gentle		Twn	1984	37,023	43,401	231	32	20	CC	
Ever Gentry		Twn	1984	37,023	43,401	231	32	20	CC	
Ever Gifted		Twn	1984	37,023	43,401	231	32	20	CC	
Ever Given		Pan	1986	46,410	53,240	270	32	20	CC	
Ever Golden		Twn	1985	37,023	43,401	231	32	20	CC	
Ever Goods		Pan	1985	46,410	53,240	270	32	20	CC	
Ever Govern		Twn	1985	37,023	43,401	231	32	20	CC	
Ever Grade		Pan	1984	37,042	43,198	231	32	20	CC	
Ever Growth		Twn	1984	37,023	43,401	231	32	20	CC	
Ever Guest		Pan	1986	46,410	53,240	270	32	21	CC	
Ever Guide		Pan	1983	37,042	43,198	231	32	20	CC	ex Cosco New York-02, Ever Guide-00
Ever Racer		Pan	1994	53,359	57,904	294	32	23	CC	
Ever Reach		Pan	1994	53,359	57,904	294	32	23	CC	
Ever Refine		Pan	1995	53,103	58,912	266	32	23	CC	
Ever Renown		Pan	1994	53,101	58,912	294	32	23	CC	
Ever Repute		Pan	1995	53,103	58,912	294	32	23	CC	
Ever Result		Pan	1994	53,103	58,912	294	32	23	CC	
Ever Reward		Pan	1994	53,103	58,912	294	32	23	CC	
Ever Right		Pan	1993	53,359	57,904	294	32	23	CC	
Ever Round		Pan	1993	53,359	57,904	294	32	22	CC	
Ever Royal		Pan	1993	53,359	58,048	294	32	22	CC	
Ever Uberty		Pan	1999	69,246	63,216	285	40	25	CC	
Ever Ultra		Pan	1996	69,218	63,388	285	40	24	CC	
Ever Unific		Pan	1999	69,246	63,216	285	40	25	CC	
Ever Union		Pan	1997	69,218	63,388	285	40	24	CC	
Ever Unique		Pan	1997	69,218	63,388	285	40	24	CC	
Ever Unison		Pan	1996	69,218	63,388	285	40	24	CC	
Ever United		Pan	1996	69,218	62,386	285	40	24	CC	ex LT United-03, Ever United-00
Ever Uranus		Pan	1999	69,246	63,216	285	40	24	CC	
Ever Urban		Pan	2000	69,200	63,216	285	40	24	CC	
Ever Useful		Pan	1999	69,200	62,700	285	40	24	CC	
Green Modest		Twn	1976	12,406	16,858	163	23	15	CC	ex Uni-Modest-02, Access-84, Galleon Topaz-82, Ever Modest-80
Green Moral		Twn	1976	12,406	16,858	163	23	15	CC	ex Uni-Moral-02, Achieve-84, Galleon Opal-84, Galleon Onyx-81, Ever Moral-80
Hatsu Eagle *		Gbr	2001	76,022	75,898	300	43	25	CC	I/a Ever Eagle
Hatsu Elite		Gbr	2002	76,022	75,898	300	43	25	CC	
Hatsu Envoy *		Gbr	2002	76,067	75,898	300	43	25	CC	I/a Ever Envoy
Hatsu Ethic *		Gbr	2002	76,067	75,898	300	43	24	CC	
Hatsu Excel *		Gbr	2002	76,022	75,898	300	43	25	CC	
Hatsu Pride *		Gbr	2003	17,887	19,309	182	28	19	CC	
Hatsu Prima		Gbr	2003	17,887	19,309	182	28	18	CC	
LT Giant		Pan	1984	37,023	43,198	231	32	20	CC	ex Ever Giant-99
LT Gleamy		Pan	1985	37,023	43,401	231	32	20	CC	ex Ever Gleamy-02, LT Gleamy-00, Ever Gleamy-00
LT Going		Pan	1983	37,042	43,198	231	32	20	CC	ex Ever Going-99
LT Guard		Pan	1983	37,042	43,198	231	32	20	CC	ex Ever Guard-02, Cosco Santos-01, Ever Guard-00
LT Peace		Pan	2002	17,887	19,309	182	28	18	CC	I/a Ever Peace
LT Pearl		Pan	2002	17,887	19,309	182	28	18	CC	
LT Power		Pan	2002	17,887	19,309	182	28	19	CC	I/a Ever Power
LT Ulysses		Pan	2000	69,200	62,700	285	40	25	CC	ex Ever Ulysses-00
LT Unicorn		Pan	2000	69,200	62,700	285	40	25	CC	I/a Ever Unicorn
LT Unity		Pan	1999	69,246	62,700	285	40	25	CC	ex Ever Unity-00
LT Ursula		Pan	1999	69,200	62,700	285	40	25	CC	ex Ever Ursula-00

Name	Eng	Flag	Year	GRT	DWT	Loa	Bm	Kts	Type	Former names
LT Utile		Pan	2000	69,246	63,216	285	40	25	CC	ex Ever Utile-00
Uni-Accord		Hkg	1997	14,796	15,300	165	27	18	CC	ex Cosco Redsea-02, Uni-Accord-01
Uni-Active		Twn	1998	14,796	15,300	165	27	18	CC	
Uni-Adroit		Twn	1998	14,807	15,511	165	27	18	CC	
Uni-Ahead		Pan	1997	14,796	15,477	165	27	18	CC	
Uni-Ample		Pan	1997	14,796	15,300	165	27	18	CC	
Uni-Angel		Pan	1997	14,796	15,300	165	27	18	CC	
Uni-Ardent		Pan	1998	14,807	15,511	165	27	18	CC	
Uni-Arise		Pan	1997	14,796	15,300	165	27	18	CC	
Uni-Aspire		Pan	1998	14,807	15,511	165	27	18	CC	
Uni-Assent		Pan	1999	14,807	15,511	165	27	18	CC	
Uni-Assure		Pan	1999	14,807	15,511	165	27	18	CC	
Uni-Chart		Pan	1992	12,405	17,446	152	26	17	CC	
Uni-Concert		Pan	1993	12,405	17,446	152	26	17	CC	
Uni-Concord		Pan	1992	12,405	17,445	153	26	17	CC	
Uni-Corona		Pan	1992	12,405	17,445	152	26	17	CC	
Uni-Crown		Pan	1992	12,404	17,446	152	26	17	CC	
Uni-Forever		Pan	1979	13,995	18,813	162	23	15	CC	ex Ever Forever-84, Green Forever-83
Uni-Fortune		Pan	1978	13,995	18,828	162	23	15	CC	ex Ever Fortune-84, Green Fortune-83
Uni-Forward		Pan	1978	13,995	18,821	162	23	15	CC	ex Ever Forward-84, Green Forward-83
Uni-Oasis		Pan	1982	18,337	26,674	180	23	15	CC	ex Ever Oasis-94
Uni-Obtain		Pan	1983	19,698	30,254	183	24	15	CC	ex Ever Obtain-94
Uni-Ocean		Pan	1982	18,337	26,674	180	23	15	CC	ex Ever Ocean-94
Uni-Onward		Pan	1982	19,698	30,254	183	24	15	CC	ex Ever Onward-94
Uni-Order		Pan	1982	18,337	26,671	180	23	15	CC	ex Ever Order-94
Uni-Orient		Pan	1982	19,698	30,254	183	24	15	CC	ex Ever Orient-94
Uni-Pacific		Pan	1999	17,887	19,309	182	28	18	CC	
Uni-Patriot		Pan	1999	17,887	19,309	182	28	18	CC	
Uni-Perfect		Pan	2000	17,887	19,100	182	28	18	CC	
Uni-Phoenix		Pan	2000	18,300	19,100	182	28	18	CC	
Uni-Popular		Pan	2000	17,887	15,418	182	28	18	CC	
Uni-Premier		Pan	2001	17,887	19,309	182	28	18	CC	
Uni-Probity		Pan	2001	17,887	19,309	182	28	18	CC	
Uni-Promote		Pan	2001	17,887	19,308	182	28	18	CC	
Uni-Prosper		Pan	2001	17,887	19,309	182	28	18	CC	
Uni-Prudent		Pan	2000	17,887	19,309	182	28	18	CC	

newbuildings : ten 74,700 grt 78,200 dwt and eight 95,000 grt 98,500 dwt container ships for 2005-7 delivery from Far Eastern builders.
* owned by subsidiary Hatsu Marine Ltd., UK

Lloyd Triestino di Navigazione SpA/Italy

Funnel: Cream with blue 'LT' below narrow blue band, blue top.
Hull: Black with white 'LLOYD TRIESTINO' and green boot-topping.

Name	Eng	Flag	Year	GRT	DWT	Loa	Bm	Kts	Type	Former names
LT Garland		Ita	1988	46,445	44,424	270	32	20	CC	ex Ever Garland-99
LT Genova		Ita	1993	38,395	41,500	234	32	21	CC	ex Nuova Genova-01
LT Glamour		Ita	1987	46,445	53,240	270	32	20	CC	ex Ever Glamour-99
LT Grace		Ita	1984	37,023	43,198	231	32	20	CC	ex Ever Grace-99
LT Greet		Ita	1984	37,042	43,293	231	32	20	CC	ex Ever Greet-99
LT Lloydiana		Ita	1989	35,629	40,196	231	32	20	CC	ex Nuova Lloydiana-00, LT Lloydiana-00, Nuova Lloydiana-99
LT Trieste		Ita	1993	38,395	41,700	234	32	21	CC	ex Nuova Trieste-00
LT Unica		Ita	2001	68,888	63,216	285	40	25	CC	
LT Universo		Ita	2001	68,888	63,216	285	40	25	CC	
LT Usodimare		Ita	2000	69,200	63,216	285	40	25	CC	

Exxon Mobil Corp.   USA

Sea River Maritime Inc./USA

Funnel: Blue with narrow white band separated from upper broad red band by further narrow white band, narrow black top.
Hull: Black with red or blue boot-topping.

Name	Eng	Flag	Year	GRT	DWT	Loa	Bm	Kts	Type	Former names
S/R American Progress		Usa	1997	26,092	45,435	183	32	14	T	ex American Progress-00
S/R Baytown		Usa	1984	32,136	59,625	238	32	15	T	ex Exxon Baytown-93
S/R Bristol Bay		Usa	1999	30,770	45,671	189	32	16	T	ex HMI Ambrose Channel-02
S/R Charlestown		Usa	1983	27,669	49,762	194	32	16	T	ex Exxon Charlestown-93
S/R Columbia Bay *	(st)	Usa	1978	94,547	188,099	290	51	14	T	ex B.T. Alaska-03

Name	Eng	Flag	Year	GRT	DWT	Loa	Bm	Kts	Type	Former names
S/R Hinchinbrook	(st)	Usa	1977	44,869	92,017	273	32	16	T	ex Overseas Ohio-00
S/R Long Beach		Usa	1987	94,999	214,853	301	51	16	T	ex Exxon Long Beach-93
S/R Mediterranean		Usa	1986	94,999	214,853	301	51	16	T	ex Exxon Mediterranean-93, Exxon Valdez-90
S/R Wilmington		Usa	1984	27,508	48,779	194	32	16	T	ex Exxon Wilmington-93

* owned by OMI Corporation q.v.

International Marine Transportation Ltd./UK

Funnel: Black with white 'IMT' on blue rectangle on large white disc.
Hull: Black or dark grey with red boot-topping.

Name	Eng	Flag	Year	GRT	DWT	Loa	Bm	Kts	Type	Former names
Alrehab		Mhl	1999	160,279	301,620	335	58	15	T	
Eagle		Mhl	1993	160,347	284,493	332	58	16	T	
Eclipse		Mhl	1989	78,244	147,500	268	43	-	T	ex Ania-93
Hawk		Mhl	2000	159,414	306,320	335	58	16	T	
Kestrel		Mhl	2000	159,414	306,278	335	58	16	T	
Magnolia	(st)	Mhl	1973	139,092	280,428	340	54	15	T	ex Mobil Petrel-93, Yanbu Star-84, Al Bilad-83, Mobil Magnolia-83
Osprey		Mhl	1999	160,279	284,893	335	58	16	T	
Ras Laffan		Mhl	1999	57,066	105,424	244	42	14	T	
Raven		Mhl	1996	160,348	301,653	332	58	15	T	
Valiant		Mhl	1999	57,066	105,476	244	42	14	T	

Fednav Ltd.   Canada

Funnel: White, red design incorporating part of maple leaf with interlinked 'F' and 'C', broad black top.
Hull: Red with dark red boot-topping.

Name	Eng	Flag	Year	GRT	DWT	Loa	Bm	Kts	Type	Former names
Arctic		Can	1978	20,236	28,418	221	23	15	Obo	
Federal Agno ‡		Phl	1985	17,821	29,643	183	23	14	BC	ex Federal Asahi-89
Federal Asahi ‡		Hkg	1999	20,659	36,500	200	24	14	B	
Federal Baffin		Brb	1995	27,078	43,732	190	31	14	B	
Federal Danube ‡		Cyp	2004	23,100	35,000	200	24	14	B	
Federal Elbe ‡		Cyp	2003	22,600	37,000	200	24	14	B	
Federal Ems ‡		Cyp	2002	22,654	37,058	200	24	14	B	
Federal Franklin		Brb	1995	27,078	43,706	190	31	14	B	
Federal Hudson		Hkg	2000	20,659	36,563	200	24	14	B	
Federal Hunter		Hkg	2001	20,659	36,563	200	24	14	B	
Federal Kivalina		Hkg	2000	20,659	36,563	200	24	14	B	
Federal Kumano ‡		Hkg	2003	20,661	36,489	200	24	14	B	
Federal Kushiro ‡		Pan	2004	19,200	32,500	-	-	-	B	
Federal Leda ‡		Cyp	2003	22,600	37,000	200	24	14	B	
Federal Maas		Brb	1997	20,837	34,372	200	24	14	B	
Federal Mackinac ‡		Atg	2004	17,000	27,000	-	-	-	B	
Federal Manitou †		Atg	2004	17,000	27,000	-	-	-	B	
Federal Matane †		Atg	2004	17,000	27,000	-	-	-	B	
Federal Oshima		Hkg	1999	20,500	36,563	200	24	14	B	
Federal Progress		Hkg	1989	21,469	36,445	177	30	14	B	
Federal Rhine		Brb	1997	20,837	34,372	200	23	14	B	
Federal Rideau		Hkg	2000	20,500	36,563	200	24	14	B	
Federal Saguenay		Brb	1996	20,837	34,372	200	23	14	B	
Federal Schelde		Brb	1997	20,837	34,372	200	23	14	B	
Federal St. Laurent		Brb	1996	20,837	34,372	200	23	14	B	
Federal Shimanto ‡		Pan	2001	19,125	32,787	190	24	14	B	
Federal Sumida ‡		Pan	1998	37,689	72,493	225	32	-	B	
Federal Venture		Hkg	1989	21,469	36,445	177	30	14	B	ex Northern Venture-02
Federal Welland		Hkg	2000	20,659	35,750	200	24	14	B	
Federal Weser ‡		Cyp	2002	21,300	35,000	200	24	14	B	
Federal Yoshino ‡		Pan	2001	19,125	32,845	190	24	14	B	
Federal Yukon		Hkg	2000	20,659	36,563	200	24	14	B	
Lake Erie		Mhl	1980	22,734	38,294	223	23	14	B	ex Federal Ottawa-95
Lake Michigan		Mhl	1981	22,734	38,294	222	23	14	B	ex Federal Maas-95
Lake Ontario		Mhl	1980	22,734	38,294	222	23	14	B	ex Federal Danube-95
Lake Superior		Mhl	1981	22,734	38,294	222	23	14	B	ex Federal Thames-95
Mecta Sea ‡		Bhs	1984	17,066	28,166	178	23	14	B	ex Union-97, Socrates-92
Orsula ‡		Hrv	1996	20,837	34,198	200	24	14	B	ex Federal Calumet-97

Evergreen Marine Corp. (Lloyd Triestino). LT TRIESTE. *Hans Kraijenbosch.*

Exxon Mobil Corp. HAWK. *Hans Kraijenbosch.*

Fednav. FEDERAL RHINE. *J. M. Kakebeeke.*

Name	Eng	Flag	Year	GRT	DWT	Loa	Bm	Kts	Type	Former names
Tecam Sea ‡		Bhs	1984	17,056	27,631	178	23	16	B	ex Alam University-98, University-95, Monte Bonita-93, Rich Alliance-89

newbuildings : two 35,000 dwt bulk carriers for 2004 delivery.
managed by Anglo-Eastern Ship Management Ltd. except † chartered fro Lauterjung or ‡ from various other owners.
Other vessels chartered-in from Oldendorff, Spar Shipping, Viken Ship Management AS (A/S J. Ludwig Mowinckels Rederi), Norway

Fortum Oil & Gas Oy Finland

Funnel: Black with diamond divided green over blue.
Hull: Black or dark blue, some with pale green or white 'NESTESHIP', red or pink boot-topping.

Name	Eng	Flag	Year	GRT	DWT	Loa	Bm	Kts	Type	Former names
Kihu		Fin	1984	13,974	22.717	161	23	14	T	
Mastera	(me2)	Fin	2003	64,259	106,208	252	44	14	T	
Natura		Fin	1993	51,161	91,263	242	40	14	T	
Palva		Fin	1986	28,292	48,376	200	30	14	T	
Sotka		Fin	1976	11,290	16,420	164	22	14	T	
Tavi		Fin	1985	13,974	19,999	161	23	14	T	
Tempera	(me2)	Fin	2002	64,259	106,034	252	44	14	T	
Tervi		Fin	1986	28,292	48,375	202	30	14	T	

newbuildings - four 25,000 dwt tankers on order from Chinese builder for 2004 delivery.

Frontline Ltd. Bermuda

Frontline Management AS/Norway

Funnel: White with light blue 'f' symbol on dark blue vertical rectangle above 'FRONTLINE'.
Hull: Black, brown or light blue with red or dark blue boot-topping.

Name	Eng	Flag	Year	GRT	DWT	Loa	Bm	Kts	Type	Former names
Ariake		Bhs	2001	159,397	298,530	333	60	15	T	ex Berge Ariake-01
Dundee		Lbr	1993	156,408	302,432	332	58	15	T	ex Golar Dundee-01
Edinburgh		Lbr	1993	156,408	302,493	332	58	15	T	ex Golar Edinburgh-01
Front Ace		Lbr	1993	144,652	275,546	325	57	15	T	ex General Ace-00, Sea Princess-93
Front Ardenne		Nis	1998	79,633	152,550	258	46	15	T	ex Ardenne-00
Front Birch		Nis	1991	78,443	151,680	267	46	14	T	ex Birch-99
Front Brabant		Nis	1998	79,633	152,550	269	46	15	T	ex Brabant-00
Front Breaker		Nis	1991	89,004	169,146	285	45	14	Obo	
Front Century †		Bhs	1998	157,976	311,189	334	58	15	T	
Front Champion †		Bhs	1998	157,976	311,286	334	58	15	T	
Front Chief †		Bhs	1999	157,863	311,224	334	58	15	T	
Front Climber		Sgp	1991	89,004	169,146	285	45	14	Obo	
Front Commander †		Bhs	1999	157,863	311,168	334	58	15	T	
Front Commodore †		Lbr	2000	159,397	298,620	333	60	15	T	ex Stena Commodore-01
Front Comor		Nis	1993	77,931	142,031	269	45	14	T	ex Comor-99
Front Crown †		Bhs	1999	157,863	311,176	334	58	15	T	ex Front President-99
Front Driver		Nis	1991	89,004	169,146	285	45	14	Obo	
Front Duchess		Sgp	1993	149,997	284,480	322	56	14	T	ex Sea Duchess-96
Front Duke		Sgp	1992	149,945	284,420	322	56	14	T	ex Sea Duke-96
Front Eagle †		Bhs	2002	160,904	309,064	333	58	-	T	l/a Moseagle
Front Emperor		Sgp	1992	77,356	147,273	274	43	14	T	ex Sea Emperor-96
Front Falcon ***		Bhs	2002	160,904	308,875	333	58	-	T	l/a Mosfalcon
Front Fighter *		Nis	1998	79,669	153,328	269	46	14	T	
Front Glory		Nis	1995	79,979	149,834	269	46	15	T	ex London Glory-97
Front Granite		Nis	1991	77,931	142,031	269	45	14	T	ex Granite-01
Front Guider		Sgp	1991	89,004	169,146	285	45	14	Obo	
Front Highness		Sgp	1991	149,945	284,317	322	56	14	T	ex Sea Highness-96
Front Hunter *		Nis	1998	79,669	153,328	269	46	14	T	
Front Lady		Sgp	1991	149,945	284,497	322	56	14	T	ex Sea Lady-96
Front Leader		Sgp	1991	89,004	169,146	285	45	14	Obo	
Front Lillo		Nis	1991	77,725	134,893	274	43	15	T	ex Lillo-01
Front Lord		Sgp	1991	149,945	282,057	322	56	14	T	ex Sea Lord-96
Front Maple		Nis	1991	78,443	151,680	267	46	14	T	ex Maple-00
Front Melody †		Lbr	2001	79,525	150,500	272	46	14	T	
Front Page		Lbr	2002	156,916	299,164	330	60	-	T	l/a Front Saga
Front Pride		Nis	1993	79,978	149,686	269	46	15	T	ex London Pride-98
Front Rider		Sgp	1992	89,004	169,146	285	45	14	Obo	
Front Sabang		Sgp	1990	153,644	285,715	328	57	14	T	ex Sabang-00, Damar-94, Argo Dione-91
Front Serenade		Lbr	2002	157,000	298,300	333	60	16	T	

Fortum Oil & Gas. TEMPERA. *Hans Kraijenbosch.*

Frontline. OPALIA (on charter to Royal Dutch Shell Group). *Hans Kraijenbosch.*

Name	Eng	Flag	Year	GRT	DWT	Loa	Bm	Kts	Type	Former names
Front Spirit		Nis	1993	77,356	147,273	274	43	14	T	ex Sea Spirit-97, Sea Empress-97
Front Splendour		Nis	1995	79,979	148,835	269	46	15	T	ex London Splendour-97
Front Stratus		Lbr	2002	156,916	299,157	330	60	-	T	
Front Striver		Sgp	1992	89,004	169,204	285	45	14	Obo	
Front Sunda		Nis	1992	77,931	142,031	269	45	14	T	ex Sunda-99
Front Symphony †		Lbr	2001	79,525	150,500	272	46	14	T	
Front Tina		Lbr	2000	159,463	298,824	333	60	16	T	
Front Tobago ‡		Lbr	1993	147,580	260,619	333	56	15	T	ex Toba-00
Front Viewer		Sgp	1992	89,004	169,146	285	45	14	Obo	
Front Warrior †		Bhs	1998	79,669	153,181	269	46	14	T	
Hakata		Bhs	2002	159,383	298,465	333	60	15	T	
Mindanao		Sgp	1998	81,265	147,447	274	48	15	T	
Opalia ++		Iom	1999	159,756	302,193	333	60	15	T	
Oscilla ++		Iom	2000	160,805	302,561	333	60	16	T	

Controlled (48%) by John Fredriksen owned Hemen Holdings.
Managed by V. Ships (UK) Ltd, V. Ships Norway AS, International Tanker Management Holding Ltd, UAE or Thome Ship Management.
* owned by 64% Hemen Holdings controlled Seatankers Management Co. Ltd, Cyprus (managed by V. Ships Norway AS or ** Wallem Shipmanagement, Hong Kong) or *** owned by fully controlled Mosvold Shipping AS, Norway.
† chartered from Dr. Peters KG fund, Germany and ‡ jointly owned by Overseas Shipholding (30%) and CMB-Euronav (30%) q.v.
++ chartered to Royal Dutch-Shell Group

Golar LNG Ltd/Bermuda

Name	Eng	Flag	Year	GRT	DWT	Loa	Bm	Kts	Type	Former names
Gimi	(st)	Lbr	1976	96,235	72,703	294	42	19	Lgc	
Golar Freeze	(st)	Lbr	1977	95,879	66,200	288	43	20	Lng	
Golar Mazo	(st)	Lbr	2000	111,835	76,210	290	47	19	Lng	
Golar Spirit	(st)	Lbr	1981	106,577	80,239	289	45	19	Lng	
Golar Winter	(st)	Nis	2004	95,800	77,000	277	43	-	Lng	
Hilli	(st)	Gbr	1975	96,235	72,703	293	42	19	Lgc	ex Golar Glacier-75
Ibnu *		Pan	1993	22,367	35,601	178	28	-	T	
Khannur	(st)	Gbr	1977	96,235	73,074	293	42	19	Lgc	
Methane Princess	(st)	Gbr	2003	93,899	77,707	277	43	-	Lng	

newbuildings : two further 95,000 grt Lng tankers on order.
* jointly owned with P.T. Pelayaran Pelumin, Indonesia.

Golden Ocean Services (UK) Ltd./UK

Funnel: Blue with gold overlapping 'GO'.
Hull: Black with red boot-topping

Name	Eng	Flag	Year	GRT	DWT	Loa	Bm	Kts	Type	Former names
Front Comanche		Atf	1999	159,423	300,133	333	60	15	T	ex Stena Comanche-01
Front Commerce		Lbr	1999	159,423	300,144	333	60	16	T	ex Stena Commerce-01
Golden Fountain *		Pan	1995	156,303	301,665	328	57	15	T	
Golden Stream *		Pan	1995	144,149	275,616	326	57	14	T	
Pacific Lagoon *		Bel	1999	163,346	305,839	333	58	15	T	

* managed by Thome Ship Management Pte. Ltd.

Gorthon Lines AB   Sweden

Funnel: Yellow with yellow curled device on blue disc.
Hull: Grey or white with red boot-topping.

Name	Eng	Flag	Year	GRT	DWT	Loa	Bm	Kts	Type	Former names
Ada Gorthon		Swe	1984	13,525	11,425	156	22	15	Ro	
Alida Gorthon		Swe	1977	12,750	14,240	141	22	15	B	
Ingrid Gorthon		Swe	1977	12,750	14,298	141	22	15	B	
Joh. Gorthon		Swe	1977	11,907	7,182	142	21	15	Ro	
Margit Gorthon		Bmu	1977	12,672	14,240	141	22	15	B	
Maria Gorthon		Swe	1984	13,533	11,491	156	22	15	Ro	
Obbola		Swe	1996	20,186	9,589	156	24	16	Ro	
Ortviken		Swe	1996	20.154	9,618	156	24	16	Ro	
Ostrand		Swe	1996	18,265	9,618	156	24	16	Ro	
Viola Gorthon		Swe	1987	18,773	10,917	166	23	20	Ro	

Part owned by Leif Hoegh & Co. ASA (49.98%) and all managed by Gorthon Fleet Services AB

The Great Eastern Shipping Co. Ltd.

India

Funnel: Yellow with 'AHB' on white diamond on red and green diagonally *divided houseflag, narrow black top.*
Hull: Grey or black with 'Great Eastern', red boot-topping.

Name	Eng	Flag	Year	GRT	DWT	Loa	Bm	Kts	Type	Former names
Jag Anjali	Ind	1986	36,512	66,203	230	32	14	T	ex Suzanne-03
Jag Arnav *	Ind	1995	38,265	71,122	225	32	14	B	ex Floral Deigo-01
Jag Arpan	Ind	1986	36,512	66,183	230	32	14	T	
Jag Laadki	Ind	1992	78,710	145,242	270	44	14	T	ex Knock Adoon-93
Jag Laila	Ind	1987	52,997	96,967	247	42	14	T	ex Singapore Spirit-03, Galaxy River-96
Jag Lakshya	Lbr	1989	79,552	139,753	267	46	14	T	ex Geres Knock-04, Sheen-99
Jag Lamha	Ind	1987	52,764	98,214	247	42	14	T	ex Sudong Spirit-03, Full Moon River-95
Jag Larjish	Ind	1985	56,456	83,660	244	43	15	T	ex Stellata-04
Jag Lata	Ind	2003	57,508	105,709	244	43	14	T	
Jag Lavanya	Ind	2004	58,400	105,000	244	43	14	T	
Jag Laxmi	Ind	1999	58,374	105,051	243	42	14	T	
Jag Leela	Ind	1999	58,374	105,148	243	42	14	T	
Jag Leena	Ind	1985	55,903	95,007	246	44	14	T	ex Magellan Spirit-03, Nikko Maru-95
Jag Leher	Ind	1986	58,853	107,544	246	43	14	T	ex Genmar Pacific-03, North Pacific-03, Nord Pacific-93
Jag Padma	Ind	1982	27,771	47,803	183	32	15	T	ex Paula Maersk-92
Jag Palak *	Ind	1985	18,542	27,402	170	26	15	T	
Jag Pankhi	Ind	2003	27,627	46,272	183	32	14	T	
Jag Pari *	Ind	1982	20,302	28,679	171	27	14	T	
Jag Pavitra	Ind	1985	28,010	50,600	183	32	15	T	ex Olivia Maersk-97, Evelyn Maersk-93
Jag Prachi	Ind	1996	25,202	44,124	182	30	14	T	ex Torm Lily-01
Jag Pradip	Ind	1996	27,627	45,683	183	32	14	T	
Jag Pragati	Ind	1985	18,542	27,402	170	26	15	T	
Jag Praja	Ind	1982	17,199	29,990	171	26	15	T	ex Rossi-95, Novorossiysk-91, World Product-82
Jag Prakash	Ind	2003	27,627	46,345	183	32	14	T	
Jag Pranam	Ind	1984	28,010	50,600	183	32	15	T	ex A.P. Moller-96
Jag Pratap	Ind	1995	27,627	45,692	183	32	14	T	
Jag Prayog	Ind	1982	17,199	29,990	171	26	15	T	ex Stavropol-95
Jag Preeti *	Ind	1981	20,302	29,138	171	27	14	T	
Jag Rani *	Ind	1984	24,643	41,545	183	31	14	B	ex Malaya-99, Spring Stork-96, Sanko Stork-86
Jag Ratna	Ind	1977	21,396	35,100	185	27	14	B	ex Captain John D.Pateras-89, Pantanassa-79
Jag Rishi *	Ind	1984	24,111	41,093	185	30	14	B	ex Spring Peacock-96, Sanko Peacock-86
Jag Vayu	Ind	1978	21,308	28,400	192	26	19	Lpg	ex Herdis-97, Helios-91, Lord Kelvin-87
Jag Vidya	Ind	1977	16,926	27,490	170	26	15	B	ex Amita-88, Syra-87
Jag Vikas	Ind	1977	16,393	26,781	177	23	16	B	ex Polychronis-89
Jag Vikram *	Ind	1980	16,910	27,463	170	26	15	B	ex Jag Kranti-89, Radhika-87, Mia-86
Nisha †	Vct	1977	16,931	27,481	170	26	15	B	ex Jag Vishnu-98, Gayatri-88, Petropolis-87, Triton-82

newbuildings - four 159,000 dwt tankers for 2004/5 delivery from South Korean builder.
* managed by Five Stars Shipping Co. Pte. Ltd., or † by The Great Eastern Shipping Co. London Ltd., UK

Grimaldi Group

Italy

Funnel: Yellow with red 'Gt' symbol or blue with either white 'I' or 'A' symbol or white 'S' within white ring.
Hull: Yellow with black 'GRIMALDI LINES' on white upperworks, red boot-topping.

Name	Eng	Flag	Year	GRT	DWT	Loa	Bm	Kts	Type	Former names
Gran Bretagna *	Ita	1999	51,714	18,461	181	32	18	Ro	
Grand Benelux *	Ita	2001	37,712	12,594	176	31	20	Ro	
Grande Africa	Ita	1998	56,642	26,195	214	32	18	Ro	
Grande Amburgo	Ita	2003	56,642	26,170	214	32	18	Ro	
Grande America	Mlt	1997	56,642	26,169	214	32	18	Ro	
Grande Atlantico	Ita	1999	56,640	26,170	214	32	18	Ro	
Grande Brasile	Ita	2000	56,642	26,170	214	32	18	Ro	
Grande Ellade *	Ita	2001	52,000	18,440	181	32	18	Ro	
Grande Europa *	Ita	1998	51,714	18,461	181	32	18	Ro	
Grande Francia §	Ita	2002	56,642	26,170	214	32	18	Ro	
Grande Italia *	Ita	2001	37,712	12,594	176	31	20	Ro	
Grande Mediterraneo *	Ita	1998	51,714	18,427	181	32	18	Ro	
Grande Napoli	Ita	2003	42,600	14,900	201	31	20	Ro	
Grande Nigeria §	Ita	2002	56,642	26,170	214	32	18	Ro	
Grande Portogallo *	Ita	2002	37,712	12,594	176	31	20	Ro	
Grande Roma	Ita	2003	42,600	14,900	201	31	20	Ro	

Name	Eng	Flag	Year	GRT	DWT	Loa	Bm	Kts	Type	Former names
Grande San Paolo		Ita	2003	56,642	26,170	214	32	18	Ro	
Grande Scandinavia *		Ita	2001	52,000	18,440	181	32	18	Ro	
Grande Spagna *		Ita	2002	37,712	12,594	176	31	20	Ro	
Laura †		Vct	1981	32,068	22,447	204	31	22	Ro	ex Laura Delmas-02, Jolly Celeste-00, Katsina-99, Anatoily Vasilyev-97
Repubblica Argentina †		Ita	1998	51,925	23,882	206	30	20	Ro	
Repubblica del Brasile †		Ita	1998	51,925	23,800	206	30	20	Ro	
Repubblica di Amalfi		Ita	1989	42,574	25,450	216	30	18	Ro	
Repubblica di Genova *		Ita	1988	42,567	25,450	216	30	18	Ro	
Repubblica di Roma §		Ita	1992	42,001	19,287	184	30	19	Ro	
Repubblica di Venezia †		Ita	1987	48,622	18,730	213	30	18	Ro	

Newbuildings : four 14,900 dwt vehicle carriers and one 26,000 dwt ro-ro vessel for 2004-6 delivery.

Ships owned by related Italian companies * Atlantica SpA di Navigazione, by † Grandi Traghetti SpA di Navigazione, by ‡ Sicula Oceanica SpA or by § Industria Armamento Meridionale SpA, who also operate other ferries and ro-ro vessels in the Mediterranean.

ACL Shipmanagement AB/Sweden

Funnel: White with blue 'ACL' over wavy line, black top.
Hull: Black with white 'ACL' symbol.

Name	Eng	Flag	Year	GRT	DWT	Loa	Bm	Kts	Type	Former names
Atlantic Cartier		Swe	1985	58,358	51,648	292	32	17	Ro	
Atlantic Companion		Swe	1984	57,255	51,648	292	32	17	Ro	ex Companion Express-94, Atlantic Companion-87
Atlantic Compass		Swe	1984	57,255	51,648	292	32	17	Ro	
Atlantic Concert		Swe	1984	57,255	51,648	292	32	17	Ro	ex Concert Express-94, Atlantic Concert-87
Atlantic Conveyor		Swe	1985	58,438	51,648	292	32	17	Ro	
Grande Argentina		Swe	2001	56,642	26,170	214	32	18	Ro	
Grande Buenos Aires		Swe	2004	56,642	26,169	214	32	18	Ro	

Hanjin Shipping Co. Ltd.   South Korea

Funnel: Orange with white 'H' inside white ring.
Hull: Black with white 'HANJIN', red boot-topping.

Name	Eng	Flag	Year	GRT	DWT	Loa	Bm	Kts	Type	Former names
Hanjin Antwerp *		Kor	1996	16,252	27,367	167	26	14	B	
Hanjin Barcelona		Pan	1992	50,792	62,723	290	32	24	CC	
Hanjin Beijing *		Kor	1996	65,893	67,115	279	40	25	CC	
Hanjin Berlin *		Kor	1997	66,403	67,236	279	40	25	CC	
Hanjin Bombay *		Kor	1994	16,252	27,029	167	26	14	B	
Hanjin Brisbane *		Kor	1997	16,252	27,327	167	26	14	B	
Hanjin Busan †		Cyp	1979	17,682	18,782	201	24	18	CC	
Hanjin Calcutta *		Kor	1997	16,270	27,365	167	26	14	B	
Hanjin Capetown		Pan	1993	76,954	147,631	274	45	13	B	
Hanjin Colombo		Pan	1994	50,792	62,850	290	32	24	CC	
Hanjin Dampier		Kor	1989	110,541	207,346	309	50	13	B	
Hanjin Gladstone		Lbr	1990	110,541	207,391	309	50	13	B	
Hanjin Haypoint		Kor	1990	77,650	151,431	274	45	13	B	
Hanjin Houston *		Kor	1995	16,232	27,209	167	26	14	B	
Hanjin Istanbul *		Kor	1997	16,270	27,369	167	26	14	B	
Hanjin Kaohsiung **		Cyp	1990	37,134	43,925	243	32	22	CC	
Hanjin Kwangyang †		Cyp	1978	14,953	20,195	187	25	17	CC	ex Ever Victory-83
Hanjin London *		Kor	1996	66,687	67,298	279	40	26	CC	
Hanjin Los Angeles		Pan	1997	51,754	62,700	290	32	24	CC	
Hanjin Madras		Kor	1990	77,650	150,431	274	45	13	B	
Hanjin Malta		Kor	1993	51,299	62,649	290	32	24	CC	
Hanjin Marseilles		Pan	1993	51,299	62,681	290	32	24	CC	
Hanjin Melbourne		Kor	1987	93,643	186,260	292	48	13	B	ex Westin Seven-89
Hanjin Nagoya		Pan	1998	51,754	62,500	290	32	24	CC	
Hanjin New Orleans		Kor	1994	37,550	70,337	225	32	13	B	
Hanjin Osaka		Pan	1992	51,754	62,681	290	32	24	CC	ex Ville de Shanghai-99, Hanjin Osaka-98
Hanjin Oslo		Pan	1998	65,469	68,993	279	40	25	CC	
Hanjin Paris		Pan	1997	66,687	68,500	279	40	25	CC	
Hanjin Penang *		Kor	1997	16,270	27,369	167	26	14	B	
Hanjin Pittsburg		Kor	1990	25,461	38,393	186	28	15	B	ex Pittsburg-93
Hanjin Pohang †		Cyp	1979	17,933	18,798	201	24	17	CC	
Hanjin Port Kembla		Pan	1993	68,243	126,267	264	41	13	B	
Hanjin Portland		Kor	1993	50,792	62,716	290	32	24	CC	
Hanjin Richards Bay		Pan	1997	75,752	149,322	269	43	14	B	

Gorthon Lines AB. ADA GORTHON. *F. de Vries.*

Grimaldi Group. GRAN BRETAGNE. *Oliver Sesemann.*

Grimaldi Group. GRANDE FRANCIA. *F. de Vries.*

Name	Eng	Flag	Year	GRT	DWT	Loa	Bm	Kts	Type	Former names
Hanjin Roberts Bank		Pan	1994	73,706	135,069	268	43	14	B	
Hanjin Rome		Pan	1998	65,469	68,955	280	40	25	CC	
Hanjin San Francisco		Kor	1996	50,792	62,681	290	32	24	CC	
Hanjin Seoul †		Cyp	1979	17,675	18,835	201	24	17	CC	
Hanjin Shanghai		Pan	1995	50,792	62,799	290	32	24	CC	
Hanjin Sydney		Kor	1987	95,513	188,117	291	48	13	B	ex Westin Nine-89
Hanjin Tacoma		Pan	1994	37,550	70,347	225	32	13	B	
Hanjin Tampa *		Kor	1995	16,252	27,209	167	26	14	B	
Hanjin Tokyo		Pan	1994	50,792	62,742	290	32	24	CC	
Hanjin Valencia		Pan	1998	51,754	62,799	290	32	24	CC	
Hanjin Vancouver **		Cyp	1990	35,745	44,764	241	32	20	CC	ex Hanjin Hamburg-90
Hanjin Washington		Pan	1997	65,643	67,272	279	40	25	CC	
Hanjin Wilmington		Pan	1997	50,792	62,799	290	32	24	CC	

newbuildings : two 31,800 dwt, two 176,000 dwt bulk carriers, two 48,000 dwt tankers and five 85,000 dwt container ships for 2004-6 delivery.
The company also operates four large Lng tankers, operating mainly in the Far East.
* owned by Korea French Banking Corp. (formed jointly by Societe Generale SA and Hanil Development Co. Ltd.)
Formerly owned now chartered from † Varship Shipping Co. Ltd., or ** from Samartzis Maritime Enterprises Co. SA, both Greece

Senator Lines GmbH/Germany

Funnel: *White with broad red band beneath blue top.*
Hull: *Black or dark grey with red or grey boot-topping.*

Name	Eng	Flag	Year	GRT	DWT	Loa	Bm	Kts	Type	Former names
America Senator **	Mys	1993	34,231	45,696	216	32	19	CC	ex DSR-America-00	
Berlin Senator ‡	Lbr	1991	37,071	47,120	237	32	21	CC		
Baykal Senator ‡	Pan	1991	37,071	47,120	237	32	21	CC	ex DSR-Senator-00, Vladivostock-91	
California Senator *	Deu	1994	34,617	45,025	216	32	21	CC	ex Sea Initiative-95, Chesapeake Bay-94, Californian Senator-94	
Canada Senator *	Lbr	1992	30,567	31,160	203	31	19	CC	ex Northern Joy-01, CMA Xingang-01, Contship Mexico-99, Northern Joy-98, Sea Vigor-97, Hyundai Tacoma-96, Sea Hawk-94, Northern Joy-93	
Hongkong Senator *	Deu	1995	34,617	45,470	216	32	21	CC		
Japan Senator **	Mys	1993	34,231	45,696	216	32	19	CC	ex Choyang Elite-98, DSR-Asia-96	
London Senator *	Deu	1994	34,454	45,696	216	32	24	CC	ex Sea Endeavour 05, Delaware Bay-94, London Senator-94	
Montreal Senator §	Bmu	1982	31,570	32,207	223	32	22	CC	ex Cast Power-03, Contship Success-99, CanMar Success-98, Alligator Excellence-95, America Maru-90	
Pacific Senator †	Lbr	1992	34,231	45,696	216	32	19	CC	ex DSR-Pacific-97	
Patmos Senator †	Lbr	1992	34,231	45,696	216	32	19	CC	ex DSR-Europe-97	
Pohang Senator †	Deu	1998	53,324	63,537	294	32	23	CC		
Port Said Senator †	Lbr	1994	19,819	22,300	174	27	19	CC	ex DSR-Port Said-00, Northern Pleasure-94	
Portugal Senator †	Deu	1998	53,324	63,645	294	32	23	CC		
Pudong Senator †	Deu	1997	53,324	62,057	294	32	23	CC		
Pugwash Senator †	Deu	1997	53,324	62,200	294	32	23	CC		
Punjab Senator †	Deu	1997	53,324	63,645	294	32	23	CC		
Pusan Senator †	Deu	1997	53,324	63,584	294	32	23	CC		
Shanghai Senator †	Lbr	1992	34,231	45,696	216	32	19	CC	ex DSR-Atlantic-97	
Washington Senator *	Deu	1994	34,454	45,455	216	32	20	CC	ex Maersk Antwerp-95, Tor Bay-94, Washington Senator-94	

80% owned affiliate company only operating chartered vessels, including * from NSB Niederelbe Schiffahrts. GmbH & Co. KG, † from Reederei F. Laeisz GmbH, both Germany q.v., ** from Prima Shipmanagement, Malaysia (Halim Mazmin Group) and managed by Anglo-Eastern Ship Management Ltd., Hong Kong (China), ‡ from Unicom or § from Maritime Consortium, Malaysia.

Hansa Mare Reederei GmbH & Co. KG   Germany

Funnel: *Black with red dot over blue wave on broad white band or charterers colours.*
Hull: *Blue or grey with red boot-topping.*

Name	Eng	Flag	Year	GRT	DWT	Loa	Bm	Kts	Type	Former names
CMA CGM Rodin	Atg	2001	27,093	33,220	210	30	22	CC	I/a Ansgaritor	
Delaware Bridge	Atg	2002	41,834	53,554	266	32	-	CC	ex HLL Atlantic-03	
Elbe Bridge	Atg	1998	40,306	52,329	261	32	24	CC	ex Mare Superum-98	
Kota Ekspres	Atg	1997	29,383	34,670	196	32	22	CC	ex Mare Africum-02	
Maersk Dammam	Atg	2003	41,834	53,511	266	32	-	CC	I/a HLL Pacific	
Maersk Dublin	Atg	1995	50,698	62,441	292	32	24	CC	ex Dragor Maersk-02	

Name	Eng	Flag	Year	GRT	DWT	Loa	Bm	Kts	Type	Former names
Mare Adriaticum		Atg	1993	9,581	12,721	150	23	17	CC	ex Mekong Stream-03, Mare Adriaticum-03, ACX Wagle-02, Mare Adriaticum-00, Rotterdam Stad-98, Mare Adriaticum-97, Sea Nordic-95, Independent Trader-94, Mare Adriaticum-94
Mare Balticum		Atg	1993	9,584	12,712	150	23	17	CC	ex X-Press Konkan-02, Mare Balticum-01, Saudi Dammam-99, Mare Balticum-99, Maersk Euro Octavo-94, Mare Balticum-93
Mare Caspium		Atg	1995	29,383	34,625	196	32	21	CC	ex ANL China-02, NYK Minerva-01, Mare Caspium-00
Mare Doricum		Atg	1995	9,590	12,705	150	22	17	CC	ex ACX Falcon-02, Mare Doricum-00, Breda Stad-98, Mare Doricum-97, Sea Nordic-95, Mare Doricum-95
Mare Gallicum		Deu	1996	29,383	34,671	196	32	22	CC	ex Ipex Emperor-02, OOCL Haven-01, Mare Gallicum-00, Acapulco-98, TMM Acapulco-97, Mare Gallicum-96
Mare Hibernum		Atg	1995	9,600	12,571	150	22	17	CC	ex ACX Seagull-02, Saudi Buraydah-00, Mare Hibernum-98
Mare Ibericum		Atg	1994	16,266	22,494	168	25	19	CC	ex Indamex Impala-03, ANL Impala-01, Mare Ibericum-01, Carina Challenger-01, Mare Ibericum-97, CSAV Ranco-97, Mare Ibericum-94
Mare Internum		Atg	1997	29,383	34,705	196	32	22	CC	
Mare Phoenicium		Atg	1999	40,306	52,330	261	32	24	CC	ex Ems Bridge-01, I/a Mare Phoenicium
Mare Thracium		Atg	1997	29,383	34,705	196	32	22	CC	ex MSC Oregon-01, Mare Thracium-00
MSC Biscay		Atg	1996	9,616	12,705	150	22	17	CC	ex Mare Tuscum-01, Ankara-01, DNOL Ankara-99, Mare Tuscum-98, CGM Jean Laborde-98, Mare Tuscum-97
MSC Scandinavia		Atg	2000	40,306	52,250	261	32	24	CC	ex Donau Bridge-04, Mare Atlanticum-01
OOCL Harmony		Atg	1997	29,750	34,800	196	32	21	CC	ex Mare Ionium-00
P&O Nedlloyd Chicago *		Cyp	1998	37,579	56,902	243	32	23	CC	
P&O Nedlloyd Cobra		Atg	1999	40,306	47,660	261	32	24	CC	ex Mare Lycium-03, Mosel Bridge-02, I/a Mare Lycium
Weser Bridge		Atg	1998	40,306	52,357	261	32	25	CC	I/a Mare Siculum
YM New York		Atg	2000	40,306	52,250	261	32	22	CC	ex Trade Tesia-03, Mare Arcticum-01
YM Savannah		Atg	2000	40,306	52,250	261	32	22	CC	ex Trade Hallie-03, Mare Caribicum-01
YM Wilmington		Atg	2000	40,306	52,250	261	32	22	CC	ex Trade Freda-03, I/a Mare Britannicum

newbuildings - three 4,700-4,800 teu container ships for 2004 delivery.
Company jointly owned by Hanseatic Lloyd Reederei and Schlussel Reederei GmbH & Co. KG, both Germany.
* managed by Hanseatic Shipping Co. Ltd., Cyprus (Schulte Group).

Hapag-Lloyd A.G.   Germany

Funnel: Orange with blue 'HL' symbol.
Hull: Black with white 'Hapag-Lloyd' and red boot-topping.

Name	Eng	Flag	Year	GRT	DWT	Loa	Bm	Kts	Type	Former names
Antwerpen Express		Deu	2000	54,437	67,145	294	32	24	CC	ex Tokyo Express-99
Berlin Express		Deu	2002	88,493	100,019	320	43	26	CC	
Bonn Express		Deu	1989	35,919	45,977	236	32	20	CC	
Bremen Express		Deu	2000	54,465	66,971	294	32	24	CC	
Dresden Express		Deu	1991	53,883	67,680	294	32	23	CC	
Dusseldorf Express		Deu	1998	53,523	66,525	294	32	23	CC	
Essen Express		Deu	1993	53,815	67,680	294	32	23	CC	
Frankfurt Express *	(2)	Sgp	1981	57,540	51,540	288	32	23	CC	
Hamburg Express		Deu	2001	88,493	100,003	320	43	26	CC	
Hannover Express		Deu	1991	53,783	67,680	294	32	23	CC	
Heidelburg Express		Deu	1989	35,919	45,977	236	32	20	CC	ex Ville De Verseau-91, Heidelberg Express-91
Hoechst Express		Deu	1991	53,833	67,680	294	32	23	CC	
Hong Kong Express		Deu	2002	88,493	100,016	320	43	26	CC	ex Berlin Express-02
Humboldt Express *		Sgp	1984	32,444	34,037	200	32	16	CC	
Kobe Express		Deu	1998	53,523	67,537	294	32	23	CC	ex Shanghai Express-02
Leverkusen Express		Deu	1991	53,783	67,680	294	32	23	CC	
London Express		Deu	1998	53,523	66,577	294	32	23	CC	
Ludwigshafen Express		Deu	1992	53,833	67,680	294	32	23	CC	
Norfolk Express		Deu	1995	36,606	45,362	245	32	24	CC	ex OOCL Atlantic-03, Norfolk Express-02, Hong Kong Express-02, Northern Majesty-96
Paris Express		Deu	1994	53,815	67,613	294	32	23	CC	ex Hamburg Express-01
Rotterdam Express		Deu	2000	54,400	66,975	294	32	24	CC	

Name	Eng	Flag	Year	GRT	DWT	Loa	Bm	Kts	Type	Former names
Santiago Express *		Sgp	1984	32,444	33,997	206	32	18	CC	ex Isla de la Plata-96, Cordillera Express-84
Shanghai Express		Deu	2002	88,493	100,006	320	43	26	CC	
Stuttgart Express		Deu	1993	53,815	67,640	294	32	23	CC	
Tokyo Express		Deu	2000	54,437	54,766	294	32	24	CC	

newbuildings - three 85,000 grt 83,700 dwt (8000 teu) on order from South Korean builder for 2005/6 delivery.
* owned by subsidiaries Hapag-Lloyd (Eastwind) Pte. Ltd. or Hapag-Lloyd (Westwind) Pte. Ltd., both Singapore.

Harren & Partners Schiffahrts GmbH Germany

Funnel: Cream with two dark sails above three waves.
Hull: Light grey with red boot-topping.

Name	Eng	Flag	Year	GRT	DWT	Loa	Bm	Kts	Type	Former names
Peoria		Lbr	1996	36,615	70,231	225	32	14	B	
Pochard		Atg	2003	22,655	37,384	199	24	14	B	l/a Panarea
Puffin		Atg	2003	22,654	37,641	199	24	14	B	
Sibulk Premier		Atg	2003	29,985	53,609	190	32	-	B	ex Sibulk Pioneer-03
VOC Galaxy *		Bhs	2002	30,928	51,201	190	32	14	B	ex Clipper Galaxy-03
VOC Gemini *		Atg	2003	30,928	51,187	192	32	14	B	ex Clipper Gemini-03

newbuildings : two 16,400 dwt tankers on order from Chinese builder for 2005 delivery.
* on charter to Van Ommeren Clipper Holdings (Clipper Group)

Hartmann Schiffahrts. GmbH & Co. KG Germany

Funnel: White with blue 'h' symbol.
Hull: Blue with red boot-topping.

Name	Eng	Flag	Year	GRT	DWT	Loa	Bm	Kts	Type	Former names
BBC Russia		Cyp	2003	12,993	17,471	143	23	-	Co	ex Atlantic Progress-03
DAL Madagascar		Lbr	2001	16,803	23,051	184	25	19	CC	ex Sagittarius-04
Mount Fuji *		Cyp	2003	22,515	40,055	182	27	-	T	
UBC Beaumont *		Cyp	1995	13,695	22,056	158	25	14	B	ex Brunes-01
UBC Saiki *		Cyp	2002	19,746	31,770	171	27	15	B	
UBC Singapore *		Cyp	2002	19,746	31,759	171	27	15	B	

newbuildings : two 36,000 dwt and seven 33,900 dwt container ships on order from 2004/5 delivery from German builders.
* owned by subsidiary Intership Navigation Co. Ltd., Cyprus.

Leif Hoegh & Co. ASA Norway

Funnel: White with blue top and houseflag interrupting white band.
Hull: Grey with blue 'HOEGH LINES', red boot-topping.

Name	Eng	Flag	Year	GRT	DWT	Loa	Bm	Kts	Type	Former names
Hoegh Galleon	(st)	Nis	1974	71,822	50,746	250	40	19	Lgc	ex Mystic Lady-00, Asake Maru-98, Mystic Lady-98, Asake Maru-98, Pollenger-87, LNG Challenger-79
Hoegh Gandria ‡	(st)	Nis	1977	96,011	71,630	288	44	20	Lgc	
Hoegh Marlin		Bhs	1977	30,931	45,065	201	31	15	BC	ex Star Marlin-91, Hoegh Marlin-87
Hoegh Mascot		Bhs	1977	30,931	45,063	201	31	15	BC	ex Mascot-03, Hoegh Mascot-94, Star Mascot-89, Hoegh Mascot-87
Hoegh Merchant		Bhs	1977	30,987	44,895	201	31	15	BC	ex Star Merchant-93, Westwood Merchant-90, Hoegh Merchant-83
Hoegh Merit		Bhs	1977	30,987	44,926	201	31	15	BC	ex Star Merit-95, Hoegh Merit-94, Star Merit-94, Westwood Merit-90, Hoegh Merit-83
Hoegh Minerva		Nis	1979	30,995	44,016	201	31	15	BC	ex Max Oldendorff-03, Hoegh Minerva-01, Star Minerva-89, Hoegh Minerva-87
Hoegh Miranda		Nis	1979	30,995	44,016	201	31	15	BC	ex August Oldendorff-03, Hoegh Mirande-01, Star Miranda-89, Hoegh Mirande-87
Hoegh Monal		Bhs	1996	36,463	49,755	200	32	16	BC	ex Saga Challenger-02
Hoegh Morus		Bhs	1997	36,463	56,801	200	32	16	BC	
Hoegh Musketeer		Bhs	1977	30,987	44,895	201	31	15	BC	ex Star Musketeer-94, Westwood Musketeer-90, Hoegh Musketeer-83
Norman Lady ‡	(st)	Nis	1973	71,469	50,922	250	40	18	Lgc	
SG Enterprise		Bhs	1997	108,083	211,485	312	51	14	B	ex Jedforest-00, SG Enterprise-98
SG Prosperity		Bhs	1996	108,083	211,201	312	51	14	B	ex Lauderdale-00, SG Prosperity-98

newbuildings : two large Lng carriers jointly owned with Mitsui OSK Lines on order from Japanese builder from 2005/6 delivery.
* owned by Societe Navale de l'Ouest subsidiary and managed by Delmas Armement, both France
‡ jointly owned with Mitsui O.S.K. Lines Ltd., Japan q.v.

Leif Hoegh & Co. (Hual AS). HUAL TRIDENT. *Hans Kraijenbosch.*

Hyundai Merchant Marine. HYUNDAI STAR. *Hans Kraijenbosch.*

Name	Eng	Flag	Year	GRT	DWT	Loa	Bm	Kts	Type	Former names

HUAL AS/Norway

Funnel: Blue with red car symbol over three blue wavy lines over blue 'HUAL' on broad white band.
Hull: Grey with black 'HUAL' on white upperworks, red boot-topping.

Name	Eng	Flag	Year	GRT	DWT	Loa	Bm	Kts	Type	Former names
Hual Africa †		Bhs	2004	57,718	21,300	200	32	-	V	
Hual America †		Bhs	2003	57,718	21,182	200	32	-	V	
Hual Asia		Bhs	2000	57,200	21,200	200	32	19	V	
Hual Dubai ‡		Pan	2004	58,947	19,121	200	32	-	V	
Hual Durban ‡		Pan	2004	58,947	19,121	200	32	-	V	
Hual Oceania ‡		Pan	2003	58,947	19,121	200	32	-	V	
Hual Seoul		Bhs	2004	57,000	21,500	200	32	-	V	
Hual Tokyo		Bhs	2004	57,000	21,500	200	32	-	V	
Hual Tracer		Nis	1981	33,236	12,961	180	29	18	V	ex Tracer-95, Hual Tracer-94
Hual Trader		Bhs	1998	56,816	16,393	200	32	20	V	
Hual Trailer *		Nis	1980	45,007	15,603	194	32	18	V	ex Hual Karinita-00, Karinita-82
Hual Tramper		Bhs	1980	33,369	12,169	180	29	17	V	Hual Rolita-00, ex Rolita-82
Hual Transit		Nis	1981	45,573	17,650	190	32	19	V	ex Hual Transita-00, Kyushu-96, Kyushu Maru-88
Hual Transporter		Bhs	1999	57,757	21,300	200	32	20	V	
Hual Trapeze *		Nis	1983	41,871	15,500	180	31	17	V	ex Hual Carmencita-00
Hual Trapper		Nis	1981	33,236	12,961	180	29	18	V	
Hual Traveller		Nis	1983	35,022	15,370	180	29	18	V	
Hual Treasure *		Bhs	1999	58,684	21,199	200	32	19	V	ex Hual Carolita-00
Hual Trekker *		Nis	1981	33,374	11,977	180	29	17	V	ex Hual Angelita-00, Angelita-82
Hual Tribute		Bhs	1988	53,578	21,835	200	32	18	V	
Hual Tricorn		Bhs	1988	52,422	23,096	200	32	18	V	ex Hual Champ-00, Auto Champ-00
Hual Trident		Bhs	1995	56,164	21,423	200	32	20	V	
Hual Trinity		Nis	1981	45,365	17,938	190	32	19	V	ex Hual Trinita-00, Yokohama-95, Yokohama Maru-88
Hual Triton		Bhs	1988	52,422	23,052	200	32	18	V	ex Auto Diana-00, l/a Auto Daewoo
Hual Triumph		Nis	1988	53,578	20,885	200	32	18	V	ex Hual Margarita-00
Hual Trooper		Bhs	1995	56,164	21,414	200	32	20	V	
Hual Trophy *		Nis	1987	53,578	20,885	200	32	18	V	ex Hual Favorita-01
Hual Tropicana *		Nis	1980	33,359	12,003	180	32	17	V	ex Hual Lisita-00, Lisita-82
Hual Trotter		Nis	1983	35,022	15,370	180	29	18	V	
Hual Troubadour		Nis	1980	33,369	12,165	180	29	17	V	ex Hual Ingrita-00, Ingrita-82
Hual Trove *		Bhs	2000	57,200	21,200	200	32	19	V	ex Hual Maritita-00

newbuildings - eight 57,000 grt 6100 car vehicle carriers on order from South Korean builder for 2004-6 delivery.
*Managed by Hoegh Fleet Services AS or * by IUM Shipmanagement AS, both Norway.*
† on long-term charter from Stamco Ship Management Co. Ltd., Greece or ‡ Cido Shipping Co. Ltd., Japan.

Hyundai Corporation   South Korea

Hyundai Merchant Marine Co. Ltd.

Funnel: White with yellow edged green triangle.
Hull: Blue with white 'HYUNDAI', red boot-topping.

Name	Eng	Flag	Year	GRT	DWT	Loa	Bm	Kts	Type	Former names
Federal		Pan	1994	51,841	61,152	275	37	24	CC	ex Hyundai Federal-03
Forest Pioneer		Pan	1998	39,548	51,300	218	32	15	Bw	
Global Victory		Pan	1996	76,068	149,155	270	43	14	B	
Global Winner		Pan	1997	81,152	161,121	280	45	14	B	
Hyundai Advance		Pan	1997	21,611	24,777	182	30	22	CC	ex Wan Hai 251-00, Hyundai Advance-98
Hyundai Atlas		Pan	1995	76,068	149,310	270	43	13	B	
Hyundai Banner		Kor	1996	151,977	281,074	330	58	15	T	
Hyundai Bridge		Pan	1998	21,611	24,766	182	30	21	CC	
Hyundai Confidence		Pan	2003	64,845	68,114	275	40	-	CC	
Hyundai Continental		Kor	1988	101,466	200,269	309	50	13	B	
Hyundai Cosmos		Kor	1986	85,678	163,256	290	45	13	B	
Hyundai Fortune		Pan	1996	64,054	68,539	275	40	25	CC	
Hyundai Freedom		Pan	1996	64,054	68,363	275	40	25	CC	
Hyundai Future		Pan	1997	21,611	24,600	182	30	21	CC	
Hyundai General		Kor	1996	64,054	68,378	275	40	25	CC	
Hyundai Glory		Pan	2004	53,352	63,404	294	32	-	CC	
Hyundai Highness		Kor	1996	64,054	68,379	275	40	25	CC	
Hyundai Highway		Pan	1998	21,611	24,799	182	30	21	CC	
Hyundai Island		Kor	1986	67,897	127,852	274	43	12	B	

Name	Eng	Flag	Year	GRT	DWT	Loa	Bm	Kts	Type	Former names
Hyundai Oceania		Kor	1983	74,052	139,887	267	43	15	B	
Hyundai Olympia		Kor	1987	93,005	186,330	292	46	13	B	
Hyundai Power		Pan	1998	76,068	135,000	269	43	14	B	
Hyundai Progress		Pan	1997	21,611	24,766	182	30	22	CC	ex Wan Hai 252-00, Hyundai Progress-98
Hyundai Prosperity		Kor	1990	77,650	151,257	274	45	13	B	
Hyundai Spirit		Pan	1993	68,093	126,051	263	41	18	B	
Hyundai Sprinter		Pan	1997	21,611	24,600	182	30	21	CC	
Hyundai Star		Pan	1995	151,592	281,199	330	58	15	T	
Hyundai Stride		Pan	1997	21,611	24,777	182	30	21	CC	
Hyundai Sun		Pan	1998	156,692	301,178	330	58	15	T	
Hyundai Universal		Kor	1990	101,604	200,100	309	50	13	B	
Hyundai Vladivostok		Cyp	1997	21,611	24,766	182	30	21	CC	ex CMA Oakland-01, Hyundai Vladivostok-99
Kiani Satu †		Pan	1997	16,660	16,717	165	26	14	C	
Oriental Green		Pan	1996	25,503	43,229	185	31	14	B	
Pacific Champ		Pan	1996	25,503	43,229	185	31	14	B	
Pacific Courage		Pan	1992	145,403	258,096	338	58	15	T	ex Stena Comfort-00, Wisteria-97
Pacific Royal		Pan	1997	25,503	43,210	185	31	14	B	
Pacific Success		Kor	1989	24,790	38,412	186	28	14	B	
Pos Challenger		Pan	1992	75,277	140,302	269	43	13	B	
Pos Harvester		Pan	1992	75,277	140,302	269	43	13	B	
Universal Brave		Pan	1997	156,692	278,900	331	58	15	T	
Universal Prime		Pan	1997	156,692	278,900	331	58	15	T	

newbuildings : two 300,000 dwt tankers and five 85,250 dwt container ships for 2006 delivery from South Korean builders.
Also owns six large Lng tankers operating mainly in the Far East.
* managed by Keoyang Shipping Co. Ltd., South Korea or † by Barber Ship Management, Malaysia.

International Shipholding Corporation USA
Central Gulf Lines Inc./USA

Funnel: White with blue symbol within blue ring, narrow black top or buff with 8-pointed white star on white edged broad red band or green with two broad white bands.
Hull: Black with red boot-topping.

Name	Eng	Flag	Year	GRT	DWT	Loa	Bm	Kts	Type	Former names
Asian Emperor		Pan	1999	55,729	21,479	200	32	20	V	
Atlantic Forest	(2)	Usa	1984	37,460	40,881	263	32	20	LC	ex Aleksey Kosygin-96
Bali Sea	(2)	Sgp	1982	29,594	22,220	175	36	13	HL	ex Super Servant 5-95, Dan Lifter-85
Banda Sea	(2)	Sgp	1982	29,594	22,239	175	36	13	HL	ex Super Servant 6-95, Dan Mover-85
Green Cove		Usa	1994	50,308	16,178	179	32	19	V	ex Shojin-00
Green Dale *		Usa	1999	50,087	15,894	179	32	19	V	ex Altair Leader-99
Green Lake		Usa	1998	57,623	22,799	200	32	19	V	ex Cygnus Leader-01
Green Point		Usa	1994	51,819	14,930	180	32	19	V	ex Triton Diamond-98
Green Wave		Usa	1980	9,751	13,130	154	21	17	C	ex Woermann Mira-84, Sloman Mira-84
Rhine Forest		Mhl	1972	35,826	44,799	261	32	18	LC	ex Bilderdyk-86

managed by LMS Shipmanagement Inc. * for Waterman Steamship Corp., both USA

Islamic Republic of Iran Shipping Lines Iran

Funnel: Red base with broad white band below green top.
Hull: Light grey with black 'IRISL' and red or green boot-topping, or black with red boot-topping

Name	Eng	Flag	Year	GRT	DWT	Loa	Bm	Kts	Type	Former names
Iran Abozar		Irn	1986	25,770	43,365	190	30	14	B	
Iran Adi		Irn	1983	22,027	37,537	186	28	15	B	ex World Fraternity-84
Iran Afzal		Irn	1983	22,027	37,588	186	28	15	B	ex Manila Faith-84, Primelock-83
Iran Akhavan		Irn	1984	20,576	34,859	198	24	15	B	ex Philippine Success-84
Iran Amanat		Irn	1983	20,576	34,859	198	24	15	B	ex Manila Pride-84
Iran Ardebil		Irn	2004	25,369	33,850	207	30	-	CC	
Iran Ashrafi		Irn	1985	25,768	43,342	190	30	14	B	
Iran Azadi		Irn	1979	20,672	35,839	180	28	15	B	ex Oinoussian Friendship-81
Iran Azarbayjan		Irn	2000	39,424	72,642	225	32	14	B	
Iran Baabael		Irn	1998	15,670	22,882	168	26	16	Co	
Iran Baakeri		Irn	1998	15,670	22,882	168	26	16	Co	
Iran Baghaei		Irn	1979	12,775	17,970	170	23	18	C	ex Ydra-93, Almas-92, Tannenbels-86, Stratherrol-82
Iran Bahonar		Irn	1983	21,959	40,325	176	32	14	T	ex Cleon-83
Iran Baluchestan		Irn	2000	16,694	22,600	174	26	16	Co	
Iran Bayan		Irn	1974	9,891	16,265	150	21	16	C	ex Arya Sepand-80, Aristonimos-75
Iran Beheshti		Irn	1979	22,048	39,026	205	26	15	T	ex Selma-82

Name	Eng	Flag	Year	GRT	DWT	Loa	Bm	Kts	Type	Former names
Iran Borhan		Irn	1975	10,205	16,265	150	21	16	C	ex Arya Gohar-80
Iran Broojerdi		Irn	1978	13,917	17,970	170	23	18	C	ex Arastou-93, Merbabu-86, Rheinbels-83, Strathelgin-82
Iran Chamran		Irn	1985	25,768	43,309	190	30	14	B	
Iran Dastghayb		Irn	1984	25,768	43,369	190	30	14	B	
Iran Deyanat		Irn	1983	25,168	44,468	200	29	15	B	ex Odinlock-84
Iran Eghbal		Irn	1986	25,768	40,345	191	30	14	B	
Iran Ehsan		Irn	1975	9,891	16,265	150	21	16	C	ex Arya Akhtar-80, Aristaios-75
Iran Entekhab		Irn	1978	20,811	35,896	180	28	15	B	ex Oinoussian Prestige 81
Iran Eshraghi		Irn	1985	25,768	43,369	190	30	14	B	
Iran Esteghial		Irn	1978	20,811	35,839	180	28	15	B	ex Oinoussian Virtue-81
Iran Ghafari		Irn	1985	25,768	43,369	190	30	14	B	
Iran Ghazi		Irn	1985	25,768	43,442	190	30	14	B	
Iran Gheyamat		Irn	1978	14,433	19,212	167	25	18	C	ex Arya Shams-80
Iran Ghodousi		Irn	1986	25,770	43,480	190	30	14	B	
Iran Gilan		Irn	2000	39,424	63,400	225	32	14	B	
Iran Golestan		Irn	2001	39,517	72,162	225	32	14	B	
Iran Hamedan		Irn	2001	39,517	72,162	225	32	14	B	
Iran Hamzeh		Irn	1986	25,770	43,288	190	30	14	B	
Iran Hesabi		Irn	1998	15,670	22,882	168	26	16	Co	
Iran Hormozgan		Irn	2000	36,014	41,962	240	32	22	CC	
Iran Ilam		Irn	2004	25,369	33,850	207	30	-	CC	
Iran Isfahan		Irn	2000	36,014	41,971	240	32	22	CC	
Iran Jamal		Irn	1985	25,768	40,422	190	30	14	B	
Iran Jomhuri		Irn	1978	20,811	35,830	180	28	15	B	ex Oinoussian Leadership-81
Iran Kashani		Irn	1984	25,768	43,309	190	30	14	B	
Iran Kerman		Irn	2000	36,014	41,978	240	32	22	CC	
Iran Kermanshah		Cyp	2001	40,609	75,249	225	32	14	B	ex Cape Tenaron-03
Iran Khorasan		Irn	2000	39,424	72,622	225	32	14	B	
Iran Khuzestan		Irn	1999	16,694	23,116	174	26	16	Co	
Iran Kordestan		Irn	1999	16,694	23,116	174	26	16	Co	
Iran Lorestan		Irn	1999	16,694	23,176	174	26	16	Co	
Iran Madani		Irn	1985	25,768	43,345	190	30	14	B	
Iran Mahallati		Irn	1978	13,914	16,905	170	23	18	C	ex Lindenbels-88, Strathewe-82
Iran Makin		Irn	1997	16,621	24,065	174	26	17	Co	
Iran Matin		Irn	1996	16,621	22,948	174	26	16	Co	
Iran Mazandaran		Irn	2000	39,424	72,642	225	32	14	B	
Iran Meezan		Irn	1975	9,888	16,265	150	21	16	C	ex Arya Sooroosh-80
Iran Mobin		Irn	1996	16,621	22,982	174	26	16	Co	
Iran Modares		Irn	1977	20,049	33,667	182	27	15	B	ex Gentle River-83, Treana-78
Iran Mufateh		Irn	1985	25,768	43,262	190	30	14	B	
Iran Nabuvat		Irn	1977	14,856	19,212	167	25	18	C	ex Arya Shahab-60
Iran Navab		Irn	1986	25,768	43,342	190	30	14	B	
Iran Piroozi		Irn	2003	25,369	33,900	207	30	-	CC	
Iran Rajai		Irn	1983	22,097	40,367	176	32	14	T	ex Ferncraig-83
Iran Sadoughi		Irn	1985	25,768	43,369	190	30	14	B	
Iran Sadr		Irn	1985	25,768	43,265	190	30	14	B	
Iran Saeidi		Irn	1986	25,768	43,369	190	30	14	B	
Iran Salam		Irn	1975	8,364	12,140	153	18	18	C	ex Arya Zar-80
Iran Sarbaz		Irn	1984	20,576	34,859	198	24	15	B	
Iran Sattari		Irn	1998	15,670	22,882	168	26	16	Co	
Iran Seestan		Irn	1999	16,694	23,176	174	26	16	Co	
Iran Sepah		Irn	1976	19,701	33,856	186	26	14	B	ex Ocean Cosmos-84
Iran Shahryar		Irn	1999	15,670	22,882	168	26	16	Co	
Iran Shariat		Irn	1983	25,168	44,468	200	29	15	B	ex Thorlock-84
Iran Shariati		Irn	1985	25,768	40,422	190	30	14	B	
Iran Sokan		Irn	1975	9,888	16,265	150	21	16	C	ex Arya Navid-80
Iran Tabatabaei		Irn	1998	15,670	22,621	168	26	16	Co	
Iran Takhti		Irn	1978	16,173	23,720	159	25	16	Co	ex Sargodha-84
Iran Taleghani		Irn	1985	25,768	43,309	190	30	14	B	
Iran Tehran		Irn	2000	36,014	41,937	240	32	22	CC	
Iran Teyfouri		Irn	1979	16,173	23,720	159	25	16	Co	ex Simba-84
Iran Vahdat		Irn	1977	14,856	19,212	167	25	18	C	ex Arya Keyhan-80
Iran Vojdan		Irn	1975	9,891	16,265	150	21	16	C	ex Arya Kay-80, Aristonidas-75
Iran Yamin		Irn	1996	16,621	22,967	174	26	17	Co	
Iran Yasooj		Irn	2004	25,369	33,850	207	30	-	CC	

Name	Eng	Flag	Year	GRT	DWT	Loa	Bm	Kts	Type	Former names
Iran Yazd		Cyp	2001	40,609	72,642	225	32	14	B	ex Cape Race-03

newbuildings - two further 25,400 grt 33,850 dwt and five 30,000 dwt container ships due for 2004/5 delivery.

Irano-Hind Shipping Co. Ltd.

Funnel: Black with green/brown diagonally quartered flag with white 'I' and 'H' in upper and lower quarters respectively.
Hull: Black with red boot-topping.

Name	Eng	Flag	Year	GRT	DWT	Loa	Bm	Kts	Type	Former names
Attar		Mlt	1994	25,885	43,706	186	30	14	B	ex Parisian Trader-00
ISI Olive		Mlt	1992	81,135	141,861	274	48	14	T	ex Mastera-02
Sattar		Mlt	1992	24,155	43,419	185	31	14	B	ex Belstar-01

Formed jointly with The Shipping Corporation of India Ltd (49%). q.v.

Ernst Jacob GmbH & Co. KG   Germany

Funnel: Black, white diagonal cross on broad blue band with blue 'J' on white centre diamond
Hull: Grey or red with red boot-topping or white with blue boot-topping.

Name	Eng	Flag	Year	GRT	DWT	Loa	Bm	Kts	Type	Former names
Ariadne Jacob		Ant	2004	41,690	72,700	225	32	14	T	
Chaleur Bay *		Mlt	2000	40,705	71,345	229	32	15	T	
Chinook **		Cym	2001	24,252	38,695	189	28	14	T	ex Glasgow-02, I/a Calinesti
Colin Jacob		Ant	2004	41,690	72,700	225	32	14	T	
Four Schooner		Cym	2000	40,037	73,083	229	32	15	T	
Four Smile		Cym	2001	81,236	160,573	274	48	14	T	
Four Sun		Cym	2003	81,236	160,292	274	48	14	T	
Jill Jacob		Cym	2003	40,037	72,909	229	32	-	T	ex Four Clipper-04
Kim Jacob		Lbr	1998	81,265	159,211	274	48	15	T	ex Celebes-98
Margara *		Cym	1999	40,705	60,913	229	32	14	T	
Max Jacob		Lbr	2000	81,565	159,211	274	48	14	T	ex Soyang-01
Oliver Jacob		Lbr	1999	81,565	157,326	274	48	14	T	ex Columbia-02
P&O Nedlloyd Yarra Valley		Mhl	2002	25,703	33,670	208	30	21	CC	ex Wehr Oste-03
Pactol River		Lbr	1981	23,100	37,270	171	30	14	T	ex Nortank Pacific-92, Pacific Current-90, Kathy O-84
Santa Ana **		Cym	2002	24,252	39,768	190	28	14	T	ex Greenock-02, I/a Diamant
Tanja Jacob		Tuv	1980	23,847	43,190	176	32	15	B	

newbuildings : two 72,700 dwt tankers for 2005 delivery from South Korean builder.
* managed by Scorpio Ship Management SAM or ** by IndoChina Ship Management (UK) Ltd.

Jahre Dahl Bergesen AS   Norway

Funnel: Various operating company or charterers colours.
Hull: Various including black with red boot-topping.

Name	Eng	Flag	Year	GRT	DWT	Loa	Bm	Kts	Type	Former names
Eurydice		Cyp	1986	52,862	94,941	244	42	14	T	ex Jahre Prince-00, Friendship Venture-87
Hyundai Explorer		Bhs	1986	39,892	43,567	244	32	21	CC	ex P&O Nedlloyd Pusan-03, Hyundai Explorer-02
Hyundai Innovator		Pan	1986	39,892	43,567	244	32	21	CC	
Hyundai Pioneer		Bhs	1986	39,892	43,567	244	32	21	CC	
Jahre Viking	(st)	Nis	1976	260,851	564,763	458	69	13	T	ex Happy Giant-91, Seawise Giant-89 (len-80)
Maersk Tampa		Bhs	1984	43,332	53,325	270	32	24	CC	ex Louis Maersk-99
MSC Parana **		Nis	1987	23,761	34,380	202	28	17	CC	ex Cielo di Valencia-02, Lynx-00, Cast Lynx-99, Norasia Mubarak-94
MSC Peru **		Nis	1987	23,761	34,380	202	28	17	CC	ex P&O Nedlloyd Falcon-03, Cielo di Livorno-01, Bear-00, Cast Bear-99, Norasia Al-Muntazah-94
MSC Pretoria		Bhs	1986	39,892	43,567	244	32	21	CC	ex Hyundai Frontier-02, Lalandia-92, Hyundai Frontier-88
Nord Sea		Iom	1980	51,771	81,561	244	42	15	T	ex Solena-00, World Fame-86
NYK Pride		Bhs	1988	39,990	43,537	245	32	21	CC	ex Hyundai Commander-00
P&O Nedlloyd Panama		Bhs	1986	39,892	43,567	244	32	21	CC	ex Hyundai Challenger-03
Prigipos		Cyp	1981	51,807	99,811	244	42	-	T	ex LMZ Sky-01, Alandia Patriot-00, Nicolas-98, Neva-95, World Dawn-90
Skauboard		Nis	1997	34,885	49,370	196	32	15	B	

Ship management company owned by AS Thor Dahl Shipping (52.5%), Bulls Tankrederi A/S-Jorgen Jahre (22.5%), Gluteus Medius AS (Tom Bergesen) and others with vessels managed by Jahre-Wallem AS (JDB 50%, Wallem 40% and B. Skaugen 10%)
* managed by Jahre-Wallem AS for Cyclops Ships Ltd., Greece or ** for Jaya-TDS Shipping Ltd (formed jointly Thor Dahl and Jaya Holdings Ltd., Mauritius)
See also Eukor (Wallenius Willhelmsen)

Name	Eng	Flag	Year	GRT	DWT	Loa	Bm	Kts	Type	Former names

Kristian Gerhard Jebsen Skipsrederi AS

Norway

Funnel: *Black with white pennant flag on broad blue band or * pale green with white 'SKS' on broad red band.*
Hull: *Black or * red with red or green boot-topping.*

Name	Eng	Flag	Year	GRT	DWT	Loa	Bm	Kts	Type	Former names
Apalis Arrow	Bhs	1983	30,767	42,149	208	32	14	BC	ex Emerald Coast-98, Star Everwin-87, Everwin-83
Avocet Arrow	Bhs	1985	27,470	39,239	199	30	15	BC	ex City of Alberni-98, Belwood-93
Barbet Arrow	Bhs	1985	27,470	39,260	199	30	15	BC	ex City of New Westminster-98, Belforest-93
Canelo Arrow	Bhs	1997	32,520	48,041	187	31	14	B	
CHL Innovator †	Sgp	1976	19,426	26,931	175	26	15	B	ex Rodney-86, Cape Rodney-85
CHL Progressor †	Sgp	1985	32,333	48,251	189	32	-	B	ex Therassia-89
Gannet Arrow	Bhs	1985	27,470	39,260	199	30	15	BC	ex City of Nanaimo-98, Beltimber-93
Jaeger Arrow	Bhs	2001	29,103	24,101	171	25	18	Cfp	
Kestrel Arrow	Bhs	1983	30,767	42,149	208	32	15	BC	ex Jade Forest-98, Star Everace-87, Everace-83
Pine Arrow	Bhs	1996	32,520	48,041	190	31	14	BC	
SKS Mersey	Nis	2003	70,933	120,499	250	44	-	Obo	
SKS Mosel	Nis	2003	70,933	121,000	250	44	-	Obo	
SKS Saluda	Nis	2003	81,270	160,000	274	50	-	T	
SKS Tagus *	Nis	1997	63,515	109,933	244	42	15	Obo	
SKS Tana *	Nis	1996	63,515	109,906	244	42	14	Obo	
SKS Tanaro *	Nis	1999	63,515	109,787	244	42	14	Obo	
SKS Tiete *	Nis	1999	63,515	109,773	244	42	14	Obo	
SKS Torrens *	Nis	1999	63,515	109,846	244	42	14	Obo	
SKS Trent *	Nis	1997	63,515	109,832	244	42	15	Obo	
SKS Trinity *	Nis	1999	63,515	109,798	244	42	14	Obo	
SKS Tugela *	Nis	1997	63,515	109,913	244	42	15	Obo	
SKS Tweed *	Nis	1996	63,515	109,832	244	42	15	Obo	
SKS Tyne *	Nis	1996	63,515	109,891	244	42	14	Obo	

newbuildings : two 82,000 grt 159,000 dwt tankers on order for 2006 delivery from South Korean builder.
* owned by SKS OBO Ltd formed jointly with Compania SudAmericana de Vapores SA (CSAV), Chile and managed by V.Ships Norway A/S
† managed for CHL Shipping B.V., Netherlands (subsidiary of TNT Shipping & Development Ltd., Australia)

Gearbulk Shipowning Ltd./Bermuda

Funnel: *Black with large white 'G'.*
Hull: *Black with white 'GEARBULK', red boot-topping.*

Name	Eng	Flag	Year	GRT	DWT	Loa	Bm	Kts	Type	Former names
Alouette Arrow	Nis	1980	12,688	14,602	159	21	16	Cp	ex Chimo-94, Finnarctis-91
Auk Arrow	Bhs	1984	27,962	43,952	188	29	13	BC	ex Heina-91
Bergen Arrow	Bhs	1984	25,063	38,800	182	29	14	BC	ex Bergen Thistle-86
Cedar Arrow	Bhs	2001	32,458	47,818	190	31	14	BC	
Condor Arrow	Nis	1979	25,846	38,008	182	29	15	BC	ex Molda-81
Cormorant Arrow	Bhs	1986	28,005	43,074	188	29	13	BC	
Crane Arrow	Bhs	1984	27,818	41,646	188	29	14	BC	ex Chelsfield-89
Eagle Arrow **	Bhs	1977	30,719	45,063	201	31	15	BC	ex Norsul Bahia-04, Cielo d'Europa-01, Star Europa-96, Cielo d'Europa-91, Star Mallard-89, Hoegh Mallard-87
Emu Arrow	Bhs	1997	36,008	51,419	200	32	14	B	
Falcon Arrow *	Bhs	1986	28,805	45,295	200	31	15	BC	ex Norsul Europa-04, Westwood Belinda-03
Finch Arrow	Bhs	1984	26,130	39,273	183	29	13	BC	ex Francois L.D.-90
Grebe Arrow	Bhs	1997	35,998	51,633	200	32	16	B	
Grouse Arrow	Bhs	1991	44,398	42,276	185	30	15	B	
Gull Arrow	Bhs	1982	25,846	38,787	182	29	16	BC	ex Horda-91
Harefield	Bhs	1985	27,818	41,651	188	29	13	BC	
Hawk Arrow	Bhs	1985	28,092	40,269	188	29	14	BC	
Ibis Arrow	Bhs	1986	28,239	42,497	188	29	14	BC	
Kite Arrow	Bhs	1997	36,008	51,800	200	32	16	B	
Kiwi Arrow	Bhs	1981	27,069	38,695	182	29	14	BC	
Linnet Arrow **	Bhs	1974	19,653	29,602	172	26	14	BC	ex Norsul Parana-04, Visayas Victory-00, Fjord Thistle-87, Ogna-82
Mandarin Arrow	Bhs	1996	35,998	51,733	200	32	16	B	
Mozu Arrow	Bhs	1992	44,398	42,276	185	30	15	B	
Nandu Arrow	Bhs	1978	25,063	38,618	182	29	14	BC	
Osprey Arrow	Bhs	1985	27,938	42,596	188	29	13	BC	
Pelican Arrow	Bhs	1982	25,846	38,787	182	29	16	BC	ex Folga-91
Penguin Arrow	Bhs	1997	36,008	51,738	200	32	16	B	
Petersfield	Bhs	1985	27,818	41,646	188	29	13	BC	
Petrel Arrow	Bhs	1985	27,824	42,964	188	29	14	BC	ex Alain L.D.-90

Kristian Gerhard Jebsen Skips. JAEGER ARROW. *F. de Vries.*

Kristian Gerhard Jebsen Skips. SKS TANA. *J. M. Kakebeeke.*

Kristian Gerhard Jebsen (Gearbulk). EMU ARROW. *Hans Kraijenbosch.*

Name	Eng	Flag	Year	GRT	DWT	Loa	Bm	Kts	Type	Former names
Plover Arrow		Bhs	1997	36,008	51,880	200	32	14	B	
Puffin Arrow		Bhs	1981	27,069	38,695	183	29	13	BC	ex Brierfield-89, La Sierra-83
Raven Arrow		Bhs	1981	24,855	38,771	182	29	14	BC	
Rhone		Bhs	1978	26,204	38,542	182	29	16	BC	ex Rokko-89, Sun Rokko-86, La Cordillera-83
Siskin Arrow		Bhs	1985	26,130	39,151	183	29	14	BC	ex Monique L.D.-90
Spruce Arrow		Bhs	2002	32,458	47,818	190	31	14	BC	
Sun Suma		Bhs	1978	26,204	38,542	182	29	16	BC	ex La Costa-84
Swan Arrow *		Bhs	1987	28,805	45,295	200	31	15	BC	ex Norsul America-04, Westwood Jago-03
Swift Arrow		Bhs	1992	44,398	42,276	185	30	15	B	
Teal Arrow		Bhs	1984	27,962	43,002	188	29	13	BC	ex Lista-91
Tern Arrow		Bhs	1986	28,239	42,570	188	29	14	BC	
Toki Arrow **		Bhs	1980	21,139	31,247	180	28	17	BC	ex Harmac Dawn-04
Toucan Arrow		Bhs	1996	35,998	51,880	200	32	16	B	
Tsuru Arrow *		Bhs	1987	28,805	45,295	200	31	15	BC	ex Norsul Vancouver-04, Westwood Cleo-02
Weaver Arrow		Bhs	1997	36,008	51,364	200	32	14	B	
Westfield		Bhs	1985	27,818	41,619	188	29	13	BC	
Wren Arrow		Bhs	1985	27,824	41,637	188	29	13	BC	ex Charles L.D.-90

newbuildings - four 32,500 grt 47,900 dwt open-hatch bulk carriers on order from Polish builder for 2004 delivery.
*Minority of 40% in Gearbulk owned by Mitsui O.S.K. Lines Ltd., Japan q.v. * managed by Borgstad or ** SMT Shipmanagement.*

Jungerhans & Co. Reedereiverwaltung　　　　　Germany

Funnel: Charterers colours
Hull: Grey with red boot-topping.

Name	Eng	Flag	Year	GRT	DWT	Loa	Bm	Kts	Type	Former names
Ara J		Atg	1998	11,153	16,833	148	25	18	CC	ex Safmarine Italia-02, SCL Italia-00, Schwerin-98, Ara J-98
City of Stuttgart		Atg	1997	18,233	26,260	177	28	20	CC	ex Klaus J-02, Irma Delmas-02, Maersk San Antonio-99, TNX Express-98, Aldebaren-97, I/a Klaus J
Helene J		Atg	1997	18,233	26,260	178	28	20	CC	ex ANL Oryx-03, Helene J-02, Fesco Express-00, Maersk Manzanillo-99, TNX Sprint-98, Antares-97, Helene J-97
Maersk Ravenna		Gib	2001	14,000	18,400	156	25	18	CC	I/a Auriga J
Maersk Rio Grande		Gib	2002	16,129	16,794	161	25	19	CC	ex Corona J-02
Maersk Rosario		Gib	2003	16,129	16,824	161	25	19	CC	ex Crux J-03
Maersk Rostock		Atg	2002	14,062	18,832	156	25	19	CC	ex Taurus J-03
Maersk Rotterdam		Gib	2002	14,062	18,400	156	25	18	CC	I/a Antares J
P&O Nedlloyd Malindi		Atg	1999	12,004	14,065	149	23	19	CC	ex Leo J-02, Castilla-99
Tausala Samoa		Atg	1998	12,004	14,174	149	23	19	CC	I/a Libra J

Kawasaki Kisen K.K. ('K' Line)　　　　　Japan

Funnel: Bright red with white 'K', above grey base.
Hull: Grey with red boot-topping.

Name	Eng	Flag	Year	GRT	DWT	Loa	Bm	Kts	Type	Former names
Akashi Bridge		Pan	1993	48,237	47,425	277	32	24	CC	
Akinada Bridge		Pan	2001	66,687	71,366	285	40	25	CC	
American Highway		Pan	2000	49,212	16,750	179	32	20	V	
Arcadia Highway		Pan	1994	49,012	15,507	180	32	20	V	
Atlantic Highway		Pan	2002	55,493	17,232	200	32	20	V	
Atlas Highway		Lbr	1987	45,742	14,487	180	32	20	V	
Baltic Highway		Pan	2001	42,238	17,828	179	32	20	V	
Bay Bridge		Lbr	1985	34,467	35,396	227	32	20	CC	
Bosphoros Bridge		Pan	1993	48,220	47,359	277	32	25	CC	
Bremen Bridge		Pan	2001	66,332	67,170	279	40	25	CC	
Californian Highway		Pan	1983	43,407	16,519	183	32	18	V	
Caribbean Highway		Pan	2002	42,238	17,866	179	32	20	V	
Century Highway No. 1		Pan	1984	43,198	15,363	186	32	18	V	
Century Highway No. 2		Pan	1985	44,616	15,509	186	32	18	V	
Century Highway No. 3		Pan	1986	46,186	14,304	186	32	18	V	
Century Highway No. 5		Pan	1986	44,969	15,380	190	32	18	V	
Chang Jiang Bridge		Pan	1992	48,237	47,425	277	32	24	CC	ex Brooklyn Bridge-01
Chicago Bridge		Pan	2001	66,332	67,170	279	40	25	CC	
Chiswick Bridge		Pan	2001	68,687	68,280	285	40	25	CC	

Kawasaki Kisen K.K. MEDITERRANEAN HIGHWAY. *Phil Kempsey.*

Kawasaki Kisen K.K. ROTTERDAM BRIDGE. *Hans Kraijenbosch.*

Name	Eng	Flag	Year	GRT	DWT	Loa	Bm	Kts	Type	Former names
Concord Bridge		Pan	1998	47,541	51,805	275	32	23	CC	
Continental Highway		Pan	2001	55,493	17,201	200	32	20	V	
Coral Highway		Pan	1987	49,439	14,597	180	32	20	V	ex Michigan Highway-95
Diamond Highway		Pan	1984	33,131	11,940	173	28	18	V	
Emden		Pan	1987	38,062	13,898	178	29	17	V	
Emerald Highway		Pan	1985	33,131	11,889	173	28	18	V	
European Highway		Pan	1999	48,039	15,057	180	32	20	V	
Genoa Bridge		Pan	2002	66,292	67,197	279	40	25	CC	
George Washington Bridge		Jpn	1986	42,000	40,928	241	32	22	CC	
Global Highway		Jpn	1982	51,087	15,148	200	32	18	V	
Golden Gate Bridge		Pan	2001	68,687	71,376	285	40	25	CC	
Henry Hudson Bridge		Jpn	1987	42,407	40,934	241	32	22	CC	
Hercules Highway		Jpn	1987	46,875	14,977	180	32	18	V	
Humber Bridge		Jpn	1988	48,305	47,539	277	32	24	CC	
Hume Highway		Pan	1985	51,235	16,169	200	32	18	V	
Indiana Highway		Jpn	2003	55,457	17,442	200	32	20	V	
James River Bridge		Pan	2001	68,687	71,336	285	40	25	CC	
Kentucky Highway		Jpn	1987	50,320	15,587	180	32	19	V	
Lions Gate Bridge		Pan	2001	68,687	71,395	285	40	25	CC	
Long Beach Bridge		Pan	2001	68,687	68,280	285	40	25	CC	
Mackinac Bridge		Jpn	1986	42,414	40,982	241	32	22	CC	
Manhatten Bridge		Pan	1987	42,394	40,934	241	32	22	CC	
Marble Highway		Pan	1984	33,131	11,907	173	28	18	V	
Mediterranean Highway		Pan	2002	55,493	17,228	200	32	20	V	
Melbourne Highway		Pan	1983	43,259	16,483	183	32	18	V	
New York Highway		Jpn	1985	45,706	13,684	180	32	18	V	
Newport Bridge		Pan	1993	48,220	47,384	277	32	25	CC	
Nippon Highway		Pan	1999	49,212	16,827	179	32	20	V	
Ocean Highway		Pan	2000	49,212	16,733	179	32	20	V	
Olympian Highway		Pan	1995	47,077	14,226	180	32	20	V	
Oriental Highway		Lbr	1980	28,997	12,434	175	27	17	V	
Orion Highway		Lbr	1984	44,576	14,384	179	32	19	V	
Pacific Highway		Pan	2000	48,039	15,127	180	32	20	V	
Pegasus Highway		Pan	1994	49,012	15,553	180	32	18	V	
Princes Highway		Pan	1986	51,233	16,191	200	32	18	V	
Rhein Bridge		Pan	1989	48,235	46,200	277	32	24	CC	
Rotterdam Bridge		Pan	2001	66,332	68,280	285	40	25	CC	
Sapphire Highway		Pan	1986	49,098	14,683	179	32	19	V	ex London Highway-94
Scandinavian Highway		Pan	1986	48,014	14,569	190	32	18	V	ex European Highway-96
Seto Bridge		Pan	1993	48,342	47,425	277	32	24	CC	
Seven Seas Highway		Pan	2001	55,493	17,232	200	32	20	V	
Shanghai Bridge		Pan	2001	68,687	68,280	285	40	25	CC	
Shenandoah Highway		Pan	1992	47,368	12,308	180	32	18	V	
Sirius Highway		Pan	1984	44,576	14,301	179	32	18	V	
Suez Canal Bridge		Pan	2002	68,687	71,359	285	40	25	CC	
Texas Highway		Jpn	2003	55,458	17,200	200	32	20	V	
Tokyo Highway		Pan	1984	45,699	13,687	180	32	18	V	
Tower Bridge		Sgp	1985	34,487	34,775	227	32	20	CC	
Triton Highway		Jpn	1987	45,783	14,484	180	32	18	V	
Tsing Ma Bridge		Pan	2002	68,687	68,280	285	40	25	CC	
Victoria Bridge		Pan	1998	47,541	51,759	275	32	23	CC	
Washington Highway		Jpn	1986	50,334	14,081	190	32	19	V	
YM Tacoma		Lbr	1989	48,235	47,351	277	32	23	CC	ex Normandie Bridge-02

newbuilldings : About 32 on order including four tankers up to 259,700 dwt, five bulk carriers up to 205,000 dwt, thirteen container ships over 53,000 dwt and three large vehicle carriers, all for 2004-6 delivery.

The company has many subsidiaries with ownership of over 210 vessels and over 30 newbuildings. Only the larger container ships and car carriers are listed above, the owned, managed and chartered fleet also including over 40 'capesize' bulk carriers (143-182,000 dwt), almost 70 'panamax' or 'handy' bulk carriers, 12 tankers, 20 Lng tankers.

See also various other chartered containerships with 'Bridge' suffix in index.

Torvald Klaveness & Co. AS

Norway

Funnel: Yellow with blue 'K' on white disc and blue edged narrow white band.

Hull: Grey or orange with red boot-topping.

Name	Eng	Flag	Year	GRT	DWT	Loa	Bm	Kts	Type
Al Mansour		Nis	2002	38,889	72,562	225	32	-	B

Name	Eng	Flag	Year	GRT	DWT	Loa	Bm	Kts	Type	Former names
Bakra		Nis	1993	37,550	70,456	225	32	13	B	ex Bakar-99, Beskydy-98
Balao		Nor	2002	28,718	50,969	190	32	-	B	
Balboa		Nis	2002	28,718	50,900	190	32	-	B	
Balder		Nis	2002	30,739	48,184	190	32	-	B	
Ballangen		Nis	1987	24,621	41,734	184	31	14	B	ex Yamburg-92, Oinoussian Fighter-89
Balsfjord		Nis	1996	37,550	70,120	225	32	13	B	ex Sumava-98
Banasol		Nis	2001	38,889	72,562	225	32	14	B	
Banastar		Nor	2001	38,889	72,700	225	32	16	B	
Bandar		Mlt	1982	46,996	81,659	259	32	15	B	ex Bulkgulf-03
Baniyas		Nis	2001	38,889	72,562	225	32	-	B	
Bardu		Lbr	1979	21,630	33,684	177	27	15	B	ex Swan Cliff-99, Bardu-95
Barkald		Nis	2002	28,912	49,900	190	32	-	B	
Bauta		Nis	1987	24,621	41,756	184	31	14	B	ex Yasnaya Polyana-92, Oinoussian Prudence-89
China Glory *		Lbr	1990	36,433	65,652	226	32	14	B	
China Hope *		Lbr	1994	38,657	70,109	225	32	14	B	
China Joy *		Lbr	1994	38,679	70,044	225	32	14	B	
China Pride *		Lbr	1990	36,433	64,619	225	32	14	B	ex Alaska-02, China Pride-02
China Spirit *		Lbr	1994	38,679	70,046	225	32	14	B	
KCL Barracuda		Pan	1984	10,880	17,722	147	23	13	B	ex Thai Ho-04, Kiwi Star-93
Probo Gull		Nis	1987	31,255	47,980	183	32	14	BO	

newbuildings - two 38,900 grt 72,450 dwt bulk carriers for 2005/7 delivery from Japanese builder.

* owned by subsidiary American Bulker KS and managed by Lasco Shipping Co., USA (see under Clipper Group)

Knutsen O.A.S. Shipping AS

Norway

Funnel: Black with two red bands.

Hull: Orange (larger vessels with white 'KNUTSEN OAS'), red boot-topping.

Name	Eng	Flag	Year	GRT	DWT	Loa	Bm	Kts	Type	Former names
Anna Knutsen	(2)	Nor	1987	69,313	129,154	257	46	14	T	
Anneleen Knutsen		Gbr	2002	24,242	35,140	183	-	-	T	
Asgard C	(2)	Nis	2000	71,850	125,772	265	43	15	Ts	ex Jorunn Knutsen-00
Betty Knutsen		Nis	1999	24,185	35,807	183	27	14	T	
Bilbao Knutsen	(st)	Nis	2004	93,450	68,530	-	-	-	Lng	
Cadiz Knutsen	(st)	Nis	2003	115,000	68,530	-	-	-	Lng	
Catherine Knutsen		Nis	1992	77,352	134,003	277	43	14	T	ex Tanana-99, Wilomi Tanana-98, Tanana-98, Wilomi Tanana-97
Elisabeth Knutsen *	(me2)	Nor	1997	71,880	124,788	265	43	14	T	
Ellen Knutsen †		Nis	1991	11,433	17,071	142	23	13	T	
Gerd Knutsen *		Iom	1996	79,244	134,510	277	44	14	T	ex Knock An-03
Hanne Knutsen	(2)	Gbr	2000	72,245	123,851	265	43	15	T	
Helene Knutsen		Nis	1992	11,737	14,848	142	23	13	T	
Hilda Knutsen		Nis	1989	11,425	14,910	142	23	13	T	
Isabel Knutsen		Gbr	2001	13,753	22,377	160	23	15	T	ex Chembulk Savannah-00
Karen Knutsen *	(2)	Lbr	1999	87,827	154,390	276	50	14	T	ex Knock Whillan-03
Kitty Knutsen		Gbr	1980	63,101	127,747	264	41	16	T	ex Norrisia-03, Gerina-87
Kristin Knutsen †		Nis	1998	12,184	19,152	148	23	15	T	
Maria Knutsen		Gbr	2001	13,753	22,377	160	23	15	T	l/a Chembulk Barcelona
Navion Europa *	(me2)	Nor	1995	73,637	130,596	265	43	15	T	ex Jorunn Knutsen-98
Navion Norvegia *		Nor	1995	73,637	130,865	265	43	15	T	ex Hanne Knutsen-98
Pascale Knutsen		Gbr	1993	11,688	14,848	142	23	13	T	
Ragnhild Knutsen		Gbr	1987	69,321	128,772	260	46	14	T	
Sallie Knutsen *	(2)	Iom	1999	87,827	154,390	276	50	14	T	ex Knock Sallie-03
Sidsel Knutsen		Nis	1993	15,806	22,625	163	23	13	T	
Synnove Knutsen †		Nis	1992	11,433	17,071	142	23	13	T	
Tordis Knutsen *		Nor	1993	66,671	123,848	265	43	14	T	
Torill Knutsen		Nis	1990	11,425	14,910	142	23	13	T	ex Vinga Knutsen-90
Tove Knutsen *		Nor	1989	60,719	112,508	243	43	14	T	
Turid Knutsen		Nis	1993	15,689	22,617	142	23	13	T	
Vigdis Knutsen *		Nor	1993	66,671	123,423	265	43	14	T	

newbuildings - two 24,242 grt 35,700 dwt and two 80,500 grt 147,500 dwt tankers on order for 2004-5 delivery.

* operated by Navion ASA (see under Teekay Shipping Corp.) or † by JO Tankers (J. O. Odfjell A/S), Norway q.v.

Name	Eng	Flag	Year	GRT	DWT	Loa	Bm	Kts	Type	Former names

Reederei Ernst Komrowski   Germany

Funnel: Charterers colours
Hull: Grey with red boot-topping.

Name	Eng	Flag	Year	GRT	DWT	Loa	Bm	Kts	Type	Former names
Bonanza		Ant	2004	39,900	74,000	225	32	14	B	
Dorian		Lbr	1994	16,191	22,426	179	25	19	CC	ex DAL Karoo-02, Dorian-01, Karawa-00, Dorian-99, Sea Bold-98, Dorian-98, Sea Bold-97, Maersk Charleston-97, TSL Bold-96, Dorian-94
Marfret Caraibes		Lux	1996	16,800	22,982	185	25	19	CC	ex CMA CGM Karukera-04, Vulkan-01, CMA CGM Karukera-01, Vulkan-01, Cap York-00, Vulkan-99, CSAV Rengo-99, Vulkan-06
Tiger Cloud		Lbr	1987	13,315	16,804	159	23	16	CC	ex Heluan-03, Dubai Confidence-98, Heluan-96, Columbus Olinda-96
TMM Hidalgo		Lbr	1997	16,793	22,900	185	25	-	CC	ex Delmas Tourville-03, Adrian-03, Ivory Star-02, TMM Manzanillo-01, Adrian-01, CSAV Barcelona-01, Adrian-99, Santa Paula-98, Adrian-97, Jan Ritscher-97

Kuwait Oil Tanker Co. (S.A.K.)   Kuwait

Funnel: Red with gold Arabic characters on green oval disc on broad white band beneath black top.
Hull: Black with red or grey boot-topping.

Name	Eng	Flag	Year	GRT	DWT	Loa	Bm	Kts	Type	Former names
Al Awdah		Kwt	1991	149,647	284,533	322	56	14	T	
Al Badiyah		Kwt	1989	26,356	35,643	183	32	13	T	
Al Deerah		Kwt	1989	26,356	35,643	183	32	13	T	
Al Funtas		Kwt	1983	160,010	294,739	336	60	14	T	ex Middletown-89, Al Funtas-87
Al Kuwaitiah		Kwt	1988	26,351	35,643	183	32	13	T	
Al Maqwa		Kwt	1983	43,970	66,652	241	32	15	T	ex West Kirby-88, Umm Al Jathathel-87
Al Sabiyah		Kwt	1988	26,356	35,644	183	32	13	T	
Al Salheia		Kwt	1998	158,503	310,453	334	58	15	T	
Al Samidoon		Kwt	1992	149,719	284,889	322	57	14	T	
Al Shegaya		Kwt	1998	158,503	310,433	334	58	15	T	
Al Shuhadaa		Kwt	1992	149,719	285,116	322	57	14	T	
Al Tahreer		Kwt	1991	149,719	284,532	322	56	14	T	
Arabiyah		Kwt	1988	75,029	121,109	250	43	13	T	
Gas Al Ahmadi		Kwt	1979	42,904	47,471	230	35	16	Lpg	ex Gas Princess-89, Gas Al Ahmadi-87
Gas Al Burgan		Kwt	1979	42,904	47,471	230	35	21	Lpg	ex Gas King-89, Gas Al Burgan-87
Gas Al-Gurain		Kwt	1993	44,868	49,874	230	37	16	Lpg	
Gas Al Minagish		Kwt	1980	42,904	47,471	231	35	16	Lpg	ex Gas Prince-89, Gas Al Minagish-87
Gas Al Mutlaa		Kwt	1993	44,868	49,874	230	37	16	Lpg	
Hadiyah		Kwt	1988	75,029	121,109	250	43	13	T	
Kazimah		Kwt	1982	160,010	294,739	336	60	14	T	ex Townsend-88, Kazimah-87
Keefan		Kwt	1982	43,970	66,652	241	32	15	T	ex Hoylake-88, Umm Al Roos-87
Warbah		Kwt	1982	43,970	66,652	241	32	15	T	ex Helsby-88, Umm Ruwaisat-87

Subsidiary of Kuwait Petroleum Corporation
† owned by Chesapeake Shipping Inc. and managed by Keystone Shipping Co., both USA or ‡ owned by Kent Petroleum Ltd., UK.

F. Laeisz Schiffahrts GmbH & Co.   Germany

Funnel: Yellow or charterers colours.
Hull: Black with red boot-topping or white with blue boot-topping.

Name	Eng	Flag	Year	GRT	DWT	Loa	Bm	Kts	Type	Former names
Bussewitz *		Lbr	1983	14,377	13,935	152	23	12	Lpg	
CMA CGM Emerald *		Deu	1997	25,499	33,950	200	30	21	CC	ex Pembroke Senator-03, P&O Nedlloyd Fos-01, ECL Europa-99, Pembroke Senator-99
Hanjin Philadephia *		Lbr	2002	50,242	58,810	282	32	24	CC	
Hanjin Phoenix *		Lbr	2002	50,242	58,423	282	32	24	CC	
Hanjin Praha †		Lbr	2001	50,242	58,423	280	32	24	CC	I/a Praha
Hanjin Pretoria †		Lbr	2002	50,242	58,768	282	32	24	CC	
Kota Pelangi *		Lbr	1996	31,131	38,650	210	32	22	CC	ex Potsdam-02, Ipex Emperor-99, Sea Elegance-97, Potsdam-96
Kota Pusaka *		Lbr	1996	31,131	38,650	210	32	22	CC	ex Pommern-02, P&O Nedlloyd Unity-01, Pommern-97, Sea Excellence-97, Pommern-96
Luise Oldendorff *		Lbr	1994	38,513	72,873	225	32	14	B	
MSC Chile *		Lbr	1997	28,701	32,500	202	31	20	CC	ex Priwall-02, Sea Panther-01, Priwall-97

Knutsen OAS Shipping. PASCALE KNUTSEN. *F. de Vries.*

F. Laeisz Schiffahrts GmbH. PITTSBURG (in Seatrade colours). *M. D. J. Lennon.*

Name	Eng	Flag	Year	GRT	DWT	Loa	Bm	Kts	Type	Former names
MSC Palermo		Lbr	1992	34,231	45,696	216	32	19	CC	ex Palermo Senator-03, DSR-Baltic-96
Panama		Lbr	1989	18,000	26,288	177	28	18	CC	ex MSC Amazonia-02, MSC Andes-01, Panama-98, Panama Senator-97, Contship Noumea-96, Panama Senator-96
Paradise N *		Lbr	1997	155,051	322,398	332	58	13	B	ex Peene Ore-02
Paris *		Lbr	1990	18,000	26,288	177	28	17	CC	ex Sunrise-97, Choyang Pride-96, Paris-93, Paris Senator-93
Pequot *		Lbr	1996	36,615	70,165	225	32	15	B	
Pilgrim **		Lbr	1994	7,743	7,721	131	20	19	R	ex Crystal Pilgrim-96
Pittsburg **		Lbr	1994	7,743	7,721	131	20	19	R	ex Pioneer-96, Crystal Pioneer-96
Powhatan *		Lbr	1995	36,615	69,045	225	32	15	B	
Pride **		Lbr	1992	7,743	7,726	131	20	19	R	ex Crystal Pride-03
Privilege **		Lbr	1992	7,743	7,726	131	20	19	R	ex Crystal Privilege-03
Puritan *		Lbr	1983	13,998	9,649	148	26	17	CC	ex Eagle Prestige-96, Puritan-93
William Oldendorff		Lbr	1997	38,215	73,726	225	32	15	B	ex Wiltrader-03, Win Trader-02

*owned or managed by Reederei F. Laeisz GmbH and ** chartered to Seatrade q.v. † owned by Dr. Peters KG fund, Germany.*
see also under Hanjin Shipping Co. Ltd. (Senator Line) and NSB Niederelbe Schiffahrts. GmbH.

Latvian Shipping Company   Latvia

Funnel: Dark brown with dark brown 'Lat' on broad white band or blue with white 'L+C' overlapping broad red band.
Hull: Black or red with red boot-topping.

Name	Eng	Flag	Year	GRT	DWT	Loa	Bm	Kts	Type	Former names
Abava		Mlt	1992	7,057	6,366	140	19	16	R	ex Chiquita Abava-93
Akademikis Vavilovs		Mlt	1985	9,552	7,673	138	23	20	R	ex Akademik N. Vavilov-91
Akademikis Zavarickis		Mlt	1986	9,552	7,673	138	23	20	R	ex Akademik Zavaritskiy-91
Alioth Star *		Mhl	1985	10,937	17,617	151	22	15	T	ex Alioth-00, Kobuleti-00, Bolshevik Kamo-93
Amata		Mlt	1991	7,392	6,231	140	19	16	R	ex Chiquita Amata-93, Amata-91, Mazoiusze-91
Antonio Gramsi		Lbr	1978	25,726	39,870	195	28	16	T	ex Antonio Gramsci-91
Aries *		Mhl	1993	18,094	29,790	175	26	14	T	ex Parnar-00
Asari		Cyp	1984	18,526	28,750	179	25	15	T	ex Georgiy Kholostyakov-92
Belgoroda		Mlt	1986	8,960	7,535	146	21	21	R	ex Byelgorod-92
Bulduri		Cyp	1983	18,625	28,750	179	25	15	T	ex Dmitriy Medvedyev-91
Davids Sikeiross		Lbr	1976	25,679	40,030	195	28	16	T	ex David Siqueiros-91
Dubulti		Mlt	1982	17,532	29,610	179	25	14	T	ex General Pliyev-91
Dzintari		Lbr	1985	10,944	16,341	152	22	15	T	ex Moris Bishop-91
Dzons Rids		Lbr	1978	25,726	39,870	195	28	16	T	ex John Reed-91
Estere		Cyp	1989	18,625	28,610	178	25	14	T	ex Esther-94
Gaida		Lbr	1991	25,803	41,465	182	30	14	T	ex Stavanger Ocean-92
Hose Marti		Lva	1978	25,726	39,870	195	28	16	T	ex Jose Marti-91
Indra		I hr	1994	21,183	28,840	179	25	14	T	ex Puikovo-94
Inga		Lbr	1990	18,625	28,610	179	25	14	T	
Kemeri		Lbr	1985	10,944	17.610	152	22	15	T	ex Yuliy Danishevshiy-91
Klements Gotvalds		Lbr	1978	25,726	39,870	195	28	16	T	ex Klement Gottwald-91
Kurzeme		Lbr	1997	18,503	23,100	160	26	15	Lpg	
Latgale		Mlt	2001	39,085	68,467	229	32	14	T	ex Inca-01
Lielupe		Lbr	1979	25,726	39,870	195	28	16	T	ex Sukhe Bator-92
Majori		Lva	1980	17,521	27,235	179	25	14	T	ex Grigoriy Nikolayev-91
Mar		Lbr	1990	18,625	28,610	178	25	14	T	
Mercure *		Mhl	1992	18,094	29,751	175	26	14	T	ex Danila-00
Ojars Vacietis		Cyp	1985	10,944	16,341	152	22	15	T	ex Oyar Vatsietis-91
Olga †		Lbr	1992	24,731	44,646	182	30	14	T	ex Gunta-95, Argo Europa-92
Pols Robsons		Lbr	1978	25,726	39,870	195	28	16	T	ex Paul Robeson-91
Pumpuri		Cyp	1987	18,526	28,750	179	25	14	T	ex Mikhail Gromov-92
Riga		Mlt	2001	39,085	68,467	229	32	14	T	ex Aztec-01
Ropazi		Cyp	1985	10,944	16,341	152	22	15	T	ex Ropazhi-93, Panteleymon Ponomarenko-91
Rundale		Cyp	1977	13,704	17,025	160	23	15	T	ex Leninsk Kuznetskiy-91
Samburga		Cyp	1976	13,704	17,200	160	23	15	T	ex Samburg-92
Skulptors Tomskis		Mlt	1986	9,552	7,673	138	23	20	R	ex Skulptor Tomskiy-91
Vidzeme		Lbr	1997	18,503	23,100	160	26	15	Lpg	
Zanis Griva		Lbr	1985	10,944	16,341	152	22	15	T	ex Zhan Griva-91
Zemgale		Mlt	2001	39,085	68,467	229	32	14	T	ex Maya-01
Zoja I		Cyp	1988	18,625	28,610	179	25	14	T	ex Don-89
Zoja II		Lva	1989	18,625	28,610	178	25	14	T	ex Kmir-90

*managed by LSC Ship Management, Latvia except * by Columbia Shipmanagement (Deutschland) GmbH, ** by Columbia Shipmanagement Ltd., Cyprus, † by A/S Dampskibs. Torm, Denmark.*

Latvian Shipping. ABAVA. *M. D. J. Lennon.*

Latvian Shipping. MERCURE (in Columbia Ship Management colours). *F. de Vries.*

Latvian Shipping. ROPAZI. *Oliver Sesemann.*

J. Lauritzen Holding A/S

Denmark

LauritzenCool AB

Funnel: Deep red base and broad blue top withblue and red arcs on broad white central band.
Hull: Red, cream or white with red/blue 'LauritzenCool', red or blue boot-topping.

Name	Eng	Flag	Year	GRT	DWT	Loa	Bm	Kts	Type	Former names
Amer Annapurna §		Lbr	1987	10,298	11,022	146	23	18	R	ex Arctic Spirit-99, Arctic Universal-97
Amer Choapa		Cyp	1987	13,312	12,848	152	24	18	R	ex Choapa-96
Amer Everest §		Cyp	1989	9,072	11,622	149	21	19	R	ex Hokkaido Rex-95
Amer Fuji §		Cyp	1990	9,070	11,540	149	21	17	R	
Amer Himalaya §		Cyp	1990	9,070	11,595	149	21	17	R	
Amer Whitney §		Cyp	1990	9,070	11,633	149	21	20	R	ex Californian Reefer-98, Humboldt Rex-94
Atlantic Reefer		Pan	1998	10,991	12,633	145	23	21	R	
Atlantik Frigo		Hrv	1989	10,366	11,000	143	23	19	R	
Chilean Reefer		Dis	1992	7,944	11,095	141	20	22	R	ex Carelian Reefer-97
Ditlev Lauritzen		Dis	1990	14,406	16,950	164	24	20	R	
Dominica †		Bhs	1993	13,077	13,981	158	24	22	R	ex Geest Dominica-97
Ivar Lauritzen		Dis	1990	14,406	16,950	165	24	19	R	
Ivory Ace		Vut	1990	10,394	10,713	150	23	20	R	
Ivory Dawn		Bhs	1991	10,412	10,600	150	23	20	R	
Ivory Girl		Vut	1996	11,438	10,432	154	24	21	R	
Ivory Tirupati §		Lbr	1989	11,438	10,432	150	23	20	R	ex Ivory Bay-89
Jorgen Lauritzen		Dis	1991	14,406	16,950	164	24	19	R	
Knud Lauritzen		Dis	1991	14,406	16,950	164	24	19	R	
Lady Korcula		Mhl	2000	11,443	12,913	155	23	20	R	
Lady Racisce		Hrv	2000	11,443	12,913	155	23	20	R	
Mexican Reefer		Pan	1994	10,203	11,575	145	22	-	R	
Pacific Reefer		Pan	1998	10,991	12,633	145	23	21	R	
Peruvian Reefer		Dis	1992	7,944	11,092	141	20	22	R	ex Savonian Reefer-97
Scandinavian Reefer		Dis	1992	7,944	11,054	141	20	22	R	
St. Lucia †		Bhs	1993	13,077	13,981	158	24	22	R	ex Geest St. Lucia-97
Summer Bay *		Bhs	1985	12,660	13,613	169	24	24	R	ex Summer Breeze-00, Chiquita Baracoa-96, Ellen D-90
Summer Flower *		Bhs	1984	12,659	13,556	169	24	22	R	ex Chiquita Baru-96, Vivian M-90
Summer Meadow *		Bhs	1985	12,659	13,584	169	24	20	R	ex Chiquita Bocas-96, Irma M-90
Summer Wind *		Bhs	1985	12,660	13,636	169	24	24	R	ex Chiquita Burica-96, Edyth L-90

* chartered from Chartworld Shipping Corp., Greece, † from Geest PLC (FII Fyffes Ltd.).
operating about 70 refrigerated ships mainly chartered from various owners including § Amer Shipping Ltd.
See also vessels chartered from Star Reefers and Leonhardt & Blumberg Reederei.
Company also involved in ReeferShip pool formed jointly with Eco Ltd. (Eastwind Transport) and Armada Shipping SA, Switzerland and also with chartered vessels in a 'handy-size' bulker pool operated with South African based Island View Shipping (Grindrod Group)

C. M. Lemos & Co. Ltd.

UK

Nereus Shipping S.A./Greece

Funnel: Yellow with blue 'L' on white houseflag, black top.
Hull: Black or grey with red boot-topping.

Name	Eng	Flag	Year	GRT	DWT	Loa	Bm	Kts	Type	Former names
Cosmic		Grc	2000	78,918	150,284	274	48	15	T	
Emerald		Grc	1986	27,535	46,793	189	32	14	B	
Majestic		Grc	2000	78,918	150,284	274	48	15	T	
North Star		Grc	1996	79,832	148,561	269	46	15	T	
Poetic		Grc	2003	78,922	150,103	274	48	15	T	
Sea Star		Grc	1996	79,832	148,435	269	46	15	T	
Topaz		Grc	1985	27,535	46,874	189	32	14	B	

newbuildings: one further 79,200 grt 153,000 dwt tanker on order from Japanese builder for 2004 delivery.

Lauritzen Reefers. IVORY ACE (in Turbana charter colours). *G. J. de Boer.*

Lauritzen Reefers. SUMMER FLOWER. *J. M. Kakebeeke.*

Name	Eng	Flag	Year	GRT	DWT	Loa	Bm	Kts	Type	Former names

Leonhardt & Blumberg Schiffahrts GmbH & Co. KG Germany

Funnel: Black with red 'x' and black '+' combined on broad white band, * black with blue single wave on white rectangle with white Maltese Cross on dark blue square in top corner or charterers colours.
Hull: Dark grey, blue or black with red boot-topping or white with blue boot-topping.

Name	Eng	Flag	Year	GRT	DWT	Loa	Bm	Kts	Type	Former names
Al Shamiah	Lbr	1998	15,988	20,840	170	25	20	CC	ex Hansa Trondheim-04, MSC Thailand-04, Hansa Trondheim-02, Direct Hawk-01, Hansa Trondheim-01, Direct Jabiru-00, Maersk Reunion-99, Hansa Trondheim-98
Al Yamamah	Lbr	2001	15,988	20,700	170	25	16	CC	ex Hansa Aalesund-04, MSC New Plymouth-04 Hansa Aalesund-02
Cap Aguilar	Lbr	2000	18,037	23,600	175	27	18	CC	ex Hansa Augustenburg-03
Cap Lobos	Lbr	1997	16,927	20,860	168	27	19	CC	ex Hansa Catalina-03, CMA Xiamen-00, P&O Nedlloyd Abidjan-99, Hansa Catalina-97
Cap Pasado	Lbr	1997	15,988	20,526	170	25	18	CC	ex Hansa Stavanger-03, Direct Condor-00, Maersk Gauteng-99, Maersk Izmir-98, Hansa Stavanger-98
Cap Pilar †	Lbr	2003	16,145	20,700	170	25	19	CC	ex H. Langeland-03
CMA CGM Mercure *	Lbr	2002	50,242	58,512	280	32	24	CC	ex HS Caribe-02, I/a Hansa Caribe
CMA CGM Neptune *	Lbr	2002	50,242	57,600	280	32	24	CC	I/a HS Colon-02, I/dn Hansa Colon
CSCL Seattle *	Lbr	2001	65,131	67,988	275	40	26	CC	I/a HS Columbia, I/dn Hansa Columbia
CSCL Xiamen *	Lbr	2000	25,369	33,899	207	30	21	CC	ex Hansa Victory-00
CSCL Yantian *	Lbr	2000	25,369	33,912	207	30	21	CC	ex Hansa Liberty-00
Dagmar Maersk	Deu	1996	50,644	62,399	292	32	24	CC	ex Hansa Atlantic-96
Damaskus	Deu	1998	16,915	21,480	168	27	19	CC	ex CMA Mersin-00, Hansa Castella-99
Delmas Kerguelen	Lbr	2002	18,334	23,493	175	27	19	CC	ex Hansa Oldenburg-03
Direct Condor	Lbr	2000	18,335	23,579	175	27	18	CC	ex Hansa Flensburg-00
Direct Jabiru	Lbr	2000	18,037	23,600	175	27	18	CC	ex Hansa Rendsburg-01
Direct Kestrel	Lbr	2000	18,037	23,600	175	27	18	CC	ex Hansa Sonderburg-01
Dorthe Maersk	Deu	1996	50,644	62,400	277	32	24	CC	ex Hansa Pacific-96
EWL Antilles	Lbr	1993	9,606	12,575	150	22	18	CC	ex Nedlloyd Curacao-97, Sea-Land Panama-95, Maya Star-94, Hansa Wismar-93
EWL West Indies	Lbr	1996	9,605	12,559	150	22	17	CC	ex Hansa Greifswald-96
H. Kirkenes †	Lbr	2002	15,988	20,463	175	27	18	CC	I/a Hansa Kirkenes
Hansa Africa	Lbr	1997	37,398	43,378	243	32	22	CC	ex ANL Excellence-03, Ville de Venus-02, Ibn Zaidoun-00, Hansa Africa-97
Hansa Bergen	Lbr	1997	15,988	20,887	170	25	20	CC	ex Maersk Windhoek-99, Maersk Gothenburg-98, Hansa Bergen-98
Hansa Bremen ‡	Lbr	1989	10,842	12,942	157	23	21	R	
Hansa Centaur	Lbr	1998	16,927	20,860	168	27	19	CC	ex Pacific Merchant-01, CMA Qingdao-00, P&O Nedlloyd Luanda-99, I/a I lansa Centaur
Hansa Challenger	Lbr	2004	30,123	35,600	-	-	-	CC	
Hansa Commodore	Lbr	1997	16,915	21,470	168	27	19	CC	
Hansa Constitution **	Lbr	1997	31,730	34,954	193	32	22	CC	ex MSC Florida-03, Hansa Constitution-98, Ibn Al Akfani-98, Hansa Constitution-97
Hansa India	Lbr	1994	37,563	43,600	243	32	22	CC	ex P&O Nedlloyd Yantian-02, Largs Bay-99
Hansa Kristiansand	Lbr	2001	15,988	20,700	170	25	16	CC	ex Kota Machan-03, Hansa Kristiansand-02
Hansa London	Lbr	1992	9,608	12,575	150	22	17	CC	ex Marfret Normandie-99, Maersk Zambezi-98, Gouritz-97, Hansa London-96, Maersk Santiago-96, Hansa London-92
Hansa Lubeck ‡	Lbr	1990	10,842	12,942	157	23	21	R	
Hansa Narvik	Lbr	1998	15,988	20,630	170	25	20	CC	ex Kota Serikat-03, Hansa Narvik-02, Direct Eagle-00, Hansa Narvik-99
Hansa Rostock	Lbr	1994	9,606	12,575	150	23	18	CC	
Hansa Stockholm ‡	Lbr	1991	10,842	12,942	157	23	21	R	
Hansa Stralsund	Lbr	1993	9,603	12,577	150	22	17	CC	ex Chile Star-98, Hansa Stralsund-97, Eagle Wave-96, Hansa Stralsund-93
Hansa Visby ‡	Lbr	1989	10,842	12,942	157	23	21	R	
HS Challenger ††	Lbr	2004	30,123	35,600	207	32	22	CC	
HS Discoverer ††	Lbr	2003	30,123	35,600	207	32	22	CC	
Kota Perdana	Lbr	1997	31,730	34,954	193	32	22	CC	ex Zim Pusan I-02, Hansa Century-98, Ibn Duraid-98, Hansa Century-97
Maersk Athens	Lbr	1998	16,915	21,473	168	27	19	CC	ex Hansa Centurion-00, CMA Kobe-00, Hansa Centurion-99
Maersk Auckland	Lbr	2003	18,334	23,493	175	27	19	CC	ex Hansa Brandenburg-03
Maersk Malaga	Deu	1998	16,927	21,563	168	27	19	CC	ex Hansa Caledonia-03, CSAV Suape-98, Hansa Caledonia-98

Name	Eng	Flag	Year	GRT	DWT	Loa	Bm	Kts	Type	Former names
Maersk Marseille		Lbr	1994	16,927	21,480	168	27	19	CC	ex CMA Inchon-00, P&O Nedlloyd Accra-99, Nedlloyd River Plate-97, Hansa Riga-94
Maersk Pireaus		Deu	1998	16,915	21,480	168	27	19	CC	ex Hansa Calypso-00, Maersk Pireaus-00, Hansa Calypso-00, CMA Hakata-00, Hansa Calypso-99
Maersk Vaasa †		Lbr	2003	16,145	20,367	170	25	19	CC	l/a H. Fyn
Maersk Ventspils		Lbr	2004	15,000	17,600	175	27	19	CC	
Maersk Vilnius		Lbr	2003	18,335	23,606	175	27	18	CC	ex Hansa Augustenburg-03
Maersk Volos		Lbr	2003	18,334	17,600	175	27	19	CC	l/a H.Freyburg, l/dn Hansa Freyburg
MB Caribe		Lbr	1993	9,609	12,582	150	22	17	CC	ex Melbridge Berlin-03, EWL Venezuela-99, Hansa Berlin-98, Eagle Wisdom-95, Hansa Berlin-93
MSC Arizona *		Lbr	2002	50,243	58,213	282	32	24	CC	ex HS Voyager-03, l/a Hansa Voyager
MSC Donata		Lbr	2002	40,108	52,806	258	32	24	CC	
MSC Lausanne *		Lbr	2002	50,243	58,486	282	32	24	CC	ex HS Explorer-02, l/a Hansa Explorer
MSC Sarah *		Lbr	1999	53,208	67,795	294	32	24	CC	ex Saudi Yanbu-02
P&O Nedlloyd Nelson		Lbr	2002	18,334	23,493	175	27	19	CC	ex Hansa Nordburg-02
TMM Chiapas		Lbr	2001	15,988	20,700	170	25	16	CC	ex Hansa Arendal-02

newbuildings : †† seven 15,000 grt container ships (H. Ronneburg etc) on order from Chinese builder, four 53,500 grt (HS Livingstone, HS Humboldt, HS Columbus and HS Barents), two 36,000 grt and four 27,000 grt container ships on order from South Korean builder.
* owned or managed by Hansa Shipping GmbH & Co. KG, ** by Hansa Shipmanagement GmbH & Co. KG, or † by Hansa Hamburg Shipping or †† Hansa Treuhard, all Germany. ‡ chartered out to LauritzenCool AB q.v.

Lithuanian Shipping Co. (LISCO)　　　　　　　Lithuania

Funnel:　White with yellow 'L' on red edged green band.
Hull:　Grey or black with red boot-topping.

Name	Eng	Flag	Year	GRT	DWT	Loa	Bm	Kts	Type	Former names
Kapitonas A. Lucka		Ltu	1980	9,965	14,550	146	21	13	B	ex Ivan Nesterov-91
Kapitonas Andzejauskas		Ltu	1978	9,965	14,550	146	21	14	B	ex Kapitonas Mesceriakov-96, Kapitan Meshcheryakov-92
Kapitonas Domeika		Ltu	1979	9,965	14,550	146	21	13	B	ex Kapitonas Vavilov-95, Kapitan Vavilov-92
Kapitonas Kaminskas		Ltu	1978	9,965	14,550	146	21	13	B	ex Kapitonas Gudin-95, Kapitan Gudin-92
Kapitonas Marcinkus		Ltu	1977	9,965	14,550	146	21	13	B	ex Kapitonas Izmiakov-96, Kapitan Izhmyakov-92
Kapitonas Serafinas		Ltu	1980	9,965	14,550	146	21	13	B	ex Kapitonas Stulov-97, Kapitan Stulov-91
Kapitonas Simkus		Ltu	1976	9,965	14,550	146	21	14	B	ex Kapitonas Chromcov-97, Kapitan Khromtsov-92
Kapitonas Stulpinas		Ltu	1981	9,965	14,320	146	21	13	B	ex Yustas Paleckis-92

Livanos Group　　　　　　　　　　　　　　　　Greece

Sun Enterprises Ltd.

Funnel:　Black with red 'L' between 'greek key' borders on broad white band.
Hull:　Grey with red boot-topping.

Name	Eng	Flag	Year	GRT	DWT	Loa	Bm	Kts	Type	Former names
Achilleus		Grc	1983	22,587	39,731	174	32	15	T	ex Sylvan Arrow-02, Mobil Challenge-92
Alfios		Grc	1983	21,963	38,452	171	30	15	T	ex Saucon-02, Mobil Enterprise-91
Aliakmon		Grc	1982	21,963	33,235	171	30	15	T	ex Samoset-02, Mobil Endurance-90
Amazon Explorer		Grc	2002	43,075	72,826	228	40	15	T	
Amazon Gladiator		Grc	2001	43,075	72,910	228	40	15	T	
Amazon Guardian		Grc	1999	43,075	72,910	228	40	15	T	
Artemis		Grc	1983	22,587	39,776	174	32	15	T	ex Royal Arrow-01, Mobil Courage-91
Atlantic Sovereign		Grc	1986	35,954	68,641	225	32	14	B	ex Southern Wealth-90, Moroiso-86
Axios		Grc	1981	21,963	33,187	171	30	15	T	ex Sacona-02, Mobil Endeavour-90
Cap Leon		Grc	2003	81,328	159,048	274	48	-	T	
Chios		Grc	1993	157,213	301,824	327	58	14	T	
Christina		Grc	1999	158,110	309,344	335	58	16	T	
Corona Fortune		Lbr	1993	91,188	172,972	303	46	-	B	ex Fortune 22-00, 0022 Decembrie 1989-94
Evros		Grc	1984	24,310	40,632	178	30	15	T	
Ioannis Zafirakis		Grc	2004	38,700	74,000	225	32	14	B	
Lita		Grc	2002	56,573	104,459	241	42	-	T	
Meandros		Grc	1988	52,159	91,680	244	42	14	T	ex Wenatchi-02, American Pegasus-99, Neptune Pegasus-94, Caribbean First-92
Seryna		Grc	1988	141,991	240,401	333	58	16	T	ex T.Y. Draco-01

newbuildings : four 45,800 dwt and one 71,000 dwt tankers for 2005/6 delivery.

Name	Eng	Flag	Year	GRT	DWT	Loa	Bm	Kts	Type	Former names

Louis Dreyfus Armateurs SAS

France

Funnel: Black with blue 'LD & C' on white band between two narrow red bands.
Hull: Black

Name	Eng	Flag	Year	GRT	DWT	Loa	Bm	Kts	Type	Former names
Charles LD		Atf	1999	88,385	171,850	289	45	14	B	
Edouard LD	(st)	Fra	1977	79,252	67,460	281	42	20	Lng	
Eric LD		Atf	1999	88,385	169,883	289	45	14	B	
Marine Hunter ‡		Mhl	1984	83,784	164,891	289	43	14	B	ex Federal Hunter-95
Philippe LD		Atf	1999	88,385	169,981	289	45	14	B	
Pierre LD		Atf	1999	87,522	172,561	289	45	16	B	

newbuildings : two 173,000 dwt bulk carriers on order from South Korean builder for 2005 delivery.
Operated by subsidiary Louis Dreyfus Armateurs SNC, the main partner in G.I.E. CETRAGPA group.
‡ on charter from Sohtorik Management, Turkey

Joint Stock Co. LUKoil

Russia

Funnel: Black with logo on white square over white above pale blue above red bands.
Hull: Black with red boot-topping.

Name	Eng	Flag	Year	GRT	DWT	Loa	Bm	Kts	Type	Former names
Astrakhan		Rus	2000	13,767	19,995	156	25	15	T	
Kogalym		Cyp	1996	21,145	32,490	179	25	14	T	ex Iver Progress-96
Maikop		Rus	1999	10,321	15,441	145	23	14	T	
Murmansk		Rus	1999	10,321	15,441	145	23	14	T	
Perm		Rus	1997	10,298	15,855	145	23	14	T	
Saint Petersburg		Rus	1999	10,321	15,541	145	23	14	T	ex Sankt-Peterburg-99
Saratov		Rus	2002	13,767	19,995	154	25	15	T	
Urai		Cyp	1995	21,183	28,840	179	25	14	T	ex Belanja-98, Pavlovsk-95
Usinsk		Rus	2002	13,815	19,800	154	25	15	T	
Volgograd		Rus	1998	10,298	15,855	145	23	14	T	

Murmansk Shipping Co./Russia

Funnel: Black with white over blue over red bands, interrupted by white square containing blue flash and 'L' above 'T', or blue with white polar bear, (or white with polar bear on broad blue band) and black top.
Hull: Grey, black or red with red boot-topping.

Name	Eng	Flag	Year	GRT	DWT	Loa	Bm	Kts	Type	Former names
Admiral Ushakov		Rus	1979	14,141	19,885	162	23	14	BC	
Aleksandr Nevskiy		Rus	1978	14,141	19,885	162	23	14	BC	
Aleksandr Sledzyuk *		Rus	1975	13,153	17,200	160	23	16	T	ex Urengoy-02
Aleksandr Suvorov		Rus	1979	14,141	19,885	162	23	14	BC	
Anatoliy Lyapidevskiy *		Cyp	1984	14,141	19,252	162	23	15	BC	
Arctic Trader *		Mlt	1994	28,420	48,170	192	32	15	R	ex Goldstar-94
Arctic Voyager *		Mlt	1994	28,420	48,131	192	32	15	B	ex Silverstar-94
Arkhangelsk *		Cyp	1983	18,627	19,943	174	25	17	Ro	
Dmitriy Donskoy		Rus	1977	14,141	19,885	162	23	14	BC	
Dmitriy Pozharskiy		Rus	1978	14,141	19,885	162	23	14	BC	
Indiga		Rus	1976	11,290	16,420	164	22	14	T	ex Lunni-03
Ivan Bogun		Rus	1981	14,141	19,885	162	23	14	BC	
Ivan Papanin		Rus	1990	14,400	10,105	166	23	17	Ro	
Ivan Susanin		Rus	1981	14,141	19,885	162	23	14	BC	
Kaliningrad		Rus	2001	13,767	19,996	156	25	15	T	
Kandalaksha		Rus	1984	18,627	19,943	177	25	17	ROl	
Kapitan Bochek *		Cyp	1982	14,141	19,252	162	23	14	BC	
Kapitan Chukhchin		Rus	1981	14,141	19,240	162	23	14	BC	
Kapitan Danilkin		Rus	1987	18,574	19,763	174	25	17	Ro	
Kapitan Kudlay *		Cyp	1983	14,009	19,252	162	23	15	BC	
Kapitan Nazarev *		Cyp	1984	14,141	19,252	162	23	15	BC	
Kapitan Sviridov		Rus	1982	14,141	19,240	162	23	14	BC	
Kapitan Vakula *		Cyp	1983	14,141	19,252	162	23	15	BC	
Kapitan Vodenko *		Cyp	1982	14,141	19,240	162	23	15	BC	
Khatanga		Rus	1987	14,937	23,050	158	26	15	T	ex Bauska-04, Nord Skagerrak-87
Kola		Rus	1983	18,627	19,943	177	25	17	ROl	
Kuzma Minin		Rus	1980	14,141	19,885	162	23	14	BC	
Magas		Rus	2000	13,767	19,996	156	25	15	T	
Mikhail Kutuzov		Rus	1979	14,141	19,885	162	23	14	BC	
Mikhail Strekalovskiy		Rus	1981	14,141	19,250	162	23	14	BC	
Monchegorsk *		Cyp	1983	18,672	19,943	177	25	17	ROl	

Leonhardt & Blumberg. HANSA INDIA. *Hans Kraijenbosch.*

LUKoil (Murmansk Shipping). YURIY ARSHENEVSKIY. *N. Kemps.*

Name	Eng	Flag	Year	GRT	DWT	Loa	Bm	Kts	Type	Former names
Norilsk *		Cyp	1982	18,627	19,942	174	25	17	ROI	
Pavel Vavilov		Rus	1981	14,141	19,240	162	23	15	BC	
Pyotr (Petr) Velikiy		Rus	1978	14,141	19,885	162	23	14	BC	
Stepan Razin		Rus	1980	14,141	19,885	162	22	15	BC	
Tim Buck *		Cyp	1983	14,141	19,240	162	23	14	BC	
Varzuga		Rus	1977	11,290	16,420	164	22	14	T	ex Uikku-03
Viktor Tkachyov		Rus	1981	14,141	19,240	162	23	15	BC	
Yemelyan Pugachev		Rus	1980	13,572	19,885	162	22	15	BC	
Yuriy Arshenevskiy		Rus	1986	18,574	19,724	177	25	17	ROI	
Yuriy Dolorukiy		Rus	1980	14,141	19,885	162	22	15	BC	

*Controlled by Joint Stock Co. LUKoil and * owned by NB Shipping Ltd. companies (managed by NB Maritime Management (Cyprus) Ltd.)*

Lundqvist Rederierna   Finland

Funnel: White with yellow diamond interrupting thin blue band on blue edged broader yellow band.
Hull: Brown or black with red boot-topping.

Name		Flag	Year	GRT	DWT	Loa	Bm	Kts	Type
Alfa Britannia		Bhs	1998	56,115	99,280	248	43	14	T
Alfa Germania		Bhs	1998	56,115	99,193	248	43	14	T
Alfa Italia		Bhs	2002	59,719	105,588	249	43	15	T
Channel Dragon		Bhs	1990	51,972	96,759	232	42	15	T
Hildegaard		Bhs	1999	56,115	99,122	248	43	14	T
Katja		Bhs	1995	52,067	97,220	232	42	15	T
Sarpen		Bhs	2002	59,719	105,655	248	43	15	T
Thornbury		Bhs	2001	56,115	99,220	248	43	15	T

MACS - Maritime Carrier Shipping GmbH & Co.   Germany

Funnel: Blue with white 'macs'.
Hull: Black with white rhinoceros symbol and 'macs', some with white band above red boot-topping.

Name		Flag	Year	GRT	DWT	Loa	Bm	Kts	Type	Former names
Amber Lagoon		Lbr	1997	23,401	31,916	187	27	17	Co	
Blue Master *		Sgp	1971	20,578	28,876	179	26	16	Co	ex Nahoda Biru-86, Blue Master-84
Diamond Land		Lbr	1981	21,826	28,042	177	27	18	Ro	ex Columbine-94, Conti Bavaria-89, Genova-86, Conti Bavaria-85, Costa Ligure-84
Green Cape	(2)	Lbr	1981	19,708	28,052	177	27	18	Ro	ex Natal-94, Bandama-92, Conti Hammonia-91, Als Dedication-89, Conti Hammonia-87, Manhattan-86, Conti Hammonia-85, Costa Arabica-84
Grey Fox		Lbr	1998	23,401	31,916	192	27	16	Co	
Purple Beach		Lbr	1998	23,401	31,916	187	27	17	Co	
Silverfjord *		Sgp	1972	20,584	28,876	179	26	15	Co	ex Chung Shing-87, Silverfjord-83
Viborg *		Sgp	1971	20,578	28,876	179	26	15	Co	ex Golden Isle-98, Tropical Isle-87, Arica-85, Taurus-81, Norbeth-78

* owned by Choosan Shipping Pte. Ltd (managed by Multinational Ship Management Inc., Philippines)

Malaysian International Shipping Corp. Berhad   Malaysia

Funnel: Blue, broad red band divided by white band with yellow star
Hull: Black or red with white 'MISC' or 'MISC Malaysia', red or grey boot-topping.

Name		Flag	Year	GRT	DWT	Loa	Bm	Kts	Type	Former names
Bunga Anggerik		Mys	1989	18,453	29,995	172	26	15	T	
Bunga Bidara		Mys	1990	17,215	23,518	177	27	18	CC	
Bunga Cenderawasih		Mys	1989	18,453	29,928	172	26	15	T	
Bunga Delima		Mys	1990	17,215	23,518	177	27	18	CC	
Bunga Kasturi		Mys	2003	156,967	299,999	330	60	-	T	
Bunga Kekaras		Mys	1995	20,378	29,990	178	30	14	T	
Bunga Kelana Dua **		Mys	1997	57,017	105,575	244	42	14	T	
Bunga Kelana Empat		Mys	1999	57,017	105,815	244	42	14	T	
Bunga Kelana Enam		Mys	1999	57,017	105,811	244	42	14	T	
Bunga Kelana Lima		Mys	1999	57,017	105,400	244	42	14	T	
Bunga Kelana Satu		Mys	1997	57,017	105,575	244	42	14	T	
Bunga Kelana Tiga		Mys	1998	57,017	105,784	244	42	14	T	
Bunga Kelana Tudjuh		Mys	2004	57,500	105,000	244	42	14	T	
Bunga Kenanga		Mys	2000	40,037	73,083	229	32	15	T	ex Four Cutter-00

Malaysian International Shipping. BUNGA MELATI SATU. *J. M. Kakebeeke.*

Malaysian International Shipping. BUNGA TERATAI 3. *Hans Kraijenbosch.*

MISC (American Eagle Tankers). EAGLE VIRGINIA. *Hans Kraijenbosch.*

Name	Eng	Flag	Year	GRT	DWT	Loa	Bm	Kts	Type	Former names
Bunga Kenari		Mys	1991	17,215	23,574	177	27	18	CC	
Bunga Kerayong		Mys	1994	12,994	18,130	160	26	13	T	
Bunga Mawar		Mys	1990	18,453	29,974	172	26	15	T	
Bunga Melati Dua		Mys	1997	22,254	32,169	177	30	14	T	
Bunga Melati Empat		Mys	1999	22,116	31,967	177	30	14	T	
Bunga Melati Enam		Mys	2000	22,116	30,000	177	30	15	T	
Bunga Melati Lima		Mys	1999	22,116	30,000	177	30	15	T	
Bunga Melati Satu		Mys	1997	22,254	32,127	177	30	14	T	
Bunga Melati Tiga		Mys	1999	22,116	31,986	177	30	15	T	
Bunga Melati Tudjuh		Mys	2000	23,000	30,000	177	30	15	T	
Bunga Melor Dua		Mys	1995	24,550	43,125	185	31	14	B	
Bunga Melor Empat		Mys	1995	24,550	43,108	185	31	14	B	
Bunga Melor Satu		Mys	1994	24,550	42,427	185	31	14	B	
Bunga Melor Tiga		Mys	1995	24,550	43,108	185	31	14	B	
Bunga Orkid Dua		Mys	1994	25,498	43,246	185	31	15	B	
Bunga Orkid Empat		Mys	1995	25,498	43,246	185	31	15	B	
Bunga Orkid Lima		Mys	1995	25,498	43,246	185	31	15	B	
Bunga Orkid Satu		Mys	1994	25,498	43,246	185	31	15	B	
Bunga Orkid Tiga		Mys	1994	25,498	43,189	185	31	15	B	
Bunga Pelangi		Mys	1992	53,521	61,428	275	37	24	CC	
Bunga Pelangi Dua		Mys	1995	53,521	61,777	275	37	24	CC	
Bunga Raya Dua		Mys	1998	39,582	48,244	258	32	24	CC	
Bunga Raya Satu		Mys	1998	39,582	48,304	258	32	24	CC	
Bunga Saga Dua		Mys	1993	39,012	74,696	225	32	14	B	
Bunga Saga Empat		Mys	1994	39,012	72,338	225	32	14	B	
Bunga Saga Enam		Mys	1998	38,489	73,056	225	32	14	B	
Bunga Saga Lapan		Mys	1998	38,489	73,207	225	32	14	B	
Bunga Saga Lima		Mys	1998	38,489	73,144	225	32	14	B	
Bunga Saga Satu		Mys	1993	39,012	73,503	225	32	14	B	
Bunga Saga Sembilan		Mys	1999	38,972	73,670	225	32	14	B	
Bunga Saga Sepuloh		Mys	1999	38,972	73,670	225	32	14	B	
Bunga Saga Tiga		Mys	1994	39,012	72,338	225	32	14	B	
Bunga Saga Tujuh		Mys	1998	38,489	73,220	225	32	14	B	
Bunga Semarak		Mys	1990	9,951	16,924	143	22	13	T	
Bunga Siantan		Mys	1991	9,951	16,924	143	22	13	T	
Bunga Tanjung		Mys	1991	18,453	29,980	172	26	14	T	
Bunga Terasek		Mys	1991	17,215	20,000	177	27	19	CC	
Bunga Teratai		Mys	1998	21,339	24,612	184	27	19	CC	ex Bunga Teratai Satu-01
Bunga Teratai Dua		Mys	1998	21,339	24,554	184	27	19	CC	
Bunga Teratai Empat		Mys	1998	21,339	24,561	184	27	19	CC	
Bunga Teratai Tiga		Mys	1998	21,339	24,554	184	27	19	CC	
Federal Bergen *		Hkg	1984	16,983	29,967	180	23	14	B	ex Thunder Bay-92, Federal Bergen-92, High Peak-90
Gangga Nagara		Mys	1997	15,888	24,110	160	26	14	B	
Marquisa		Mys	1997	16,041	26,391	169	26	14	B	
Pernas Amang		Mys	1987	36,369	64,944	225	32	14	B	
Quasar **		Mys	1989	52,500	97,197	247	42	14	T	ex Freja Svea-97, Paola-89
Sea Maestro		Mys	1997	15,888	24,000	160	26	14	B	
Sea Maiden		Phl	1997	15,888	24,000	160	26	14	B	
Sulu Warrior		Phl	1985	19,340	33,024	175	27	14	B	ex Handy Bonita-96, Mar Bonita-94, Reina del Mar-90, Jovian Lotus-89, Sanko Symphony-85

newbuildings - ten tankers between 67,000-298,000 dwt, one 83,700 dwt container ship and eleven LNG tankers for 2004-6 delivery.
Controlled (62.4%) by national oil company Petronas Group (Petroleum Nasional Berhad).
Also own or manage 10 Lng tankers (excluding newbuildings) and 21 bulk carriers with 'Handy' prefix, 8 managed by Transasia Pool, Singapore
* on charter to Fednav Ltd. q.v. and ** managed by Anglo-Eastern Ship Management (Singapore) Pte. Ltd.

American Eagle Tankers/Bermuda

Funnel: White with dark blue 'AET' symbol incorporating ships bow and six small red dashes, narrow black top.
Hull: Orange with red boot-topping.

Name	Eng	Flag	Year	GRT	DWT	Loa	Bm	Kts	Type	Former names
Eagle Albany		Sgp	1998	57,929	107,160	247	42	14	T	
Eagle Anaheim		Sgp	1999	57,929	107,160	247	42	14	T	
Eagle Aries *		Sgp	1985	19,832	29,998	174	28	14	T	ex NOL Aries-00, Neptune Aries-97
Eagle Atlanta		Sgp	1999	57,929	107,160	247	42	14	T	
Eagle Augusta		Sgp	1999	58,156	105,345	244	42	14	T	

Name	Eng	Flag	Year	GRT	DWT	Loa	Bm	Kts	Type	Former names
Eagle Auriga		Sgp	1993	55,962	102,352	241	42	14	T	ex Neptune Auriga-94
Eagle Austin		Sgp	1998	58,156	105,000	244	42	14	T	
Eagle Baltimore		Sgp	1996	57,456	99,405	253	44	14	T	
Eagle Beaumont		Sgp	1996	57,456	99,448	253	44	14	T	
Eagle Birmingham		Sgp	1997	57,456	99,343	253	44	14	T	
Eagle Boston		Sgp	1996	57,456	99,328	253	44	14	T	
Eagle Carina		Sgp	1993	52,504	95,639	247	42	14	T	ex Neptune Carina-94
Eagle Centaurus		Sgp	1992	52,504	95,644	247	42	14	T	ex Neptune Centaurus-94
Eagle Charlotte		Sgp	1997	57,949	107,169	247	42	14	T	
Eagle Columbus		Sgp	1997	57,949	107,166	247	42	14	T	
Eagle Corona		Sgp	1993	52,504	79,993	235	42	14	T	ex Neptune Corona-94
Eagle Memphis		Sgp	1987	53,483	104,499	236	43	13	T	ex Neptune Pisces-95
Eagle Milwaukee		Sgp	1987	53,483	104,385	236	43	13	T	ex Neptune Phoenix-95
Eagle Otome		Sgp	1994	52,504	95,663	247	42	14	T	ex Neptune Otome-00
Eagle Phoenix		Sgp	1998	56,346	105,500	241	42	14	T	ex Paola I-01
Eagle Sagitta *		Sgp	1996	28,433	47,172	183	32	15	T	ex NOL Sagitta-00
Eagle Subaru		Sgp	1994	52,504	95,675	247	42	14	T	ex Neptune Subaru-99
Eagle Tacoma		Sgp	2002	57,950	107,123	247	42	14	T	
Eagle Tampa		Sgp	2003	58,166	107,123	247	42	14	T	
Eagle Toledo		Sgp	2002	58,166	107,092	247	42	14	T	
Eagle Trenton		Sgp	2003	58,166	107,123	247	42	14	T	
Eagle Tucson		Sgp	2003	58,166	107,123	247	42	14	T	
Eagle Vela *		Sgp	1996	28,433	47,172	183	32	15	T	ex NOL Vela-00
Eagle Vermont		Sgp	2002	161,233	318,338	333	60	16	T	
Eagle Virginia		Sgp	2002	161,233	318,338	333	60	16	T	

*Managed by Eagle Shipmanagement or * by Neptune Shipmanagement, both Singapore.*

PNSL Holdings Berhad

Subsidiary, associated with Tong Joo Shipping Pte. Ltd., owning 6 vessels and controlling Anglo-Eastern Ship Management Ltd., Hong Kong and Pacific Basin Bulk Shipping, Hong Kong (23 bulk carriers and 2 newbuildings) all operating mainly in Far Eastern waters.

The Anglo-Eastern Group/Hong Kong (China)

Ship management subsidiary formed by amalgamation of Denholm Ship Management Ltd and Anglo-Eastern Ship Management.

Compagnie Maritime Marfret   France

Funnel: *Blue with red 'MF', black top.*
Hull: *Black with red boot-topping.*

Delmas Forbin		Lbr	2003	18,334	23,579	175	27	18	CC	ex Durande-03, I/a Hansa Sonderburg
Providence		Fra	1995	16,252	23,334	179	25	19	CC	ex Nordcloud-96

Martime-Gesellschaft fur Maritime Diens. GmbH.   Germany

Funnel: *Large blue 'M' or charterers colours.*
Hull: *Grey with red boot-topping.*

Alianca Bahia		Lbr	2002	25,587	33,940	201	30	21	CC	ex Kassandra-02
Alianca Shanghai		Lbr	1998	25,499	34,116	200	30	21	CC	ex P&O Nedlloyd Eagle-03, Columbus Texas-01, Gallia-98
Barbarossa		Atg	1980	16,868	21,569	164	29	18	CC	ex Nuova Australia-98, Zura Bhum-96, Barbarossa-94, Alum Bay-94, Sea Progress-92, Hoechst Express-91, JSS Britannia-88, JSS Los Angeles I-86, JSS Los Angeles-86, Barbarossa-86, Ibn Al-Akfani-83, I/a Barbarossa
Cap Bonavista		Lbr	1999	25,535	33,917	200	30	21	CC	ex P&O Nedlloyd La Spezia-02, I/a Cap Bonavista
Cap Cortes		Lbr	1997	16,211	20,983	168	27	21	CC	ex Fresena-03, Cabo Creus-03, Monte Rosa-01, Azteca-00, Columbus la Plata-99, Fresena-98
Cap Delgado		Lbr	2000	25,535	34,026	200	30	21	CC	ex P&O Nedlloyd Salerno-02, Cap Delgado-00
Cap Ortegal		Lbr	1998	25,500	34,362	199	30	21	CC	ex CMA CGM Delacroix-02, Cap Ortegal-00, Gemini-98
Cap Reinga		Lbr	1998	16,211	20,976	168	28	21	CC	ex Columbus Coromandel-04, I/a Hispania
Columbus Florida		Lbr	1997	16,211	21,008	168	27	21	CC	ex Fiducia-97

Name	Eng	Flag	Year	GRT	DWT	Loa	Bm	Kts	Type	Former names
CSAV Rio Amazonas		Lbr	1987	20,344	29,358	181	29	20	CC	ex Dolores-03, P&O Nedlloyd Nina-02, Dolores-01, Kota Sempena-01, Zim Chicago-00, Dolores-99, City of Haifa-99, Dolores-98, Nelson Bay-98, Dolores-94, OOCL Breeze-93, Dolores-91, ScanDutch Gallia-90, Dolores-87
CSCL Lianyungang		Lbr	2001	25,535	33,900	200	30	21	CC	ex Katharina-01
CSCL Longkou		Lbr	2001	25,535	33,917	200	30	21	CC	ex Juturna-01
CSCL Yantai		Lbr	2001	25,535	33,900	200	30	21	CC	l/a Jasmin
Eyrene		Lbr	1993	21,034	29,931	182	28	19	CC	ex CSAV Seoul-03, Norasia Seoul-01, CSAV Seattle-00, P&O Nedlloyd San Jose-00, Nedlloyd San Jose-98, Eyrene-93
Helvetia		Lbr	1996	15,859	20,084	167	27	19	CC	ex Columbus Pacific-03, Sea Amazon-97, Helvetia-96, Columbus Olinda-96, Helvetia-96
Igloo Moon		Lbr	1987	10,195	13,125	142	22	16	Lpg	ex Gaschem Moon-87
Igloo Star		Lbr	1986	10,195	13,125	142	22	16	Lpg	ex Gaschem Star-86
Kota Permasan		Lbr	1994	21,034	29,931	182	28	19	CC	ex Elisabeth-99, Cielo di Los Angeles-99, Elisabeth-94

Mediterranean Shipping Co. SA Switzerland

Funnel: Cream with cream 'MSC' on black disc, narrow black band below black top.
Hull: Black with red boot-topping.

Name	Eng	Flag	Year	GRT	DWT	Loa	Bm	Kts	Type	Former names
MSC Adele		Mus	1986	21,633	31,205	187	28	17	CC	ex Norasia Sharjah-94
MSC Alexa		Pan	1996	42,307	51,000	243	32	22	CC	
MSC Alexandra		Pan	1987	31,340	41,771	199	32	18	BC	ex MSC Orinoco-99, Toluca-99, MSC Nicole-99, Toluca-98
MSC Alice		Pan	1976	35,535	38,984	252	31	23	CC	ex OOCL Explorer-95, Oriental Explorer-91, Seapac Princeton-83, Oriental Statesman-81 (len-82)
MSC Alpana *		Pan	1978	28,060	28,153	204	31	20	CC	ex Indfex SCI-02, Angela-01, Zim Beijing-01, Angela-99, Oregon Star-98, Angela-97, Uruguay Express-96, Alemania Express-92
MSC Alyssa		Pan	2001	43,575	61,487	274	32	23	CC	
MSC Anahita *		Pan	1985	34,285	36,377	224	32	20	CC	ex CMC Pearl-04, Harbour Bridge-02
MSC Anastasia		Pan	1970	16,670	21,307	181	28	20	CC	ex POL Baltic-95, Leverkusen Express-90, CGM Lorraine-86, Leverkusen Express-85, pt.ex Leverkusen-78 (len/wid-78)
MSC Angela *		Pan	1975	12,364	17,110	159	23	18	C	ex Mananjary-93, Mungo-90, Calvados-83
MSC Aniello		Pan	2000	40,631	56,916	260	32	23	CC	
MSC Annamaria		Pan	1987	21,633	31,205	187	28	17	CC	ex Norasia Al-Mansoorah-94
MSC Antonia		Pan	1985	22,667	33,864	188	28	18	CC	ex Mixteco-94, Birthe Oldendorff-93, Ville de Castor-92, DSR Oakland-92, London Senator-91, ScanDutch Hispania-89, Commander-87, Astoria-86, World Champion-85
MSC Arabia §		Mlt	1972	14,453	21,834	171	23	16	CC	Zim Odessa I-04, Heung-A Carmen-98, Leeward-96, Lizard-85, Neckar Express-84, Freienfels-80, Aristarchos-75
MSC Ariane *		Pan	1970	10,837	14,714	153	23	20	C	ex Ninghai-91, Tausala Samoa-90, Santa Clara-84, Torm America-83, Goldenfels-81, Atlantica Montreal-76, Goldenfels-72
MSC Atlantic *		Pan	1991	37,071	46,975	237	32	21	CC	ex Rostock Senator-02, DSR-Rostock-00
MSC Augusta		Mlt	1986	21,648	31,205	187	28	17	CC	ex Norasia Pearl-94
MSC Aurora *		Pan	1971	13,276	18,534	175	23	19	CC	ex Aurora-94, Acadia-86, Atlantica Genova-76, Gruenfels-71 (len-73)
MSC Barbara		Pan	2002	73,819	85,250	304	40	25	CC	
MSC Brianna		Pan	1986	40,177	43,288	244	32	19	CC	ex Neptune Jade-97
MSC Carole *		Pan	1980	16,600	21,936	179	23	15	Co	ex Vega-03, Seaboard Santiago-02, Vega-02, Pamina-83, CP Hunter-81, Pamina-80
MSC Camille *	(2)	Pan	1970	15,769	16,070	174	26	21	Co	ex MSC Diego-98, Diego-94, San Francisco-86
MSC Carina *		Pan	1986	42,260	45,725	241	32	22	CC	ex MSC Europe-03, Rainbow Bridge-02
MSC Carla †		Pan	1986	35,953	43,300	241	32	20	CC	ex Hanjin Longbeach-01
MSC Carmen *		Pan	1979	20,391	21,457	186	27	21	CC	ex Nuova Rosandra-93, Pancaldo-89 (conv Ro-89)

Mediterranean Shipping Co. MSC ARIANE. *J. M. Kakebeeke.*

Mediterranean Shipping Co. MSC CHIARA. *J. M. Kakebeeke.*

Mediterranean Shipping Co. MSC LEVINA. *J. M. Kakebeeke.*

Name	Eng	Flag	Year	GRT	DWT	Loa	Bm	Kts	Type	Former names
MSC Chelsea *		Pan	1983	17,468	25,412	166	29	18	CC	ex Concordia-04, Hyundai Inchon-95, Concordia-95, Nedlloyd Seoul-95, Red Sea Eureka-93, Concordia-92, Incotrans Pacific-90, Concordia-87, JSS Los Angeles-86, Concordia-86, ScanDutch Concordia-85, Concordia-83
MSC Chiara		Pan	1988	31,430	41,828	199	32	18	BC	ex TMM Morelos-01, Morelos-00
MSC Claudia *	(2)	Pan	1971	50,303	35,737	261	32	24	CC	ex Oceanus Osaka-95, Kamakura Maru-88
MSC Clorinda		Pan	1981	32,238	30,714	222	32	23	CC	ex Ace Concord-94, Neptune Accord-86, Kawana-84, Ace Concord-82
MSC Corinna		Pan	1984	32,703	38,466	207	32	20	CC	ex Med Singapore-97, Ville de Sirius-94, Rhein Express-91, Verhaeren-84
MSC Corsica ††		Mhl	1980	27,994	27,631	204	31	20	CC	ex Safmarine Infant-02, SCL Infanta-00, Author-99, Benarmin-82, Author-81
MSC Cristiana *		Pan	1984	17,700	20,221	184	25	18	Co	ex Absalon-03, Kota Maha-01, Absalon-00, Kenya Star I-00, Absalon-99, Presidente Sarmiento-98, Lanka Abhaya-87, Andalusia-85, Euro Star-84
MSC Daniela *		Pan	1972	11,506	15,967	155	23	16	Co	ex MSC Aniello-99, Aniello-94, Jogoo-80, Turmalin-78
MSC Deila *		Pan	1979	20,391	21,457	186	27	21	Ro	ex Nuova Piave-93, Da Mosto-89 (conv Ro-89)
MSC Denisse *		Pan	1977	28,176	23,058	204	31	21	CC	ex CanMar Force-01, Caraibe-00
MSC Diego		Pan	1999	40,631	56,889	260	32	23	CC	
MSC Don Giovanni		Pan	1996	29,181	41,583	203	31	19	CC	ex Jean-96, l/a Jean Lykes
MSC Dymphna		Pan	1988	36,420	43,224	241	32	22	CC	ex Hanjin Rotterdam-98
MSC Edna		Pan	1977	35,599	38,686	252	31	23	CC	ex OOCL Educator-96, Oriental Educator-88, Seapac Lexington-83, Oriental Researcher-81, l/a Oriental Chevalier
MSC Eleonora *		Pan	1994	28,892	41,667	203	31	20	CC	ex MSC Beijing-03, Trade Cosmos-02, Sea Excellence-96, Trade Cosmos-95
MSC Eliana *		Pan	1970	13,875	14,258	187	23	18	CC	ex Ming Hope-90, Ho Ming-77, Hai Mou-73 (len-79)
MSC Eleni		Pan	2004	53,500	67,800	294	32	24	CC	
MSC Emilia S *		Pan	1970	10,932	14,336	153	23	20	Co	ex Emilia S-94, Sternenfels-80
MSC Emma		Pan	2003	53,500	67,800	294	32	24	CC	
MSC Eyra *		Pan	1982	21,586	21,370	203	25	20	CC	ex Pelineo-04, Miden Agan-02, Maersk Toronto-00, Miden Agan-97, CMA Le Cap-95, Kapitan Kozlovskiy-95 (len-89)
MSC Federica *	(2)	Cyp	1974	21,296	21,101	209	27	18	CC	ex MSC Gina-99, Gina-94, Water Gina-91, Gina S-90, Australia-86, Malmros Monsoon-84
MSC Floriana		Pan	1986	21,648	31,205	187	28	17	CC	ex Princess-95, Norasia Princess-94
MSC Francesca *		Pan	1971	10,837	14,819	153	23	20	Co	ex Francesca-94, Stockenfels-80
MSC Gabriella *		Pan	1983	13,038	17,330	158	23	15	Co	ex Pearl Merchant-01, New Hailong-95, Ciudad de Buenaventura-93, Webber's Post-88, Nedlloyd Cristobal-86, Giahara-86, Woermann Wangoni-85, Family Irini-84
MSC Germany ‡		Lbr	1978	38,991	40,849	240	32	21	CC	ex Genua Express-03, Nurnberg Express-00, Nurnberg Atlantic-93, Nurnberg Express-87
MSC Gianna *		Pan	1983	27,758	42,077	209	30	15	BC	ex Hellen C-03, Jolly Ebano-01, Hellen C-00, Ellen Hudig-97
MSC Gina		Pan	1999	40,631	56,889	260	32	23	CC	
MSC Giovanna		Pan	1987	27,103	25,904	178	32	18	CC	ex MSC Provence-99, Dubrovnik Express-99, Koper Express-96
MSC Giorgia		Pan	1985	22,667	33,823	188	28	18	CC	ex Maya-94, DSR Yokohama-93, Tokyo Senator-91, ScanDutch Massilia-88, Azuma-87, Pacific Pride-86
MSC Giulia		Pan	1970	16,670	21,185	181	28	21	CC	ex POL Gulf-93, Ludwigshafen-90, Ludwigshafen Express-90, pt ex Ludwigshafen-79 (len/wid-79)
MSC Grace *		Pan	1991	13,861	17,298	155	23	16	Co	ex Putney Bridge-02, Melanesian Chief-00, Putney Bridge-99, Mikhail Tsarev-97, Zim Rio-96, Mikhail Tsarev-94, Contship Columbus-93, Mikhail Tsarev-93
MSC Himalaya §		Mlt	1978	27,297	33,621	228	29	19	CC	ex Himalaya-02, MSC Himalaya-02, Evge-01, Smart River-99, YS Prosperity-92, Oriental Premier-86, Oriental Expert-83 (len-83)
MSC Hina		Pan	1984	21,585	21,370	203	25	20	CC	ex Leixoes-03, MSC Melbourne-01, Leixoes-98, Tikhon Kiselyev-95

Name	Eng	Flag	Year	GRT	DWT	Loa	Bm	Kts	Type	Former names
MSC Ilaria *		Pan	1977	20,408	16,167	181	27	18	CC	ex Antigoni-00, Norasia Toronto-00, Antigoni-99, MSC Granada-99, Antigoni-98, UB Tiger-98, Malacca Glory-98, Alkistis-96, Eastern Trader-95, Golfo de Chiriqui-95, Ciudad de Quito-84
MSC Imma		Pan	1983	27,758	42,077	209	30	17	BC	ex Princess Stefanie-04, Jolly Avorio-01, Princess Stefanie-00, Prince Nicolas-00, Cornelis Verolme-97
MSC India *		Pan	1991	13,258	17,298	155	23	16	Co	ex Albert Bridge-02, Kiribati Chief-01, Niugini Chief-01, Chekiang-99, Albert Bridge-98, Nedlloyd Everest-97, Aleksandr Marinesko-95, Orient Shreyas-95, Aleksandr Marinesko-93
MSC Ingrid *		Pan	1999	53,208	67,678	294	32	25	CC	ex Saudi Jeddah-02
MSC Insa *	(3)	Pan	1972	51,608	40,227	269	32	27	CC	ex Maersk Tacoma-96, North Sea-94, Elbe Maru-89
MSC Ireland §§		Atg	1999	14,241	18,425	159	24	18	CC	ex Jork Venture-02
MSC Jade *		Pan	1986	36,514	43,293	241	32	20	CC	ex Hanjin Yokohama-01
MSC Jasmine		Pan	1988	31,430	41,828	199	32	18	BC	ex TMM Oaxaca-00, Contship Houston-97, Oaxaca-96
MSC Jessica *		Pan	1980	23,291	23,930	202	30	19	CC	ex Columbus Olivos-01, Alianca Hamburgo-98, Columbus Olivos-97, Monte Pascoal-96, Columbus Olivos-95, Monte Pascoal-90, Dunedin-86
MSC Jordan *		Lbr	1993	37,071	47,120	237	32	21	CC	ex Sovcomflot Senator-03
MSC Katie		Pan	1977	35,599	38,908	252	31	23	CC	ex OOCL Executive-95, Oriental Executive-89 (len-81)
MSC Katherine Ann		Pan	1985	17,700	20,169	184	25	18	CC	ex Alter Ego-04, Kota Mutiara-01, Alter Ego-00, Dr. Juan B. Alberdi-98, Lanka Amitha-87, Aquitania-85, I/a Eurosun
MSC Katrina		Pan	1979	30,249	27,738	203	31	21	CC	ex Gulf Spirit-97, Eagle Pride-95, Gulf Spirit-94, OOCL Blossom-93, Gulf Spirit-91, Incotrans Spirit-86
MSC Kerry		Pan	1995	37,323	45,530	240	32	22	CC	ex Ville de Norma-98
MSC Lara *		Pan	1994	28,892	38,270	203	31	20	CC	ex MSC Bruxelles-04, Trade Apollo-02, Jadroplov Trader-95, Chesapeake Bay-95, Sea Excellence-94, Trade Sol-94
MSC Laura		Pan	2002	75,590	80,000	300	40	24	CC	
MSC Lauren		Pan	1982	32,238	30,790	222	32	25	CC	ex OOCL Charisma-93, Oriental Patriot-91
MSC Laurence		Pan	1977	32,341	30,937	222	32	23	CC	ex Dragon Komodo-97, NOL Coral-96, Neptune Coral-96
MSC Leanne §§		Pan	1983	17,702	20,128	184	25	18	Co	ex Honour-03, MSC Leanne-03, Honour-03, Kota Molek-01, Delmas Surville-00, Honour-99, Ocean Sirius-95, Lanka Asitha-89, Laredo-84
MSC Levina		Pan	1989	36,420	43,140	241	32	21	CC	ex Hanjin Le Havre-98
MSC Lieselotte *		Pan	1983	21,586	21,370	203	25	20	CC	ex Aveiro-03, Tiger Sea-02, Aveiro-02, Nikolay Tikhonov-95 (len-89)
MSC Loretta		Pan	2002	73,819	85,801	304	40	25	CC	
MSC Ludovica		Pan	2003	75,590	85,882	304	40	25	CC	
MSC Luisa		Pan	2002	75,000	84,920	304	40	25	CC	
MSC Magali *		Pan	1980	33,113	38,485	231	32	23	CC	ex Amber I-03, APL Amber-01, NOL Amber-00, Neptune Amber-96
MSC Malin *		Pan	1982	21,586	21,370	203	25	20	CC	ex Pelado-04, Tavira-03, Maersk Montreal-00, Tavira-97, Kapitan Kanlevskiy -95 (len-89)
MSC Maria *		Pan	1985	21,586	21,370	203	26	20	CC	ex Delphic Spirit-03, Zim Seoul-99, Delphic Spirit-99, MSC Uruguay-98, Miden River-98, Spevde Vradeos-97, Algoa Bay-95, Professor Tovstykh-95
MSC Maria Laura		Pan	1988	36,343	42,513	229	32	20	CC	ex Sea Cheetah-00, Cap Verde-00, CGM La Perouse-98, Ville de la Fontaine-93, La Fontaine-92, CGM La Perouse-91
MSC Marianna		Pan	2002	73,819	85,250	304	40	25	CC	ex MSC Loraine-02
MSC Marina		Pan	2003	75,000	85,250	300	40	25	CC	
MSC Martina		Pan	1993	37,398	43,378	243	32	22	CC	ex Maersk Hong Kong-97, Hansa America-93
MSC Matilde *		Pan	1999	53,208	67,615	294	32	25	CC	ex Saudi Jubail-02
MSC Maya		Pan	1988	35,598	43,184	242	32	21	CC	ex Maersk Levant-04, MSC Jamie-02, Hanjin Seattle-98
MSC Mee May		Pan	1970	16,670	21,185	181	29	21	CC	ex Mee May-94, Erlangen Express-86, Incotrans Progress-82, Erlangen Express-81, Erlangen-79 (len/wid-79)
MSC Melissa		Pan	2002	73,819	85,250	304	40	25	CC	

Name	Eng	Flag	Year	GRT	DWT	Loa	Bm	Kts	Type	Former names
MSC Michaela		Pan	2002	73,819	85,797	304	40	25	CC	
MSC Michele		Pan	1971	16,670	21,185	181	29	21	CC	ex Michele-94, Incotrans Pacific-86, Hoechst Express-84, Incotrans Promise-83, Hoechst Express-81, Hoechst-79 (len/wid-79)
MSC Mirella *		Pan	1989	27,103	25,904	178	32	18	CC	ex Zagreb Express-99
MSC Monica		Pan	1993	37,398	43,378	243	32	22	CC	ex Ville d'Aquila-97, Hansa Asia-93
MSC Natalia *		Pan	1986	40,177	43,403	244	32	21	CC	ex MSC California-01, Vision-99, Choyang Vision-98, Neptune Garnet-96
MSC Nederland *		Pan	1992	37,071	47,120	237	32	21	CC	ex Vladivostok Mariner-03, Vladivostok Senator-02
MSC Nerissa		Pan	2004	53,500	67,800	294	32	24	CC	
MSC Nicole		Pan	1989	31,430	41,828	199	32	18	BC	ex Contship America-00, Monterrey-00, MSC Lima-98, Nedlloyd Montevideo-98, Monterrey-97
MSC Nigeria §§		Atg	1994	11,062	15,166	158	23	18	CC	ex P&O Nedlloyd San Pedro-01, Kent Merchant-99, Maersk Libreville-98, Antje-97, Lanka Amila-97, Antje-94
MSC Nuria	(2)	Pan	1977	44,154	39,454	249	32	19	CC	ex Australian Venture-96
MSC Patagonia ¶		Cyp	1984	16,517	22,233	166	27	18	CC	ex Heicon-99, Sea Victory-97, Heicon-97, CSAV Rauten-96, Heicon-95, CSAV Rubens-95, Heicon-94, CGM Iguacu-94, Calapadria-93, Red Sea Energy-91, Belgian Senator-90, Euro Texas-89, Heicon-88
MSC Patricia *		Pan	1990	13,651	18,150	166	24	14	Co	ex Torm America-02, Tisno-98, Torm America-97, Vardar Delmas-92, Vardar-91
MSC Paola *		Pan	1978	20,295	19,974	202	26	22	CC	ex Safmarine Nomzi-01, Nomzi-00, Boringia-95
MSC Peggy		Pan	1984	32,696	38,981	207	32	20	CC	ex Atlantic Bridge-98, CMBT Maeterlinck-97, Med Barcelona-96, Ville de Canopus-94, ScanDutch Helvetia-91, Maeterlinck-89
MSC Perle *		Pan	1983	17,414	25,329	166	29	18	CC	ex Corona-03, Nautic I-02, City of Dublin-00, City of Antwerp-98, City of London-97, Pacific Span-93, Incotrans Pacific-90, ScanDutch Arcadia-90, Korean Senator-88, Corona-87, Atlantic Corona-85, Corona-84, ScanDutch Corona-84, Corona-83
MSC Pioneer		Bhs	1986	39,892	43,567	244	32	21	CC	ex Hyundai Pioneer-04, P&O Nedlloyd Miami-03, Hyundai Piomeer-02
MSC Provence ‡‡		Mlt	1979	17,304	14,520	170	25	19	CC	ex City of Liverpool-03, Zim Liverpool I-00, Mor Canada-99, Nikolay Golovanov-94
MSC Rafaela		Pan	1996	42,307	51,210	243	32	22	CC	
MSC Rebecca *		Pan	1997	37,879	42,926	243	32	-	CC	ex Grand Concord-97
MSC Regina		Pan	1999	40,631	56,890	200	32	23	CC	
MSC Romania II ‡		Lbr	1979	16,471	19,261	179	25	18	CC	ex MSC Genova-02, Shanghai-98, MSC Shanghai-98, Heung-A Strait-97, Zim Genova-95, Zim Koper-91, Enterprise-88, TFL Enterprise-86, Eagle Faith-85, TFL Enterprise-85, Alltrans Enterprise-82, Incotrans Enterprise-82, TFL Enterprise-81, Alltrans Enterprise-79
MSC Rosa M *		Cyp	1978	20,418	20,185	186	27	23	Ro	ex Rosa M-94, D'Albertis-87
MSC Rossella		Pan	1993	37,396	43,878	243	32	22	CC	ex Ville de Carina-97, Hansa Europe-93
MSC Sabrina		Pan	1989	35,598	43,078	243	32	21	CC	ex Hanjin Oakland-98
MSC Samia	(2)	Pan	1973	40,944	35,480	265	32	26	CC	ex Maersk Kobe-94, Verrazano Bridge-93
MSC Sandra		Pan	2001	43,575	61,468	274	32	23	CC	
MSC Sariska *		Pan	1971	13,276	18,836	175	23	18	CC	ex MSC Alexa-96, Alexa-94, Carmen Mare-87, Ville de Zenith-86, Carmen Mare-86, Passero-85, Ruhr Express-85, Geyerfels-80, Seatrain Bremen-80, Geyerfels-79, Seatrain Valley Forge-78, Atlantic Livorno-77, l/a Geyerfels (len-74)
MSC Serena *		Pan	1977	38,991	40,624	241	32	21	CC	ex Zim Eilat I-02, New York Express-98, Maersk Algeciras-96, Stuttgart Express-92 (len-85)
MSC Sharjah §		Mlt	1972	14,453	21,876	171	23	16	CC	ex Zim Constantza I-04, Heung-A Grace-98, Grace-98, Carmen Carina-95, Biscay-86, Fulda Express-84, Frankenfels-80, Aristandros-74
MSC Shaula *		Pan	1977	20,295	19,974	202	26	21	CC	ex MSC Mbashi-00, Mbashi-99, CMBT America-96, Fionia-95

108

Mediterranean Shipping Co. MSC MICHAELA. *J. M. Kakebeeke.*

Mediterranean Shipping Co. MSC SONIA. *J. M. Kakebeeke.*

Name	Eng	Flag	Year	GRT	DWT	Loa	Bm	Kts	Type	Former names
MSC Sintra §§		Atg	2000	14,241	18,425	159	24	18	CC	ex Jork Valiant-02
MSC Socotra §		Lbr	1980	35,065	43,070	246	32	23	CC	ex Astoria Bridge-03, Transworld Bridge-99
MSC Sonia	(2)	Pan	1972	50,646	40,929	261	32	24	CC	ex Sea Dominance-96, Double Haven-95, Rhine Maru-95
MSC Sophie		Pan	1993	37,398	43,294	243	32	22	CC	ex Maersk Colombo-97, Hansa Australia-93
MSC Stefania		Pan	1969	23,881	24,245	213	30	23	CC	ex Stefania-94, Shireen-88, Crescent-88, Hakozaki Maru-81
MSC Suez *		Pan	1993	37,071	47,120	237	32	21	CC	ex Hamburg Senator-02
MSC Teresa *	(2)	Pan	1974	22,042	20,770	209	27	22	CC	ex MSC Rafaela-96, Rafaela S-94, Seagull-88, Tavara-86, Tamara-84
MSC Tina *		Pan	1986	42,259	45,721†	249	32	22	CC	ex Ambassador Bridge-04
MSC Trinidad †		Pan	1984	31,248	37,933	203	32	18	CC	ex Jaguar-03, Maipo-02
MSC Valeria *		Pan	1970	10,837	14,666	153	23	15	C	ex Tamaitai Samoa-91, Santa Monica-84, Torm Africa-83, Deneb-81, Gutenfels-80, Atlantica New York-73, Gutenfels-72
MSC Vanessa		Pan	2003	75,590	85,844	300	40	25	CC	
MSC Venice ‡		Lbr	1978	16,471	19,261	179	25	18	CC	ex MSC Osaka-98, Osaka-97, Zim Osaka-96, Liberty-88, TFL Liberty-86
MSC Veronique		Pan	1976	32,341	30,934	222	32	23	CC	ex NOL Pearl-97, Neptune Pearl-96
MSC Vietnam ††		Pan	1981	26,787	25,745	208	31	19	CC	ex Nefeli I-03, Zim Shekou-00, Nefeli I-99, MSC Durban-99, Nefeli I-98, Hanjin Chungmu-98, Korean Wonis Seven-89
MSC Viviana		Pan	2003	75,000	85,250	304	40	25	CC	
MSC Zrin §§		Mlt	1994	29,912	35,100	201	32	18	CC	ex CSAV Peru-01, Zrin-98, Columbus Bahia-98, Alemania Express-97, MSC Zrin-96, Zrin-94, Antoine de Padoue-94
Pelat *		Cyp	1982	21,586	21,370	203	25	20	CC	ex MSC Eyra-04, Pelat-04, Lisboa-02, P&O Nedlloyd Ottawa-00, Sea-Land Canada-99, Lisboa-97, Kapitan Gavrilov-95 (len-89)

newbuilding - About 25 owned container ships on order from South Korean builders for 2004-7 delivery, including three 7960TEU ('S' class), four 4300TEU and three 6252TEU (chartered from Costamare)

World's second largest container carrier (by vessels and capacity) - see other chartered ships with 'MSC' prefix in index

* managed by Pacific Marine Services Ltd., Hong Kong (associated with Univan, Singapore)

† owned by Technomar Shipping Inc., †† byTarget Marine SA, ‡ by Ciel Shipmanagement SA, ‡‡ by Sarlis Container Services SA, § by Goldenport Shipmanagement Ltd., all Greece, # by Oost Atlantic Lijn BV, Netherlands, ¶ by Islamar Shipmanagement Co. Ltd., Cyprus, § by Dr. Peters KG fund, Germany or §§ various other owners..

Mitsui O.S.K. Lines Ltd.　　　　　　　　　　Japan

Funnel: Bright red.

Hull: Light blue or grey with green waterline and red boot-topping.

Name	Eng	Flag	Year	GRT	DWT	Loa	Bm	Kts	Type	Former names
African Ruby		Pan	1994	81,803	147,638	278	45	15	T	
Ambassador Norris		Pan	2001	27,955	45,290	180	32	15	T	
APL Chiwan		Pan	1995	59,622	63,440	299	37	24	CC	ex MOL Tyne-02, Tyne-01
APL Dubai		Pan	1995	60,133	62,905	300	37	24	CC	ex MOL Rhine-02, Rhine-01
APL Ningpo		Pan	1995	58,531	61,470	300	37	24	CC	ex MOL Loire-02, La Loire-01
APL Qingdao		Pan	1995	58,923	61,489	300	37	23	CC	ex MOL Mosel-02, Mosel-00
Aquarius Ace		Pan	1998	36,615	14,353	175	29	15	V	
Astral Ace		Pan	2000	36,615	14,280	175	29	18	V	
Atlantic Hero		Pan	1992	51,984	96,687	232	42	13	T	ex Stena Concertina-99
Atlantic Liberty		Pan	1995	164,373	311,625	330	58	15	T	
Atlantic Prosperity		Pan	1996	164,373	310,000	330	58	15	T	
Atlixco		Pan	1982	41,697	18,217	199	30	18	V	ex Clover Ace-99
Azalea Ace		Pan	1979	27,874	12,672	175	27	18	V	ex Sevenseas-92, Sevenseas Highway-88
Bravery Ace *		Pan	2000	52,276	17,686	189	32	20	V	
Brilliant Ace		Pan	1987	47,505	14,189	180	32	17	V	
Camellia Ace		Pan	1994	55,336	18,938	200	32	18	V	
Cattleya Ace		Vut	1988	56,823	18,762	199	32	21	V	
Comet Ace		Pan	2000	36,615	14,283	175	29	18	V	

Mitsui OSK Lines. AMBASSADOR NORRIS. *J. M. Kakebeeke.*

Mitsui OSK Lines. MOL PROMISE. *Hans Kraijenbosch.*

Mitsui OSK Lines. POLARIS ACE. *Phil Kempsey.*

Name	Eng	Flag	Year	GRT	DWT	Loa	Bm	Kts	Type	Former names
Cosmos Ace *		Pan	1998	46,346	15,439	182	31	19	V	
Cosmo Spirit *		Lbr	1985	37,841	13,295	175	29	18	V	ex Excelsior-99, Young Skipper-91
Cosmos Venture *		Lbr	1986	46,051	17,750	188	31	18	V	
Courageous Ace *		Pan	2003	56,439	19,927	198	32	-	V	
Crystal Ace		Pan	1983	27,566	10,538	161	27	16	V	
Dynamic City		Pan	1990	140,850	243,850	325	58	16	T	ex Diamond City-00
Dynamic Express		Pan	1993	25,644	42,253	180	31	14	T	
Eternal Ace *		Pan	1988	55,380	18,701	200	32	19	V	
Euro Spirit *		Lbr	1998	46,346	15,483	188	31	19	V	
Frontier Ace *		Pan	2000	52,276	17,693	189	32	20	V	
Frontier Express		Pan	1993	40,721	68,520	229	32	14	T	
Glorious Ace		Jpn	1981	46,047	17,743	190	32	18	V	
Harmony Ace *		Pan	1992	47,819	14,256	180	32	19	V	
Heroic Ace		Pan	2002	56,439	19,879	198	32	-	V	
Iris Ace		Pan	1983	33,521	16,461	190	32	19	V	ex Rainbow Ace-93
Lambert Maru *		Pan	1986	98,661	197,981	300	50	15	O	
Maple Ace II *		Lbr	1992	38,349	15,361	188	28	18	V	
Martorell		Pan	2003	57,789	19,531	200	32	-	V	
Mercury Ace		Jpn	1985	44,979	16,603	176	29	17	V	
MOL Advantage		Pan	2001	66,332	66,532	279	40	25	CC	
MOL Ambition †		Iom	1997	23,734	30,461	188	30	21	CC	ex City of London-04, CGM Caravelle-01, City of London-98
MOL Bravery		Pan	1995	41,114	39,788	245	32	23	CC	ex Alligator Bravery-01
MOL Columbus		Pan	1991	41,144	40,331	245	32	21	CC	ex Alligator Columbus-00
MOL Discovery		Pan	1991	42,812	40,499	253	32	22	CC	ex Alligator Discovery-01, OOCL Shanghai-98, Alligator Discovery-96
MOL Elbe		Jpn	1990	50,352	58,112	292	32	23	CC	ex Elbe-01
MOL Efficiency		Pan	2002	53,822	63,160	294	32	24	CC	
MOL Encore		Pan	2003	53,096	61,441	294	32	24	CC	
MOL Endeavor		Pan	2003	53,096	61,441	294	32	24	CC	
MOL Endurance		Pan	2003	53,096	61,441	294	32	24	CC	
MOL Enterprise		Pan	2004	53,600	49,600	294	32	24	CC	
MOL Eternity		Jpn	1985	35,234	33,637	205	32	19	CC	ex Southern Cross Maru-01
MOL Excellence		Pan	2003	53,822	50,800	294	32	24	CC	
MOL Expeditor		Pan	2003	53,822	62,800	294	32	24	CC	
MOL Express		Pan	2003	53,400	62,800	294	32	24	CC	
MOL Fortune		Lbr	1986	40,354	41,513	226	32	20	CC	ex Alligator Fortune-01
MOL Glory		Lbr	1986	39,283	40,817	226	32	20	CC	ex Aligator Glory-01
MOL Golden Wattle		Lbr	1986	40,354	41,474	226	32	19	CC	ex Alligator Hope-01
MOL Integrity		Pan	2001	66,332	66,800	279	40	25	CC	
MOL Ingenuity		Pan	1992	50,204	58,986	292	32	24	CC	ex MOL Danube-02, Danube-01
MOL Initiative		Pan	1988	50,030	59,488	290	32	23	CC	ex La Seine-02
MOL Liberty		Pan	1986	42,117	38,512	246	32	22	CC	ex Alligator Liberty-02
MOL Maas		Lbr	1995	60,133	62,905	300	37	23	CC	ex Maas-01
MOL Miracle		Pan	1991	41,495	40,330	245	32	21	CC	ex Alligator Miracle-02, Alligator America-99
MOL Performance		Pan	2001	74,071	74,453	294	40	27	CC	
MOL Precision		Pan	2002	71,902	72,300	293	40	25	CC	
MOL Pride *		Lbr	1988	41,126	40,192	245	32	21	CC	ex Alligator Pride-01
MOL Priority		Pan	2002	74,071	74,453	294	40	26	CC	
MOL Progress		Pan	2002	71,902	72,300	293	40	25	CC	
MOL Promise		Pan	2002	71,902	72,300	293	40	25	CC	
MOL Solution		Pan	2001	71,902	72,300	293	40	25	CC	
MOL Thames		Pan	1990	50,628	59,056	290	32	23	CC	ex Thames-00
MOL Triumph		Lbr	1988	43,082	40,540	253	32	22	CC	ex Alligator Triumph-01
MOL Wellington		Pan	1979	32,163	29,888	216	32	22	CC	ex Wellington Maru-01, Canberra Maru-87
MOL Wisdom		Pan	1995	41,114	59,814	245	32	23	CC	ex Alligator Wisdom-01
Mona Century *		Pan	2000	87,523	172,036	289	45	15	B	
Mona Liberty		Sgp	1992	77,195	151,533	273	43	14	B	ex Kohju-01
Mona Linden *		Pan	2000	84,507	170,473	289	45	14	B	
Neptune Ace *		Pan	1985	44,979	16,560	176	29	17	V	
Ocean Spirit *		Lbr	1985	47,561	16,770	191	32	19	V	ex San Laurel-97, Nissan Laurel-95
Oriental Phoenix *		Lbr	1985	27,658	11,824	159	28	17	V	
Pearl Ace *		Pan	1994	45,796	15,194	188	31	18	V	
Pegasus Ace		Pan	1998	36,615	14,348	175	29	19	V	
Planet Ace *		Pan	1992	38,349	15,327	188	28	18	V	
Polaris Ace		Pan	1997	46,346	15,522	182	31	19	V	

Name	Eng	Flag	Year	GRT	DWT	Loa	Bm	Kts	Type	Former names
Progress Ace		Pan	2003	57,789	19,512	200	32	-	V	
Prominent Ace		Pan	2004	57,789	13,500	200	32	-	V	
Sapphire Ace		Pan	1993	45,796	15,204	188	31	18	V	
Solar Wing *		Lbr	1988	41,604	13,224	187	32	19	V	
Splendid Ace *		Pan	2003	56,439	19,893	198	32	-	V	
Sun Ace		Pan	1981	29,973	13,051	179	27	17	V	
Triumph Ace *		Pan	2000	55,880	20,131	194	32	20	V	
Universal Spirit *		Lbr	1985	39,948	13,025	173	30	19	V	ex Sanwa-98, Sanwa Maru-91
Victory Ace		Pan	1985	36,026	16,068	200	28	18	V	(len-87)
World Spirit		Lbr	1998	37,949	14,101	175	29	19	V	

newbuildings : About 48 on order including 16 vehicle carriers, plus eight tankers and six bulk carriers over 100,000 dwt.
* managed by M. O. Ship Management Co. Ltd./Japan † chartered from Andrew Weir Shipping Ltd., UK

MOL Tankship Management Ltd./UK

Name	Eng	Flag	Year	GRT	DWT	Loa	Bm	Kts	Type	Former names
Asian Progress II *	Sgp	2000	160,079	314,026	333	60	15	T	
Bandaisan	Pan	2000	149,282	281,037	330	60	15	T	
Chinook Maiden	Pan	1996	27,915	45,217	180	32	14	T	
Diamond Hope *	Pan	1995	146,865	259,999	322	58	15	T	
Diamond Jasmine *	Pan	1999	152,041	281,050	330	60	16	T	
Glen Maye	Mlt	1992	79,595	140,991	272	46	14	T	
Glen Roy	Mlt	1992	79,479	144,100	273	43	14	T	
Ibukisan *	Pan	2000	160,079	299,999	330	60	15	T	
Ikomasan *	Pan	2000	160,079	299,986	333	60	15	T	
Iwatesan *	Pan	2003	159,912	300,667	333	60	-	T	
Kaimon *	Pan	1991	142,463	258,076	324	56	15	T	
Kaimon II *	Pan	2002	160,079	314,014	333	60	15	T	
Kaminesan *	Pan	2003	159,813	303,896	333	60	-	T	
Katori *	Pan	1995	146,510	259,999	324	56	15	T	
Maracas Bay	Bhs	1998	20,573	30,977	175	28	15	T	
Midnight Sun	Pan	1997	27,915	45,219	180	32	14	T	
Millennium Explorer	Pan	2000	57,000	97,850	241	42	15	T	
Mitsumine *	Pan	1993	149,323	260,995	330	59	15	T	
Naparima	Pan	1996	20,573	30,947	175	28	15	T	
Nariva	Bhs	1998	20,573	30,977	175	28	15	T	
Ohminesan *	Pan	1996	151,039	259,984	333	60	15	T	
Oriental Venture	Pan	1992	154,071	281,018	330	59	14	T	
Orion Trader *	Pan	1998	151,039	267,736	333	60	15	T	
Pacific Wave	Pan	1992	54,935	96,099	242	42	14	T	
Perseus Trader *	Pan	2003	160,066	299,992	333	60	-	T	
Rokkosan *	Pan	2003	160,066	300,257	333	60	-	T	
Ryuohsan *	Pan	2000	149,282	281,050	330	60	16	T	
Selene Trader *	Pan	2003	159,912	299,991	333	60	-	T	
Vega Trader *	Pan	2003	159,813	299,985	333	60	-	T	
Washusan *	Pan	2002	152,041	281,050	330	60	16	T	
Welsh Venture	Pan	1991	151,127	280,491	330	56	14	T	
Yohteisan *	Pan	2000	149,282	281,050	330	60	16	T	

* owned or managed by subsidiary International Energy Transport Co. Ltd..
MOL is probably the world's second largest shipping group with many subsidiaries owning about 250 vessels (23 million tonnes deadweight), in addition to which there are about 150 managed vessels and many under charter. Only the largest container ships, tankers and vehicle carriers are listed, in addition to which there are numerous bulk carriers, wood-chip carriers, product tankers and over 30 jointly owned Lng carriers.

A. P. Moller-Maersk   Denmark

Funnel: Black with white seven-pointed star on broad light blue band.
Hull: Light blue with black 'Maersk Line' or 'MAERSK SEALAND', red boot-topping.

Name	Eng	Flag	Year	GRT	DWT	Loa	Bm	Kts	Type	Former names
A. P. Moller	Dis	2000	91,560	104,750	347	43	25	CC	
Adrian Maersk	Dis	1998	14,120	17,375	155	25	18	CC	
Agnete Maersk	Dis	1998	14,120	17,375	155	25	18	CC	
Albert Maersk	Dis	1998	14,120	17,375	155	25	18	CC	
Alva Maersk	Dis	1998	14,120	17,375	155	25	18	CC	
Anna Maersk	Dis	2003	93,496	109,000	352	43	25	CC	
Arnold Maersk	Dis	2003	93,496	109,000	352	43	25	CC	
Arthur Maersk	Dis	2003	93,496	105,750	352	43	25	CC	
Axel Maersk	Dis	2003	93,496	109,000	352	43	25	CC	
Caroline Maersk	Dis	2000	91,560	104,700	347	43	25	CC	

Name	Eng	Flag	Year	GRT	DWT	Loa	Bm	Kts	Type	Former names
Carsten Maersk		Dis	2000	91,560	104,750	347	43	25	CC	
Cecilie Maersk		Dis	1994	20,842	28,550	190	28	18	CC	
Charlotte Maersk		Dis	2002	91,000	104,000	347	43	25	CC	
Chastine Maersk		Dis	2001	91,560	104,750	347	43	25	CC	
Christian Maersk		Dis	1992	18,979	25,375	176	28	18	CC	
Claes Maersk		Dis	1994	20,842	28,550	190	28	18	CC	
Clara Maersk		Dis	1992	18,979	25,275	176	28	18	CC	
Clementine Maersk		Dis	2002	91,921	104,750	347	43	25	CC	
Clifford Maersk		Dis	1999	91,560	104,700	348	43	25	CC	
Columbine Maersk		Dis	2002	91,921	110,000	347	43	25	CC	
Cornelia Maersk		Dis	2002	91,921	104,750	347	43	25	CC	
Cornelius Maersk		Dis	2000	91,560	104,700	347	43	25	CC	
Dirch Maersk		Dis	1996	50,698	62,418	292	32	24	CC	
Donax		Sgp	2001	61,764	79,000	245	42	15	T	ex Maersk Prosper-01
Eli Maersk		Dis	2000	159,187	259,999	333	58	16	T	
Ellen Maersk		Dis	2000	159,187	308,491	333	58	16	T	
Else Maersk		Dis	2000	159,187	308,491	333	58	16	T	
Eugen Maersk		Dis	1993	158,475	298,900	344	56	14	T	ex British Vigilance-02, Emma Maersk-97
Glasgow Maersk		Gbr	1999	50,698	62,400	292	32	24	CC	
Greenwich Maersk		Gbr	2000	50,698	62,228	292	32	24	CC	
Hans Maersk		Dis	1993	18,360	23,257	160	26	16	Lpg	
Helene Maersk		Dis	1993	18,360	23,270	160	26	16	Lpg	
Henning Maersk		Dis	1994	18,360	23,267	160	26	16	Lpg	
Henriette Maersk		Dis	1994	18,360	23,267	160	26	16	Lpg	
Jakob Maersk		Dis	1991	23,878	36,160	185	27	16	Lpg	
Jane Maersk		Dis	1990	23,878	36,160	185	27	16	Lpg	
Jens Maersk		Dis	2001	30,166	27,300	216	32	23	CC	
Jepperson Maersk		Dis	2001	30,166	35,097	216	32	22	CC	
Jesper Maersk		Dis	1991	23,878	36,160	185	27	16	Lpg	
Jessie Maersk		Dis	1991	23,878	36,160	185	27	16	Lpg	
Johannes Maersk		Dis	2001	30,166	27,300	216	32	23	CC	
Josephine Maersk		Dis	2002	30,166	27,300	216	32	23	CC	
Karen Maersk		Dis	1996	81,488	82,135	318	43	25	CC	
Kate Maersk		Dis	1996	81,488	84,900	318	43	25	CC	
Katrine Maersk		Dis	1997	81,488	84,900	318	43	25	CC	
Kirsten Maersk		Dis	1997	81,488	90,456	318	43	25	CC	
Knud Maersk		Dis	1996	81,488	84,900	318	43	25	CC	
Laura Maersk		Dis	2001	50,721	63,200	266	37	24	CC	
Laust Maersk		Dis	2001	50,721	63,000	266	37	24	CC	
Leda Maersk		Dis	2001	50,721	63,200	266	37	24	CC	
Lexa Maersk		Dls	2001	50,721	63,400	266	37	24	CC	
Lica Maersk		Dis	2001	50,721	63,400	266	37	24	CC	
Luna Maersk		Dis	2002	50,721	63,400	266	37	25	CC	
Madison Maersk		Dis	1991	52,181	60,350	294	32	23	CC	
Maersk Ahram ††		Egy	1998	14,063	17,728	155	25	18	CC	
Maersk Curlew		Gbr	1983	52,175	99,800	236	40	15	T	ex Maersk Dorset-97, Bin He-95, Dorthe Maersk-92
Maersk Garonne		Fra	2003	50,698	62,007	282	32	24	CC	
Maersk Gateshead		Iom	2002	50,686	62,242	292	32	24	CC	
Maersk Gironde		Atf	2002	50,698	62,007	292	32	24	CC	
Maersk Holyhead		Ven	2000	18,500	23,000	159	26	18	Lpg	
Maersk Koper §§		Gbr	1963	17,618	15,170	202	24	18	CC	ex Sea Adventure-02, Maersk Constanza-00, Sea Adventure-99, Sea-Land Adventurer-89, pt ex San Francisco-78
Maersk Perth ø		Lbr	2001	32,322	39,300	211	32	22	CC	l/a Meta
Maersk Plymouth ø		Lbr	2000	32,322	39,300	211	32	22	CC	ex Alexandra-00
Maersk Rhine §§		Dis	1999	22,181	35,000	171	31	14	T	ex Ras Maersk-00
Maersk Riga		Dis	2001	22,184	34,999	171	27	14	T	ex Roy Maersk-03
Maersk Rosyth		Gbr	2003	22,184	34,811	171	27	14	T	
Maersk Tacoma §		Pan	1982	36,238	44,142	241	32	24	CC	ex Luna Maersk-96, Newport Bay-92, Luna Maersk-91
Maersk Toledo §§		Iom	1985	43,332	53,325	270	32	22	CC	ex Lindo Maersk-00, Mc-Kinney Maersk-90
Maersk Trieste §§		Dis	1983	43,332	53,310	270	32	24	CC	ex Leise Maersk-99, Regina Maersk-95
Magleby Maersk		Dis	1990	52,181	60,350	294	32	23	CC	
Majestic Maersk		Dis	1990	52,181	60,639	294	32	23	CC	
Marchen Maersk		Dis	1988	52,191	60,639	294	32	23	CC	
Maren Maersk		Dis	1989	52,191	60,639	294	32	23	CC	

114

A. P. Moller. ARNOLD MAERSK. *Hans Kraijenbosch.*

A. P. Moller. MAERSK ROSYTH. *J. M. Kakebeeke.*

A. P. Moller. OLGA MAERSK. *Hans Kraijenbosch.*

Name	Eng	Flag	Year	GRT	DWT	Loa	Bm	Kts	Type	Former names
Margrethe Maersk		Dis	1989	52,191	60,639	294	32	23	CC	
Marie Maersk		Dis	1990	52,181	60,350	294	32	23	CC	
Marit Maersk		Dis	1988	52,191	60,639	294	32	23	CC	
Mathilde Maersk		Dis	1989	52,191	60,640	294	32	23	CC	
Mayview Maersk		Dis	1991	52,181	60,350	294	32	23	CC	
Mc-Kinney Maersk		Dis	1991	52,181	60,350	294	32	23	CC	
Mette Maersk		Dis	1989	52,191	60,639	294	32	23	CC	
Millennium Maersk		Dis	2000	159,187	308,491	333	58	16	T	
Nele Maersk		Dis	2000	27,300	30,420	199	30	21	CC	
Nexø Maersk		Dis	2001	27,733	30,420	199	30	21	CC	
Nicolai Maersk		Dis	2000	27,733	30,420	199	30	21	CC	
Nicoline Maersk		Dis	2000	27,733	30,191	199	30	21	CC	
Niels Maersk		Nis	1991	11,822	16,259	158	21	15	Lpg	ex Ravnanger-98, Salacgriva-91
Nkossa II ***		Bhs	1992	44,493	48,162	230	37	16	Lpg	ex Inger Maersk-96
Nora Maersk		Dis	2000	27,733	30,194	199	30	21	CC	
Nysted Maersk		Dis	2001	27,733	30,194	197	30	21	CC	
Olga Maersk		Dis	2003	34,202	41,028	237	32	-	CC	
Olivia Maersk		Dis	2003	34,000	31.410	237	32	-	CC	
Oluf Maersk		Dis	2003	34,000	31,400	237	32	-	CC	
Paula Maersk		Dis	2000	61,764	84,999	245	42	15	T	
Peter Maersk		Dis	1999	61,764	110,000	245	42	15	T	
Ras Maersk		Dis	2003	22,181	34,999	171	27	14	T	
Regina Maersk		Dis	1996	81,488	82,135	318	43	25	CC	
Ribe Maersk		Dis	2004	22,181	35,000	171	27	14	T	
Richard Maersk		Dis	2001	22,184	34,909	171	27	14	T	
Ribe Maersk		Dis	2004	22,161	35,000	171	27	14	T	
Robert Maersk		Dis	2003	22,181	34,801	171	27	14	T	
Romo Maersk		Dis	2004	22,161	35,000	171	27	14	T	
Safmarine Ibhayi ø		Lbr	2000	32,322	39,300	211	32	22	CC	ex Maersk Pelepas-03, Heike-01
Safmarine Ikapa ø		Lbr	2001	32,322	39,300	211	32	22	CC	ex MSC Canada-03, Liwia-02
Sally Maersk		Dis	1998	91,560	104,696	348	43	25	CC	
Sea-Land Achiever **		Usa	1984	57,075	59,869	290	32	18	CC	ex Galveston Bay-02, Sea-Land Achiever-94, Leyla A-88, American Alabama-87
Sea-Land Atlantic **		Usa	1985	57,075	58,943	290	32	19	CC	ex Karen H-88, American Oklahoma-87
Sea-Land Champion *		Gbr	1995	49,985	59,840	292	32	24	CC	
Sea-Land Charger *		Gbr	1997	49,985	59,961	292	32	24	CC	
Sea-Land Comet *		Gbr	1995	49,985	59,840	292	32	24	CC	
Sea-Land Commitment **		Usa	1985	57,075	58,869	290	32	19	Cc	ex OOCL Inspiration-00, CGM Ile de France-93, Sea-Land Commitment-91, Marguerite-88, American California-87
Sea-Land Defender **		Usa	1900	32,029	30,379	257	31	20	CC	
Sea-Land Developer **		Usa	1980	32,629	30,296	257	31	20	CC	
Sea-Land Eagle *		Gbr	1997	49,985	59,961	292	32	24	CC	
Sea-Land Endurance **		Usa	1980	32,629	30,224	257	31	20	CC	
Sea-Land Explorer **		Usa	1980	32,629	30,298	257	31	20	CC	
Sea-Land Express **		Usa	1980	32,629	30,422	257	31	20	CC	
Sea-Land Florida **		Usa	1984	57,075	58,943	290	32	19	CC	ex Nedlloyd Holland-00, Catherine K-88, American New York-87
Sea-Land Freedom *		Mhl	1980	32,629	30,416	257	31	20	CC	
Sea-Land Independence **		Usa	1980	32,629	30,374	257	31	20	CC	
Sea-Land Innovator **		Usa	1980	32,629	30,341	257	31	20	CC	
Sea-Land Integrity **		Usa	1984	57,075	58,869	290	32	19	CC	ex Virginia-88, Jacqueline-88, American Virginia-87
Sea-Land Liberator **		Usa	1980	32,629	30,250	227	31	20	CC	
Sea-Land Mariner *		Mhl	1980	32,629	30,489	257	31	20	CC	
Sea-Land Mercury *		Gbr	1995	49,985	59,840	292	32	24	CC	
Sea-Land Meteor *		Gbr	1996	49,985	59,938	292	32	24	CC	
Sea-Land Motivator **		USA	1984	47,667	46,987	261	32	21	CC	ex Raleigh Bay-94, Elizabeth L-88, American New Jersey-87
Sea-Land Patriot **		Usa	1980	32,629	30,225	257	31	20	CC	
Sea-Land Performance **		Usa	1985	57,075	58,869	290	32	19	CC	ex Ruth W-88, American Washington-87
Sea-Land Pride **		Usa	1985	47,667	47,171	261	32	21	CC	ex Galveston Bay-94, Mary Anne-88, American Kentucky-87
Sea-Land Quality **		Usa	1985	57,075	58,869	290	32	19	CC	ex Patricia M-88, American Illinois-87
Sea-Land Racer *		Gbr	1997	49,985	59,964	292	32	24	CC	
Sea-Land Voyager **		Usa	1980	32,629	30,390	257	31	20	CC	
Sine Maersk		Dis	1998	91,560	104,696	348	43	25	CC	

Name	Eng	Flag	Year	GRT	DWT	Loa	Bm	Kts	Type	Former names
Skagen Maersk		Dis	1999	91,500	104,700	348	43	25	CC	
Sofie Maersk		Dis	1999	91,500	104,696	348	43	25	CC	
Sorø Maersk		Dis	1999	91,500	104,696	348	43	25	CC	
Sovereign Maersk		Dis	1997	91,560	104,886	348	43	25	CC	
Susan Maersk		Dis	1997	91,560	104,886	348	43	25	CC	
Svend Maersk		Dis	1999	91,500	104,896	348	43	25	CC	
Svendborg Maersk		Dis	1998	91,560	104,696	348	43	25	CC	
Tâsinge Maersk		Dis	1994	20,842	28,550	190	28	18	CC	ex Maersk California-02, Caroline Maersk-97
Thies Maersk		Dis	1992	16,982	21,825	162	28	18	CC	ex Cornelia Maersk-01
Thurø Maersk		Dis	1991	16,982	21,825	162	28	18	CC	ex Chastine Maersk-01
Tove Maersk		Dis	1992	16,982	21,825	162	28	18	CC	ex Charlotte Maersk-01
Troense Maersk		Dis	1992	16,982	21,825	162	28	18	CC	ex Maersk Colorado-03, Clifford Maersk-97

newbuildings - about 46 deep-sea vessels currently on order including a 300,000 dwt tanker, five 105,750 dwt, six 67,600 dwt and six 51,100 dwt container ships for 2004-6 delivery.
Worlds largest container carrier (by vessels and capacity) - see other chartered ships with 'Maersk' prefix or suffix in index.
* owned by subsidiary Chesham Containerships Ltd., UK (managed by InterSea Operations Ltd.) or ** managed by U.S. Ship Management Inc.
†† owned by subsidiaries Maersk Egypt SAE, Egypt or *** by Gas Management, Denmark.
ø on charter from Reederei Stefan Patjens, # from Quadrant Bereederungs. GmbH, both Germany,† from Marlow Navigation Co. Ltd., ‡ from Delphic Shipping Co. Ltd.(Uniship (Hellas) Shipping & Trading SA), Greece, § from Unique Shipping (Hong Kong) Ltd and ¶ managed by ASP Ship Management Pty. Ltd., Australia or §§ various other owners.

A.P. Moller Singapore Pte. Ltd./Singapore

Name	Eng	Flag	Year	GRT	DWT	Loa	Bm	Kts	Type	Former names
Effie Maersk		Sgp	2000	159,187	307,190	333	58	16	T	
Elisabeth Maersk		Sgp	1999	159,187	307,190	333	58	-	T	
Emilie Maersk		Sgp	1999	159,187	307,190	333	58	-	T	
Emma Maersk		Sgp	1995	158,475	299,700	344	56	14	T	ex Ellen Maersk-97
Maersk Aberdeen		Sgp	1999	14,130	17,720	155	25	18	CC	
Maersk Antwerp		Sgp	1999	14,063	17,720	155	25	18	CC	
Maersk Atlantic		Sgp	1999	14,063	17,720	155	25	18	CC	ex Swan River Bridge-00, Maersk Atlantic-99
Maersk Cloud *		Sgp	1983	30,588	11,164	167	28	17	V	ex Rich Victoria-89
Maersk Crest *		Sgp	1983	30,572	11,430	167	28	17	V	ex Rich Queen-89
Maersk Malacca		Sgp	1990	49,779	56,049	294	32	24	CC	ex Munkebo Maersk-03, Alsia-93
Maersk Merlion		Sgp	1990	49,874	55,971	294	32	24	CC	ex Marstal Maersk-03, Arosia-93
Maersk Pointer		Sgp	2001	61,764	79,000	245	42	15	T	
Maersk Pride		Sgp	1999	61,764	110,000	245	42	15	T	
Maersk Prime		Sgp	1999	61,764	110,000	245	42	15	T	
Maersk Princess		Sgp	2003	61,764	105,000	245	42	15	T	
Maersk Sea *		Sgp	1987	27,887	7,902	158	27	19	V	
Maersk Sun *		Sgp	1987	27,887	7,894	158	27	19	V	
Maersk Taiki *		Sgp	1998	44,219	12,490	179	32	19	V	
Maersk Taiyo *		Sgp	1996	44,219	13,778	179	32	19	V	
Maersk Teal *		Sgp	1998	44,219	12,490	179	32	19	V	
Maersk Tide *		Sgp	1997	44,219	12,490	179	32	19	V	
Maersk Wave *		Sgp	2000	51,770	12,473	180	32	20	V	
Maersk Wind *		Sgp	2000	51,720	12,473	180	32	20	V	
Sea-Land Intrepid		Sgp	1997	49,985	59,000	292	32	24	CC	
Sea-Land Lightning		Sgp	1996	49,985	59,938	292	32	24	CC	
Sea-Land Value		Sgp	1984	47,667	44,751	261	32	21	CC	ex Kim D-88, American Utah-87

* on charter to Wallenius-Wilhelmsen q.v.

The Maersk Co. Ltd./UK

Name	Eng	Flag	Year	GRT	DWT	Loa	Bm	Kts	Type	Former names
Burgos		Mex	1998	17,980	23,293	159	26	18	Lpg	ex Maersk Humber-00
Gosport Maersk		Gbr	2000	50,698	51,100	292	32	24	CC	
Grasmere Maersk		Gbr	2000	50,698	51,100	292	32	24	CC	
Loch Rannoch ‡	(2)	Gbr	1998	75,526	130,031	270	46	14	T	
Maersk Alaska †		Usa	1975	40,594	30,866	239	31	21	CC	ex SP5 Eric G. Gibson-99, pt. Adrian Maersk-94, pt. Axel Maersk-84 (len-78, len-84)
Maersk Arizona †		Usa	1975	40,594	30,866	239	31	21	CC	ex LTC Calvin P. Titus-99, pt. Albert Maersk-95, pt. Adrian Maersk-84 (len-78, len-84)
Maersk Arun		Gbr	1999	14,063	14,175	155	25	18	CC	
Maersk Avon		Gbr	1999	14,063	17,728	155	25	18	CC	
Maersk Carolina †		Usa	1998	50,698	62,229	292	32	24	CC	
Maersk Constellation †		Usa	1980	20,529	21,213	182	27	18	Ro	ex Elisabeth Maersk-88, C.R. Marseille-88, Elisabeth Maersk-87

Name	Eng	Flag	Year	GRT	DWT	Loa	Bm	Kts	Type	Former names
Maersk Gareloch		Gbr	2002	50,698	62,242	292	32	24	CC	
Maersk Georgia †		Usa	1998	50,698	62,400	292	32	24	CC	ex Gudrun Maersk-02
Maersk Missouri †		Usa	1998	50,698	62,226	292	32	24	CC	ex Gerd Maersk-02
Maersk Rugen ‡‡		Iom	2001	22,181	34,999	171	27	14	T	ex Maersk Ramsey-03
Maersk Rapier		Iom	2000	22,181	35,000	171	27	15	T	ex Robert Maersk-00
Maersk Regent		Gbr	2003	22,181	35,000	171	27	14	T	
Maersk Rhode Island †		Usa	2002	22,161	34,801	171	27	14	T	l/a Maersk Ramsey
Maersk Richmond		Gbr	2003	22,181	35,000	171	27	14	T	
Maersk Rochester		Iom	2000	22,181	35,000	171	27	15	T	
Maersk Rouen ‡‡		Iom	2000	22,181	35,000	171	27	15	T	ex Maersk Rye-03
Maersk Scotland *		Iom	1991	11,822	16,263	158	21	15	Lpg	ex Risanger-98, Saulkrasti-91
Maersk Virginia †		Usa	2002	50,686	62,009	292	32	24	CC	ex Maersk Geelong-03
Marienborg		Gbr	1990	17,700	21,238	161	28	18	CC	ex Thorkil Maersk-01
North Sea Producer		Iom	1983	52,434	99,800	236	40	15	T	ex Dagmar Maersk-96
Safmarine Concord **		Bel	1988	18,037	26,152	177	28	17	CC	ex Zoe Delmas-00, Concord-99, CMBT Concord-97, Hansa Concord-95, POL East-93, Ville de Mars-92
Safmarine Cotonou **		Bel	1986	21,054	29,800	182	29	18	CC	ex Maersk Cotonou-00, Nomaza-98, Mediterraneo-98, Zim Australia-96, Nedlloyd van Linschoten-94, ScanDutch Edo-89, Santa Catarina-86
Safmarine Nolizwe		Mhl	1981	20,799	25,070	186	28	20	CC	ex Nolizwe-01, CMB Plantin-94, Plantin-89
Thomas Maersk		Dis	1994	18,859	25,368	176	28	18	CC	ex Maersk Tennesse-02, Thomas Maersk-97
Tinglev Maersk †		Dis	1994	18,859	25,431	176	28	18	CC	ex Maersk Texas-02, Tinglev Maersk-97
Tobias Maersk		Gbr	1990	17,700	21,229	161	28	18	CC	ex TRSL Antares-96, Tobias Maersk-95
Torben Maersk		Gbr	1990	17,700	21,238	161	28	18	CC	
Trein Maersk		Gbr	1990	17,700	21,229	161	28	18	CC	ex TRSL Arcturus-97, Trein Maersk-95

* managed by Maersk Co. (IOM.) Ltd. or ** by Safmarine Ship Management, South Africa.
† owned by Maersk Line Ltd., USA, (who also own six other vessels long-term chartered to US military fleet)
‡ managed by BP Shipping Ltd., UK or ‡‡ chartered from Chemikalien Seetransport GmbH, Germany

Safmarine Ltd./South AfricaChem

Funnel: *Grey with blue above white above orange bands, narrow black top; grey or cream with two blue bands, narrow black top.*
Hull: *White with 'Safmarine', red or green boot-topping.*

Name	Eng	Flag	Year	GRT	DWT	Loa	Bm	Kts	Type	Former names
Maersk Constantia *	(2)	Bel	1979	52,615	50,027	258	32	22	CC	ex S.A. Waterberg-01
Oranje		Zaf	1991	27,103	29,651	178	32	18	CC	ex Safmarine Oranje-04, S.A. Oranje-00, Oranje-96
S.A. Helderberg *	(2)	Bel	1977	52,615	49,579	258	32	21	CC	
S.A. Sederberg *	(2)	Bhs	1978	52,615	48,878	258	32	21	CC	
S.A. Winterberg *	(2)	Bhs	1978	52,615	50,017	258	32	22	CC	ex Transvaal-95, S.A. Winterberg-92
Safmarine Asia		Iom	1985	21,887	31,290	189	28	17	CC	ex CMBT Asia-00, Norasia Samantha-94 (len-89)
Safmarine Europe		Iom	1985	21,887	31,290	189	28	17	CC	ex CMBT Europe-00, Norasia Susan-94 (len-89)

managed by Safmarine Ship Management.
* on charter from Danaos until end of 2004 q.v.

A/S J. Ludwig Mowinckels Rederi Norway

Viken Ship Management AS

Funnel: *Yellow with narrow blue band on white band on broad red band beneath black top*
Hull: *Black, grey or brown, or dark green with red boot-topping.*

Name	Eng	Flag	Year	GRT	DWT	Loa	Bm	Kts	Type	Former names
Daviken *		Bhs	1987	23,306	34,752	222	23	14	B	ex Malinska-97
Erviken		Nis	2004	87,400	160,000	-	-	-	T	
Federal Fuji *		Bhs	1986	17,814	29,536	183	23	14	B	
Federal Polaris *		Bhs	1985	17,815	29,536	183	23	14	B	
Goviken *		Bhs	1987	23,306	34,752	222	23	14	B	ex Omisalj-97
Inviken *		Bhs	1986	17,313	30,070	189	23	15	B	ex Bar-97
Kronviken		Nis	1988	79,544	152,385	267	46	14	T	ex Eurus-97, Golar Jane-91
Morviken		Bhs	1999	37,695	72,000	225	32	14	B	ex Far Eastern Jennifer-00
Nordic Rio		Bhs	2004	82,650	159,600	-	-	-	T	
Norviken		Bhs	1998	37,695	72,495	225	32	14	B	ex Far Eastern Wendy-00
Sandviken		Bhs	1986	23,271	34,750	222	23	-	B	ex Petka-00
Solviken *		Nis	1989	79,544	152,385	267	46	14	T	ex Corus-97, Golar Colleen-91
Utviken *		Bhs	1987	17,191	30,052	189	23	16	B	ex C. Bianco-95, Bijelo Polije-92

* on charter to Fednav Ltd., Canada q.v.

A. P. Moller (Singapore). ELIZABETH MAERSK. *Hans Kraijenbosch.*

A. P. Moller (Safmarine). SAFMARINE COTONOU. *Hans Kraijenbosch.*

National Shipping Co. Of Saudi Arabia. NCC BAHA. *F. de Vries.*

Vista Ship Management AS

Funnel: Yellow with narrow blue band on white band on broad red band beneath black top or * blue with red/black 'T' on broad white band.
Hull: Black, grey or brown with red boot-topping.

Name	Eng	Flag	Year	GRT	DWT	Loa	Bm	Kts	Type	Former names
Borga		Nor	1992	66,671	123,665	265	43	14	T	ex Marie Knutsen-94
Fosna		Nis	1992	52,157	96,314	232	42	14	T	
Grena		Bhs	2003	80,691	148,553	278	46	-	T	
Molda		Nis	1994	52,157	96,347	238	42	14	T	

The National Shipping Company of Saudi Arabia · Saudi Arabia

Funnel: White with yellow palm tree and crossed swords between two narrow green bands, narrow black top.
Hull: Green with yellow 'NSCSA', red or blue boot-topping.

Name	Flag	Year	GRT	DWT	Loa	Bm	Kts	Type	Former names
Abqaiq	Bhs	2002	159,990	302,986	333	58	16	T	
Al Farabi †	Sau	1986	26,464	41,158	178	32	14	T	
Ghawar	Bhs	1996	163,882	300,361	340	56	15	T	
Harad	Bhs	2001	159,990	303,115	333	58	17	T	l/a Hellespont Burnside
Hawtah	Bhs	1996	163,882	300,361	340	56	15	T	
Matjam	Bhs	2002	159,990	303,115	333	58	17	T	
NCC Arar *	Nis	1982	14,627	23,016	159	23	14	T	ex Austanger-90
NCC Asir *	Nis	1982	14,627	23,016	159	23	16	T	ex Bow Explorer-90, Grenanger-90
NCC Baha *	Nis	1985	15,817	24,728	172	28	14	T	ex Bow Falcon-90, Fjellanger-90, Northern Falcon-89, Portela-88
NCC Jizan **	Nis	1976	17,561	28,025	171	25	17	T	ex Bow Saint-90, Torvanger-90
NCC Jouf **	Nis	1976	17,561	28,080	171	25	17	T	ex Bow Saturn-90, Porsanger-90
NCC Jubail **	Nis	1996	23,197	37,449	183	32	16	T	
NCC Madinah **	Nis	1976	17,561	28,060	171	25	17	T	ex Bow Selene-90, Nordanger-90
NCC Mekka **	Nis	1995	23,197	37,272	183	32	16	T	
NCC Najran **	Nis	1976	17,561	28,025	171	25	17	T	ex Bow Sirius-90, Risanger-90
NCC Riyad **	Nis	1994	23,197	37,252	183	32	16	T	
NCC Tihamah **	Nis	1977	17,561	28,088	171	25	17	T	ex Bow Solar-90, Brimanger-90
NCC Yamamah **	Nis	1977	17,561	28,053	171	25	17	T	ex Bow Stellar-90, Spinanger-90
Ramlah	Bhs	1996	163,882	300,361	340	56	15	T	
Safaniyah	Bhs	1997	163,882	300,361	340	56	15	T	
Safwa	Bhs	2002	159,990	302,977	333	58	16	T	
Saudi Abha	Sau	1983	44,171	42,600	249	32	18	Ro	
Saudi Diriyah	Sau	1983	44,171	42,600	249	32	18	Ro	
Saudi Hofuf	Sau	1983	44,171	42,600	249	32	18	Ro	
Saudi Tabuk	Sau	1983	44,171	42,600	249	32	18	Ro	
Uqba Ibn Nafi	Sau	1985	28,195	42,825	180	32	14	T	
Watban	Bhs	1996	163,882	300,361	340	56	15	T	

* owned by subsidiary National Chemical Carriers Ltd., and managed by Mideast Ship Management Ltd or ** by Odfjell ASA , Norway q.v.
† owned by Arabian Chemical Carriers (formed jointly with United Arab Shipping Co. SAG) and managed by Mideast Ship Management Ltd, UAE.

Navigation Maritime Bulgare · Bulgaria

Funnel: Yellow with broad red band.
Hull: Black with red boot-topping.

Name	Flag	Year	GRT	DWT	Loa	Bm	Kts	Type	Former names
Adalbert Antonov	Bgr	1979	23,363	38,510	202	28	14	B	
Aleko Konstantinov	Bgr	1985	12,554	15,442	159	23	17	CC	
Alexander Dimitrov	Mlt	1985	23,609	38,524	199	28	15	B	
Balgarka	Mlt	2002	24,700	41,425	186	30	14	B	ex Dolly-04
Balkan	Bgr	1975	15,865	24,386	185	23	14	B	
Belmeken	Bgr	1973	16,151	23,738	185	23	15	B	
Bogdan	Mlt	1997	10,220	14,011	142	22	13	B	
Bulgaria	Bgr	1978	30,596	52,975	215	32	14	B	
Dimitrovsky Komsomol	Mlt	1985	23,444	38,545	201	28	15	B	
General Vladimir Zaimov	Bgr	1973	16,150	23,661	185	23	15	B	
Geo Milev	Bgr	1985	12,174	14,814	159	23	18	C	
Georgi Grigorov	Mlt	1986	23,540	38,518	199	28	15	B	
Jordanka Nikolova	Bgr	1979	23,363	38,400	202	28	14	B	
Kamenitza	Bgr	1980	16,188	24,150	185	23	14	B	
Kapitan Georgi Georgiev	Bgr	1980	16,188	24,150	185	23	14	B	

Name	Eng	Flag	Year	GRT	DWT	Loa	Bm	Kts	Type	Former names
Kom		Mlt	1997	10,220	13,971	142	22	13	B	
Koznitsa		Bgr	1984	16,502	24,100	185	23	14	B	
Liliana Dimitrova		Bgr	1982	23,779	38,135	202	28	16	B	
Malyovitza		Bgr	1983	16,188	24,456	184	23	14	B	
Midjur		Mlt	1992	13,834	21,537	168	25	13	B	
Milin Kamak		Bgr	1979	16,166	24,596	185	23	14	B	
Okoitchitza		Bgr	1982	16,188	24,148	184	23	14	B	
Perelik		Mlt	1998	10,220	13,900	142	22	13	B	
Persenk		Mlt	1998	10,228	13,887	142	22	13	B	
Petimata OT RMS		Bgr	1978	23,363	38,400	202	28	14	B	
Peyo Yavorov		Bgr	1984	12,554	15,104	159	23	18	C	
Plana		Mlt	1991	13,834	19,985	169	25	13	B	
Plovdiv		Mlt	1989	11,982	14,101	157	23	16	CC	ex Nedlloyd Marne-97, Armada Sprinter-97, Nedlloyd Marne-96, Waterdrager-91
Rila		Bgr	1977	16,166	24,354	185	23	14	B	
Rodina		Bgr	1978	30,596	52,975	215	32	14	B	
Rodopi		Bgr	1978	16,166	24,708	185	23	14	B	
Rojen		Bgr	1978	16,166	24,500	185	23	14	B	ex Sakar-78
Rousse		Mlt	1989	11,982	14,101	157	23	16	CC	ex Nedlloyd Musi-97, Wateraids-91, Kariba-91, Wateraids-91, CMB Effort-90, Wateraids-89
Sakar		Mlt	1995	13,957	21,591	168	25	13	B	
Shipka		Bgr	1979	16,166	24,285	185	23	14	B	
Slavianka		Bgr	1978	16,166	24,685	185	23	14	B	
Sofia		Mlt	1988	11,977	13,800	157	23	16	CC	ex Nedlloyd Maas-96, Waterkoning-91, Contship Singapore-90, Waterkoning-89, AEL America-89, Waterkoning-88
Svilen Russev		Bgr	1982	23,779	38,142	202	28	14	B	
Trapezitsa		Bgr	2003	13,967	21,250	169	25	-	B	
Tzarevetz		Mlt	1998	13,965	21,470	169	25	-	B	
Vitosha		Bgr	1977	16,166	25,864	185	23	14	B	
Vola 1		Mlt	1992	13,834	20,620	168	25	13	B	ex Vola-03
Yordan Lutibrodski		Vct	1986	23,589	38,519	198	28	15	B	

Part owned (43.7%) by British Orient Holdings.

Neptune Orient Lines Ltd.   Singapore

Funnel: Blue with horizontal blue and diagonal green triple wave design on broad white band, narrow black top or dark blue with white eagle and stars on red band (APL vessels)

Hull: Light grey with blue 'NOL' or black with white 'APL' with red or dark grey boot-topping

Name	Flag	Year	GRT	DWT	Loa	Bm	Kts	Type	Former names
Alba †	Sgp	1997	38,520	73,049	225	32	14	B	ex Hawthorn-01, NOL Sirius-00
APL Agate	Sgp	1997	65,475	63,693	272	40	24	CC	ex NOL Agate-00
APL Alexandrite	Sgp	1992	49,716	59,603	288	32	25	CC	ex MOL Ideal-02, APL Alexandrite-02, Neptune Alexandrite-01
APL Almandine	Sgp	1993	49,716	59,560	288	32	23	CC	ex Tokyo Bay-98, Neptune Almandine-96
APL Amazonite	Sgp	1993	49,716	59,603	288	32	24	CC	ex APL Sweden-01, NOL Amazonite-00, Osaka Bay-97, NOL Amazonite-96, Neptune Amazonite-95
APL Cairo	Sgp	2001	25,305	34,133	207	30	21	CC	
APL China *	Usa	1995	64,502	67,432	276	40	24	CC	
APL Coral	Sgp	1998	65,475	64,145	275	40	24	CC	ex NOL Coral-01
APL Cyprine	Sgp	1997	65,475	64,156	272	40	24	CC	ex NOL Cyprine-00
APL Germany §	Lbr	2003	66,462	67,109	281	40	-	CC	
APL Hong Kong §	Lbr	2002	66,573	67,009	280	40	-	CC	
APL Ireland §	Lbr	2002	66,462	67,009	280	40	-	CC	
APL Iris	Sgp	1998	63,900	62,693	272	40	24	CC	ex NOL Iris-01
APL Jade	Sgp	1995	53,519	66,647	294	32	24	CC	ex NOL Sheratan-98, l/a Neptune Sheratan
APL Japan	Sgp	1995	64,502	66,520	276	40	24	CC	
APL Kennedy	Sgp	1988	61,296	54,665	275	39	24	CC	ex President Kennedy-03
APL Korea *	Usa	1995	64,502	66,370	276	40	24	CC	
APL Orchid	Sgp	1984	13,488	18,437	161	25	17	CC	ex Eagle Orion-99, Dragon Nias-97, Neptune Jasper-96, Anro Adelaide-93, Neptune Jasper-89
APL Pearl	Sgp	1998	65,475	64,050	275	40	24	CC	ex NOL Pearl-99
APL Pusan	Sgp	2002	25,305	34,122	207	30	21	CC	ex Indamex Chesapeake-04, APL Pusan-02
APL Philippines	Usa	1996	64,502	66,370	276	40	24	CC	

Name	Eng	Flag	Year	GRT	DWT	Loa	Bm	Kts	Type	Former names
APL Singapore *		Usa	1995	64,502	66,370	276	40	24	CC	
APL Spain §		Lbr	2004	66,300	66,100	281	40	-	CC	
APL Spinel		Sgp	1996	53,519	66,511	294	32	24	CC	ex NOL Spinel-98
APL Thailand *		Usa	1995	64,502	66,370	276	40	24	CC	
APL Topaz		Sgp	1989	47,893	51,534	276	32	24	CC	ex America-01, President Hoover-99, NOL Topaz-98, Neptune Topaz-96
APL Tourmaline		Sgp	1995	52,086	60,323	294	32	24	CC	ex MOL Innovation-04, MOL Tourmaline-03, APL Tourmaline-02, NOL Tourmaline-98
APL Tulip		Sgp	1984	13,488	18,437	161	25	17	CC	ex NOL Beryl-99, Neptune Beryl-97, Anro Fremantle-93, Neptune Beryl-89
APL Turquoise		Sgp	1996	52,086	60,323	294	32	24	CC	ex NOL Turquoise-98
Indamex Dalian		Sgp	2002	25,305	34,133	207	30	21	CC	ex APL Dalian-03
Indamex Malabar		Sgp	2001	25,305	34,122	207	30	21	CC	ex APL Jeddah-03
MOL Vigor		Sgp	1995	53,519	66,565	294	32	24	CC	ex MSC Louisiana-03, APL Garnet-02, NOL Seginus-98, Neptune Seginus-95
MOL Vision		Sgp	1995	53,519	65,598	294	32	24	CC	ex MSC Maryland-03, APL Sardonyx-02, NOL Sardonyx-98, Neptune Sardonyx-96
MSC Hudson		Sgp	1997	63,900	62,693	272	40	26	CC	ex APL Iolite-03, NOL Iolite-00
New Confidence		Pan	2001	13,764	16,400	154	25	19	CC	
New Dynamic		Pan	2001	13,764	16,400	154	25	19	CC	
Pole ‡		Iom	1997	38,520	73,049	225	32	14	B	ex Polaris-02, NOL Castor-00
President Adams *		Usa	1988	61,296	53,613	275	39	24	CC	
President Grant *		Usa	1988	47,893	51,437	276	32	24	CC	ex NOL Ruby-98, Neptune Ruby-96
President Jackson *		Usa	1988	61,296	53,613	275	39	24	CC	
President Polk *		Usa	1988	61,296	53,613	275	39	24	CC	
President Truman *		Usa	1988	61,296	53,613	275	39	24	CC	
President Wilson *		Usa	1989	47,893	51,534	276	32	24	CC	ex NOL Zircon-98, Neptune Zircon-96

*managed by Neptune Shipmanagement Services (Pte.) Ltd., Singapore, except * by subsidiary American Ship Management LLC, USA.*
† managed by Gemini Shipmanagement Ltd., Isle of Man or ‡ by Augustea Ship Management S.r.l., Italy.
§ chartered from Japanese owners or finance groups.

Nippon Yusen Kaisha (NYK Line)   Japan

Funnel: Black with two narrow red bands on broad white band.
Hull: Black with red boot-topping.

Name	Eng	Flag	Year	GRT	DWT	Loa	Bm	Kts	Type	Former names
ACX Hibiscus		Pan	1997	18,502	24,581	193	28	20	CC	
ACX Lily		Lbr	1990	16,731	22,375	185	28	19	CC	
ACX Marguerite		Pan	1998	18,602	24,300	193	28	20	CC	ex NYK Virgo-02
Alioth Leader		Pan	1998	51,790	14,909	180	32	19	V	
Anna **		Nis	1978	39,710	17,224	196	30	19	V	ex Hojin Maru-89
Aquarius Leader		Pan	1998	57,623	22,815	200	32	19	V	
Baltic Leader		Pan	1982	27,424	10,449	161	27	16	V	ex Brava-99, Jinyo Maru-87
Bellona		Pan	1985	45,495	15,160	184	32	18	V	ex Centry Leader No. 2-94
Bijin		Pan	1988	47,521	14,126	180	32	17	V	
Blue Hawk		Lbr	1978	40,711	14,407	186	32	18	V	
Bujin		Pan	1993	41,931	17,189	196	29	18	V	
California Jupiter *		Lbr	1986	41,668	38,438	248	32	22	CC	
California Mercury		Jpn	1987	41,442	38,538	248	32	22	CC	
Cape Charles		Pan	1986	41,843	38,449	249	32	22	CC	
Cape May		Jpn	1986	42,145	38,217	248	32	22	CC	ex Yamataka Maru-91
Cassiopeia Leader		Pan	1999	57,455	21,547	200	32	19	V	
Century Leader No.1		Pan	1984	45,422	11,772	180	32	18	V	
Century Leader No.3		Jpn	1986	44,830	14,154	179	32	18	V	
Century Leader No.5		Jpn	1986	50,867	15,293	200	32	18	V	
Champion Peace		Pan	1999	56,249	106,042	241	42	15	T	
Champion Pride		Pan	1998	58,141	99,997	244	42	13	T	
Columbia Leader		Pan	1987	38,659	13,491	182	30	18	V	ex Green Bay-01
Crown Emerald		Pan	1996	10,519	10,351	152	23	18	R	
Crown Garnet		Pan	1996	10,519	10,322	152	23	21	R	
Crown Jade		Pan	1997	10,519	10,332	152	23	21	R	
Crown Opal		Pan	1997	10,519	10,332	152	23	21	R	
Crown Ruby		Pan	1997	10,519	10,338	152	23	21	R	
Crown Sapphire		Pan	1997	10,519	10,334	152	23	21	R	
Crown Topaz		Pan	1999	10,527	10,318	152	23	21	R	
Cygnus Reefer		Lbr	1990	8,818	9,679	144	22	20	R	

Neptune Orient Line. APL HONG KONG. *Hans Kraijenbosch.*

Neptune Orient Line. PRESIDENT ADAMS. *Hans Kraijenbosch.*

Nippon Yusen Kaisha. AQUARIUS LEADER. *M. D. J. Lennon.*

Name	Eng	Flag	Year	GRT	DWT	Loa	Bm	Kts	Type	Former names
Delphinus Leader		Pan	1998	57,391	21,514	200	32	19	V	
Dresden		Pan	2000	37,237	12,743	177	32	19	V	
Eijin		Pan	1982	41,195	14,361	180	32	18	V	ex Eijin Maru-85
Eufonia **		Pan	1981	27,163	10,480	165	28	18	V	ex Yujin-92, Yujin Maru-85
Fanta **		Pan	1983	36,437	13,732	190	29	16	V	ex Evviva-98, Madonna-93, Aso Maru-90
Festa **		Pan	1983	36,439	13,656	190	29	16	V	ex Amagi Maru-90
Fontana		Pan	1977	52,214	16,602	196	30	19	V	ex Ryujin Maru-88
Fuji		Lbr	1984	47,751	16,204	190	32	18	V	ex Fuji Maru-90
Galaxy Harvest		Pan	1988	8,519	8,800	142	21	19	R	ex Gallant Harvest-93
Ganta		Pan	1978	25,431	11,311	165	27	17	V	ex Beach-90, Pioneer Racer-90
Gas Aries *		Lbr	1991	44,493	50,357	230	37	16	Lpg	
Gas Capricorn *		Lbr	2003	46,021	49,999	230	37	16	Lpg	
Global Harvest		Pan	1993	8,520	8,752	144	21	19	R	
Glorious Harvest		Pan	1989	8,519	8,830	142	21	19	R	ex Glorious Express-93
Hakone		Pan	1983	35,309	29,733	212	32	21	CC	ex Hakone Maru-99
Heijin *		Pan	1989	47,521	14,366	180	32	18	V	
Hercules Leader		Pan	1998	57,449	21,523	200	32	19	V	
Hojin *		Vut	1990	55,470	18,273	200	32	19	V	
Hotaka Maru		Pan	1980	32,654	36,022	227	31	22	CC	ex California Orion-98, Japan Apollo-92
Hudson Leader		Pan	1987	47,707	14,104	180	32	18	V	ex Green Lake-01
Jingu Maru *		Jpn	1992	42,164	17,216	196	32	18	V	
Jinsei Maru		Jpn	1990	55,489	17,914	199	32	19	V	
Jupiter Diamond		Sgp	1978	45,998	14,687	214	29	18	V	
Kaga		Jpn	1988	51,047	59,188	289	32	23	CC	
Kaijin *		Pan	1994	41,931	17,183	196	29	18	V	
Kamakura *		Pan	1988	50,462	59,441	290	32	23	CC	
Katsuragi *		Pan	1990	50,437	59,418	292	32	23	CC	ex Kowloon Bay-98, Katsuragi-96
Kitano		Jpn	1990	50,618	59,804	288	32	23	CC	
Koh Jin		Vut	1981	49,844	19,712	199	32	18	V	
Leo Leader		Pan	1999	57,566	22,733	200	32	19	V	
Linden Pride *		Pan	2001	46,021	49,999	230	37	16	Lpg	
Nada V *		Pan	1984	43,101	14,820	186	32	18	V	
New Nada *		Pan	1992	47,519	14,180	180	32	19	V	
Nippon *		Pan	2002	159,613	298,399	333	60	15	T	
Nobleza		Lbr	1983	29,933	11,428	164	28	18	V	ex Meijin-92, I/a Caribbean Breeze
NYK Andromeda *		Pan	1998	75,637	81,819	300	40	23	CC	
NYK Antares *		Pan	1997	75,637	81,819	300	40	23	CC	
NYK Aphrodite *		Pan	2003	75,484	81,171	300	40	-	CC	
NYK Apollo *		Pan	2002	75,484	81,171	300	40	-	CC	
NYK Aquarius		Pan	2003	75,484	81,171	300	40	-	CC	
NYK Aretmis		Pan	2003	75,484	81,171	300	40	-	CC	
NYK Argus		Pan	2004	75,500	81,000	300	40	-	CC	
NYK Athena		Pan	2003	75,484	81,171	300	40	-	CC	
NYK Canopus		Pan	1998	76,847	82,275	300	40	23	CC	
NYK Castor *		Pan	1998	76,847	82,275	300	40	23	CC	
NYK Kai *		Pan	1993	50,606	59,658	288	32	24	CC	ex Kai-95
NYK Leo *		Pan	2002	75,201	77,900	300	40	27	CC	
NYK Libra		Pan	2002	75,201	77,900	300	40	26	CC	
NYK Loadstar *		Pan	2001	75,201	77,900	300	40	27	CC	
NYK Lynx		Pan	2002	75,201	77,950	300	40	26	CC	
NYK Lyra *		Pan	2002	75,201	78,000	300	40	26	CC	
NYK Pegasus *		Pan	2003	76,199	80,270	300	40	25	CC	
NYK Phoenix *		Pan	2003	76,199	80,270	300	40	25	CC	
NYK Procyon *		Pan	1995	60,117	63,179	300	37	22	CC	
NYK Sirius		Pan	1998	76,847	82,271	300	40	23	CC	
NYK Springtide *		Pan	1992	43,213	39,394	253	32	23	CC	
NYK Starlight *		Pan	1991	43,327	39,015	251	32	23	CC	
Orion Diamond		Vut	1982	53,251	15,396	214	32	18	V	
Orion Leader		Pan	1999	57,513	21,526	200	32	19	V	
Orion Reefer		Pan	1989	8,818	9,643	144	22	20	R	
Pacific Aries		Lbr	1985	27,267	11,678	158	28	17	V	
Pacific Leader		Pan	1983	47,129	16,138	184	32	17	V	ex Prospero-99, Jinkai Maru-90
Pegasus Diamond		Jpn	1986	47,164	13,068	180	32	18	V	
Pegasus Leader		Pan	1999	57,566	22,747	200	32	19	V	
Perseus Leader		Pan	1999	57,449	21,503	200	32	19	V	
Phoenix Diamond		Pan	1988	47,068	13,162	180	32	18	V	

Name	Eng	Flag	Year	GRT	DWT	Loa	Bm	Kts	Type	Former names
Pioneer Leader **		Pan	1980	41,116	17,859	200	32	17	V	
Procyon Leader		Pan	2000	51,259	17,361	180	32	19	V	
Provider *		Lbr	1978	30,575	31,227	215	31	24	CC	ex NYK Provider-00, P&O Nedlloyd Otago-00, Provider-99, NYK Providence-98, Neptune Rhodonite-96, Hira II-91, Hira Maru-87
Ryujin		Pan	1993	47,737	14,080	180	32	19	V	
Satsuma		Bhs	1993	150,167	258,019	332	58	15	T	
Silver Paradise		Pan	1998	58,141	105,161	244	42	15	T	
Sirius Leader		Pan	2000	51,496	16,451	180	32	19	V	
Southern Harvest		Sgp	1990	8,483	8,946	141	23	19	R	ex Serene Harvest-00
Splendid Harvest		Lbr	1988	8,483	8,955	141	21	19	R	
Supreme Harvest		Vut	1988	8,483	8,937	141	21	19	R	
Taizan		Pan	2002	160,084	300,405	333	60	15	T	
Tajima		Pan	1996	148,330	258,096	333	60	16	T	
Takachiho II		Pan	1998	149,376	280,889	330	60	16	T	
Takamatsu Maru *		Jpn	1987	145,635	254,008	321	58	14	T	
Takasago Maru *		Jpn	1999	149,376	281,050	330	60	16	T	
Takasuzu *		Pan	2000	152,139	279,989	330	60	16	T	
Tateyama		Pan	2002	160,072	300,373	333	60	15	T	
Tenryu		Lbr	1999	152,139	281,050	330	60	16	T	
Tohdoh		Pan	1991	149,356	258,096	330	59	15	T	
Tokachi *		Pan	1999	149,376	280,973	330	60	16	T	
Triton Reefer		Lbr	1990	8,818	9,683	144	22	18	R	
Tsurusaki *		Pan	2002	154,338	300,838	333	60	-	T	
Vega Leader		Pan	2000	51,496	16,396	180	32	19	V	
Wild Cosmos		Pan	1998	9,859	10,097	150	22	20	R	
Wild Heather		Pan	1998	9,859	10,114	150	22	20	R	
Wild Jasmine		Pan	1998	9,859	10,110	150	22	20	R	
Wild Lotus		Pan	1998	9,859	10,139	150	22	20	R	
Wild Peony		Pan	1998	9,859	10,110	150	22	20	R	

newbuildings - about 48 large vessels on order including eight bulk carriers over 170,000 dwt, ten container ships over 71,000 dwt and 13 vehicle carriers.
* managed by NYK Ship Management Co. Ltd., Japan or ** NYK Ship Management, Hong Kong.
The company is one of the world's largest operators of ships, its many subsidiaries owning over 250 vessels (17 million tonnes deadweight) and with a further 500 vessels on charter. In addition to the large container ships, vehicle carriers and tankers listed, the company also owns, manages or operates 26 large Lng tankers, 20 wood-chip carriers, numerous other bulk carriers and tankers.
See also Stolt-Nielsen Group and A/S Damps. Torm.

Nordcapital GmbH   Germany
E.R. Schiffahrt GmbH & Cie.

Funnel: Charterers colours.
Hull: Blue with pink boot-topping or charterers colours.

Name	Eng	Flag	Year	GRT	DWT	Loa	Bm	Kts	Type	Former names
ANL Pacific		Lbr	2003	39,941	50,900	264	32	24	CC	ex CMA CGM New York-03, I/a E.R. New York
APL Canada		Lbr	2001	65,792	68,025	277	40	26	CC	ex E.R. Canada-01
APL Denmark		Sgp	2002	65,792	67,935	277	40	26	CC	ex E.R. Denmark-02
APL India		Sgp	2002	65,792	68,025	277	40	26	CC	ex E.R. India-02
APL Sweden		Sgp	2002	65,792	68,025	277	40	26	CC	ex E.R. Sweden-02
China Star		Lbr	1996	30,280	35,962	202	32	22	CC	ex E.R. Darwin-02, Ganges-02, Hanjin Genoa-00
CMA CGM Aegean		Lbr	1996	30,280	35,966	202	32	22	CC	ex E.R. Brisbane-03, Pan Crystal-02
CMA CGM Constellation		Deu	1998	36,603	45,383	232	32	23	CC	ex Safmarine Vinson-03, E.R. Melbourne-02, Congo-02, Choyang Honour-01
CMA CGM Marmara		Lbr	1998	30,280	35,798	202	32	22	CC	ex CSCL Nile-03, Nile-02, Hyundai Nobility-01
CMA CGM Turkey		Lbr	1998	30,280	35,848	202	32	22	CC	ex CSCL Indus-03, Indus-02, Hyundai Infinity-01
CMA CGM Yantian		Lbr	2003	39,941	53,000	264	32	24	CC	I/a E.R. Yantian
Copiapo		Lbr	1998	26,125	30,720	196	30	19	CC	I/a E.R. Santiago
Cosco Long Beach		Pan	2004	85,000	93,000	300	43	25	CC	
Cosco Seattle		Pan	2004	85,000	93,000	300	43	25	CC	
Cosco Shenzen		Pan	2004	85,000	93,000	300	43	25	CC	I/dn E.R. Shenzen
Cosco Vancouver		Pan	2004	85,000	93,000	300	43	25	CC	
Cosco Yokohama		Pan	2004	85,000	93,000	300	43	25	CC	
CSCL Fuzhou		Lbr	2000	25,500	33,855	207	30	21	CC	ex E.R. Lubeck-01, E.R. Fuzhou-01
CSCL Kobe		Lbr	2001	66,289	67,500	277	40	26	CC	I/a E.R. Kobe

Name	Eng	Flag	Year	GRT	DWT	Loa	Bm	Kts	Type	Former names
CSCL Los Angeles		Lbr	2001	66,289	67,500	277	40	26	CC	I/a E.R. Los Angeles
CSAV Shanghai		Lbr	1998	26,125	30,721	196	30	19	CC	ex Aconcagua-99 I/a E.R. Hamburg
E.R. Albany		Lbr	1996	30,280	35,966	202	32	22	CC	ex Rhein-02, Zim Sydney-00
E.R. Auckland		Lbr	2004	40,000	53,000	264	32	24	CC	I/a E.R. Wellington
E.R. Dallas		Lbr	2004	60,000	67,170	294	32	25	CC	
E.R. Denver		Lbr	2004	60,000	67,170	294	32	25	CC	
E.R. Durban		Lbr	1999	16,803	23,075	185	26	19	CC	ex Direct Falcon-03, Griffin Clio-99
E.R. Hobart		Lbr	1994	22,736	33,523	188	28	18	CC	ex Mosel-02, Zim Koper-98, Hyundai Longview-96
E.R. Kingston		Lbr	2003	39,941	50,900	264	32	24	CC	ex CMA CGM Kingston-03, I/a E.R. Kingston
E.R. Savannah		Lbr	2004	60,000	67,170	294	32	25	CC	
E.R. Sydney		Lbr	1998	36,603	45,400	232	32	23	CC	ex YM Napoli-04, Amazonas-02, Choyang Zenith-01, I/a Zenith Globe
E.R. Wellinghton		Lbr	2004	40,000	53,000	264	32	24	CC	I/a E.R. Auckland
Indamex Mumbai		Lbr	1996	30,280	35,962	202	32	22	CC	ex E.R. Canberra-03, Donau-02, Hanjin Dalian-00
Indamex Tuticorin		Lbr	1999	25,630	33,855	207	30	21	CC	ex E.R. Stralsund-03, Maersk Mendoza-02, I/a E.R. Stralsund
Maersk New Orleans	Deu		2002	27,322	33,800	212	30	22	CC	ex E.R. Wilhelmshaven-02
Maersk Newark		Lbr	2002	26,200	33,800	212	30	22	CC	ex E.R. Cuxhaven-02
Maersk Newcastle		Lbr	2003	26,200	33,800	212	30	22	CC	ex E.R. Elsfleth-03
Maersk Norfolk		Lbr	2003	27,322	33,800	212	30	22	CC	ex E.R. Bremen-03
Maersk Valencia		Lbr	1999	25,630	33,855	207	30	21	CC	ex E.R. Copenhagen-99
OOCL France		Lbr	2001	66,289	67,591	277	40	26	CC	ex E.R. Paris-01
OOCL Germany		Lbr	2000	66,289	67,660	277	40	26	CC	ex E.R. Berlin-01
OOCL Los Angeles		Lbr	2000	66,289	67,500	277	40	26	CC	I/a E.R. Pusan
OOCL Malaysia		Lbr	2000	66,289	66,298	277	40	26	CC	ex E.R. Seoul-00
OOCL New York		Lbr	1999	66,289	67,660	277	40	26	CC	I/a E.R. Hong Kong
OOCL Shanghai		Lbr	1999	66,289	67,473	277	40	26	CC	I/a E.R. Shanghai
P&O Nedlloyd Magellan		Lbr	2000	66,289	67,557	277	40	26	CC	I/a E.R. Amsterdam
P&O Nedlloyd Torres		Lbr	2000	66,289	67,500	277	40	26	CC	I/a E.R. Felixstowe
P&O Nedlloyd Vespucci		Lbr	2000	66,289	67,566	277	40	26	CC	I/a E.R. London
Panatlantic		Lbr	1995	16,175	22,900	185	26	19	CC	ex Quadrant Express-99
Safmarine Cunene		Lbr	2002	27,332	33,800	212	30	22	CC	ex E.R. Bremerhaven-02
Safmarine Zambezi		Lbr	2002	27,322	34,608	212	30	22	CC	ex E.R. Helgoland-02

newbuildings : seven 110,000 dwt (8,200 teu), four 93,000 dwt (7,500 teu), one further 5,040 teu (67,170 dwt), six 45,400 dwt (2,824 teu) and four 34,500 dwt (2,550 teu) containerships on order from South Korean and German builders for 2004-7 delivery.

Shipping subsidiary of Erck Rickmers' investment group Nordcapital Ges. Fur Unternehmensbeteiligungen mbH & Cie.

Norddeutsche Vermogensanlage GmbH & Co.   Germany

Funnel: Charterers colours
Hull: Black or red with red boot-topping.

Name	Eng	Flag	Year	GRT	DWT	Loa	Bm	Kts	Type	Former names
APL Arabia *		Lbr	2000	54,415	66,895	294	32	24	CC	ex MOL Vigilance-03, Vantage-03, MOL Vantage-02, APL Arabia-02, I/a Northern Grace
APL Egypt *		Lbr	2000	54,415	66,922	294	32	24	CC	ex MOL Virtue-03, APL Egypt-02
APL Malaysia *		Lbr	2000	54,415	66,910	294	32	24	CC	ex MOL Value-03, APL Malaysia-02, I/a Northern Glance
Barcelona Bridge		Lbr	2003	41,078	48,874	260	32	-	CC	ex Northern Delicacy
Bangkok Express		Lbr	2003	75,590	85,400	300	40	25	CC	
Busan Express		Lbr	2003	75,590	85,400	300	40	25	CC	
Cap Frio *		Lbr	2001	25,713	33,900	208	30	21	CC	ex Northern Endeavour-03, Andhika Loreto-01
Cap Matapan *		Lbr	2001	25,713	33,900	208	30	21	CC	ex Northern Endurance-03, Andhika Fatima-01
Cebu	(2)	Lbr	1984	15,575	27,468	163	25	13	B	ex Zambesi-95, Irazu-95, Swift Wings-93, Usuki Pioneer-87
Conti Arabian ‡		Lbr	1990	18,000	26,288	177	28	18	CC	ex Delmas Mascareignes-03, Kaedi-02, Conti Arabian-00, Maruba Challenger-00, Conti Arabian-97, Arabian Senator-97
Duburg ‡		Lbr	1990	18,000	26,288	177	28	18	CC	ex Kota Perkasa-02, Japan Senator-98
Gluecksburg ‡		Phl	1988	18,037	26,152	177	28	17	CC	ex MSC Quito-02, Gluecksburg-01, P&O Nedlloyd Chile-00, CMBT Himalaya-97, CGM Iguacu II-96, Glucksburg-94, Ville de Neptune-92
Indamex Godavari *		Lbr	1997	36,606	45,131	245	32	23	CC	ex MSC Bursa-04, P&O Nedlloyd Barcelona-02, Northern Diversity-98

Nippon Yusen Kaisha. NYK ARTEMIS. *Phil Kempsey.*

Nordcapital (E.R. Schiffahrts). CSCL KOBE. *Hans Kraijenbosch.*

Name	Eng	Flag	Year	GRT	DWT	Loa	Bm	Kts	Type	Former names
Lamon Bay ‡		Lbr	1985	16,910	20,485	177	25	17	CC	ex Eagle Comet-98, Lamon Bay-97, Choyang Sun-96, Lamon Bay-91
Los Angeles Express		Lbr	2003	75,590	85,400	300	40	-	CC	ex Northern Magnum-03
Luetjenburg ‡		Lbr	1995	37,323	45,530	239	32	23	CC	ex Garden Bridge-03, Heaven River-00, Lutjenburg-98
MSC Ans		Pan	2004	53,500	67,800	294	32	24	CC	
MSC Ela		Pan	2004	53,500	67,800	294	32	24	CC	
MSC Lisa		Pan	2004	53,500	67,800	294	32	24	CC	
MSC Ornella		Pan	2004	53,500	67,800	294	32	24	CC	
Northern Devotion		Lbr	2004	35,697	34,100	-	-	-	CC	
Northern Distinction		Lbr	2004	35,697	34,100	-	-	-	CC	
Northern Magnitude		Lbr	2004	75,590	85,400	300	40	25	CC	
NYK Freesia		Lbr	2001	25,713	33,900	208	30	21	CC	ex Cap Salinas-04, Northern Enterprise-03, Andhika Lourdes-02
P&O Nedlloyd Damietta *		Lbr	1997	36,606	44,117	245	32	23	CC	ex OOCL Europe-02, P&O Nedlloyd Damietta-01, Northern Divinity-97
Peking Senator **		Deu	1997	53,324	63,527	294	32	23	CC	ex Cho Yang Ark-00
Penang Senator **		Deu	1997	53,324	63,533	294	32	23	CC	ex Cho Yang Atlas-01
Portland Senator **		Deu	1997	53,324	63,645	294	32	23	CC	ex Cho Yang Alpha-01
Potomac Bridge *		Lbr	2003	41,078	48,923	260	32	-	CC	ex Northern Decency-03
San Francisco Express		Lbr	2004	75,590	85,400	300	40	25	CC	
Shanghai Express		Lbr	2003	75,590	85,400	300	40	25	CC	
Tiger Sky ‡		Lbr	1991	16,236	23,596	163	28	17	CC	ex Mildburg-02, Direct Condor-99, Mildburg-96, Contship Australia-95
Troyburg ‡		Lbr	1988	18,037	26,070	177	28	17	CC	ex MSC Callao-02, Troyburg-98, NOL Koi-98, Deppe Florida-96,Troyburg-94, Ville de Venus-93
Yokohama Senator *		Lbr	1998	53,324	63,615	294	32	23	CC	ex Cho Yang Ace-01

Newbuildings : two 95,000 grt, three further 75,000 grt, four 53,500 grt and three 35,000 grt container ships from Far Eastern builders.
* owned by subsidiary 'NRG' Norddeutsche Reederei Beteiligungsgesellschaft mbH & Co. and ** managed by Reederei F. Laeisz GmbH.
‡ owned by Norddeutsche subsidiary Engineering Consulting & Management GmbH (acquired 1999 from H. Schuldt)

Dampskibsselskabet 'Norden' A/S   Denmark

Funnel: Black with narrow red band on broard white band.
Hull: Black or dark blue with red boot-topping.

Name	Eng	Year	GRT	DWT	Loa	Bm	Kts	Type
Nord Amalie	Bhs	2004	30,000	55,000	-	-	-	B
Nord Stealth	Dis	2001	56,346	105,300	239	42	14	T
Nordafrika	Sgp	2003	25,561	37,462	180	32	-	T
Nordamerika	Dis	2000	23,740	35,775	183	27	14	T
Nordasia	Dis	1998	57,009	105,994	244	42	13	T
Nordatlantic	Dis	2001	56,346	105,322	239	42	15	T
Nordeuropa	Dis	2000	23,740	35,752	183	27	14	T
Nordpacific	Dis	2003	56,346	105,344	239	42	14	T

newbuildings - six 25,000 grt 38,500 dwt bulk carriers on order from Japanese/Chinese builders for 2004/5 delivery.
30% owned by Torm, who are bidding for full ownership.

Novorossiysk Shipping Co.   Russia

Funnel: Blue with red and black intertwined ropes between narrow diagonal blue bands on broad diagonal white band.
Hull: Black, brown or red with red boot-topping.

Name	Eng	Year	GRT	DWT	Loa	Bm	Kts	Type	Former names
Adygeja *	Lbr	1982	36,782	61,341	225	32	14	T	ex Norse Venture-86
Akademik Pustovoyt	Rus	1980	50,776	88,723	229	42	15	Ts	ex Viking Eagle-86
Akademik Vereshchagin	Mlt	1989	18,625	28,610	179	25	14	T	
Aleksandr Pokryshkin *	Lbr	1987	37,884	67,980	243	32	15	T	
Boris Livanov	Rus	1986	16,502	23,920	185	23	15	B	
Elbrus *	Mlt	2004	28,000	46,080	183	32	14	T	
General Tyulenev	Rus	1983	37,916	67,980	243	32	15	T	
General Zamora	Ven	1993	39,036	68,198	224	32	15	T	ex Amity-01

Dampsskibs. Norden. NORDAFRIKA. *Hans Kraijenbosch.*

Novorossiysk Shipping. NOVOROSSIYSK. *M. D. J. Lennon.*

Novorossiysk Shipping. TULA. *F. de Vries.*

Name	Eng	Flag	Year	GRT	DWT	Loa	Bm	Kts	Type	Former names
Geroi Sevastopolya		Rus	1979	29,983	55,870	207	32	15	T	ex Jalunga-86, Viking Gull-85
Grigoriy Nesterenko *		Mlt	1986	18,625	28,610	179	25	14	T	
Ilya Erenburg		Rus	1987	10,949	15,970	152	22	15	T	
Kaluga *		Lbr	2003	62,395	114,800	250	44	-	T	
Kapitan Koziar *		Lbr	1985	45,353	76,324	244	32	14	Obo	ex Badak-92
Kapitan Ostashevskiy		Rus	1980	30,196	67,958	220	35	13	T	ex Laura-86, World Flora-86
Kapitan Putilin *		Lbr	1985	44,921	76,279	244	32	14	Obo	ex Mercedes-89
Kapitan Stankov *		Lbr	1985	45,278	76,324	244	32	14	Obo	ex Palacio-89
Kapitan Zhuravlyov *		Mlt	1985	45,278	76,284	245	32	14	Obo	ex Dodsland-89
Kazan *		Lbr	2003	62,395	115,727	250	44	-	T	
Kazbek *		Mlt	2004	28,000	46,080	183	32	14	T	
Khirurg Vishnevskiy		Rus	1988	10,949	15,970	152	22	15	T	
Khudozhnik Moor		Rus	1983	16,502	24,110	185	23	14	B	
Krasnodar *		Lbr	2003	62,395	115,605	250	44	-	T	
Krymsk *		Lbr	2003	62,395	115,605	250	44	-	T	
Kuban *		Lbr	2000	56,076	106,562	243	42	14	T	I/a Moscow Glory
Leonid Sobolyev		Rus	1985	16,502	23,940	184	23	14	B	
Leonid Utesov		Rus	1989	10,949	15,970	152	22	15	T	
Marshal Bagramyan *		Lbr	1984	37,884	67,980	243	32	15	T	
Marshal Chu(y)kov *		Lbr	1984	37,916	67,980	243	32	15	T	
Marshal Vasilyevskiy		Rus	1982	37,916	67,980	243	32	15	T	
Mashuk *		Mlt	2004	28,000	46,000	183	32	14	T	
MCT Alioth *		Lbr	1999	12,358	17,563	149	24	15	T	ex Alioth-04
MCT Almak *		Lbr	1999	12,358	17,561	149	24	15	T	ex Almak-03
MCT Altair *		Lbr	1999	12,358	17,553	149	24	15	T	ex Altair-03
MCT Arcturus *		Lbr	1999	12,358	17,563	149	24	15	T	ex Arcturus-03
Mekhanik Slauta		Rus	1980	37,734	60,952	220	35	14	T	ex Goya-86, Viana I-86, Astro Aries-86
Moskovskiy Festival *		Mlt	1985	18,526	28,750	179	25	15	T	
Moscow *		Lbr	1998	56,076	99,600	243	42	15	T	
Moscow Kremlin *		Lbr	1998	56,076	106,521	243	42	15	T	
Moscow River *		Lbr	1999	56,075	106,552	243	42	15	T	
Moscow Stars *		Lbr	1999	56,076	106,450	243	42	14	T	
Moscow University *		Lbr	1999	56,076	106,521	243	42	15	T	
Moskovskiy Festival *		Mlt	1985	18,526	28,750	179	25	15	T	
Novorossiysk *	(2)	Mlt	1994	16,940	13,480	169	24	17	Ro	
Pamir *		Mlt	2004	28,000	46,000	183	32	14	T	
Pob(y)eda		Rus	1981	37,916	67,980	243	32	15	T	
Pyotr (Petr) Shmidt *		Mlt	1987	18,526	28,610	179	25	14	T	
Ruby		Lbr	2004	28,000	46,000	183	32	14	T	
Sergey Lemesh(y)ev		Rus	1983	16,502	24,110	185	23	14	B	
Sochi *		Mlt	1996	16,940	23,025	169	24	17	Ro	
Sorokaletiye Pobedy *		Lbr	1985	38,916	67,980	243	32	15	T	
Stena Concord		Lbr	2004	27,500	47,400	183	32	-	T	
Stena Consul		Lbr	2004	27,500	47,400	183	32	-	T	
Taganrog *		Lbr	1996	26,218	40,713	181	32	14	T	
Taman *		Lbr	1996	26,218	40,818	181	32	15	T	
Tambov *		Lbr	1996	26,218	40,727	181	32	14	T	
Temryuk *		Lbr	1996	26,218	40,584	181	32	14	T	
Tikhoretsk *		Lbr	1996	26,218	40,791	181	32	14	T	
Tikhvin *		Lbr	1996	26,218	40,727	181	32	15	T	
Timashevsk *		Lbr	1996	26,218	40,584	181	32	15	T	
Tomsk *		Lbr	1997	26,218	40,703	181	32	15	T	
Trogir *		Mlt	1995	26,218	40,727	181	32	14	T	
Troitsk *		Lbr	1996	26,218	40,816	181	32	15	T	
Tula *		Lbr	1997	26,218	40,584	181	32	14	T	
Tver *		Lbr	1996	26,218	40,743	181	32	15	T	
Valeriy Chkalov *		Mlt	1988	18,625	28,610	179	25	14	T	
Vera Mar(y)etskaya		Rus	1983	16,508	24,110	185	23	14	B	
Vladimir Kokkinaki *		Mlt	1986	18,526	28,750	179	25	15	T	
Vladimir Vysotskiy		Rus	1988	10,949	15,970	152	22	15	T	
Yevgeniy Titov *		Mlt	1986	18,625	28,640	179	25	14	T	

newbuildings : three further 46,000 dwt tankers for 2004 delivery, four 57,000 grt 105,000 dwt and six 26,000 grt 47,000 dwt tankers on order for 2005/6 delivery all from South Korean and Croatian builders.
Owned by Government of The Republic of Russia and * managed by subsidiary Novoship (UK) Ltd., UK.

NSB Niederelbe Schiffahrtsges. mbH & Co. KG — Germany

Funnel: Blue with blue 'NSB' on white diamond or blue 'N' on square on broad white band or charterers colours.
Hull: Black, blue or dark grey with red boot-topping.

Name	Eng	Flag	Year	GRT	DWT	Loa	Bm	Kts	Type	Former names
ANL Pioneer	Deu	1987	10,811	13,464	147	23	15	CC	ex MSC Kiwi-02, Everett Express-01, Doria-00, OOCL Admiral-98, Doria-97, Sea-Land Mexico-94, Doria-94, Contship Asia-91, Ocean Asia-88, Doria-88
Buxcrown	Deu	1989	18,000	26,288	177	28	17	CC	ex Kota Pertama-01, Buxcrown-98, Singapore Senator 95
Buxfavourite	Deu	1997	25,713	34,083	206	30	21	CC	ex CSCL Yingkou-03, Sea Puma-01, Buxfavourite-98
Buxmaster	Deu	1986	16,250	23,465	163	28	18	CC	ex Cotonou Star-02, Buxmaster-01, WEC Rotterdam-01, Buxmaster-98, CMB Melody-96, Red Sea Endurance-92, Ville de Pluton-91
Buxsailor	Deu	1993	16,282	23,465	163	28	19	CC	ex City of York-03, Buxsailor-01, CSAV Salerno-00, Libra Houston-00, CMBT Amboseli-98, Contship Atlantic-97
Buxsund	Deu	1994	16,269	23,465	165	28	19	CC	ex Maersk Shimizu-02, Contship Europe-98
Cap Ferrato	Lbr	2002	25,375	33,864	207	30	21	CC	
Cap Velas	Deu	1994	19,819	22,273	174	27	19	CC	ex Northern Happiness-03, Kairo-00, DNOL Kairo-99, Kairo-98, Northern Happiness-94
Caribbean Sea	Deu	1996	37,549	44,731	241	32	24	CC	ex MSC Madrid-03, Sea-Land Endeavour-01, Sea Endeavour-96, Caribbean Sea-96
CMA CGM Albatross	Deu	1997	25,713	34,083	206	30	22	CC	ex Conti Bilbao-03, Brasilia-02, Sea-Land Brasil-99, l/a Conti Bilbao
CMA CGM Balzac	Deu	2001	73,172	77,941	300	40	26	CC	ex Conti Paris-01
CMA CGM Baudelaire	Deu	2001	73,172	77,946	300	40	26	CC	ex Conti Lyon-01
CMA CGM Capella	Deu	1995	35,595	42,673	240	32	22	CC	ex Ville de Capella-02, Northern Honour-95
CMA CGM Eagle	Deu	1997	25,713	27,200	205	27	20	CC	ex Conti Cartagena-03, MSC Provence-01, Sea-Land Argentina -00, l/a Conti Cartagena
CMA CGM Falcon	Deu	1998	25,713	33,995	206	30	21	CC	ex CSCL Nantong-03, Sea Leopard-01, Buxhansa-98
CMA CGM Hugo	Pan	2004	85,000	100,000	-	-	-	CC	
CMA CGM La Bourdonnais	Deu	1993	16,262	23,276	163	28	19	CC	ex CGM La Bourdonnais-00, CMBT Serengeti-98, Contship Pacific-97
CMA CGM Verlaine	Deu	2001	73,172	77,900	300	40	26	CC	l/a Buxcliff
CMA CGM Vernet	Deu	1994	35,595	42,673	240	32	22	CC	ex Northern Pioneer-02, Ville de Sagitta-01, l/a Northern Pioneer
CMA CGM Vivaldi	Pan	2004	85,000	100,000	-	-	-	CC	
CMA CGM Voltaire	Lbr	2001	73,172	77,900	300	40	26	CC	l/a Buxcoast
Conti Albany	Deu	1997	31,730	34,790	193	32	22	CC	ex ANL Albany-03, Conti Albany-03, Contship Optimism-02, l/a Conti Albany
Conti Asia	Deu	1993	16,282	23,596	163	28	18	CC	ex Contship Asia-98
Conti Barcelona	Deu	1991	16,236	23,596	164	28	17	CC	ex Tiger Speed-01, Conti Barcelona-01, Maersk Barcelona-01, Conti Barcelona-99, New York Express-98, Conti Barcelona-97, Contship Barcelona-96
Conti Esperance	Deu	1996	31,730	34,800	193	32	22	CC	ex Contship Romance-03, l/a Conti Esperance
Conti Germany	Deu	1992	16,236	23,596	164	28	17	CC	ex MSC Victoria-01, Contship Germany-98
Conti Jork	Deu	1990	16,236	23,596	163	28	17	CC	ex Kota Permas-00, Conti Jork-99, Contship Jork-97
Conti La Spezia	Deu	1990	16,236	23,596	163	28	17	CC	ex MSC Amazonia-01, Buxlady-99, Contship La Spezia-95
Conti Malaga *	Deu	1998	25,713	24,083	205	27	20	CC	ex MSC Chile-02, Sea-Land Uruguay-01, Conti Malaga-98
Conti Singapore *	Deu	1994	16,259	23,465	165	28	18	CC	ex Maersk Bangkok-00, Conti Singapore-98
Cosco Tianjin *	Deu	2000	65,918	68,263	279	40	26	CC	ex Hanjin Geneva-03, Conti Porto-00
CSAV Santos	Deu	1995	16,259	23,465	163	30	18	CC	ex Buxhill-03, Indamex Malabar-03, Buxhill-02, Contship Ticino-98
Hanjin Amsterdam *	Deu	1999	66,500	67,900	279	40	26	CC	l/a Conti Canberra
Hanjin Basel *	Mhl	2003	65,918	68,200	279	40	26	CC	ex Hanjin Lisbon-03
Hanjin Brussels *	Deu	2000	66,500	67,900	279	40	26	CC	ex Conti Brussel
Hanjin Cairo *	Deu	2001	65,131	68,045	275	40	-	CC	
Hanjin Chicago *	Lbr	2003	65,918	68,037	278	40	26	CC	
Hanjin Copenhagen *	Deu	1999	66,278	68,996	279	40	26	CC	ex Conti Darwin-99
Hanjin Gothenburg *	Deu	2002	65,131	68,045	275	40	-	CC	l/a Conti Goteborg
Hanjin Helsinki *	Mhl	2002	67,500	68,045	275	40	-	CC	
Hanjin Lisbon *	Lbr	2003	65,918	67,979	279	40	26	CC	
Hanjin Madrid *	Mhl	2003	65,918	67,979	279	40	26	CC	

131

Name	Eng	Flag	Year	GRT	DWT	Loa	Bm	Kts	Type	Former names
Hanjin Ottawa *		Deu	2000	66,278	68,834	278	40	26	CC	ex Conti Melbourne-00
Hanjin Taipei *		Deu	2001	65,131	68,086	275	40	25	CC	
Hanjin Vienna *		Deu	2000	65,918	68,263	279	40	26	CC	ex Conti Lissabon-00
Ibn Sina		Deu	1993	34,454	45,470	216	32	24	CC	ex Tokyo Senator-97, Sea Progress-96, Tokyo Senator-94
Indamex Alabama *		Deu	1997	31,730	34,731	193	32	22	CC	ex Conti Welington-03, Contship Vision-03, I/a Conti Wellington
Kairo		Deu	1994	19,819	22,246	174	27	19	CC	ex Northern Delight-03, Zim Chicago II-01, Kota Sejati-00, Northern Delight-99, P&O Nedlloyd Dubai-99, Dubai Bay-98, Nedlloyd Sao Paulo-96, Northern Delight-94
MSC Alessia *		Hkg	2001	75,590	84,920	304	40	25	CC	
MSC Flaminia *		Deu	2001	75,000	84,920	304	40	24	CC	I/a Buxclipper
MSC Florentina		Pan	2003	75,000	85,000	304	40	25	CC	
MSC France *		Deu	1993	16,236	23,596	163	28	18	CC	ex Conti France-03, Maersk Jakarta-99, Conti France-98, Contship France-98
MSC Ilona *		Deu	2001	75,590	84,920	304	40	25	CC	I/a Buxcomet
MSC Italy *		Lbr	1994	42,323	41,570	242	32	22	CC	ex Norasia Sharjah-02
MSC Maureen		Pan	2003	75,590	85,832	304	40	25	CC	
MSC Munich *		Lbr	1994	42,323	41,570	242	32	22	CC	ex Norasia Hong Kong-02, MSC Houston-99, Norasia Hong Kong-98
MSC Spain *		Deu	1998	25,713	34,051	206	30	21	CC	ex Conti Valencia-03, Lykes Hunter-01, Ivaran Hunter-99, Sea Tiger-98, Conti Valencia-98
MSC Switzerland *		Deu	1996	42,336	41,460	242	32	22	CC	ex Norasia Singa-02
MSC Sydney *		Deu	1990	16,236	23,596	163	28	17	CC	ex Conti Sydney-03, MSC Senegal-01, Conti Sydney-99, Direct Currawong-98, Contship Ipswich-95, I/a Contship Sydney
P&O Nedlloyd Beirut		Deu	1994	19,819	22,246	174	27	19	CC	ex Northern Felicity-03, CMA Los Angeles-00, Northern Felicity-99, P&O Nedlloyd Dammam-99, Dammam Bay-98, Nedlloyd Salvador-96, Northern Felicity-94
P&O Nedlloyd Hunter Valley		Lbr	2002	25,375	33,817	(197)	30	23	CC	
P&O Nedlloyd Newark *		Deu	1997	31,730	34,894	193	32	22	CC	ex Contship Nobility-03, Conti Brisbane-97
Pacific Link		Pan	2004	85,000	100,000				CC	
Rejane Delmas		Deu	1994	16,282	23,276	163	28	18	CC	ex Contship New Zealand-97
Rialto Bridge *		Deu	1996	37,549	44,647	241	32	24	CC	ex Safmarine Kimley-03, Sea-Land Mistral-02, White Sea
San Pedro Bridge		Deu	1996	37,549	44,690	241	32	24	CC	ex Sea-Land Initiative-00, Sea Initiative-96, Sargasso Sea-96
Vancouver		Deu	1997	24,053	27,100	205	27	20	CC	ex Ivory Star 1-03, Conti Seattle-02, CCNI Antartico-02, Sea Lynx-00, Conti Seattle-97
Ville d'Aquarius		Deu	1996	40,465	49,229	259	32	24	CC	ex Lykes Tiger-03, Ville d'Aquarius-02
Ville d'Orion		Deu	1997	40,465	49,208	259	32	23	CC	ex ANL California-03, Ville d'Orion-03
Ville de Mimosa		Deu	1997	40,400	49,238	259	32	23	CC	
Ville de Taurus		Deu	1997	40,400	49,238	259	32	23	CC	
Yellow Sea *		Deu	1996	37,549	44,765	241	32	24	CC	ex City of Edinburgh-03, Humen Bridge-02, Sea-Land Victory-00, Yellow Sea-96
YM Athens *		Deu	2000	66,278	67,900	279	40	26	CC	ex Hanjin Athens-03, Conti Melbourne-00
YM Kwang Yang		Deu	1995	16,270	23,130	163	28	18	CC	ex Buxmoon-03, Maersk Osaka-02, Contship Lavagna-98
YM Pearl River I		Mhl	1989	18,000	26,288	177	28	19	CC	ex Conti Hong Kong-03, MSC Guayaquil-01, Conti Hong Kong-99, MSC Guayaquil-98, Nedlloyd Zaandam-97, Buxmerchant-95, Choyang Star-94, Hongkong Senator-91
YM Surabaya		Deu	1994	16,270	23,130	163	28	17	CC	ex Indamex New Delhi-03, Kota Perwira-00, Contship Italy-98

*newbuildings - ten 85,000 grt, two 55,000 grt and eight 95,000 grt container ships for Conti KG funds.
Company associated with W. Harms GmbH & Co. KG. and * managed for Conti Reederei, Germany.*

Odfjell ASA   Norway

Funnel: White with blue diagonal chain link symbol, black top
Hull: Orange with blue 'ODFJELL SEACHEM', red or black boot-topping

Bow Andes ‡		Chl	1977	17,561	28,021	171	25	17	T	ex Bow Sun-98

NSB Niederelbe Schiffs. CMA CGM BALZAC (in charterers colours). *Phil Kempsey.*

NSB Niederelbe Schiffs. MSC ILONA (in charterers colours). *Hans Kraijenbosch*

Name	Eng	Flag	Year	GRT	DWT	Loa	Bm	Kts	Type	Former names
Bow Cardinal		Nis	1997	23,196	37,479	183	32	16	T	
Bow Cecil		Nis	1998	23,206	37,545	183	32	16	T	
Bow Cedar		Nis	1996	23,196	37,455	183	32	16	T	
Bow Century		Nis	2000	23,206	37,438	183	32	16	T	
Bow Chain		Nis	2002	23,190	37,518	183	32	16	T	
Bow Cheetah *		Grc	1988	22,637	40,257	171	32	14	T	ex Santa Anna-00, Falkanger-91, Fort Cheetah-89, Northern Cheetah-88
Bow Clipper		Nis	1995	23,197	37,221	183	32	16	T	
Bow Eagle		Nis	1985	15,829	24,728	172	28	14	T	ex Northern Eagle-89, Mangueira-88
Bow Fagus		Nis	1995	23,197	37,221	183	32	16	T	
Bow Faith		Nis	1997	23,196	37,479	183	32	16	T	
Bow Favour		Nis	2001	23,190	37,467	183	32	16	T	
Bow Fighter *		Nis	1982	20,478	35,100	174	32	15	T	
Bow Firda		Nis	2003	23,190	37,000	183	32	16	T	
Bow Flora		Nis	1998	23,206	37,369	183	32	16	T	
Bow Flower		Nis	1994	23,197	37,221	183	32	16	T	
Bow Fortune		Nis	1999	23,206	37,395	183	32	16	T	
Bow Heron *		Nis	1979	20,362	35,210	174	32	15	T	ex Iver Heron-91
Bow Hunter		Nis	1983	14,627	23,002	158	23	15	T	
Bow Lady		Nis	1978	18,438	32,227	171	26	17	T	ex Golar Petrosun-89
Bow Lancer *		Nis	1980	20,478	35,050	174	32	15	T	ex Berganger-90
Bow Leopard *		Nis	1988	22,637	40,257	171	32	14	T	ex Fort Leopard-89, Northern Leopard-88
Bow Lion *		Nis	1987	22,637	40,272	171	32	14	T	ex Fort Lion-89, Northern Lion-88
Bow Merkur †		Nis	1975	17,561	27,954	171	25	17	T	ex Bow Fortune-98
Bow Pacifico ‡		Chl	1982	12,198	15,200	161	23	15	T	ex Bow Saphir-01
Bow Panther *		Nis	1986	22,714	40,263	171	32	14	T	ex Northern Panther-89
Bow Peace *		Grc	1987	28,001	45,655	177	32	14	T	ex Peaceventure L-00
Bow Petros *		Nis	1984	22,589	37,250	174	32	14	T	ex Petros-92, Owl Petros-84, Atlas Petros-84
Bow Pioneer		Nis	1982	14,627	23,016	158	23	15	T	
Bow Power *		Grc	1987	28,001	39,571	177	32	14	T	ex Powerventure L-00
Bow Pride *		Grc	1987	28,001	39,586	177	32	14	T	ex Pridevenure L-00
Bow Prima *		Grc	1987	28,001	45,655	177	32	14	T	ex Primaventure L-00
Bow Princess **		Nis	1976	18,438	32,329	171	26	15	T	ex Golar Petrosea-89
Bow Prosper *		Grc	1987	28,008	39,574	177	32	14	T	ex Prosperventure L-00
Bow Puma *		Grc	1986	22,714	40,091	171	32	14	T	ex Santa Maria-91, Finnanger-91, Fort Puma-89, Northern Puma-86
Bow Queen **		Nis	1975	18,262	32,362	171	26	15	T	ex Golar Petrotrade-89
Bow Saturn †		Nis	1976	17,561	28,085	171	25	17	T	ex Bow Star-98
Bow Sea		Nis	1978	17,561	28,084	171	25	17	T	
Bow Sky †		Nis	1977	17,561	28,085	171	25	17	T	
Bow Spring †		Nis	1976	17,561	28,160	171	25	17	T	
Bow Star		Nis	2004	29,900	40,000	183	32	-	T	
Bow Sun		Nis	2003	29,965	40,000	183	32	-	T	l/a Multicarrier
Bow Transporter *		Lbr	1983	22,587	39,738	174	32	14	T	ex Owl Transporter-92, Atlas Transporter-84
Bow Viking		Gbr	1981	19,639	33,695	183	30	16	T	ex Mauranger-90, Kaupanger-81

newbuildings - four 40,000 dwt tankers for 2004/5 delivery from Polish builder.
* managed by Ceres Hellenic Shipping Enterprises Ltd, Greece q.v., partners in Seachem Pool
† owned by Salhus Shipping AS, Norway or ** managed by Hanseatic Shipping Co. Ltd., Cyprus
‡ jointly owned by Odfjell y Vapores SA, Chile and CSAV, managed by Southern Shipmanagement (Chile) Ltd. q.v.
See also time-chartered vessels under The National Shipping Company of Saudi Arabia, Saudi Arabia.

J. O. Odfjell A/S   Norway

JO Tankers AS

Funnel: *Blue with white interlinked 'JO' symbol.*
Hull: *Orange with blue 'JO TANKERS', red boot-topping*

Name	Eng	Flag	Year	GRT	DWT	Loa	Bm	Kts	Type	Former names
Bryggen		Nis	1981	15,393	26,328	173	23	14	T	ex Jo Elm-03, Lake Anne-91
Jo Acer		Nis	2004	18,500	30,000	170	26	-	T	
Jo Ask		Nld	1997	12,317	19,087	148	23	16	T	
Jo Betula		Nis	2003	15,992	25,032	159	25	-	T	
Jo Birk		Nis	1982	22,772	39,293	175	32	16	T	
Jo Brevik		Nis	1986	19,685	33,490	183	30	15	T	
Jo Cedar		Nld	1994	22,415	36,733	182	32	15	T	
Jo Clipper		Nld	1981	19,889	33,695	183	30	15	T	ex Polux-81
Jo Eik		Nis	1998	12,249	19,234	148	23	16	T	

Odfjell ASA. BOW SUN. *Hans Kraijenbosch.*

J. O. Odfjell A/S (JO Tankers). JO ELM (since renamed BRYGGEN). *N. Kemps.*

Name	Eng	Flag	Year	GRT	DWT	Loa	Bm	Kts	Type	Former names
Jo Gran	(2)	Nis	1980	23,194	37,532	175	32	16	T	ex Johnson Chemstar-88
Jo Kiri		Pan	2003	11,769	19,508	145	24	14	T	
Jo Lind	(2)	Nld	1982	19,809	33,532	183	30	15	T	ex Johnson Chemspan-88
Jo Lonn		Nld	1982	21,568	39,273	175	32	16	T	
Jo Oak		Nis	1983	22,772	39,270	175	32	16	T	
Jo Rogn	(2)	Nis	1980	23,189	37,572	175	32	14	T	ex Johnson Chemsun-88
Jo Selje		Nld	1993	22,380	36,800	182	32	15	T	
Jo Sequoia		Nis	2003	23,129	37,622	183	32	15	T	
Jo Sycamore		Nis	2000	23,200	37,500	183	32	15	T	
Jo Sypress		Nld	1998	22,415	36,752	182	32	15	T	
Jo Spruce		Nld	1993	22,415	36,778	182	32	15	T	

Managed by JO Tankers AS; also see A/S Borgestad ASA and Knutsen O.A.S. Shipping A/S, both Norway.

Rudolf A. Oetker   Germany
Hamburg-Sudamerikanische Dampfschiffahrts-ges (HSDG)

Funnel: *White with red top or buff (Furness Withy).*
Hull: *Red or white with red boot-topping. Black with green boot-topping (Furness Withy).*

Cap Carmel	Lbr	2003	25,705	33,600	207	30	22	CC	
Cap Finisterre	Deu	1991	29,841	32,675	200	32	18	CC	
Cap Melville	Lbr	2003	25,705	33,545	207	30	22	CC	
Cap Nelson	Deu	2004	25,705	33,545	207	30	22	CC	
Cap Polonia	Deu	1990	29,739	33,221	200	32	18	CC	
Cap Roca	Lbr	1990	35,303	42,221	234	32	21	CC	ex New York Express-96, Berlin Express-93, POL Jos-92, Berlin Express-91
Cap San Antonio	Lbr	2001	40,085	50,200	257	32	23	CC	
Cap San Augustin	Lbr	2001	40,085	51,087	257	32	23	CC	
Cap San Lorenzo	Lbr	2001	40,085	51,045	257	32	23	CC	
Cap San Marco	Lbr	2001	40,085	51,087	257	32	23	CC	
Cap San Nicolas	Lbr	2001	40,085	51,101	257	32	22	CC	
Cap San Raphael	Lbr	2002	40,085	51,059	257	32	22	CC	
CMA CGM Pasteur	Lbr	1990	29,739	33,222	200	32	19	CC	ex CGM Pasteur-01, Cap Trafalgar-99
Monte Cervantes	Deu	2004	46,000	78,500	-	-	-	CC	
Monte Olivia	Deu	2004	46,000	78,500	-	-	-	CC	
Monte Pascoal	Deu	2004	46,000	78,500	-	-	-	CC	
Monte Rosa	Deu	2004	46,000	78,500	-	-	-	CC	
Monte Sarmiento	Deu	2004	46,000	78,500	-	-	-	CC	
Monte Verde	Deu	2004	46,000	78,500	-	-	-	CC	
NYK Fantasia	Lbr	2003	25,705	33,795	208	30	21	CC	ex Cap Palmas-03
Polar Argentina †	Lbr	1992	10,629	10,588	150	23	21	R	ex Horntide-98, Polar Argentina-98, Gordian-95
Polar Brasil †	Lbr	1992	10,629	10,588	150	23	21	R	ex Hornstream-98, Polar Brasil-98, Numerian-95
Polar Chile †	Lbr	1993	10,629	10,620	150	23	21	R	ex Trajan-96
Polar Colombia †	Lbr	1992	10,629	10,593	150	23	21	R	ex Appian-95
Polar Ecuador †	Lbr	1992	10,629	10,452	150	23	21	R	ex Justinian-96
Polar Uruguay ‡	Lbr	1993	10,629	10,593	150	23	21	R	ex Hadrian-96
Santa Rosa	Lbr	1997	25,190	41,363	186	30	14	B	ex Northern Glory-97
Santos Express	Deu	2004	25,705	33,545	207	30	22	CC	

All managed by Columbus Shipmanagement GmbH with † operating in Star Reefers or ‡ in LauritzenCool pools.

Alianca Navegacao e Logistica Ltd./Brazil

Funnel: *Yellow with broad white over red bands beneath black top, black triangular 'A' on white band or HSDG colours.*
Hull: *Blue with white 'ALIANCA', red boot-topping.*

Alianca Brasil	Bra	1994	28,397	32,984	200	32	18	CC	
Alianca Europa	Bra	1994	28,397	32,984	200	32	18	CC	
Alianca Sao Paulo *	Lbr	2003	25,703	33,741	208	-	-	CC	ex Rio Verde-03
Alianca Urca	Bra	1981	24,270	23,520	185	28	17	CC	ex Columbus Canterbury-02, Monte Rosa-96
Copacabana	Bra	1984	20,995	26,848	179	31	18	CC	
Flamengo	Bra	1985	20,994	26,868	179	31	18	CC	
Leblon	Bra	1982	24,270	23,560	185	28	16	CC	ex Columbus California-00, Monte Cervantes-93
Lily	Bra	1984	28,347	47,043	201	27	15	B	ex Arpoador-85

newbuildings: two 43,900 grt container ships due for 2004 delivery.
* Owned by MPC Munchmeyer, Germany

Rudolf A. Oetker (HSDG). CAP ROCA. *Hans Kraijenbosch.*

Rudolf A. Oetker (Alianca). ALIANCA EUROPA. *Hans Kraijenbosch.*

Name	Eng	Flag	Year	GRT	DWT	Loa	Bm	Kts	Type	Former names

Ellerman Line

Funnel: Buff with narrow white band below narrow black top
Hull: Owners colours.

Name	Eng	Flag	Year	GRT	DWT	Loa	Bm	Kts	Type	Former names
City of Glasgow *		Grc	1978	14,050	15,270	157	25	18	CC	ex Express-98, Choyang Express-98, Express-93, MSC Laura-90, Zim Guam-90, Express-88, Durga Osaka-87, Express-87, Nedlloyd Express-86, TFL Express-86, Alltrans Express-80
City of Tunis **		Atg	1994	19,819	20,252	174	27	19	CC	ex Northern Harmony-94

* on charter from Costamare, Greece, ** from Schiffahrtskontor Rendsburg Gmbh (Reederei Karl Schluter GmbH), Germany

Maritime Services Aleuropa GmbH/Germany

Funnel: White with red half-circle on broad blue top above broad green band.
Hull: White.

Name	Eng	Flag	Year	GRT	DWT	Loa	Bm	Kts	Type	Former names
Carlos Fischer		Lbr	2002	33,005	43,067	204	32	20	Tfj	
Ouro do Brasil		Lbr	1993	15,218	19,519	173	26	20	Tfj	
Premium do Brasil		Lbr	2003	33,005	43,002	205	32	20	Tfj	
Sol do Brasil		Lbr	1994	15,218	19,653	173	26	20	Tfj	

Managed for Group Fischer, Brazil.

Ofer Brothers (Holdings) Ltd.   Israel

Funnel: Various charters colours.
Hull: Various.

Name	Eng	Flag	Year	GRT	DWT	Loa	Bm	Kts	Type	Former names
Atlantic Fortune		Mlt	1994	26,136	44,820	187	30	14	B	ex Aqua Crest-01, Halla Neptune-98
Cap Blanco		Mlt	1984	32,150	37,042	203	32	15	CC	ex CGM Magellan-97, Andes-94
Cap Domingo		Mlt	1984	31,446	34,680	201	32	19	CC	ex Alianca Mexico-99, Cap Corrientes-98, Laser Pacific-96, Bo Johnson-93
Car Bridge I		Pan	1981	41,368	17,344	199	30	17	V	ex Zimcar 1-01, Delborg-00, Primavera-96, Jinto Maru-89
Car Star 1 *		Cyp	1981	41,363	17,427	199	30	17	V	ex Thonborg-99, Margherita-96, Jinmu Maru-90
Carmel Bio-Top **		Lbr	2004	17,500	15,052	186	25	-	CC	
Carmel Eco-Fresh **		Lbr	2003	18,931	15,052	186	25	-	CC	l/a Rio Alexandre
Carmel Exotic		Bhs	1972	9,207	8,026	148	20	18	R	ex Galia Carmel-96, Vosges-86, Zira-75 (len-80)
Carmel Topaz		Bhs	1972	9,207	8,365	148	20	18	R	ex Avocado Carmel-96, Vendee-86, Zaida-75 (len-79)
City of Istanbul *		Cyp	1979	24,270	24,320	184	28	19	CC	ex Columbus Queensland-03
Columbus Canada *		Cyp	1979	24,080	22,995	184	28	18	CC	ex CMB Memling-94, Monte Sarmiento-86, Columbus Canterbury-83
Columbus Victoria *		Cyp	1979	24,081	23,165	168	28	19	CC	ex Oregon Star-94, Columbus Louisiana-91
CSCL Qingdao		Mlt	2001	39,941	50,953	260	32	24	CC	
CSCL Rotterdam		Mlt	2002	39,500	50,863	260	32	24	CC	
CSCL Tianjin		Mlt	2001	39,941	50,953	260	32	24	CC	
Dafnis		Mlt	1981	13,586	16,728	160	24	15	Co	ex Bonny-98, Zagreb-95
Durban Star III		Mlt	1982	15,611	22,918	166	27	16	Co	ex Hillary-99, Earnest Venture-96
India Lotus		Mlt	1981	36,263	39,967	239	32	22	CC	ex Zim Haifa I-02, Zim Savannah-98, M.Savannah-90, Zim Savannah-90
Kestrel I		Mlt	1988	30,824	25,684	202	31	17	CC	ex Pelican I-03, Zim Antwerp I-02, Asia Opal-02, LT Mediterranea-99, Nuova Mediterranea-99, Genova-96, Erna Oldendorff-81, H. Cegielski-91
Mombasa Star		Pan	1979	15,879	22,954	166	27	15	C	ex Valerie I-00, Concord Asia-96, Grand Wing-86
MSC Andalucia II *		Mlt	1978	20,408	21,857	181	27	17	CC	ex Lora-02, MSC Andalucia-02, Lora-00, Norasia Alexandria-00, Lora-99, Diana-96, Asean Unity-94, Ciudad de Pasto-93 (con C-95)
Ori A		Pan	1978	14,741	21,513	163	24	14	T	ex Marina-94, Terutoku Maru-93
Philippine Star		Mlt	1986	22,667	33,852	188	28	19	CC	ex Zim Mumbai 1-02, MSC Cameroon-01, Zim Shanghai-01, Vesta-95, Ville de Vesta-94, Japan Sea-93, Ville de Vesta-89, Pacific Prosperity-88
Qingdao Star		Mlt	1985	22,667	32,934	188	28	18	CC	ex CSCL Huangpu-02, Zim India-00, Zim Singapore-98, Vega-95, Ville de Vega-94, Pacific Progress-88
SCI Gaurav		Lbr	1992	37,071	47,120	237	32	21	CC	ex German Senator-02, Choyang Volga-98
Sea Fortune		Mlt	1983	25,107	42,964	193	30	16	B	ex Asian Fortune-97, Theofano Livanos-94
TMM Monterey		Gbr	2003	39,941	50,813	260	32	24	CC	

138

Ofer Brothers. CAP DOMINGO (on Hamburg Sud charter). *Hans Kraijenbosch.*

Ofer Brothers (Associated Bulk Carriers). FERNIE. *N. Kemps.*

Name	Eng	Flag	Year	GRT	DWT	Loa	Bm	Kts	Type	Former names
White Swan *		Cyp	1989	30,824	26,132	202	31	17	CC	ex Zim Hamburg I-02, Asia Jade-02, LT Nipponica-99, Nuova Nipponica-99, Trieste-96, T. Wenda-91
Zim Adriatic		Mlt	1982	36,263	39,967	239	32	22	CC	ex Adriatic-97, Zim Iberia-97
Zim California		Isr	2002	53,453	62,740	294	32	24	CC	
Zim Dalian *		Cyp	1990	36,584	44,025	241	32	23	CC	ex Choyang Victory-98
Zim Florida		Lbr	1992	37,071	46,975	237	32	21	CC	ex St. Petersburg Mariner-03, St. Petersburg Senator-02
Zim Keelung		Mlt	1981	36,263	39,967	239	32	22	CC	ex M.Keelung-91, Zim Keelung-91
Zim Marseille		Mlt	1981	31,694	28,615	222	31	21	CC	ex Azov Sea-01, Asia Crown-01, APL Monterrey-01, Asia Crown-00, Zim Osaka-98, Asia Crown-96, California Ceres-96, Shin-Kashu Maru-81
Zim Mediterranean		Isr	2002	53,453	62,686	294	32	24	CC	
Zim Novorossiysk		Mlt	1977	15,560	18,834	187	25	21	CC	ex Gulf Glory-02, Penang Glory-01, Hanjin Kunsan-98, Ever Valiant-85
Zim Ravenna I *		Cyp	1990	36,584	44,014	240	32	22	CC	ex Choyang Glory-98
Zim Singapore		Lbr	1992	37,071	47,120	237	32	21	CC	ex Korea Star-03, Moscow Mariner-02, Moscow Senator-02, Choyang Moscow-98
Zim Virginia		Isr	2002	53,453	62,740	294	32	24	CC	

Newbuildings : three 55,000 grt 67,000 dwt and four 54,700 dwt container ships on order for 2004/5 delivery..
*Owned by Ofer (Ships Holding) Ltd except * by subsidiary Kotani Shipmanagement Ltd, Cyprus formed jointly with Zodiac Maritime Management Agencies Ltd., UK. ** chartered from Horizont Shipping GmbH, Germany.*

Associated Bulk Carriers (London) Ltd/UK

Funnel: Dark blue with white 'ABC' on black rectangle ('B' on vertical red panel)
Hull: Black or blue with red or blue boot-topping.

Name		Flag	Year	GRT	DWT	Loa	Bm	Kts	Type	Former names
Buccleuch *		Bmu	1993	90,820	182,675	284	47	13	B	
Cotswold		Bmu	1986	80,578	151,016	289	45	14	B	
Duhallow		Bmu	1993	63,240	122,774	266	41	14	B	
Eridge *		Bmu	1993	63,153	122,792	266	41	14	B	
Fernie *		Bmu	1996	63,153	122,292	266	41	14	B	
Grafton *		Bmu	1996	63,153	122,301	266	41	14	B	
Heythrop		Bmu	1996	85,364	165,729	288	44	13	B	
Irfon *		Bmu	1996	84,921	165,628	288	44	13	B	
Kildare		Bmu	1996	108,083	211,320	312	50	14	B	ex SGC Express-98
Meynell		Bmu	1997	93,629	185,767	292	48	15	B	ex SG Universe-98
New Forest		Bmu	1996	93,629	185,688	292	48	15	B	ex SGC Foundation-98
Ormond		Bmu	1986	96,794	187,025	300	47	13	B	
Pytchley		Bmu	1996	92,194	179,869	290	46	14	B	ex SGC Capital-98
Quorn		Bmu	1996	92,194	179,869	290	46	14	B	ex SG China-98
Rutland		Bmu	1997	85,848	170,013	292	46	14	B	ex SG Fortune-98
Snowdon		Bmu	1998	85,848	170,013	292	46	14	B	I/a SG Creation
Taunton		Bmu	1986	95,835	186,324	300	47	13	B	ex Marine Crusader-89
Ullswater		Bmu	1990	63,106	114,741	266	42	14	B	
Vine		Bmu	1990	63,106	114,975	266	42	14	B	
Waterford		Bmu	1990	77,113	149,513	270	43	12	B	
York		Bmu	1990	77,113	149,513	270	43	13	B	
Zetland		Bmu	1985	74,003	145,905	267	43	13	B	ex Mosbulk-90

*Managed by Zodiac Maritime Agencies Ltd. and * owned by Unique Shipping (HK) Ltd., Hong Kong.*

S. A. Monegasque d'Administration Maritime et Aerienne (SAMAMA)/Monaco

Funnel: Blue with either blue 'Z' on white disc, or black top.
Hull: Black with red boot-topping.

Name		Flag	Year	GRT	DWT	Loa	Bm	Kts	Type	Former names
Alanya		Gbr	1986	27,012	38,792	183	29	13	B	ex Rio Purus-93
Amber		Pan	1986	93,509	181,884	290	46	13	B	ex Concorde Spirit-99, Concorde Maru-91
Andes Mountains		Lbr	1983	7,988	8,410	142	20	18	R	ex Greenland Rex-95
APL Emerald		Sgp	1980	40,077	47,841	260	32	23	CC	ex President Eisenhower-98, Neptune Jade-84
APL Ivory		Sgp	1980	40,077	47,841	260	32	23	CC	ex President F.D. Roosevelt-98, Neptune Garnet-84 (len-81)
Atlas Mountains		Pan	1982	8,041	8,778	140	21	18	R	ex Winfast Reefer-96, Frontier Reefer-94, Kijima-89
Brazil Star		Lbr	1983	100,912	201,227	299	50	12	B	ex Tsukuba Maru-94
Broadgate		Lbr	1984	20,986	35,287	176	28	14	B	ex Marine Royal-95, Unyo Maru-88
Brother Glory *		Gbr	1998	27,105	46,211	190	31	13	B	
Cape Eagle		Pan	1993	81,589	161,475	280	45	14	B	
Cape Falcon		Pan	1993	81,589	149,480	280	45	14	B	

140

Name	Eng	Flag	Year	GRT	DWT	Loa	Bm	Kts	Type	Former names
Cape Hawk		Gbr	1995	81,589	161,425	280	45	14	B	
Cape Kestrel		Pan	1993	81,589	160,849	280	45	14	B	
Cape Osprey *		Gbr	1996	81,589	161,448	280	45	14	B	ex Sanko Oriole-03
Captain Aysuna		Pan	1986	16,080	26,914	168	27	13	B	ex New Venus-97, Helm Star-92, Liberty Star-88
CMA CGM Normandie		Gbr	1991	53,409	60,173	276	37	24	CC	ex Nedlloyd Normandie-01, CGM Normandie-95
CMA CGM Sapphire		Lbr	1991	36,627	44,013	240	32	22	CC	ex Grand Vision-03, Choyang Giant-01
Fuji Mountain		Lbr	1988	6,545	7,183	146	19	18	R	ex Copihue-97
Green Mountain		Pan	1983	7,777	8,488	142	20	17	R	ex Manila Tiger-95, Reefer Tiger-89
Hanjin Pennsylvania		Lbr	2002	50,000	58,000	282	32	24	CC	
Highgate		Gbr	1985	29,660	46,650	196	32	17	BC	ex Colima-96
Hyde Park		Lbr	1982	22,103	38,892	174	32	14	T	ex Stolt Reliant-96, Stolt Luisa Pando-90, M. Luisa de Pando-83
Hyundai Admiral		Pan	1992	51,836	61,152	275	37	24	CC	
Hyundai Baron		Pan	1992	51,836	61,152	275	37	24	CC	
Hyundai Discovery *		Pan	1996	64,054	51,120	275	40	25	CC	
Hyundai Dominion		Pan	2001	74,373	60,494	304	40	26	CC	
Hyundai Emperor *		Pan	1992	51,836	61,152	275	37	26	CC	
Hyundai Independence *		Pan	1996	64,054	68,537	275	40	25	CC	
Hyundai Kingdom		Pan	2001	74,373	80,551	304	40	26	CC	
Hyundai Liberty *		Gbr	1996	64,054	68,539	275	40	25	CC	
Hyundai National		Pan	2001	74,373	60,494	304	40	26	CC	
Hyundai Patriot		Pan	2001	74,373	60,494	304	40	26	CC	
Hyundai Republic		Pan	2001	74,373	80,000	304	40	26	CC	
Irongate		Lbr	1982	92,614	179,618	299	48	13	B	ex Kinokawa-96, Kinokawa Maru-93
Kenwood Park		Lbr	1982	22,103	39,015	174	32	14	T	ex Stolt Resolute-96, Stolt Maria Pando-90, A. Maria de Pando-83
Kota Perabu		Pan	1990	16,731	22,734	185	28	19	CC	ex Millenia Tower-03, ACX Rose-00
Kyushu Star		Lbr	1982	73,657	142,936	270	43	14	B	ex Kitaura Maru-95
Lake Phoenix		Gbr	1992	7,303	8,075	134	21	19	R	ex Amber Rose-96
London Tower		Pan	1994	17,651	23,884	183	28	19	CC	ex Nantai Queen-99
Lucky Transporter		Lbr	1984	15,763	26,650	167	26	14	B	ex Prime Unity-96, Maersk Pine-92, Mercury Island-90
Lykes Commander		Gbr	1994	30,971	36,999	202	32	21	CC	ex TMM Mexico-01, Sea Guardian-96, Mexico-94
Maersk Darwin		Gbr	1996	51,938	60,348	294	32	23	CC	ex ANL Indonesia-03, Indonesia-02, APL Indonesia-01
Maersk Doha *		Gbr	1996	51,938	60,348	294	32	23	CC	ex P&O Nedlloyd Caribbean-03, Germany-02, APL Germany-02, OOCL Germany-98
Maersk Dundee		Nld	1996	51,931	60,348	294	32	23	CC	ex France-03, APL France-01, OOCL France-98
Marine Phoenix		Gbr	1994	7,313	7,957	134	21	19	R	ex Amber Lily-97
Moorgate		Pan	1990	25,965	45,875	190	31	13	B	ex Federal Kumano-97
Morning Cloud		Pan	1983	36,304	66,755	230	32	15	B	ex Morning Camellia-90, Panamax Neptune-86
Mulungisi		Lbr	1984	9,057	9,340	149	21	19	R	ex Koala-95
Noa		Pan	1985	26,014	43,590	186	30	14	B	ex Soarer Adonis-97
Northgate		Pan	1984	93,049	179,422	299	48	13	B	ex Kii Maru-97
Northumberland		Gbr	1990	11,822	16,137	158	21	15	Lpg	ex Nelly Maersk-03, Reinanger-98, Anne-Laure-97, Sloka-93
Nuevo Leon		Pan	1994	30,971	36,887	202	32	20	CC	ex TMM Nuevo Leon-03, Nuevo Leon-00
P&O Nedlloyd Pinta		Gbr	1994	30,971	36,887	202	32	20	CC	ex Contship Inspiration-02, TMM Yucatan-01, Yucatan-00
P&O Nedlloyd Xiamen		Lbr	1991	36,627	44,006	242	32	22	CC	ex Choyang World-01
Pacific Quest		Lbr	1983	31,403	32,631	218	32	21	CC	ex Richmond Bridge-98, Hyundai Portland-97, Maersk Rotterdam-94, Richmond Bridge-93
Peggy Dow		Ant	1985	11,335	10,570	155	23	23	R	
Regents Park		Gbr	1984	15,163	23,169	171	24	15	T	ex Lacerta-96, R.F. Potomac-94, Mercantil Parati-91, Jacuhy-88
Richmond Park		Lbr	1984	15,163	23,814	171	24	15	T	ex Tamara I-96, R.F. Carioca-93, Mercantil Cabo Frio-92, Jutahy-88
River Phoenix		Gbr	1993	7,313	8,044	134	21	19	R	ex Clover Moon-99, Dover Phoenix-97
Sandra Azul *		Gbr	1994	60,117	63,163	300	37	23	CC	ex NYK Altair-01
Sandra Blanca		Gbr	1995	60,117	63,014	300	37	23	CC	ex NYK Vega-01
Santa Barbara		Lbr	1992	43,213	39,402	253	32	23	CC	ex NYK Surfwind-99
Santa Cruz *		Gbr	1991	43,209	38,970	252	32	23	CC	ex NYK Sunrise-99
Santa Monica		Lbr	1991	43,213	39,376	253	32	23	CC	ex NYK Seabreeze-99
Sea Phoenix		Pan	1992	7,303	8,056	134	21	19	R	ex Amber Cherry-96
Seagate		Pan	1989	17,590	28,836	170	27	14	C	ex Alabama Rainbow-01
Shetland		Iom	1981	14,102	18,270	153	25	17	Lpg	ex Maersk Shetland-01, Svendborg Maersk-94

Name	Eng	Flag	Year	GRT	DWT	Loa	Bm	Kts	Type	Former names
Silvergate		Pan	1987	37,025	68,158	225	32	14	B	ex Glory Hope-97
Somerset		Iom	1981	14,046	18,270	153	25	17	Lpg	ex Maersk Somerset-01, Sally Maersk-93
Southgate		Lbr	1982	15,274	25,417	161	25	14	B	ex Menina Elisa-93, Oriental Swan-89
Springwood		Lbr	1984	22,009	37,694	188	28	14	B	ex Spring Hawk-93, Sanko Hawk-86
Stafford		Iom	1984	14,102	18,270	153	25	17	Lpg	ex Maersk Stafford-01, Sine Maersk-93, Olga Maersk-92
Stonegate		Lbr	1984	107,083	187,011	305	51	13	B	ex Sunny Ocean-98, River Star-97
Suffolk		Iom	1984	14,102	18,270	153	25	17	Lpg	ex Maersk Suffolk-01, Sofie Maersk-93, Oluf Maersk-92
Summer Phoenix *		Gbr	1993	7,326	8,041	134	21	19	R	ex Spring Phoenix-01, Windward Phoenix-99
Surrey		Iom	1982	14,102	18,270	153	25	17	Lpg	ex Maersk Surrey-01, Svend Maersk-93
Sussex		Iom	1981	14,102	18,270	153	25	17	Lpg	ex Maersk Sussex-01, Susan Maersk-92
Tiger Bridge		Lbr	1994	16,708	24,444	183	28	19	CC	ex Libra Australia II-02, Libra Australia-00
Tiger Shark		Pan	1991	17,156	22,219	186	28	18	CC	ex Recife-01, Pacific Vista-98, Tokyo Bridge-98,
Tineke		Ant	1984	11,335	10,510	155	23	23	R	
TMM Sonora		Gbr	1994	30,971	36,887	202	32	21	CC	ex Houston Express-00, Sonora -99
Ural Mountains		Lbr	1984	8,063	8,238	142	20	18	R	ex Mistrau-95
Ville d'Antares		Gbr	1997	40,400	49,000	259	32	23	CC	
Ville de Tanya		Gbr	1998	40,480	49,238	259	32	23	CC	
Ville de Virgo		Gib	1997	40,400	49,238	259	32	23	CC	
White Mountain		Lbr	1983	6,533	8,160	137	20	17	R	ex Iceland Rex-94

newbuildings: four 45,000 grt vehicle carriers from Chinese builder.

* managed by Zodiac Maritime Agencies Ltd., UK, who also have 50% interest in Associated Bulk Carriers

Zim Israel Navigation Co. Ltd./Israel

Funnel: White with seven gold stars (four above three) between two blue bands.
Hull: White or grey with green boot-topping, or black with white 'ZIM' and red boot-topping.

Name	Eng	Flag	Year	GRT	DWT	Loa	Bm	Kts	Type	Former names
Blue Sky		Lbr	1983	93,052	166,013	290	47	15	B	ex Hadera-03
Zim America		Isr	1990	37,209	47,230	236	32	21	CC	
Zim Asia		Isr	1996	41,507	45,850	254	32	21	CC	
Zim Atlantic		Isr	1996	41,507	45,850	254	32	21	CC	
Zim Barcelona		Mlt	2004	53,450	54,740	294	32	24	CC	
Zim Britain †		Gbr	1978	14,050	15,270	157	25	18	CC	ex MSC Chiwan-99, Ratana Pailin-97, ACX Jasmin-94, TSK Melody-91, Korean Senator-89, Democracy-88, Durga Felixstowe-87, TFL Democracy-86
Zim Canada		Isr	1990	37,209	47,230	236	32	21	CC	
Zim Chicago ‡		Mlt	1985	37,814	53,726	243	32	19	CC	ex Zim Venezia II-02, Alma A-01, Houston-00, Houston Express-97, Sea Premier-94, CGM Paris-94, Maersk Tacoma-88, C. R. Paris-87
Zim China		Isr	1997	41,200	46,250	254	32	21	CC	
Zim Europa		Isr	1997	41,507	45,850	254	32	21	CC	
Zim Hong Kong		Isr	1992	37,209	47,230	236	32	21	CC	
Zim Iberia		Isr	1998	41,507	46,350	254	32	21	CC	
Zim Israel		Isr	1992	37,209	47,230	236	32	22	CC	
Zim Italia		Isr	1991	37,209	47,230	236	32	21	CC	
Zim Jamaica		Isr	1997	41,507	45,850	254	32	21	CC	
Zim Japan		Isr	1991	37,209	47,230	236	32	21	CC	
Zim Korea		Isr	1991	37,209	47,230	236	32	21	CC	
Zim Panama		Gbr	2002	53,453	55,000	294	32	24	CC	
Zim Pacific		Isr	1996	41,507	45,850	254	32	21	CC	
Zim U.S.A.		Isr	1997	41,200	46,250	254	32	21	CC	

48.9% owned by Ofer Bros. controlled Israel Corporation, 48.6% owned by Government of Israel.

† owned by Ciel Shipmanagement SA, ‡ by Goldenport Shipmanagement Ltd., both Greece

See other chartered ships with 'Zim' prefix in index.

Reederei Claus-Peter Offen GmbH & Co.   Germany

Funnel: Black with white Maltese Cross on broad blue band edged with narrow white bands, or charterers colours.
Hull: Black, light grey or red with red boot-topping.

Name	Eng	Flag	Year	GRT	DWT	Loa	Bm	Kts	Type	Former names
Canmar Promise		Lbr	1997	21,531	30,202	182	30	20	CC	ex Santa Giorgina-03, P&O Nedlloyd Rio Grande-03, Santa Giorgina-97
Columbus New Zealand		Lbr	2002	45,200	52,800	281	32	25	CC	ex P&O Nedlloyd Resolution-02, Santa Rosanna-02

Ofer Brothers (SAMAMA). KENWOOD PARK. *N. Kemps.*

Ofer Brothers (SAMAMA). SHETLAND. *Hans Kraijenbosch.*

Ofer Brothers (SAMAMA). URAL MOUNTAINS. *J. M. Kakebeeke.*

Name	Eng	Flag	Year	GRT	DWT	Loa	Bm	Kts	Type	Former names
Delmas Bourgainville		Deu	1994	21,054	29,610	182	29	20	CC	ex P&O Nedlloyd Hawkes Bay-03, P&O Nedlloyd Durban-02, Nedlloyd van Nassau-99, Santa Maddalena-95
Maersk Abidjan		Lbr	1995	15,859	20,156	167	28	19	CC	ex San Cristobal-01, Lykes Hawk-00, San Cristobal-99, CGM Saint Exupery-98, Equinox-97, San Cristobal-95
Maersk Accra		Lbr	1993	15,778	20,326	166	28	19	CC	ex San Isidro-01, P&O Nedlloyd Lome-00 San Isidro-98
Maersk Apapa		Lbr	1996	15,859	20,200	167	28	19	CC	ex San Francisco-01, Lykes Raven-00, Ivaran Raven-99, San Francisco-98, Contship Brasil-97, Francsico-96, San Francisco-96
Mercosul Palometa		Lbr	1993	15,778	20,278	167	28	19	CC	ex P&O Nedlloyd Zanzibar-01, San Vicente-99, CGM Santos Dumont-98, San Vicente-97
OOCL Korea		Lbr	2001	66,500	67,796	277	40	24	CC	l/a Santa Victoria
OOCL Thailand		Lbr	2002	65,289	67,644	277	40	24	CC	l/a Santa Virginia
P&O Nedlloyd Abidjan		Lbr	2000	25,294	32,391	207	30	22	CC	ex MOL San Paulo-02, P&O Nedlloyd Abidjan-01, Santa Alexandra-00
P&O Nedlloyd Accra		Lbr	2000	25,294	32,321	207	30	22	CC	ex MOL Salvador-02, P&O Nedlloyd Accra-01, Santa Arabella-00
P&O Nedlloyd Agulhas		Lbr	2000	25,294	32,308	207	30	22	CC	ex MOL Paraguay-02, P&O Nedlloyd Agulhas-01, Santa Annabella-00
P&O Nedlloyd Algoa		Lbr	2000	25,294	32,323	207	30	22	CC	ex MOL Parana-02, P&O Nedlloyd Algoa-01, l/a Santa Adriana
P&O Nedlloyd Apapa		Lbr	2001	25,294	32,299	207	30	22	CC	ex MOL Santos-02, P&O Nedlloyd Apapa-01, l/a Santa Alina
P&O Nedlloyd Bantam		Lbr	2001	37,113	39,300	243	32	23	CC	l/a Santa Cristina
P&O Nedlloyd Botany		Lbr	2002	45,803	53,452	281	32	25	CC	l/a Santa Ricarda
P&O Nedlloyd Chusan		Lbr	2001	37,113	40,018	243	32	23	CC	ex Santa Celina-01
P&O Nedlloyd Dejima		Lbr	2001	37,113	40,102	243	32	23	CC	l/a Santa Catalina
P&O Nedlloyd Encounter		Lbr	2002	45,803	53,410	281	32	25	CC	l/a Santa Rebecca
P&O Nedlloyd Mairangi		Lbr	2002	45,803	53,115	281	32	25	CC	ex Santa Rufina-02
P&O Nedlloyd Olinda		Lbr	2000	37,113	40,018	243	32	23	CC	l/a Santa Carlotta
P&O Nedlloyd Palliser		Lbr	2002	45,803	53,081	281	32	25	CC	l/a Santa Romana
P&O Nedlloyd Remuera		Lbr	2002	45,803	53,328	281	32	25	CC	l/a Santa Rafaela
P&O Nedlloyd Salsa		Lbr	1997	21,531	30,173	182	30	20	CC	ex Santa Giannina-02, P&O Nedlloyd Kingston-02, l/a Santa Giannina
P&O Nedlloyd Samba		Lbr	1991	21,049	30,007	182	28	18	CC	ex Santa Monica I-03, P&O Nedlloyd Dubai-00, P&O Nedlloyd van Nes-99, Nedlloyd van Nes-98, Genoa Senator-95, Santa Monica-94
P&O Nedlloyd Seattle		Lbr	1995	36,028	45,170	246	32	24	CC	ex Chesapeake Bay-98, Santa Ana-95
P&O Nedlloyd Singapore		Lbr	1999	21,583	30,135	183	30	20	CC	l/dn Santa Fabiola
P&O Nedlloyd Surat		Lbr	2000	37,113	40,125	243	32	22	CC	ex Santa Carolina-01
P&O Nedlloyd Tema		Lbr	1996	15,859	20,219	167	28	19	CC	ex San Fernando-02, Lykes Condor-01, Ivaran Condor-99, San Fernando-98
Puerto Limon		Lbr	1996	15,859	20,058	167	28	19	CC	ex San Felipe-02, Columbus Mexico-01, Lykes Eagle-00, Ivaran Eagle-99, San Felipe-98
San Clemente		Lbr	1994	15,778	20,219	167	28	19	CC	ex Cielo del Chile-03, San Clemente-01, Columbus Bahia-01, San Clemente-99
San Lorenzo		Lbr	1993	15,778	20,278	167	28	19	CC	ex Columbus Ohio-02, Altamira-00, San Lorenzo 1-98, San Lorenzo-97
Santa Elena		Lbr	1995	36,028	45,170	246	32	24	CC	ex Maersk Rotterdam-01, New York Senator-98, Santa Elena-95
Santa Federica		Lbr	1998	21,583	29,700	182	30	20	CC	ex P&O Nedlloyd Santiago-02, l/a Santa Frederica
Santa Felicita		Lbr	1999	21,583	30,135	183	30	20	CC	ex P&O Nedlloyd Seoul-02, l/dn Santa Felicita
Santa Fiorenzo		Lbr	1998	21,583	30,007	183	30	20	CC	ex P&O Nedlloyd Arica-02, l/a Santa Fiorenzo
Santa Francesca		Lbr	1998	21,583	30,029	183	30	20	CC	ex P&O Nedlloyd Sao Paulo-02, l/a Santa Francesca
Santa Giovanna		Lbr	1996	21,531	30,201	182	30	20	CC	ex P&O Nedlloyd Amazonas-01, Santa Giovanna-01, P&O Nedlloyd Amazonas-01, Nedlloyd Amazonas-99, Santa Giovanna-96
Santa Giuliana		Lbr	1996	21,531	30,201	182	30	19	CC	ex P&O Nedlloyd Orinoco-01, Nedlloyd Orinoco-99, Santa Giuliana-96
Santa Giulietta		Lbr	1997	21,531	30,252	182	30	20	CC	ex P&O Nedlloyd Parana-02, l/a Santa Giulietta
Santa Isabella		Lbr	1986	21,049	30,007	182	29	18	CC	ex P&O Nedlloyd Dammam-01, Santa Isabella-99, P&O Nedlloyd Salvador-98, Santa Isabella-97, Nedlloyd van Cloon-97, ScanDutch Helvetia-89, l/a Holsten Sea

Reederei Claus-Peter Offen. P&O NEDLLOYD CHUSAN. *Hans Kraijenbosch.*

Reederei Claus-Peter Offen. P&O NEDLLOYD PALLISER. *Hans Kraijenbosch.*

Name	Eng	Flag	Year	GRT	DWT	Loa	Bm	Kts	Type	Former names
Santa Margherita		Lbr	1994	21,054	29,744	182	29	20	CC	ex P&O Nedlloyd Caribbean-02, P&O Nedlloyd Douala-01, Cielo di Livorno-99, Santa Margherita-94
Sydney Express		Lbr	2002	45,803	53,462	281	32	25	CC	ex P&O Nedlloyd Pegasus-03, I/a Santa Roberta

newbuildings : nine 110,000 dwt (9200 teu), eleven 60,000 grt and various smaller containers ships due 2005-7 from German and Far Eastern builders.

Egon Oldendorff OHG Germany

Funnel: *Grey with white 'EO' on broad blue band, or charterers colours.*
Hull: *Grey, black or red with red boot-topping*

Name	Eng	Flag	Year	GRT	DWT	Loa	Bm	Kts	Type	Former names
Albert Oldendorff		Lbr	1984	30,150	41,600	198	32	16	BC	ex Hoegh Dyke
Alice Oldendorff *		Lbr	2000	28,747	48,000	190	32	14	B	
Alwine Oldendorff		Lbr	1990	35,350	66,088	225	32	13	B	ex Tatry-98
Anna Oldendorff *		Lbr	1994	11,263	18,355	148	23	14	B	
Antonie Oldendorff		Lbr	1999	13,781	20,427	149	23	14	BC	
Auguste Oldendorff §		Sgp	2001	11,194	18,320	148	23	14	B	
Bernhard Oldendorff †		Lbr	1991	43,332	77,548	245	32	14	Bu	ex Yeoman Burn-94
Carl Oldendorff *		Lbr	2002	19,822	31,350	172	27	14	B	
Caroline Oldendorff		Lbr	1993	13,696	22,160	157	25	13	B	
Cathrin Oldendorff *		Lbr	2003	19,883	31,643	172	27	14	B	
Christiane Oldendorff		Lbr	1996	19,354	29,516	181	26	14	Co	ex Tamaya-99, Christiane Oldendorff-96
Christoffer Oldendorff †		Lbr	1981	37,959	62,732	228	32	14	Bu	ex CSL Innovator-93, Atlantic Huron-88, Pacific Peace-86
Conrad Oldendorff §		Pan	2002	39,727	76,623	225	32	14	B	
Cora Oldendorff §		Lbr	1999	26,010	45,659	186	30	-	B	
Crowley Americas *		Lbr	1988	19,689	13,925	164	24	26	Ro	ex UND Marmara-03, Tjoet Nya Dhien-97, Rosa Dan-94, Caracas-93, Rosa Dan-92, Stena Dan-91, Rosa Dan-88
Dora Oldendorff §		Phl	2000	26,080	45,000	181	30	15	B	
Dorothea Oldendorff		Lbr	1993	13,696	22,145	158	25	14	B	
Dorthe Oldendorff		Lbr	1994	13,712	22,059	158	25	14	B	
Eckert Oldendorff *		Lbr	1983	18,220	29,338	162	26	13	BC	ex Texas Gal-04, Eckert Oldendorff-03, Global Asia-00, Eckert Oldendorff-99, Captain Padon-91, Hyundai No.22-89
Eduard Oldendorff *		Lbr	2001	19,882	31,640	172	27	14	B	
Edward Oldendorff		Lbr	1984	30,061	41,600	198	32	16	BC	ex Hoegh Duke-01
Edwine Oldendorff §		Sgp	2000	11,194	18,315	148	23	13	B	
Elisabeth Oldendorff		Lbr	1992	13,696	22,154	158	25	14	B	
Elise Oldendorff		Lbr	1997	13,781	20,427	149	23	14	BC	
Elsa Oldendorff *		Pan	1998	14,397	24,021	154	26	13	B	ex Stellar Kohinoor-02
Erna Oldendorff *		Lbr	1994	11,264	18,355	148	23	14	B	
Ernst Oldendorff		Lbr	1997	16,405	26,045	172	25	14	B	ex Jan Hus-98
Frederike Oldendorff §		Lbr	1997	26,586	48,224	189	31	14	B	ex Mercury Trader-03
Gebe Oldendorff *		Pan	1998	14,762	23,510	155	26	14	B	ex J. Captain Trader-02
Georgia Gal		Lbr	1983	18,220	29,364	162	26	13	BC	ex Eibe Oldendorff-04, Global America-00, Eibe Oldendorff-99, Captain Bougainville-91, Hyundai No.23-89
Gerdt Oldendorff		Mlt	1998	25,791	44,114	199	30	15	B	
Gertrude Oldendorff *		Lbr	2001	19,882	31,635	172	27	14	B	
Gisela Oldendorff		Lbr	1997	13,781	20,100	149	23	14	B	
Gitta Oldendorff		Nis	1984	30,150	41,600	198	32	16	BC	ex Hoegh Dene-01
Gretke Oldendorff		Lbr	1994	13,712	22,050	158	25	14	B	
Hans Oldendorff		Lbr	1997	17,630	28,233	181	25	15	B	ex City of Newcastle-98
Hedwig Oldendorff §		Pan	2001	38,391	73,435	225	32	14	B	
Heinrich Oldendorff ¶		Lbr	2001	39,819	73,926	225	32	16	B	I/a Elbe River
Helena Oldendorff *		Lbr	1984	18,469	28,354	196	23	14	B	ex Noble River-86
Henry Oldendorff		Lbr	1998	16,405	26,031	172	25	14	B	ex Jan Zelivsky-98
Hinrich Oldendorff		Lbr	2000	19,883	31,632	172	27	14	B	
Hugo Oldendorff		Mlt	1998	25,791	44,144	199	30	14	B	
Ilsabe Oldendorff		Lbr	1996	19,354	29,512	181	26	14	Co	ex CSAV Livorno-02, Ilsabe Oldendorff-01, Cielo di Monfalcone-99, Andacollo-98, Ilsabe Oldendorff-97
Imme Oldendorff *		Lbr	1999	28,078	48,913	190	32	14	B	ex Royal Chance-03
Ingrid Oldendorff *		Lbr	1984	30,150	41,600	198	32	16	BC	ex Hoegh Drake-01
Jobst Oldendorff *		Lbr	1995	14,743	23,569	155	26	13	B	ex Tinker Bell-03

Egon Oldendorff. ALWINE OLDENDORFF. *Hans Kraijenbosch.*

Egon Oldendorff. MATHILDE OLDENDORFF. *J. M. Kakebeeke.*

Name	Eng	Flag	Year	GRT	DWT	Loa	Bm	Kts	Type	Former names
Julia Oldendorff *		Lbr	2000	13,066	20,567	153	24	17	Co	
Lily Oldendorff *		Lbr	2003	19,883	31,350	172	27	14	B	
Linda Oldendorff		Lbr	1995	39,279	75,275	225	32	14	B	
Lucas Oldendorff *		Lbr	2002	19,882	31,643	172	27	14	B	
Lucy Oldendorff		Lbr	1992	13,696	22,160	157	25	14	B	
Ludolf Oldendorff §		Phl	2000	26,010	45,578	186	30	-	B	
Lydia Oldendorff *		Lbr	1998	13,066	20,526	153	24	17	Co	
Margret Oldendorff		Lbr	1992	17,726	24,190	177	27	18	CC	ex NDS Proteus-03, MSC Damas-03, Margret Oldendorff-02, CCNI Austral-99
Mathilde Oldendorff		Lbr	1999	13,781	20,427	149	23	14	BC	
Max Oldebdorff §		Lbr	1997	26,586	48,225	189	31	14	B	ex Million Trader-03
May Oldendorff *		Lbr	1997	26,040	45,205	188	31	14	B	ex Houyu-03
Mina Oldendorff §		Phl	1999	26,010	45,630	186	30	-	B	
MSC Maracaibo *		Lbr	1999	13,066	20,567	153	24	17	Co	ex Georg Oldendorff-03, Libra Ecuador-02, CSAV Estambul-00, Georg Oldendorff-00
Paul Oldendorff §		Hkg	2003	21,185	35,117	178	28	14	B	
Regina Oldendorff *		Lbr	1986	18,121	28,031	195	23	16	B	ex St. Croix-86
Rio Branco		Lbr	1998	13,066	20,501	153	24	17	Co	ex Julius Oldendorff-03, P&O Nedlloyd Djibouti-00, I/a Julius Oldendorff
Rio Grande *		Lbr	1998	13,066	20,567	153	24	17	Co	ex Friedrich Oldendorff-03, Cielo del Peru-01, Friedrich Oldendorff-01
Rio Negro *		Lbr	1999	13,066	20,567	153	24	17	Co	ex Hermann Oldendorff-03
Rio Rubio *		Lbr	1999	13,066	20,567	153	24	17	Co	ex Johann Oldendorff-02
Rixta Oldendorff		Lbr	1986	18,121	28,031	195	23	16	B	ex Manila Spirit-86
Rosanne *		Lbr	1976	32,173	22,691	206	31	21	Ro	ex Daisy-00, Euroshipping 2-97, Magnitogorsk-96
Roxanne *		Lbr	1976	32,173	21,002	206	31	21	Ro	ex Nicole-00, Kotlini-97, Komsomolsk-95
Sophie Oldendorff †		Lbr	2000	41,428	70,034	225	32	14	Bu	
Tasman Adventurer *		Atg	1992	15,901	21,679	165	26	16	Co	ex Helga Oldendorff-99, FMG Mexico-99, Helga Oldendorff-96, POL Europe-95
Tasman Discoverer *		Atg	1992	15,900	21,763	165	26	16	Co	ex Henrietta Oldendorff-99, FMG Santiago-99, Henrietta Oldendorff-96, POL Asia-95
Tasman Explorer *		Lbr	1987	17,101	22,800	187	23	16	Co	ex T.A.Explorer-99, Dietrich Oldendorff-89
Tasman Mariner *		Atg	1989	15,504	20,430	166	23	15	Co	ex Beate Oldendorff-00, T.A.Discoverer-99, Beate Oldendorff-91
Tasman Navigator *		Lbr	1988	15,504	20,380	182	24	16	Co	ex Maria Oldendorff-00, T.A.Adventurer-99, Maria Oldendorff-91
Tasman Voyager *		Lbr	1987	17,101	22,800	187	23	16	Co	ex Johanna Oldendorff-03, Tasman Voyager-02, T.A.Voyager-99, Johanna Oldendorff-89, Begonia-89, Johanna Oldendorff-87
Tete Oldendorff *		Lbr	2000	19,070	31,051	172	27	14	B	
Theodor Oldendorff ¶		Lbr	1999	12,192	17,786	141	23	13	B	
Trina Oldendorff *		Lbr	2000	13,066	20,500	153	24	17	Co	ex Cielo del Caribe-03, Trina Oldendorff-01
Wilhelmine Oldendorff ¶		Lbr	1999	12,192	17,786	141	23	13	B	ex Rio Topaz-03, Wilhelmine Oldendorff-02
Yeoman Brook ‡		Lbr	1991	43,332	77,548	245	32	14	B	
Zella Oldendorff		Lbr	2001	39,893	73,931	225	32	-	B	ex Trave River-01

newbuildings - two 39,900 grt 73,100 dwt bulk carriers for 2004/5 delivery from Chinese builders.
* managed by subsidiary Oldendorff Carriers GmbH & Co. KG
† operated in joint Pool with CSL Group Inc., Canada or ‡ on time charter to Foster Yeoman Ltd until 2011.
§ on time-charter from various owners (currently about 81 such vessels) or ¶ on bareboat charter from MPC with purchase option

Reederei "NORD" Klaus E. Oldendorff Ltd.   Cyprus

Funnel: Grey with white 'N' inside white ring on broad blue band or charterers colours.
Hull: Light grey with red or black boot-topping.

Name	Eng	Flag	Year	GRT	DWT	Loa	Bm	Kts	Type	Former names
Cala Palamos		Cyp	1994	14,169	20,255	165	25	19	CC	ex Nordpartner-01, Cielo del Cile-01, Nordpartner-99, San Miguel-96
Cala Palos		Cyp	2003	25,407	33,853	207	30	22	CC	ex Nordatlantic-03
Cala Pilar		Cyp	1997	16,252	22,420	179	25	19	CC	ex City of Stuttgart-02, Safmarine Inyathi-01, Nordriver-01, Pacific Eagle-01, Nordriver-00, Bogata-99, Nordriver-98
CMA CGM Colombie		Deu	1997	24,053	27,100	206	27	20	CC	ex CSAV Livorno-03, Nordhawk-02, Libra Buenos Aires-01, Zim Sao Paulo-99, Panbrasil-98, I/a Nordhawk
CMA CGM Romania		Iom	2003	25,407	33,900	207	30	22	CC	ex Nordbaltic-03

Reederei 'NORD' Klaus E. Oldendorff. NORDMILLENNIUM. *Hans Kraijenbosch.*

Schiffs. Oltmann. CIELO DI SAN FRANCISCO. *Hans Kraijenbosch.*

Name	Eng	Flag	Year	GRT	DWT	Loa	Bm	Kts	Type	Former names
Delmas Kenya		Cyp	1991	11,998	14,190	157	23	17	CC	ex Nordcliff-02, New Achiever-01, Nordcliff-00, Tui Pacific-01, Nordcliff-97, Lanka Asitha-97, Nordcliff-91
Libra Patagonia		Cyp	1997	16,252	22,330	179	25	19	CC	ex Nordcloud-03, Niver Austral-99, Nordcloud-98
Lykes Envoy		Cyp	2003	25,407	34,133	207	30	22	CC	ex Nordpacific-03
MOL Sprinter		Cyp	1996	16,264	22,386	178	25	19	CC	ex Malacca Star-03, Nordsea-01, Nordseas-01, Pacific Voyager-01, Nordsea-00, Panaustral-98, Nordsea-97
Nordbay		Cyp	1999	156,417	301,438	330	58	15	T	
Nordbeach		Cyp	1991	11,998	14,100	157	23	17	CC	ex Abidjan Star-99, Nordbeach-98, X-Press Mumbai-97, Lanka Aruna-96, Nordbeach-92
Nordcoast		Deu	1997	16,264	22,350	179	25	19	CC	ex Safmarine Nahoon-02, DAL East London-02, Nordcoast-01, Alianca Parana-00, Nordcoast-00, CSAV Buenos Aires-99, Nordcoast-97
Nordeagle		Cyp	1997	24,053	27,100	206	27	20	CC	ex Libra Houston-01, CSAV Seoul-00, Panatlantic-99, Nordeagle-97
Nordelbe		Cyp	2001	40,605	75,259	225	32	14	B	
Nordems		Cyp	2001	40,605	75,253	225	32	14	B	
Nordenergy		Cyp	2003	161,306	319,174	333	60	16	T	
Nordfalcon		Cyp	1997	24,053	27,100	206	27	20	CC	ex CSAV Taipei-01, Panamerican-99, Nordfalcon-97
Nordgulf		Cyp	1998	57,148	105,176	244	42	15	T	
Nordisle		Cyp	1998	57,148	89,999	244	42	15	T	
Nordlake		Cyp	1994	16,202	22,450	179	25	19	CC	ex CSAV Lonquimay-98, Nordlake-96
Nordlight		Cyp	1998	57,148	89,999	244	42	15	T	
Nordmark		Cyp	1998	57,148	89,999	244	42	15	T	
Nordmars		Cyp	2004	40,000	74,999	225	32	14	T	
Nordmax		Cyp	1995	39,027	72,516	225	32	14	B	
Nordmed		Cyp	2003	25,368	33,900	207	30	22	CC	
Nordmerkur		Cyp	2004	40,000	74,999	225	32	14	T	
Nordmillennium		Cyp	2000	156,417	302,000	331	58	15	T	
Nordmoritz		Cyp	1995	39,027	72,610	225	32	14	B	
Nordmosel		Cyp	2001	40,605	75,080	225	32	14	B	
Nordneptune		Cyp	2004	40,000	74,999	225	32	14	T	
Nordocean		Cyp	1998	57,148	105,170	244	42	15	T	
Nordpacific		Cyp	2003	25,368	33,900	207	30	22	CC	
Nordpol		Cyp	1994	14,619	20,275	167	25	17	CC	ex Indamex Taj-02, Abidjan Star II-00, Nordpol-99, TNX Mercury-98, Nordpol-98, San Marino-97, Nordpol-94
Nordpower		Cyp	2003	161,308	319,012	333	60	16	T	
Nordrhine		Cyp	2001	40,605	75,080	225	32	14	B	
Nordsky		Cyp	1990	11,998	14,140	157	23	17	CC	ex Peru Star-00, Nordsky-97, Alaska-96, Nordsky-92, Karawa-92, Nordsky-92
Nordstar		Cyp	1998	16,803	23,007	185	25	19	CC	ex P&O Nedlloyd Pampas-02, Nordstar-01, Niver Austral-00, Nordstar-99, CSAV Rio Uruguay-99
Nordstrand		Cyp	1993	30,526	34,079	205	32	19	CC	ex Nautic-00, Nordstrand-99, Byron Bay-98, Nordstrand-97, Med Marseilles-96, Saint Corentin-94
Nordstrength		Cyp	1998	57,148	89,999	244	42	15	T	
Nordsun		Cyp	1991	11,998	14,140	157	23	17	CC	ex Chile Star II-99, Kent Scout-98, CGM La Bourdonnaise-97, Nordsun-97, Lanka Abhaya-97, Nordsun-92
Nordtrave		Cyp	2001	40,605	75,080	225	32	14	B	
Nordvenus		Lbr	2004	40,000	74,999	225	32	14	T	
Nordweser		Cyp	2001	40,605	75,321	225	32	14	B	

newbuildings - four 40,000 grt 72,000 dwt product tankers for 2004 delivery from South Korean builder.

Fred. Olsen & Co.   Norway

Funnel: Black with red band.
Hull: Dark grey or red with red or pink boot-topping.

Name	Eng	Flag	Year	GRT	DWT	Loa	Bm	Kts	Type	Former names
Knock Allan *		Lbr	1992	78,710	145,242	274	44	14	T	
Knock Clune *		Nis	1993	78,843	147,048	274	44	14	T	
Knock Dee		Lbr	1974	63,057	128,358	256	41	16	T	ex Solva-89, Afran Wave-82, Wind Endeavour-77
Knock Dun *		Lbr	1994	78,843	147,048	274	44	14	T	
Knock Muir *		Lbr	1996	79,001	146,268	274	44	14	T	

Name	Eng	Flag	Year	GRT	DWT	Loa	Bm	Kts	Type	Former names
Knock Stocks *		Lbr	1993	78,710	145,242	274	44	14	T	
Knock Taggart		Pan	1974	69,183	140,905	270	43	16	T	ex Agamemnon-87, London Enterprise-85

*Owned by subsidiary Red Band AS, Norway (operated by First Olsen Tankers Ltd., Liberia) and * managed by V.Ships Norway AS.*

Schiffahrts. Oltmann Verwaltung GmbH   Germany

Funnel: Mainly in charterers colours.
Hull: Dark grey with red boot-topping.

Name	Flag	Year	GRT	DWT	Loa	Bm	Kts	Type	Former names
APL Brazil	Pan	2004	40,952	55,461	261	32	-	CC	
Cielo di San Francisco	Deu	1998	25,359	33,964	207	30	20	CC	ex Ute Oltmann-99
Libra Buenos Aires	Atg	2000	25,381	33,937	207	30	22	CC	CMA CGM Chili-02, JPO Aquarius-01,
Montebello	Deu	1998	25,361	33,919	207	30	21	CC	ex Anika Oltmann-99, Montebello-99, Anika Oltmann-98
Trade Rainbow	Atg	2001	25,361	33,900	207	30	22	CC	ex TCL Challenger-02, JPO Aries-01
Zim Houston III	Atg	1993	10,742	14,111	163	22	17	CC	ex Lukas-99, Kaedi-99, Kano-98, Lukas-98

newbuildings : five container ships between 25,600 grt and 60,000 grt from German and Far Eastern builders for 2004/6 delivery.

OMI Marine Services LLC   USA

Funnel: Black with large white 'O' on broad red band edged with narrow white bands.
Hull: Brown or blue with red boot-topping

Name		Flag	Year	GRT	DWT	Loa	Bm	Kts	Type	Former names
Alma		Lbr	1988	18,055	29,999	166	27	13	T	ex Palmyra-90
Amazon		Mhl	2002	28,539	47,275	183	32	-	T	
Ashley		Mhl	2001	23,217	37,270	183	27	-	T	
Bandar Ayu		Pan	1993	21,804	36,345	180	28	15	T	
Charente		Mhl	2001	23,740	35,751	183	27	-	T	
Dakota		Mhl	2002	81,270	159,435	274	48	-	T	
Delaware		Nis	2002	85,000	159,169	274	48	-	T	
Elbe		Lbr	1984	38,529	66,800	231	32	15	T	ex Mantinia-89, Urania Coulouthros-89
Fox		Mhl	2004	23,200	37,000	183	27	14	T	
Guadalupe		Mhl	2000	28,539	47,037	183	32	14	T	ex Alam Bakti-00
Hudson		Mhl	2000	81,093	152,592	274	48	-	T	ex Front Sun-03
Isere		Mhl	1999	22,848	35,406	185	27	15	T	
Loire		Mhl	2004	23,200	37,106	183	27	14	T	
Madison		Lbr	2000	23,842	35,833	183	27	14	T	ex Nina-01
Marne		Mhl	2001	23,217	37,230	183	27	-	T	l/a Ruby Star
Moselle		Mhl	2003	28,567	47,038	183	32		T	
Neches		Mhl	2000	28,539	47,052	183	32	14	T	ex Alam Bayu-00
Nile		Lbr	1981	41,471	64,716	229	32	15	T	ex Ogden Nile-84
Ohio		Mhl	2001	23,235	37,278	183	27	-	T	l/a Borak
Orontes		Mhl	2002	23,235	37,383	183	27	-	T	
Ottawa		Mhl	2003	42,771	70,296	228	32		T	
Pecos		Mhl	1998	81,565	157,406	274	48	14	T	
Potomac		Mhl	2000	81,093	152,592	274	48	-	T	ex Front Sky-03
Rhone		Mhl	2000	23,740	35,769	183	27	-	T	ex Prospero-01
Rosetta		Mhl	2003	28,567	47,037	183	32	14	T	
Sabine		Mhl	1998	81,565	157,331	274	48	14	T	
Sacramento		Mhl	1998	81,565	157,411	274	48	14	T	
San Jacinto		Mhl	2002	28,539	47,038	183	32	15	T	
Seine		Mhl	1999	22,848	35,407	185	27	15	T	
Settebello	(st)	Lbr	1983	152,374	322,446	346	57	14	T	
Shannon		Lbr	1981	18,105	28,888	187	27	14	T	ex Nordholm-96, Nina-95
Somjin		Mhl	2001	83,723	160,183	274	48	14	T	
Tamar		Mhl	2003	43,000	70,100	228	32	-	T	
Tandjung Ayu		Pan	1993	21,804	38,406	180	28	15	T	
Trinity		Lbr	2000	23,842	35,833	183	27	14	T	ex Snipe-01
Volga		Lbr	1987	41,471	59,998	229	32	15	T	ex Ogden Volga-84

*newbuildings : five 23,200 grt 37,000 dwt tankers for 2004/5 delivery (to be named **Ganges**, **Garonne**, **Saone**, **Fox** and **Tiber**)*

Name	Eng	Flag	Year	GRT	DWT	Loa	Bm	Kts	Type	Former names

Onassis Group   Monaco

Olympic Shipping and Management S.A.

Funnel: Orange, large white disc with blue/yellow pennant and five interlocking coloured rings above and below
Hull: Black with red boot-topping

Name	Eng	Flag	Year	GRT	DWT	Loa	Bm	Kts	Type	Former names
Calliroe Patronicola	Grc	1985	17,879	29,608	183	23	15	B	
Olympic Faith	Grc	1991	81,192	147,457	274	45	14	T	
Olympic Flair	Grc	1991	81,192	147,396	274	45	14	T	
Olympic Galaxy	Pan	1982	35,417	64,931	225	32	14	B	ex Ikan Bawal-86
Olympic Legacy	Grc	1996	160,129	302,789	332	58	14	T	
Olympic Legend	Grc	2003	160,083	308,500	333	60	15	T	
Olympic Liberty	Grc	2003	160,083	304,992	333	60	15	T	
Olympic Loyalty	Grc	1993	160,129	303,184	332	58	15	T	
Olympic Melody	Grc	1984	17,879	29,640	182	23	14	B	
Olympic Mentor	Grc	1984	17,879	29,693	182	23	14	B	ex Patricia R-88, Calliroe Patronicola-84
Olympic Merit	Grc	1985	17,879	29,611	182	23	14	B	
Olympic Miracle	Pan	1984	17,879	29,670	182	23	14	B	
Olympic Serenity	Grc	1991	52,127	96,733	232	42	13	T	
Olympic Spirit II	Grc	1997	52,197	96,773	232	42	13	T	
Olympic Sponsor	Grc	1994	52,196	96,547	232	42	13	T	
Olympic Symphony	Grc	1990	52,086	96,547	232	42	13	T	

newbuildings : two 82,000 grt 156,000 dwt tankers due for 2004 delivery from Japanese builder (Olympic Future and Olympic Flag)

Orient Overseas (International) Ltd.   Hong Kong (China)

Orient Overseas Container Line Ltd. (OOCL)

Funnel: Yellow with red and gold flower.
Hull: Light grey with red 'OOCL', orange with white 'OOCL' or black with red boot-topping.

Name	Eng	Flag	Year	GRT	DWT	Loa	Bm	Kts	Type	Former names
China Act *	Sgp	1995	77,135	151,688	270	43	15	B	
China Fortune *	Sgp	1992	77,096	149,402	270	43	15	B	
China Prosperity *	Sgp	1986	83,474	151,013	288	45	14	B	
OOCL Ability †	Pan	1997	16,750	24,346	183	28	19	CC	
OOCL Acclaim †	Pan	1997	16,750	23,850	183	28	18	CC	
OOCL Ambition †	Pan	1997	16,750	23,850	183	28	18	CC	
OOCL America	Hkg	1995	66,047	67,741	276	40	24	CC	
OOCL Authority †	Pan	1997	16,750	23,850	183	28	18	CC	
OOCL Belgium	Hkg	1998	39,174	40,972	245	32	21	CC	
OOCL Britain	Hkg	1996	66,046	67,958	276	40	24	CC	
OOCL California	Hkg	1995	66,046	67,765	276	40	24	CC	
OOCL Chicago	Hkg	2000	66,677	67,278	277	40	25	CC	
OOCL China	Hkg	1996	66,046	67,625	276	41	24	CC	
OOCL Envoy	Hkg	1979	37,238	39,766	251	32	25	CC	ex China Container-91 (len-82)
OOCL Exporter	Hkg	1976	41,266	41,587	275	31	22	CC	ex Oriental Chief-89 (len-82)
OOCL Fair	Hkg	1987	40,980	44,448	241	32	21	CC	ex Oriental Fair-89
OOCL Faith	Hkg	1985	40,980	44,448	241	32	21	CC	ex Veracruz-98, TMM Veracruz-97, Vera Cruz-96, OOCL Faith-96, Oriental Faith-89
OOCL Fidelity	Hkg	1987	40,980	44,477	241	32	21	CC	ex Brooklyn Bridge-91
OOCL Fortune	Hkg	1985	40,978	44,433	241	32	21	CC	ex Oriental Fortune-89
OOCL Freedom	Hkg	1985	40,978	44,452	241	32	21	CC	ex Eagle Malaysia-98, OOCL Freedom-96, Oriental Freedom-89
OOCL Friendship	Hkg	1987	41,664	45,863	241	32	22	CC	ex Anahuac-98, Eagle Anahuac-97, OOCL Friendship-96, Oriental Friendship-89
OOCL Hong Kong	Hkg	1996	66,046	67,637	276	40	24	CC	
OOCL Japan	Hkg	1995	66,046	67,752	276	40	24	CC	
OOCL Long Beach	Hkg	2003	89,097	99,508	323	43	25	CC	
OOCL Melbourne †	Hkg	2003	34,610	43,093	235	32	22	CC	
OOCL Montreal	Hkg	2003	55,994	47,840	294	32	24	CC	
OOCL Netherlands	Hkg	1997	66,016	67,700	276	40	24	CC	
OOCL Ningpo	Hkg	2004	89,000	99,500	323	43	25	CC	
OOCL Osaka †	Pan	2003	34,610	43,093	235	32	22	CC	
OOCL Rotterdam	Hkg	2004	89,097	99,500	323	43	25	CC	
OOCL San Francisco	Hkg	2000	66,677	67,286	277	40	25	CC	

OMI Marine Services. VOLGA. *F. de Vries.*

Onassis Group. OLYMPIC MENTOR. *Hans Kraijenbosch.*

Orient Overseas Container Line. OOCL NETHERLANDS. *Phil Kempsey.*

Name	Eng	Flag	Year	GRT	DWT	Loa	Bm	Kts	Type	Former names
OOCL Shenzhen		Hkg	2003	89,097	99,518	323	43	25	CC	
OOCL Singapore		Hkg	1997	66,086	67,480	276	40	24	CC	
OOCL Sydney †		Sgp	2003	34,610	43,093	235	32	22	CC	
OOCL Xiamen †		Pan	2003	34,610	43,093	235	32	22	CC	

newbuildings: ten 89,000 grt 99,500 dwt (7,700 teu) and four 66,100 dwt container ships for 2004-6 delivery from South Korean builder
* owned by subsidiary Chinese Maritime Transport Ltd., Taiwan.
† on charter from various Japanese owners or finance houses.

Associated Maritime Co. (Hong Kong) Ltd.

Name	Eng	Flag	Year	GRT	DWT	Loa	Bm	Kts	Type	Former names
New Ace		Lbr	1987	52,967	88,878	244	40	14	T	ex Atlantic Ace-92
New Alliance		Lbr	1998	56,311	106,118	241	42	14	T	
New Amber		Lbr	1987	50,272	89,601	244	40	15	T	ex Sidelia-99
New Ambition		Lbr	1987	52,967	88,761	244	40	14	T	ex Ambition-91
New Amity		Lbr	1998	56,311	106,120	241	42	14	T	
New Argosy		Lbr	1987	52,967	88,782	244	40	14	T	ex Atlantic Argosy-92
New Assurance		Lbr	1986	50,272	81,274	244	40	15	T	ex Atlantic Assurance-92
New Circassia		Pan	1999	163,346	306,009	333	58	15	T	l/a Golden Circassia
New Fortuner		Lbr	1992	78,958	146,041	277	44	14	T	
New Valor		Lbr	1992	156,317	281,598	328	57	13	T	
New Vanguard		Hkg	1998	159,423	300,058	333	60	14	T	
New Venture		Lbr	1992	156,307	291,640	328	57	13	T	
New Victory		Lbr	1993	156,307	291,613	328	57	14	T	
New Vista		Hkg	1998	159,423	300,149	333	60	14	T	
New Vitality		Lbr	1993	153,808	290,691	330	56	15	T	
Pacific Enterprise		Hkg	1996	79,542	149,363	270	44	14	B	
Pacific Navigator		Hkg	1997	85,711	165,779	288	44	-	B	
Pacific Vitality		Hkg	1996	85,711	165,794	288	45	-	B	

Subsidiary formed jointly with Ming Wah Shipping Co. Ltd, Hong Kong (China).

Overseas Shipholding Group   USA

Funnel: Blue with white 'OSG' ('S' having waves in lower part), black top.
Hull: Black with red boot-topping.

Name	Eng	Flag	Year	GRT	DWT	Loa	Bm	Kts	Type	Former names
Ania		Mhl	1994	53,341	94,847	245	42	14	T	
Beryl		Mhl	1994	53,341	93,302	245	42	14	T	
Bravery *		Mhl	1994	58,091	110,461	247	42	14	T	ex Seabravery II-02, Unisina-00
Chrismir *		Lbr	1997	81,329	159,829	280	45	-	B	
Compass 1 *		Pan	1992	52,552	97,078	247	42	14	T	ex Stena Compass-00, Hawaiian Prince-96, Seto Bride-93, Seto Bridge-92
Crown Unity *		Pan	1996	156,852	300,482	330	58	14	T	
Delphina		Mhl	1989	22,972	39,673	186	27	14	T	
Denali †		Usa	1978	94,647	188,099	290	51	14	T	ex B.T. San Diego-94
Diane *		Mhl	1987	38,241	64,140	229	32	-	T	
Eclipse		Mhl	1989	78,244	147,500	268	43	-	T	ex Ania-93
Eliane		Mhl	1994	53,341	94,813	245	42	14	T	
Equatorial Lion *		Mhl	1997	156,880	273,539	330	58	15	T	
Kenai †	(st)	Usa	1979	64,329	123,114	265	42	17	T	
Koto Queen ††		Pan	2001	16,963	28,492	169	27	14	B	
Majestic Unity *		Pan	1996	156,852	300,549	330	58	14	T	
Marine Columbia †		Usa	1974	67,856	138,698	271	44	16	T	ex OMI Columbia-98, Ogden Columbia-85, Arkas-83, Susanne Onstad-80
Mary Ann *		Mhl	1986	38,241	64,239	229	32	14	T	l/a Joyce
Matilde *		Mhl	1997	81,329	160,013	280	45	-	B	
Meridian Lion ‡		Mhl	1997	156,880	300,349	330	58	15	T	
Neptune		Mhl	1989	22,946	40,085	186	27	14	T	
Nordvind ††		Pan	2002	29,980	53,553	190	32	-	B	
Odin **	(me)	Bhs	2001	65,676	96,900	265	43	15	T	ex Navion Odin-03
Olympia *		Lbr	1990	144,193	258,076	326	57	14	T	
Overseas Ann *		Mhl	2001	157,883	309,327	335	58	15	T	
Overseas Boston †		Usa	1974	61,212	122,753	261	41	16	T	ex Seatiger-81
Overseas Cathy		Mhl	2004	62,371	112,700	250	44	14	T	
Overseas Chicago †	(st)	Usa	1977	44,869	90,638	273	32	16	T	
Overseas Chris *		Mhl	2001	157,883	308,700	335	58	15	T	
Overseas Donna *		Mhl	2000	157,883	309,498	335	58	15	T	
Overseas Fran		Mhl	2001	62,385	112,700	250	44	14	T	

Name	Eng	Flag	Year	GRT	DWT	Loa	Bm	Kts	Type	Former names
Overseas Harriette		Usa	1977	15,531	25,515	173	23	15	B	
Overseas Josefa Camejo		Mhl	2001	62,385	112,200	250	44	14	T	
Overseas Joyce		Usa	1987	48,017	16,141	269	42	16	V	
Overseas Marilyn		Usa	1978	15,531	25,515	173	23	15	B	
Overseas Mulan *		Mhl	2002	161,233	319,029	333	60	16	T	
Overseas New Orleans		Usa	1983	24,816	43,644	201	27	15	T	ex Exxon Yorktown-89, Hunter Armistead-84
Overseas New York †	(st)	Usa	1977	44,869	91,843	273	32	16	T	
Overseas Philadelphia		Usa	1982	21,446	43,648	201	27	14	T	ex Exxon Princeton-89, Eileen Ingram-84
Overseas Portland *		Mhl	2001	62,385	112,700	250	44	14	T	
Overseas Rosalyn *		Mhl	2003	161,233	291,850	333	60	15	T	
Overseas Shirley		Mhl	2001	62,385	112,056	250	44	14	T	
Overseas Sophie		Mhl	2003	62,371	112,700	250	44	14	T	
Overseas Washington †	(st)	Usa	1978	44,906	91,967	273	32	16	T	
Pacific Ruby *		Mhl	1994	53,830	84,999	247	42	15	T	ex Burwain Electra-95
Pacific Sapphire *		Mhl	1994	53,830	96,173	247	42	15	T	ex Burwain Helena-95
Polystar **		Nis	1994	77,697	151,300	270	43	14	B	
Prince William Sound †	(st)	Usa	1975	64,340	123,936	268	41	17	T	
Raphael *		Mhl	2000	157,883	308,700	335	58	15	T	
Rebecca		Mhl	1994	53,341	94,872	245	42	14	T	
Regal Unity		Mhl	1997	164,371	309,966	330	58	16	T	
Sovereign Unity		Mhl	1996	164,371	309,892	330	58	16	T	
Tanabe *		Bhs	2002	159,383	298,561	333	60	16	T	
Tonsina †		Usa	1978	64,329	122,805	265	42	17	T	
Traveller **		Nor	1978	63,294	127,545	264	41	16	T	ex Polytraveller-03
Uranus		Mhl	1988	22,046	39,451	186	27	14	T	
Vega		Mhl	1989	22,972	39,710	186	27	14	T	

owned by OSG Ship Management Inc.(managed by North American Ship Agencies Inc.), * by OSG Ship Management (UK) Ltd., UK or ** managed by OSG Ship Management, Norway. † managed by Alaska Tanker Co. LLC, †† by Shoei Kisen Kaisha Ltd., Japan

‡ on charter from German finance house and managed by Columbia Shipmanagement (Deutschland) GmbH

OSG owns 51% of Rasmussen Ship Management, Norway. See also Navion ASA (under Teekay)

Royal P&O Nedlloyd N.V. Netherlands

Funnel: Blue with orange band.

Hull: Black, blue or grey with white 'P&O Nedlloyd', red or blue boot-topping.

Name	Eng	Flag	Year	GRT	DWT	Loa	Bm	Kts	Type	Former names
Arafura		Gbr	1991	37,902	44,541	241	32	18	CC	
City of Cape Town	(2)	Gbr	1977	52,055	47,196	259	32	23	CC	ex Table Bay-96, Tolaga Bay-91, Table Bay-82, Barcelona-81, Table Bay-79
Colombo Bay		Gbr	1995	50,350	59,093	292	32	22	CC	
Genua Express *		Bhs	1982	32,114	32,841	211	32	19	CC	ex Nedlloyd Colombo-03
Heemskerck **	(2)	Nld	1978	51,982	49,730	259	32	23	CC	ex Transvaal-87
Jervis Bay		Gbr	1992	50,235	59,093	292	32	22	CC	
Nedlloyd Africa *		Nld	1992	48,508	50,792	266	32	21	CC	
Nedlloyd America *		Nld	1992	48,508	50,620	266	32	21	CC	
Nedlloyd Asia *		Nld	1991	48,508	50,620	266	32	21	CC	
Nedlloyd Clarence *		Nld	1983	33,405	38,351	210	32	18	CC	ex Ibn Bajjah-97, Nedlloyd Clarence-95, Algeciras Bay-94, Ibn Bajjah-94, Nedlloyd Clarence-91, Clarence-88, Nedlloyd Clarence-86
Nedlloyd Clement *		Nld	1983	33,405	37,581	210	32	19	CC	ex Clement-88, Nedlloyd Clement-86
Nedlloyd Europa *		Nld	1991	48,508	50,792	266	32	21	CC	
Nedlloyd Hongkong *		Nld	1994	56,248	55,238	279	38	23	CC	
Nedlloyd Honshu *		Nld	1995	56,248	55,238	279	38	24	CC	
Nedlloyd Oceania *		Nld	1992	48,508	50,620	266	32	21	CC	
Newport Bay		Gbr	1993	50,350	59,093	292	32	22	CC	
Oriental Bay §		Gbr	1989	50,538	59,285	291	32	23	CC	
P&O Nedlloyd Adelaide *	(2)	Bhs	1977	52,007	49,262	259	32	23	CC	ex Aramac-00, Nedlloyd Houtman-98, Largs Bay-90, Nedlloyd Houtman-86, Largs Bay-82, Nedlloyd Houtman-80
P&O Nedlloyd Adriana †		Lbr	2003	26,833	34,567	210	30	21	CC	ex Adriana Star-03
P&O Nedlloyd Auckland *		Nld	1999	31,207	38,400	210	32	22	CC	
P&O Nedlloyd Barentsz *		Nld	2000	66,526	67,785	278	40	25	CC	
P&O Nedlloyd Barossa Valley ¶		Cyp	2002	27,093	34,638	210	30	22	CC	ex P&O Nedlloyd Barossa-02, I/a Kynouria

Name	Eng	Flag	Year	GRT	DWT	Loa	Bm	Kts	Type	Former names
P&O Nedlloyd Brisbane		Nld	1985	37,814	53,726	243	32	20	CC	ex Nedlloyd Tokyo-97, Raleigh Bay-96, Sea Cavalier-94, Nedlloyd Tokyo-94, Maersk Toyko-90, C.R.Toyko-87
P&O Nedlloyd Buenos Aires *		Nld	1984	23,790	29,730	183	31	17	CC	ex Nedlloyd van Noort-98
P&O Nedlloyd Cook		Gbr	2001	80,654	83,370	300	43	24	CC	
P&O Nedlloyd Drake		Gbr	2000	66,590	67,500	278	40	25	CC	
P&O Nedlloyd Genoa		Mhl	1998	31,333	37,845	210	32	22	CC	
P&O Nedlloyd Houston *		Nld	1983	23,930	30,040	183	31	17	CC	ex Nedlloyd van Neck-98
P&O Nedlloyd Houtman *		Nld	2001	80,654	88,967	300	43	24	CC	
P&O Nedlloyd Hudson		Nld	2000	66,526	67,900	278	40	25	CC	
P&O Nedlloyd Jakarta *		Nld	1998	31,333	38,170	210	32	22	CC	
P&O Nedlloyd Juliana †		Lbr	2003	26,833	34,315	210	30	22	CC	ex Juliana Star-03
P&O Nedlloyd Kobe		Gbr	1998	80,600	82,700	300	43	24	CC	
P&O Nedlloyd Kowloon *		Nld	1998	80,600	82,700	300	43	24	CC	
P&O Nedlloyd Los Angeles *		Bhs	1980	30,175	23,678	206	31	21	CC	ex Nedlloyd Zeelandia-98, Zeelandia-86, Java Winds-84, Nedlloyd Zeelandia-83, Benattow-82, Zeelandia-80
P&O Nedlloyd Marita		Lbr	2003	40,000	32,000	210	30	21	CC	ex Marita Star-04
P&O Nedlloyd Marseille		Gbr	1998	31,333	37,845	210	32	19	CC	
P&O Nedlloyd Mercator *		Nld	2000	66,526	67,785	278	40	25	CC	
P&O Nedlloyd Nina †		Gbr	1981	31,207	30,684	200	32	22	CC	ex P&O Nedlloyd Malacca-02, P&O Nedlloyd Khaleej-00, P&O Nedlloyd Piraeus-00, Asia Star-99, Maersk Hakata-99, Choyang Sydney-98, Singapore Express-96, Neptune Lazuli-94, Gebe Oldendorff-93, Tadeusz Kosciuszko-92
P&O Nedlloyd Pessoa		Atg	2001	16,803	22,967	185	25	20	CC	ex P&O Nedlloyd Lagos-02, I/a Gloria
P&O Nedlloyd Regina †		Lbr	2004	40,000	32,000	210	32	19	CC	I/dn Regina Star
P&O Nedlloyd Rotterdam		Nld	1998	80,942	82,700	300	43	24	CC	
P&O Nedlloyd Shackleton		Gbr	2001	80,654	87,343	300	43	24	CC	
P&O Nedlloyd Southampton *		Gbr	1998	80,942	82,702	300	43	24	CC	
P&O Nedlloyd Stuyvesant *		Nld	2001	80,654	87,343	300	43	24	CC	
P&O Nedlloyd Sydney *		Nld	1998	31,333	38,400	210	32	22	CC	
P&O Nedlloyd Taranaki †		Gbr	1981	30,080	27,930	200	32	20	Ro	ex Australia Star-99, Pyrmont Bridge-96, Heinrich Oldendorff-93, Kazimierz Pulaski-92
P&O Nedlloyd Tasman		Gbr	1999	66,526	67,900	278	40	24	CC	
P&O Nedlloyd Valentina †		Lbr	2004	40,000	32,000	210	32	19	CC	I/dn Valentina Star
P&O Nedlloyd Veracruz *		Nld	1984	23,790	29,730	183	31	18	CC	ex Nedlloyd van Diemen-98
Peninsular Bay		Gbr	1989	50,538	59,285	290	32	23	CC	
Providence Bay		Gbr	1994	50,350	59,093	292	32	22	CC	ex Shenzen Bay-94
Repulse Bay		Gbr	1992	50,350	59,093	292	32	22	CC	
Shenzen Bay		Gbr	1994	50,350	59,093	292	32	22	CC	
Singapore Bay		Gbr	1993	50,350	59,093	292	32	23	CC	

newbuildings - eight 75,000 grt (**Manet Star**, **Michelangelo Star**, **Miro Star**, **Mordrian Star** + 4 others) and four 26,700 grt (**Rio Taku**, **Rio Telsin**, **Rio Thelson**, **Rio Thompson**) container ships for 2004-7 delivery to German subsidiary Blue Star Reederei.
Controlled by Koninklijke Nedlloyd Groep NV with 25% shareholding by P&O Steam Navigation Co.
* owned by subsidiaries P&O Nedlloyd BV, Netherlands or † by Blue Star Line Ltd. or Blue Star Ship Management Ltd, both UK.
** managed for Scheepvaart Maats. Noordkaap, Netherlands ‡ chartered from Danz und Tietjens KG, (managed by BBC - Burger Bereederungs Contor GmbH), both Germany, ¶ from Efshipping Co. SA, Greece or § from Zodiac Maritime Agencies Ltd., UK (see Ofer Bros.)
Also see other chartered ships with 'P&O Nedlloyd' or 'Nedlloyd' prefixes in index.

Farrell Mediterranean Express/USA

Argonaut	(st)	Usa	1979	17,902	16,401	186	24	20	CC	
Endeavor		Usa	1991	23,953	31,829	181	31	18	CC	ex Ibn Khaldoun-97, China Sea-94, CMB Drive-91
Endurance		Usa	1991	23,953	31,829	181	31	18	CC	ex Ibn Jubayr-97, I/a CMB Dolphin
Enterprise		Usa	1992	23,953	31,829	181	31	18	CC	ex Ibn Zuhr-97, CMB Dawn-92

Papachristidis Ltd.   UK

Funnel: Blue with broad above narrow blue bands, interupted by blue 'FBP' within blue ring on white disc.
Hull: White with red boot-topping.

Hellespont Alhanbra *		Mhl	2001	234,006	441,893	380	68	16	T	
Hellespont Fairfax		Grc	2002	234,006	442,470	380	68	16	T	
Hellespont Metropolis *		Grc	2002	234,006	441,893	380	68	16	T	
Hellespont Tara		Mhl	2002	234,006	442,000	380	68	16	T	

managed by Hellespont Steamship Corp., Greece anf * ordered jointly with Loews Corp.(49%)

Overseas Shipholding Group. ODIN. *Hans Kraijenbosch.*

Royal P&O Nedlloyd. P&O NEDLLOYD BAROSSA VALLEY. *Hans Kraijenbosch.*

Royal P&O Nedlloyd. P&O NEDLLOYD JAKARTA. *Phil Kempsey.*

Polish Ocean Lines (Polskie Linie Oceaniczne)   Poland

Chinese-Polish Joint Stock Shipping Co. (Chinsko-Polskie Towarzystwo Okretowe SA)

Funnel: *Cream with cream 'C' and white 'P' on broad red band, narrow black top.*
Hull: *Grey with white 'CHIPOLBROK', green boot-topping.*

Name	Eng	Flag	Year	GRT	DWT	Loa	Bm	Kts	Type	Former names
B. Prus		Cyp	1979	16,869	24,400	171	25	17	Co	ex Concordia Sun-87, Hoegh Sun-84, Costa Mediterranea-83, Concordia Sun-82
Carnival		Mlt	1977	18,772	27,739	171	26	17	Co	ex Cai Lun-91, Willine Tysla-86, Tysla-82
Ceynowa		Mlt	1982	14,056	15,622	157	24	16	C	
Chipolbrok Moon		Hkg	2004	24,000	27,000	200	28	-	Co	
Chipolbrok Sun		Cyp	2004	24,336	27,000	200	28	-	Co	
Chong Ming		Chn	1993	18,177	22,109	170	28	16	Co	
Chopin		Cyp	1988	13,930	18,144	159	23	15	Co	
Ever Happy		Mlt	1977	18,846	27,817	171	26	17	Co	ex Da Yu-91, Hoegh Cape-86, Tsu-85, Barber Tsu-84, Tsu-81, Thalatta-77
Hua Tuo		Chn	1983	14,163	15,753	155	23	16	C	
Jan Dlugosz		Cyp	1984	15,246	15,622	157	25	16	C	
Jia Xing		Chn	1992	18,177	22,109	170	28	16	Co	ex Bao Zheng-92
Leopold Staff		Cyp	2004	24,000	27,000	200	28	-	Co	
Li Bai		Chn	1988	13,843	18,114	159	23	15	Co	
Lu Ban		Chn	1981	14,169	16,152	155	23	16	C	
Lu Xun		Chn	1988	13,843	18,144	159	23	15	Co	
Moniuszko		Mlt	1989	13,938	18,144	159	23	15	Co	
Norwid		Mlt	1998	18,202	22,258	170	28	16	Co	
Pokoj		Cyp	1977	18,846	27,937	171	26	17	Co	ex Terrier-86, Hoegh Carrier-86, Terrier-85, Barber Terrier-84, Terrier-81
Szymanowski		Cyp	1991	18,184	22,313	170	28	16	Co	
Taixing		Hkg	1997	18,207	22,271	170	28	16	Co	
Wieniawski		Mlt	1992	18,208	22,130	170	28	16	Co	
Wladyslaw Orkan		Cyp	2003	24,336	27,000	200	28	-	Co	
Yong Xing		Mlt	1998	18,207	22,309	170	28	16	Co	

Polish Steamship Co. (Polska Zegluga Morska)   Poland

Funnel: *Black with red band between two narrow yellow bands, and shield with white letters 'PZM' and trident.*
Hull: *Black, blue or grey or (§) yellow with red boot-topping.*

Name	Eng	Flag	Year	GRT	DWT	Loa	Bm	Kts	Type	Former names
Armia Krajowa ‡		Vut	1991	41,266	73,505	229	32	14	B	
Armia Ludowa		Mlt	1987	21,458	33,640	195	25	15	B	
Balgarka		Mlt	2004	24,700	41,425	-	-	-	B	
Bataliony Chlopskie #		Pol	1988	21,460	33,618	195	25	14	B	
Daria *		Cyp	1995	25,190	41,260	186	30	14	B	ex Taria-95
Delia †		Cyp	1997	25,206	41,185	186	30	14	B	
Diana *		Cyp	1997	25,206	41,425	186	30	14	B	
Dorine *		Cyp	1998	25,065	41,488	186	30	14	B	
Gardno ††		Mhl	1980	11,632	16,753	159	22	14	B	ex Kopalnia Miechowice-93
General Grot-Rowecki		Mlt	1985	23,409	38,498	199	28	14	B	
Huta Zgoda		Pol	1974	9,117	14,176	146	21	15	B	
Ignacy Daszynski		Mlt	1988	21,437	33,639	195	25	14	B	
Irma		Cyp	2000	21,387	34,948	200	24	15	B	
Iryda		Cyp	1999	21,387	34,939	200	24	14	B	
Isa		Cyp	1999	21,387	34,939	200	24	14	B	
Isadora		Cyp	1999	21,387	34,948	200	24	14	B	
Isolda		Cyp	1999	21,959	34,949	200	24	14	B	
Jamno ††		Mhl	1980	11,632	16,733	159	22	14	B	ex Kopalnia Gottwald-93
Kaliope §		Bhs	1995	11,542	16,888	149	23	14	T	ex Fjordnes-97
Kopalnia Borynia		Mlt	1989	8,893	11,899	144	19	14	B	
Kopalnia Halemba		Mlt	1990	8,897	11,715	144	19	14	B	
Kopalnia Rydultowy		Mlt	1990	8,897	11,702	144	19	14	B	
Kopalnia Sosnowiec		Pan	1974	9,117	14,179	146	21	15	B	
Kopalnia Zofiowka		Pan	1975	9,117	14,176	147	21	15	B	
Legiony Polskie ‡		Vut	1991	41,237	73,505	229	32	14	B	
Maciej Rataj		Mlt	1985	21,531	33,750	199	25	15	B	
Major Hubal		Mlt	1985	21,531	33,725	199	25	15	B	
Mamry II ††		Mhl	1979	11,676	16,653	159	22	15	B	ex Mamry-04, Kopalnia Siemianowice-93

Papachristidis. HELLESPONT METROPOLIS. *Hans Kraijenbosch.*

Polish Ocean Lines. CARNIVAL. *J. M. Kakebeeke.*

Name	Eng	Flag	Year	GRT	DWT	Loa	Bm	Kts	Type	Former names
Mitrope		Mlt	1999	11,530	15,718	149	23	13	T	
Nida ††		Bhs	1993	9,815	13,400	143	21	14	B	ex Nidanes-99, I/a Nida
Nogat		Cyp	1999	11,848	17,064	149	23	13	B	
Odra ††		Bhs	1992	9,818	13,790	143	21	14	B	ex Odranes-99, I/a Odra
Oksywie #		Pol	1987	21,460	33,580	195	25	14	B	ex Wladyslaw Gomulka-91
Orla		Mlt	1999	11,848	17.064	149	23	14	B	
Orleta Lwowskie ‡		Vut	1991	41,238	73,505	229	32	14	B	
Penelope §		Bhs	1996	11,829	15,329	149	23	14	T	
Pilica		Mlt	1999	11,540	16,900	149	23	14	B	
Polska Walczaca ‡		Vut	1992	41,220	73,505	229	32	13	B	
Pomorze Zachodnie **		Pol	1985	16,696	26,696	180	23	14	B	
Powstaniec Listopadowy		Mlt	1985	21,531	33,767	199	25	15	B	
Powstaniec Styczniowy		Mlt	1986	21,531	33,780	195	25	14	B	
Reduta Ordona		Mlt	1978	20,357	33,490	198	24	15	B	ex Feliks Dzierzynski-90
Rega		Bhs	1995	11,542	16,880	149	23	14	C	ex Fossnes-02
Rodlo		Mlt	1985	21,531	33,742	199	25	15	B	
Rolnik		Pan	1975	9,117	14,176	146	21	15	B	
Ros ††		Mhl	1980	11,676	16,693	159	22	14	B	ex Kopalnia Myslowice-93
Solidarnosc ‡		Vut	1991	41,252	73,470	229	32	14	B	
Stanislaw Kulczynski		Mlt	1988	21,456	33,627	195	25	14	B	
Szare Szeregi ‡		Vut	1991	41,191	73,505	229	32	14	B	
Talty ††		Pan	1979	11,676	16,728	159	22	14	B	ex Kopalnia Szombierki-93
Uniwersytet Slaski		Mlt	1979	20,357	33,470	198	24	16	B	
Wadag ††		Mhl	1980	11,632	16,753	159	22	14	B	ex Kopalnia Siersza-93
Walka Mlodych		Mlt	1978	20,357	33,485	198	24	15	B	
Warta ††		Bhs	1992	9,815	13,756	144	21	12	B	ex Wartanes-99
Wigry ††		Mhl	1979	11,676	16,653	159	22	14	B	ex Kopalnia Jastrzebie-93
Wisla ††		Vut	1992	9,815	13,770	143	21	13	B	ex Wislanes-99
Ziemia Chelminska **		Pol	1984	16,699	26,642	180	23	14	B	
Ziemia Cieszynska		Mhl	1992	17,464	26,264	180	23	14	B	ex Lake Carling-03, Ziemia Cieszynska-93
Ziemia Gnieznienska **		Pol	1985	16,696	26,696	180	23	14	B	
Ziemia Gornoslaska		Mhl	1990	17,427	26,209	180	23	14	B	ex Lake Charles-03, Ziemia Gornoslaska-91
Ziemia Lodzka		Mhl	1992	17,458	26,264	180	23	14	B	ex Lake Champlain-03, Ziemia Lodzka-92
Ziemia Suwalska **		Pol	1984	16,696	26,605	180	23	14	B	
Ziemia Tarnowska **		Pol	1985	16,705	26,678	180	23	14	B	
Ziemia Zamojska **		Pol	1984	16,696	26,605	180	23	14	B	

newbuildings - four 21,500 grt 38,000 dwt bulk carriers from Chinese builder for 2005 delivery.

* owned or ** managed by Polstream Oceantramp Ltd,, † owned or †† managed by Polstream Shortramp Ltd. or § owned by Polstream Tankers # owned by Polich Shipping Company (Zogluga Polska Spolka Akcyjna) or ‡ on long term charter from Dansk Investeringsfond or K/S Difko companies, Denmark (all managed by Polstream Oceantramp Ltd.)

PowerGen plc UK

Funnel: *Green with yellow and white symbol, black top.*
Hull: *Black with red boot-topping.*

Name	Eng	Flag	Year	GRT	DWT	Loa	Bm	Kts	Type	Former names
Lord Hinton		Gbr	1986	14,201	22,447	155	25	12	B	
Sir Charles Parsons		Gbr	1985	14,201	22,530	155	25	12	B	

managed by Lothian Shipping Services (London) Ltd.

KG Projex-Schiffahrts. GmbH & Co. Germany

Funnel: *White lower half and dark blue upper part with white 'PX' between narrow pale blue wavy bands or charterers colours.*
Hull: *Blue with pale blue wavy bands on bows, red boot-topping.*

Name	Eng	Flag	Year	GRT	DWT	Loa	Bm	Kts	Type	Former names
Champion		Gbr	1998	23,897	30,416	188	30	21	CC	ex Lykes Falcon-02, CSAV Rimac-00, Mediterraneo-99, Champion-98
CSCL Barcelona		Atg	2001	30,024	36,019	208	32	22	CC	ex Bonny-01
CSCL Fos		Hkg	2001	30,024	35,977	208	32	22	CC	I/a Bosun
CSCL Genoa		Atg	2001	30,026	36,189	208	32	22	CC	ex Bravo-01
CSCL Jakarta		Hkg	2001	30,024	35,980	208	32	22	CC	I/a Bella
CSCL Kelang		Hkg	2001	30,024	36,003	208	32	22	CC	I/a Chief
CSCL Napoli		Hkg	2002	30,024	35,971	208	32	22	CC	I/a Mentor

Polish Steamship Co. ISADORA. *Hans Kraijenbosch.*

Polish Steamship Co. POLSKA WALCZACA. *F. de Vries.*

Name	Eng	Flag	Year	GRT	DWT	Loa	Bm	Kts	Type	Former names
Glory		Atg	1996	23,897	30,447	188	30	20	CC	ex Cap Vincent-01, Glory-00, Crowley Americas-99, Glory-99, Pacifico-98
Harmony		Atg	1994	16,927	21,480	168	27	19	CC	ex MSC Fado-03, P&O Nedlloyd Beirut-02, DNOL Beirut-99, UB Tiger-98, Beirut-97, Contship Egypt-95, Harmony-94
Mate	Deu		2004	30,024	36,000	208	32	22	CC	
MSC Atlas		Atg	1992	9,600	12,583	150	23	17	CC	ex OPDR Gran Canaria-02, City of Istanbul-01, Major-98, Saudi Buraydah-98, Sea-Land Colombia-97, Maersk Bogota-94, I/a Major
Noble		Atg	1992	9,601	12,583	150	23	17	CC	ex Maersk Asia Tertio-95, Noble-94, Kairo-92
P&O Nedlloyd Brunel		Gbr	1997	23,897	30,416	188	30	21	CC	ex Master I-03, Master-02, CMA CGM Paris-02, Lykes Kestrel-01, MOL Europe-00, Maersk Miami-99, I/a Master
P&O Nedlloyd Chania		Atg	1992	9,601	12,583	150	22	17	CC	ex Grand-03, OPDR Tenerife-02, Sprinter-01, Maersk Douala-99, Maersk Recife-96, Sea-Land Salvador-95, Ankara-94
Safmarine Letaba		Atg	1997	23,897	30,502	188	30	20	CC	ex Primus-02, CSAV Guayas-99, Primus-99, Sea Parana-99, Primus-97
Triumph		Atg	1994	16,915	21,478	168	27	19	CC	ex P&O Nedlloyd Everest-03, Triumph-01, P&O Nedlloyd Lagos-99, Nedlloyd Lagos-98, Nedlloyd Rio-97, I/a Triumph
Trophy		Atg	1990	24,495	31,584	182	31	18	CC	ex Choyang Trader-98, Asian Senator-97, I/a Trophy

Schiffahrtskontor Rendsburg GmbH   Germany

Funnel: Blue or charterers colours.
Hull: Black or green with red boot-topping.

Name	Eng	Flag	Year	GRT	DWT	Loa	Bm	Kts	Type	Former names
Cala Pinar del Rio		Lbr	1993	14,961	20,140	167	25	17	CC	ex Norasia Chicago-01, CSAV New York-00, Westermuhlen-00, Nedlloyd Singapore-96, Westermuhlen-93
DAL Karoo		Atg	1998	23,986	30,259	188	30	21	CC	ex Westerhamm-02, Actor-01, Westerhamm-99
P&O Nedlloyd Coleridge		Lbr	1994	15,908	22,340	168	27	20	CC	ex Westerhever-03, Maersk Durban-99, Westerhever-98, Maersk Rio Grande-97, CCNI Atacama-96, Westerhever-94
Tuscany Bridge *		Atg	1997	23,896	30,291	188	30	21	CC	ex Westerburg-03, Lykes Achiever-01, Westerburg-98, Maersk La Plata-98, Westerburg-97
Westerdeich		Lbr	1994	15,908	22,343	168	27	19	CC	ex Indamex Liberty-03, Westerdeich-02, Indamex Washington-02, Kota Serika-00, Zim Santos-99, Westerdeich-99, Zim Santos-96, Westerdelch-96, Maersk Rlo Grande-96, TSL Gallant-96, Westerdeich-94
Westerems		Lbr	1997	23,896	30,600	188	30	21	CC	ex ANL Addax-03, Westerems-02, Lykes Voyager-01, Westerems-98, Maersk Cordoba-98, Westerems-97
Westerland **		Cyp	2002	30,047	35,768	207	32	-	CC	ex Alianca Hamburgo-03
Westermoor *		Lbr	2001	30,047	35,653	208	32	-	CC	

newbuildings : one 30,123 grt container ship on order from Polish builder.
* managed for Peterson Reederei or ** Mar-Con GmbH & Co. KG.

Reederei Karl Schluter GmbH & Co. KG

Funnel: Blue with blue 'N' on broad white band, plain black or charterers colours.
Hull: Various charterers colours.

Name	Eng	Flag	Year	GRT	DWT	Loa	Bm	Kts	Type	Former names
Atlantic Castle		Atg	2001	16,807	24,765	176	23	14	B	ex Cedar-03
Cosco Norfolk		Cyp	1994	35,944	43,025	240	32	21	CC	ex Choyang Phoenix-01, Ville de Lyra-97, Northern Trust-94
MSC Bremen		Iom	1997	29,115	40,100	196	32	22	CC	ex Lykes Innovator-03, Safmarine Erebus-02, CMBT Erebus-01, Northern Vision-97
MSC China		Atg	1996	29,115	40,114	196	32	22	CC	ex Ming Fidelity-00, Hyundai Fidelity-98, Northern Valour-96
MSC Manaus		Atg	1990	24,344	31,552	182	31	18	CC	ex Kota Salam-02, German S-01, City of Haifa-01, CMA Dalian-00, German S-98, German Senator-98
MSC Rio Plata		Atg	1997	29,115	40,080	196	32	22	CC	ex Northern Vitality-02, Ming Trusty-01, Hyundai Trusty-98, I/a Northern Vitality
MSC Salvador		Atg	1997	29,115	40,080	196	32	22	CC	ex Safmarine Everest-02, CMBT Everest-01, I/a Northern Victory

PowerGen plc. SIR CHARLES PARSONS. *F. de Vries.*

Schiffs. Rendsburg. WESTERMOOR. *Hans Kraijenbosch.*

Name	Eng	Flag	Year	GRT	DWT	Loa	Bm	Kts	Type	Former names
MSC Uruguay		Atg	1996	29,115	40,087	196	32	22	CC	ex Northern Virtue-01, Hyundai Majesty-99, Northern Virtue-96
Northern Dignity		Cyp	1995	36,606	45,217	240	32	22	CC	ex Ville de Gemina-02, Ming Gemina-01, Ville de Gemina-98, Northern Dignity-95
Northern Fortune		Atg	1991	30,509	30,685	195	31	19	CC	ex Canmar Trader-03, Northern Fortune-02, Zim Ashdod I-01, OOCL Dragon-01, CMA Kawasaki-00, Northern Fortune-98, Zim Ravenna-98, Northern Fortune-97, Zim Brisbane-97, Valencia Senator-95, Northern Fortune-94, A. Abraham-94
YM Hanoi		Atg	1985	10,256	13,085	147	23	18	CC	ex Wild Eagle-04, Sinar Bitung-02, Freeport-00, Freeport Express-98, Merchant-97, Independent Merchant-97, Alpha-93, Contship America-93, Ocean America-89, Wild Eagle-88

newbuildings: two 66,700 dwt and one 31,500 dwt container ships for 2005/6 delivery.

Reederei Bertram Rickmers GmbH & Cie.   Germany

Funnel: Black with houseflag (white 'R' on red over green) on broad white band, or charterers colours.
Hull: Black, pale blue or green with red boot-topping.

Name	Eng	Flag	Year	GRT	DWT	Loa	Bm	Kts	Type	Former names
Andreas †		Lbr	1998	26,131	30,723	196	30	20	CC	ex CGM Renoir-01, I/a Andreas Rickmers
APL Mumbai		Mhl	2003	21,932	24,277	196	28	-	CC	ex Saylemoon Rickmers-04
Asta Rickmers ‡		Mhl	2001	14,278	15,315	159	26	21	CC	ex Hub Racer-01, Asta Rickmers-01
Bibi *		Cyp	1979	17,128	22,378	178	27	18	Co	
Camilla Rickmers		Mhl	1996	16,801	23,045	184	25	19	CC	ex CSAV Livorno-00, Camilla Rickmers-00, CCNI Anakena-98, Camilla Rickmers-96
Carla Rickmers ‡		Mhl	2000	14,278	15,299	159	26	21	CC	
CCNI Antofagasta §		Lbr	1999	22,817	35,466	171	31	16	Co	ex CSAV Barcelona-03, CCNI Antofagasta-02, CSAV Barcelona-02, CCNI Antofagasta-01, Contship Mexico-01, CCNI Antofagasta-99
CCNI Arauco ‡		Lbr	1999	28,148	44,593	185	32	15	Co	
CCNI Austral		Lbr	1999	22,817	35,000	171	31	17	CC	ex CSAV Genova-03, Lykes Challenger-00, I/a Marie Rickmers
CCNI Chagres ‡		Lbr	1997	28,148	45,070	185	32	15	Co	ex Anna Rickmers-98
CCNI Potrerillos ‡		Lbr	1997	28,148	45,070	185	32	15	Co	I/a Lara Rickmers
Clipper Emperor		Mhl	2000	38,878	74,381	225	32	14	B	ex Pacemperor-03
CMA CGM Licorne		Lbr	1998	16,801	23,028	185	25	19	CC	ex Fiona Rickmers-04, Libra Barcelona-03, Fiona Rickmers-02, La Hispaniola-02, Zim Soa Paulo I-01, Paranagua-99, I/a Fiona Rickmers
CMA CGM St. Laurent †		Deu	1998	10,752	14,086	163	22	16	CC	ex Laurita-02, Melbridge Pearl-99, Laurita Rickmers-98
CMA CGM St. Martin †		Mhl	1998	10,752	14,040	163	22	16	CC	ex CGM Basse-Terre-01, Lilly Rickmers-98
CSAV Atlanta		Lbr	1998	26,131	30,730	196	30	20	CC	I/a Clasen Rickmers
CSAV Itajai ‡		Mhl	1997	24,053	28,352	205	27	20	CC	ex Johan Rickmers-03, APL Chile-02, Sea Cougar-99, I/a Conti Oakland
CSAV Manzanillo		Atg	1996	16,800	22,900	184	25	19	CC	ex Pacific Challenger-01, Christa Rickmers-99, CCNI Arauco-98, Christa Rickmers-96
Deike Rickmers		Lbr	1996	16,801	23,100	184	25	19	CC	ex P&O Nedlloyd Kowie-03, Deike Rickmers-01, CSAV Genova-00, Deike Rickmers-00, Scorpio Challenger-99, Deike Rickmers-97, Panatlantic-97, I/a Deike Rickmers
Delmas Cartier		Mhl	1996	16,801	23,028	185	25	19	CC	ex Etha Rickmers-02, CSAV Tokyo-02, Zim Vancouver-01, Etha Rickmers-99, CCNI Antarctico-99, Panamerican-97, CCNI Antartico-96, Etha Rickmers-96
Direct Kea		Lbr	1998	26,131	30,726	196	30	20	CC	ex CMA CGM Cezanne-01, CGM Cezanne-99, I/a Alice Rickmers
Direct Tui		Lbr	1998	26,131	30,721	196	31	20	CC	ex Contship Washington-02, I/a Albert Rickmers
Dorothea Rickmers		Lbr	1998	16,801	23,027	184	25	19	CC	ex WAL Ulanga-03, Dorothea Rickmers-01
Elisabeth Rickmers †		Atg	1995	16,801	23,190	185	25	19	CC	ex Delmas Joinville-03, Elisabeth Rickmers-03, Pacific Discovery-01, Elisabeth Rickmers-99, CSAV Santos-97, I/a Elisabeth Rickmers
Ernst Rickmers		Mhl	2002	14,278	15,313	159	26	21	CC	
Felicitas Rickmers ‡		Mhl	1997	24,053	28,366	205	27	20	CC	ex Sea Jaguar-02, Conti Jacksonville-97

Reederei Bertram Rickmers. CCNI POTRERILLOS. *C. J. Dornom.*

Reederei Bertram Rickmers. ERNST RICKMERS. *J. M. Kakebeeke.*

Name	Eng	Flag	Year	GRT	DWT	Loa	Bm	Kts	Type	Former names
Ghana Star I		Mhl	1996	24,046	32,482	174	31	19	CC	ex Hamburgo-02, P&O Nedlloyd Ottawa-01, Superba Bridge-00, CCNI Aysen-00, Maersk Montevideo-98, CCNI Aysen-96
Helene Rickmers †		Mhl	1998	16,801	23,106	184	25	19	CC	ex Lykes Crusader-02, Helene Rickmers-01, CCNI Arica-01, Helene Rickmers-98
Jacky Rickmers		Deu	2004	22,000	24,200	196	28	-	CC	
Jock Rickmers ‡		Mhl	2001	14,278	15,273	159	26	21	CC	ex APL Magnolia-01, I/a Jock Rickmers
Leon *		Cyp	1979	17,128	22,267	178	27	18	C	ex Nacional Vitoria-96, Sonora-94, Gina Luisa-82
Mabel Rickmers		Deu	1997	10,743	14,191	163	23	17	CC	ex Kribi-98, I/a Mabel Rickmers
Madeleine Rickmers		Deu	1997	16,801	22,900	184	25	19	CC	ex Sagittarius Challenger-01, Madeleine Rickmers-97
Marfret Normandie		Lux	1993	10,778	14,069	163	22	17	CC	ex Maria Rickmers-02, Melbridge Palm-01, Maria Rickmers-98, Karawa-98, Maria Rickmers-97, Karawa-96, Maria Rickmers-95, CCNI Guayas-94, I/a Maria Rickmers
Marfret Provence		Lux	1998	26,131	30,725	196	30	19	CC	ex CGM Matisse-98, Andre Rickmers-98
Maya Rickmers		Mhl	2004	51,350	57,000	286	32	25	CC	
Merida *		Cyp	1979	17,128	22,229	178	27	19	C	ex Silvia Sofia-87
Moni Rickmers		Deu	2004	22,000	24,200	196	28	-	CC	
New Orient		Atg	1992	9,601	12,583	150	22	17	CC	ex R.C.Rickmers-99, Nedlloyd Caldera-98, Sea-Land Mexico-95, TSL Bold-94, R.C.Rickmers-92
Nina Rickmers		Deu	2004	22,000	24,200	196	28	-	CC	
Norasia Bavaria		Lbr	1997	16,801	22,900	184	25	19	CC	ex CSAV Busan-03, Zim Seattle-01, Pictor Challenger-99, Denderah Rickmers-97
Norasia Sindh		Atg	1995	16,800	22,900	185	25	19	CC	ex Rickmer Rickmers-03, Columbus Hong Kong-02, Sassandra Challenger-01, Rickmer Rickmers-00, CSAV Rosario-98, Rickmer Rickmers-95
Norasia Valparaiso		Lbr	2002	51,364	58,341	286	32	25	CC	ex Cathrine Rickmers-02
P&O Nedlloyd Mahe		Lbr	1998	11,925	14,381	150	23	18	CC	ex Marine Rickmers-02, Fanal Mariner-01, Marine Rickmers-99
Pacmonarch ‡		Mhl	2000	38,878	74,381	225	32	14	B	
Paul Rickmers		Lux	1993	10,733	14,191	163	22	17	CC	ex MSC Caribbean-03, Paul Rickmers-02, Kamina-97, Zim Argentina-96, Paul Rickmers-94
Rickmers Antwerp †		Mhl	2003	23,119	29,912	193	28	19	Co/hl	ex Cape Dart-02
Rickmers Genoa †		Lbr	2004	23,119	29,900	193	28	19	Co/hl	
Rickmers Hamburg †		Mhl	2002	23,119	29,980	193	28	19	Co/hl	
Rickmers Jakarta		Mhl	2004	23,119	29,750	193	28	19	Co/hl	ex Genoa-03
Rickmers New Orleans		Mhl	2003	23,119	30,095	193	28	19	Co/hl	
Rickmers Seoul		Mhl	2003	23,119	30,151	193	28	19	Co/hl	
Rickmers Shanghai †		Mhl	2003	23,119	30,000	193	28	19	Co/hl	
Rickmers Singapore †		Mhl	2002	23,119	30,018	193	28	19	Co/hl	
Rickmers Tokyo †		Mhl	2002	23,119	30,000	193	28	19	Co/hl	ex Cape Delgardo-02
Robert Rickmers		Mhl	2003	16,802	23,063	185	25	16	CC	ex E.R. Stettin-03
Sandy Rickmers ‡		Cyp	2002	14,290	14,901	159	26	21	CC	I/a Mirko Rickmers
Sea Puma ‡		Mhl	1998	26,125	30,738	196	30	19	CC	ex Crowley Lion-01, CSAV Boston-99, I/a Willi Rickmers
Seagreen **		Cyp	1986	13,335	16,882	158	23	15	CC	ex Celia-02, Vogtland-99, Damaskus-94, Contship Egypt-93, Vogtland-91
Sungreen **		Cyp	1987	13,335	17,088	158	23	16	CC	ex Vilma VIII-02, Havelland-99
Tete Rickmers ‡		Mhl	2000	14,278	15,317	158	26	21	CC	
Togo Star		Mhl	1996	24,046	32,482	174	31	19	CC	ex Santiago-02, CCNI Chiloe-00, Maersk Curitiba-98, CCNI Chiloe-96
Zim Caribe IV		Mhl	1997	10,743	14,099	163	22	17	CC	ex Sophie Delmas-98, Mai Rickmers-97
Zim Mexico III		Atg	1993	10,778	14,120	163	22	17	CC	ex Peter Rickmers-99, Kaiama-99, Peter Rickmers-94
Zim Sao Paulo II		Mhl	1997	16,801	22,900	185	25	19	CC	ex Ursula Rickmers-01

newbuildings : ten 55,150 grt, three 51,350 grt, four 36,000 grt, one 23,000 grt and four 17,000 grt container ships for 2004-6 delivery.
* operated by subsidiary Rickmers-Linie (Cyprus) Ltd. (managed by Technomar Shipping Inc., Greece) and § owned by Hans Carl Rickners.
** managed by Carimar, Cuba, † by Columbus Shipmanagement GmbH, Germany, ‡ by Uniteam Marine Shipping GmbH, Germany/Cyprus.

Rigel Schiffahrts GmbH & Co. KG   Germany

Funnel: Blue with black 'R' on six-pointed white star on black-edged red disc on narrower white band.
Hull: Blue with red boot-topping.

Name	Eng	Flag	Year	GRT	DWT	Loa	Bm	Kts	Type	Former names
Alsterstern		Iom	1994	11,426	17,080	161	23	15	T	

Rigel Schiffs. RHONESTERN. *F. de Vries.*

Sanko Steamship. SANKO ROBUST. *Hans Kraijenbosch.*

Name	Eng	Flag	Year	GRT	DWT	Loa	Bm	Kts	Type	Former names
Donaustern		Iom	1995	11,426	17,078	161	23	14	T	
Havelstern		Iom	1994	11,423	17,080	161	23	14	T	
Isarstern		Iom	1995	11,426	17,078	161	23	14	T	
Rheinstern		Iom	1993	11,423	17,080	161	23	14	T	
Rhonestern		iom	2000	14,400	21,871	162	27	15	T	
Themsestern		Iom	2000	14,400	21,871	162	27	15	T	
Travestern		Iom	1993	11,423	17,080	161	23	14	T	
Weichselstern		Iom	1999	14,331	21,950	162	27	15	T	
Wolgastern		Iom	1999	14,331	21,950	162	27	15	T	

*newbuildings: four 25,000 grt 37,300 dwt tankers for 2004/5 delivery (to be named **Geestestern, Huntestern** and **Leinestern**)*

Ernst Russ GmbH & Co Germany

Funnel: *Black, red 'ER' bordered by narrow red bands or charterers colours.*
Hull: *Black or grey with red boot-topping.*

Name	Eng	Flag	Year	GRT	DWT	Loa	Bm	Kts	Type	Former names
Mercosul Pescada		Lbr	1996	16,800	22,984	184	25	19	CC	ex Sofia Russ-01, CSAV Vancouver-00, Sofia Russ-00, Cielo del Venezuela-99, Sofia Russ-99, CSAV Rungue-98, Sofia Russ-96
WAL Urundi		Lbr	1996	16,801	23,043	185	25	19	CC	ex Helene Russ-01, CMA Rotterdam-00, Helene Russ-99, CSAV Rio de Janeiro-98, I/a Helene Russ

The Sanko Steamship Co. Ltd. Japan

Funnel: *Light green with two red rings around red disc on broad white band.*
Hull: *Light green with white 'SANKO LINE', red boot-topping.*

Name	Eng	Flag	Year	GRT	DWT	Loa	Bm	Kts	Type	Former names
Ansac Asia *		Lbr	1998	19,882	33,945	178	28	14	B	
Gas Diana **		Lbr	2000	46,021	49,999	230	37	16	Lpg	
Gas Leo		Lbr	1990	44,493	50,357	230	37	16	Lpg	
Gas Scorpio		Lbr	1995	44,546	49,679	230	37	16	Lpg	
Gas Taurus **		Lbr	2001	46,021	48,500	230	37	16	Lpg	
Noto Gloria		Lbr	1992	42,286	49,412	224	36	15	Lpg	
Oval Nova *		Lbr	1993	44,549	50,357	230	37	16	Lpg	
Pacific Century *		Lbr	1991	44,493	50,357	230	37	15	Lpg	
Sanko Ability		Lbr	2002	50,199	83,657	239	38	-	T	
Sanko Advance		Lbr	2002	50,199	83,657	239	38	-	T	
Sanko Amity		Lbr	2002	50,199	84,999	239	38	-	T	
Sanko Brave		Pan	2003	56,500	105,400	239	42	14	T	
Sanko Dynasty		Pan	1999	57,331	106,664	241	42	14	T	ex Pacific Libra-03
Sanko Eagle		Lbr	1997	18,108	27,868	169	27	14	B	ex Aqua Crystal-03, Alpha Cosmos-01
Sanko Oasis		Pan	1995	81,058	161,192	280	45	14	T	
Sanko Quality		Lbr	1994	52,498	95,628	247	42	14	T	
Sanko Radiance †		Lbr	1994	25,676	42,529	185	31	15	B	
Sanko Rainbow †		Lbr	1994	25,676	42,529	185	31	15	B	
Sanko Rally *		Lbr	1994	25,676	42,529	185	31	15	B	
Sanko Ranger		Vut	1995	25,676	42,529	185	31	14	B	
Sanko Rejoice		Lbr	1994	25,676	42,529	185	31	15	B	
Sanko Robust ‡		Lbr	1995	25,676	42,529	185	31	15	B	
Sanko Rose		Lbr	1995	25,676	42,529	185	31	14	B	
Sanko Royal §		Lbr	1995	25,676	42,529	185	31	15	B	
Sanko Sincere		Jpn	1998	29,688	50,655	195	32	15	C	
Sanko Spring		Lbr	1998	29,688	50,655	195	32	15	C	
Sanko Stream		Lbr	1998	29,688	50,655	195	32	15	C	
Sanko Summit		Lbr	1999	29,688	50,655	195	32	15	C	
Sanko Supreme		Lbr	1999	29,688	50,655	195	32	15	C	
Sanko Unity		Pan	2000	159,577	298,920	333	60	15	T	
Sea Cattleya		Hkg	1984	22,135	38,885	181	31	14	B	ex Sanko Cattleya-87

newbuildings - two 71,000 dwt tankers and eleven bulk carriers between 50,000-73,700 dwt on order from Japanese builders.
* managed by Sanko Ship Management Co. Ltd. or ** by Anglo-Eastern Shipmanagement (Singapore) Pte. Ltd., both Japan.
† owned by Seven Seas Carriers AS, Norway, ‡ by Temm Maritime Co. Ltd., Japan or § by Eurasia International (Schulte Group) q.v.

Saudi Arabian Oil Co.
Saudi Arabia

Vela International Marine Ltd/UAE

Funnel: Plain blue or blue with white 'VELA' below two narrow white bands (top of 'V' merged with lower band).
Hull: Light grey or blue with red boot-topping.

Name	Eng	Flag	Year	GRT	DWT	Loa	Bm	Kts	Type	Former names
Al Bali Star	Lbr	1994	162,181	291,435	333	58	14	T	
Al Mahad	Sau	1982	29,240	48,530	177	32	14	T	ex World Crane-83
Al Safaniya	Sau	1982	29,240	48,582	177	32	14	T	ex World Athenian-83
Aldebaran Star	Lbr	2003	60,387	115,999	248	43	-	T	
Alnasi Star	Lbr	2004	150,000	300,000	-	-	-	T	
Alphard Star	Lbr	1995	159,222	301,858	333	56	14	T	
Altair Star	Lbr	2004	150,000	300,000	-	-	-	T	
Aries Star	Lbr	2003	164,292	316,478	333	60	15	T	
Capricorn Star	Lbr	2003	164,292	316,507	333	60	15	T	
Carina Star	Lbr	1994	159,766	305,668	332	58	14	T	
Columba Star	Lbr	1989	126,724	304,622	328	57	14	T	ex Golar Klementine-90
Dorado Star	Lbr	1989	126,724	304,622	328	57	14	T	ex Golar Cordelia-90
Gemini Star	Lbr	1995	159,222	301,862	333	56	14	T	
Hamal Star	Lbr	1994	158,680	301,550	332	58	14	T	
Hydra Star	Lbr	1994	159,766	305,846	332	58	14	T	
Leo Star	Lbr	2002	164,292	317,000	333	60	15	T	
Libra Star	Lbr	1993	162,181	291,435	333	58	14	T	
Markab Star	Lbr	1994	158,680	301,569	332	58	14	T	
Mars Glory	Lbr	2000	157,831	299,089	332	58	15	T	
Mirfak Star	Lbr	1994	158,680	301,542	332	58	14	T	
Orion Star	Lbr	1994	159,766	305,783	332	58	14	T	
Pherkad Star	Lbr	1995	158,680	301,569	332	58	14	T	
Phoenix Star	Lbr	1993	162,181	291,435	333	58	14	T	
Pisces Star	Lbr	2002	164,292	316,808	333	60	15	T	
Polaris Star	Lbr	1994	158,680	301,591	332	58	14	T	
Shaula Star	Lbr	1994	158,680	301,591	332	58	14	T	
Suhail Star	Lbr	1994	159,222	301,862	333	56	14	T	
Venus Glory	Lbr	2000	157,831	299,089	332	58	15	T	

Schepers & Co.
Germany

Funnel: Dark blue with red boot-topping.
Hull: Black with black 'S' on red diamond on white square.

Name	Eng	Flag	Year	GRT	DWT	Loa	Bm	Kts	Type	Former names
APL Venezuela	Atg	2001	35,645	42,211	220	32	22	CC	I/a Carolina
Catalina del Mar	Esp	1986	16,250	23,465	163	28	17	CC	ex Karin S-04, WEC Rotterdam-03, Karin S-01, CSAV Rio de la Plata-96, CSAV Rupanco-96, Buxwind-94, Red Sea Energy-94, Ville de Jupiter-94, Contship Success-94, Koala Success-92, Westerdam-91, Ville de Jupiter-91
CSAV Peru	Deu	1998	25,624	33,914	207	30	21	CC	ex NYK Esperanza-03, Laura S-02, Lykes Innovator-01, TMM Manzanillo-00, Laura S-99, I/a Thea S
CSAV Shenzhen	Atg	2003	27,227	33,232	200	32	21	CC	ex Jandavid S-03
Heinrich S	Deu	1998	25,624	33,914	207	30	20	CC	ex Zim Singapore I-02, I/a Heinrich S
Inga S	Atg	1995	11,964	14,464	150	23	18	CC	
Jan S	Atg	1996	18,166	26,337	179	28	19	CC	ex Helene Delmas-01, SCL Zaandam-00, P&O Nedlloyd Zaandam-99, CMBT Africa-97, Morecombe Bay-97, CMBT Africa-96, I/a Jan S
Julius S	Deu	2004	25,630	33,600	-	-	-	CC	
Maersk Nassau	Atg	2003	27,227	33,216	200	32	-	CC	ex Torge S-04, Superior Container-03
Michaela S	Deu	1997	25,361	33,976	207	30	21	CC	ex Contship Spirit-03, Michaela S-97
MSC Panama	Atg	1995	11,964	14,454	150	23	18	CC	ex Katrin S-03, Santa Paula-97, Katrin S-95
NYK Pasion	Atg	2002	25,370	33,742	207	30	22	CC	ex NYK Passion-03, Montemar Salvador-03, I/a Harald S
P&O Nedlloyd Pantanal	Deu	1997	25,361	33,936	207	30	21	CC	ex Kerstin S-97
Safmarine Kei	Atg	2002	25,630	33,500	207	30	22	CC	ex Thea S-02
Sakura	Atg	1995	11,964	14,454	150	23	18	CC	ex Bernhard S-04, MOL Manaus-02, Bernhard S-01
Zim Buenos Aires	Atg	1995	16,316	23,130	164	28	18	CC	ex Libra Buenos Aires-99, Marlene S-97

newbuilding : one 25,630 grt 33,500 dwt (Julia S) and four 36,000 grt 43,200 dwt (Adelheid S/Tim S) container ships for 2004-6 delivery.

Schoeller Holdings Ltd.
Germany

Columbia Shipmanagement Ltd./Cyprus

Funnel: Buff with blue 'CSM' on red band or charterers colours.
Hull: Green or red with red boot-topping.

Name	Eng	Flag	Year	GRT	DWT	Loa	Bm	Kts	Type	Former names
Alpina	Mhl	2003	16,418	27,112	166	-	-	B	
Bay Bridge	Lbr	1985	34,467	35,375	227	32	20	CC	
Cape Ann	Cyp	1993	10,837	15,566	158	23	17	Co	ex Silver Dawn-03, Maersk Melbourne-98, Silver Dawn-98, Mumbai Bay-97, Silver Dawn-96, Universal Bahana-96
Cape Arago	Cyp	1992	10,837	15,566	158	23	17	Co	ex Silver Sky-03, Maersk Singapore-98, Silver Sky-98, Global Bahana-96
Cape Baker	Mhl	2002	84,586	164,487	274	50	-	T	ex Decathlon-03
Cape Balboa	Mhl	2002	84,586	164,236	274	50	-	T	ex Pentathlon-03
Cape Bata	Mhl	2003	81,310	160,289	274	48	-	T	ex Sea Eagle-03
Cape Benat † **	Lbr	1998	21,165	29,133	179	25	14	T	
Cape Bille *	Mhl	2003	25,108	35,089	176	31	14	T	
Cape Bird *	Mhl	2003	25,108	35,070	176	31	14	T	
Cape Bon *	Mhl	2003	25,108	35,089	176	31	14	T	
Cape Bowen	Mhl	2003	81,310	159,988	274	48	-	T	ex Matissie-03
Cape Bruny	Mhl	2004	25,000	35,000	176	31	14	T	
Cape Conway	Hkg	1985	17,280	22,312	170	27	17	Co	ex Delmas Tourville-02, C.D.Pointe Noire-91, C.R.Pointe Noire-90
Cape Darby *	Mhl	2001	23,132	30,537	193	28	19	Co	
Cape Darnley ‡	Mhl	2003	23,132	30,346	193	28	19	Co	
Cape Delfaro	Lbr	2004	23,132	30,000	193	28	19	Co	
Cape Delgarde	Mhl	2003	23,132	30,000	193	28	19	Co	
Cape Denison	Mhl	2002	23,132	30,396	193	28	19	Co	
Cape Don	Mhl	2002	23,132	30,537	193	28	19	Co	
Cape Falcon	Mhl	2003	14,308	16,421	155	25	-	CC	
Cape Ferro	Mhl	2003	14,308	16,584	155	25	-	CC	
Cape Frio	Mhl	2003	14,308	16,400	155	25	-	CC	
Cape Norviega	Mhl	1998	17,609	24,116	183	28	18	CC	ex Justice Container-03
Cape Preston	Hkg	1983	17,210	22,351	170	27	17	Co	ex Delmas Bougainville-01, C.D.Douala-91, C.R.Douala-90
Cape York	Cyp	1983	17,210	22,351	170	27	17	Co	ex Delmas Durville-02, Griffin Star-98, Australia Current-98, Delmas Joinville-96, C.D.Abidjan-91, C.R.Abidjan-90
CMA CGM Magallanes	Mhl	2002	23,132	30,586	193	28	19	Co	ex Cape Dyer-03
CSAV Genova	Mhl	2002	23,132	30,000	193	28	19	Co	ex Cape Dorchester-03
Golden Isle ‡	Mhl	2003	23,132	30,000	193	28	17	Co	
J. Shartava	Mhl	2004	24,000	35,000				T	
MSC Normandie	Mhl	1983	20,345	28,422	174	28	18	CC	ex New Challenge-02, DAL Reunion-02, Catherine Delmas-00, Sea Commerce-97, Usambara-87, Victoria Bay-86, Usambara-84
Norasia Malabar	Mhl	1998	17,609	23,752	183	28	19	CC	ex Cape Negro-03, Ace Container-03
SKS Senne	Mhl	2003	81,270	159,385	274	48	-	T	
SKS Sinni	Nis	2003	81,270	159,367	274	48	-	T	
SKS Sira	Mhl	2002	81,270	159,453	274	48	-	T	
Tasman Endeavour	Cyp	1994	18,451	23,000	185	28	19	CO	ex Caribbean Challenger-03
Tasman Provider	Cyp	1994	18,451	23,683	185	28	19	CO	ex Meridian Challenger-03, Delmas Forbin-02, Meridian Challenger-00
Voyager *	Mhl	2002	79,525	149,991	272	46	15	T	

newbuildings: About 24 large vessels on order including eight 35,000 dwt tankers and eight 37,800 dwt container ships.
* managed by Columbia Shipmanagement (Deutschland) GmbH or ** by Columbia Shipmanagement (Netherlands) BV
‡ time-chartered until 2008 from German KG fund Lloyd Funhausen. † managed for Knohr & Burchard GmbH or ‡ for Hanse Bereederungs GmbH, both Germany

Hanse Bereederungs GmbH

Name	Eng	Flag	Year	GRT	DWT	Loa	Bm	Kts	Type	Former names
Calanda	Mhl	2000	16,418	27,321	166	27	14	B	
Cape Banks *	Lbr	1997	21,162	32,758	179	25	14	T	ex Chembulk Hong Kong-02, Cape Banks-97
Cape Bear **	Lbr	1997	21,165	32,682	179	25	14	T	ex Chembulk Vancouver-02, Cape Bear-97
Cape Blanc **	Lbr	1998	21,165	28,400	179	25	14	T	

Saudi Arabian Oil. PISCES STAR. *Hans Kraijenbosch.*

Schepers & Co. APL VENEZUELA. *Hans Kraijenbosch.*

Schoeller Holdings (Columbia). CAPE BON. *Hans Kraijenbosch.*

Name	Eng	Flag	Year	GRT	DWT	Loa	Bm	Kts	Type	Former names
Cape Henry ‡		Lbr	1992	10,376	12,835	147	24	17	CC	ex Safmarine Athi-02, Cape Henry-02, Avon-98, Halla Liberty-98, Kinabalu-97, Tiger Ocean-96, ACX Aster-95, Ratana Manee-94, TSL Bravo-93, Cape Henry-92
Cape North		Lbr	1998	17,285	22,800	175	27	20	CC	ex Tiger Pearl-03, Cape North-01, Maersk Skagen-99, I/a Cape North
Cape Sable ‡		Gib	1996	10,917	13,700	151	24	18	CC	
Cape Santiago *		Mhl	2002	14,241	18,402	159	24	18	CC	ex MSC Yaounde-03, Cape Santiago-02
Cape Serrat *		Mhl	2002	14,241	18,402	159	24	19	CC	ex MOL Sahara-02, Cape Serrat-02
Cape Spear ‡		Lbr	1998	10,917	13,623	151	24	18	CC	ex MSC Coimbra-03, Cape Spear-01
Eagle Excellence ‡		Lbr	1995	17,285	22,148	175	27	20	CC	ex Cape Natal-96
Ernst Salomon ‡		Lbr	1999	38,888	74,002	225	32	14	B	ex Far Eastern Queen-01
Ever Shining		Pan	1999	39,052	74,345	225	32	14	B	
Gertrud Salamon ‡		Pan	2000	38,888	74,078	225	32	14	B	ex Far Eastern Media-01
Hong Kong Star ‡		Mhl	1998	17,285	22,148	175	27	20	CC	ex Cape Norman-03, Tiger Breeze-02, Cape Norman-01, Sea-Land Europe-99, Maersk Ankara-99, Cape Norman-98
Maria Salamon		Pan	2001	38,888	74,117	225	32	14	B	ex Far Eastern Glory-01
MOL Brasilia ‡		Lbr	1992	10,396	12,854	147	24	17	CC	ex Cala Porlamar-03, Cape Horn I-02, Otway-99, Maersk Davao-99, Cape Horn I-98, Eagle Star -98, Cape Horn I-97, Maersk La Paz-96, Cape Horn-94, TSL Gallant-94, Cape Horn-92
MSC Perth ‡		Lbr	1993	29,912	35,071	201	32	20	CC	ex Cape Race-03, MSC Argentina-02, Cape Race-01, CSAV Callao-99, Copiapo-98, Jean Bosco-95, Yucatan-94, Jean Bosco-93
Ningbo Star		Lbr	1998	17,285	22,339	175	29	20	CC	ex Cape Nati-03, Tiger Island-02, Cape Nati-02, Sea-Land Mediterranean-99
P&O Nedlloyd Inca ‡		Cyp	1992	10,396	12,854	147	24	17	CC	ex Cape Hatteras-03, Cala Panama-03, Cape Hatteras-02, Maersk Cebu-00, Cape Hatteras-98, Eagle Dawn-98, Cape Hatteras-95, ACX Iris-95, Cape Hatteras-93
P&O Nedlloyd Thekwini ‡		Lbr	1997	10,197	13,623	151	24	18	CC	ex Cape Scott-02, Independent Leader-99, I/a Cape Scott
TS Hongkong ‡		Lbr	1996	10,917	13,623	151	24	18	CC	ex Cape Spencer-03, Fanal Merchant-00, Grafton-99, Cape Spencer-99
TS Osaka ‡		Lbr	1997	10,925	13,741	151	24	18	CC	ex Cape Sorrell-03, Independent Concept-99, Cape Sorrell-97
Willi Salomon †		Lbr	2000	38,888	74,000	225	32	14	B	ex Far Eastern Harvest-01

italic managed by Columbia Shipmanagement (Deutschland) GmbH or ** by Columbia Shipmanagement (Netherlands) BV
† managed by DFM Ltd., Poland or ‡ owned by Dr. Peters KG fund, Germany.

The Schulte Group Germany

Funnel: Dark grey with broad light blue band containing red disc with light blue 'SL' within large 'H'.
Hull: Dark grey with red boot-topping.

Name		Flag	Year	GRT	DWT	Loa	Bm	Kts	Type	Former names
ANL Emblem *		Cyp	2002	35,589	40,995	232	32	22	CC	ex CMA CGM Gauguin-04, Arnold Schulte-02
Antonia Schulte		Deu	2004	25,369	33,900	-	-	-	CC	
Caecilia Schulte *		Lbr	1995	10,749	14,148	163	22	17	CC	ex CGM Cayenne-02, Caecilia Schulte-99, Atika Delmas-98, CMBT Antarctica-98, Caecilia Schulte-96
Christiane Schulte *		Lbr	2001	27,000	33,871	210	30	22	CC	
CMA CGM Chardin *		Cyp	2002	35,589	40,995	232	32	22	CC	I/a Friedrich Schulte
CMA CGM Claudel *		Lbr	2002	27,093	34,662	210	30	22	CC	I/dn Auguste Schulte
Karthago *		Lbr	1994	14,619	20,275	166	25	17	CC	ex Renate Schulte-01, Libra Houston-97, Renate Schulte-96, Europa Express-95, Renate Schulte-94
Kasper Schulte		Cyp	2004	41,503	72,718	225	32	14	T	
Konrad Schulte		Cyp	2004	18,160	23,400	175	27	20	CC	
P&O Nedlloyd Andes *		Lbr	2001	26,626	34,717	210	30	22	CC	ex P&O Nedlloyd Rose-01, I/a Anna Schulte
P&O Nedlloyd Acapulco *		Lbr	2001	26,718	34,643	210	30	21	CC	I/a Marianne Schulte
P&O Nedlloyd Aconcagua *		Lbr	2001	26,626	34,717	210	30	22	CC	I/a Susanne Schulte
P&O Nedlloyd Antisana *		Lbr	2001	26,718	34,677	210	30	22	CC	ex Thekla Schulte-01
P&O Nedlloyd Atacama *		Lbr	2001	26,718	33,871	210	30	22	CC	I/a Henrika Schulte

The Schulte Group. CHRISTIANE SCHULTE. *J. M. Kakebeeke.*

The Schulte Group (Dorchester). CCNI ANGOL (in charterers colours). *Phil Kempsey.*

The Schulte Group (Dorchester). CIELO DI BAFFIN. *Hans Kraijenbosch.*

Name	Eng	Flag	Year	GRT	DWT	Loa	Bm	Kts	Type	Former names
P&O Nedlloyd Curacao		Lbr	1993	9,602	12,577	150	23	17	CC	ex Judith Schulte-98, Maersk Conakry-98, Fas Lattaquie-96, Judith Schulte-96, Libra Barcelona-95, Judith Schulte-95, TSL Gallant-94, Judith Schulte-94
P&O Nedlloyd Takoradi *		Lbr	1995	16,800	23,001	185	25	20	CC	ex Lissy Schulte-01, CSAV Rubens-98, Lissy Schulte-95
Philipp Schulte		Cyp	2004	18,160	23,579	175	27	20	CC	
Safmarine Pakistan **		Cyp	1998	15,929	22,020	168	27	21	CC	ex Francisca Schulte-03, Maersk San Jose-99, I/a Francisca Schulte

newbuildings : about 15 including tankers to 72,600 dwt and container ships to 34,600 dwt for 2004/5 delivery mainly from Chinese builders.
Owned by Bernhard Schulte and * managed by Vorsetzen Bereederungs und Schiffahrtskontor GmbH & Co. KG, both Germany.
** owned by Reederei Thomas Schnlte Gmbh, Germany.

Atlantic Marine Partnership/Bermuda

Name	Eng	Flag	Year	GRT	DWT	Loa	Bm	Kts	Type	Former names
Bernhard Schulte		Cyp	1994	14,366	20,275	166	25	-	CC	ex Tema Star II-00 Bernhard Schulte-99, Maersk Paita-98, TMM Tuxpan-97, Calapedra-96, Contship Tahiti-95, Bernhard Schulte-94
CMA CGM Wallaby		Bmu	1998	16,281	22,330	179	25	19	CC	ex Hans Schulte-02, Cabo Creus-01, Hans Schulte-98
Sophie Schulte		Gib	1996	10,730	14,148	163	22	17	CC	ex Marfret Guyane-03, Sophie Schulte-03, CMA CGM Oyapock-02, X-press Annapurna-01, Sophie Schulte-00
Weser Stahl		Cyp	1999	28,564	47,257	192	32	12	Bu	

Dorchester Maritime Ltd./Isle of Man

Name	Eng	Flag	Year	GRT	DWT	Loa	Bm	Kts	Type	Former names
Aglaia *		Mhl	2001	14,278	15,315	159	26	22	CC	I/a Sandy Rickmers
Amalthea *		Cyp	2001	14,290	14,901	159	26	22	CC	ex CSAV Valencia-03, CCNI Ancud-01
CCNI Anakena *		Mhl	1998	28,148	44,575	185	32	15	Co	I/a Valdermosa
CCNI Ancud *		Mhl	1998	28,148	44,575	185	32	15	Co	
CCNI Angol *		Mhl	1998	28,148	46,376	185	32	15	Co	I/a Valdivia
CCNI Atacama *		Mhl	1998	28,148	46,376	185	32	15	Co	I/a Valbella
Cielo di Baffin		Iom	1986	16,282	27,350	170	23	15	T	ex Maersk Baffin-01, Rasmine Maersk-96
Cielo di Biscaglia		Iom	1986	16,282	27,350	170	23	15	T	ex Maersk Biscay-01, Ras Maersk-97
Johann Schulte		Iom	1997	15,180	17,914	155	23	16	Lpg	
Kindia *		Iom	1999	16,986	21,184	168	27	20	CC	ex Indamex Kindia-03, Kindia-02
Maersk Rhone		Iom	1999	22,181	35,000	171	27	14	T	ex Rita Maersk-03
Wilhelm Schulte		Iom	1997	15,180	17,900	155	23	16	Lpg	

* managed by Gemini Shipmanagement Ltd., Isle of Man

Hanseatic Shipping Co. Ltd./Cyprus

Name	Eng	Flag	Year	GRT	DWT	Loa	Bm	Kts	Type	Former names
Antje Schulte †		Atg	1997	15,929	22,015	168	27	21	CC	ex Alianca Rotterdam-01, Antje Schulte-00, CGM Mascareignes-99, CGM Santos Dumont II-99, Alianca America-98, CSAV Reloncav-98, Antje Schulte-97
Charlotte Schulte		Cyp	1992	14,858	20,270	167	25	17	CC	ex Argentina-95, Argentina Express-95, Argentina-93, Charlotte Schulte-92
Cielo del Baltico		Nis	1986	16,282	27,350	170	23	15	T	ex Maersk Baltic-01, Magdelena-97, Rita Maersk-96
Cielo di Barents		Nis	1986	16,282	27,350	170	23	15	T	ex Maersk Barents-02, Edzard-97, Maersk Barents-97, Robert Maersk-97
Cielo di Bothnia		Nis	1986	16,282	27,350	170	23	15	T	ex Maersk Bothnia-01, Rebecca-97, Maersk Bothnia-97, Romo Maersk-97
Direct Eagle		Sgp	2000	17,167	21,152	169	27	18	CC	ex Spica-00
Donata Schulte *		Cyp	2001	26,718	34,717	210	30	22	CC	
Fabian Schulte †		Atg	1997	15,929	22,015	168	27	21	CC	ex Maersk Cabello-98, Fabian Schulte-97
Henriette Schulte *		Cyp	1997	16,281	22,352	179	25	19	CC	ex CSAV Brasilia-98, Henriette Schulte-97
Immanuel Kant		Nis	1983	12,240	16,228	159	21	15	Lpg	
Libra Ecuador *		Cyp	1997	16,281	22,361	192	25	19	CC	ex Helen Schulte-03, Direct Kiwi-03, Helen Schulte-99, Libra Houston-98, Helen Schulte-97
MSC Ulsan		Bhs	2002	40,300	51,020	258	32	24	CC	
NDS Prodigy		Cyp	1985	22,211	17,773	182	28	20	Ro	ex Silkeborg-98, Hudson-97, Yuriy Maksaryov-96
NDS Progress		Cyp	1979	22,211	17,872	181	28	20	Ro	ex Atlantic Hope-97, Skulptor Zalkalns-95
NDS Prominence		Vct	1982	22,211	17,773	181	28	20	Ro	ex Atlantic Herald-03, NDS Prominence-03, Atlantic Herald-97, Georgiy Pyasetskiy-95

Name	Eng	Flag	Year	GRT	DWT	Loa	Bm	Kts	Type	Former names
NDS Provider		Cyp	1979	22,186	17,665	182	28	20	Ro	ex Global Wind-98, Nikolay Cherkasov-96
P&O Nedlloyd Altiplano		Cyp	2001	26,582	33,871	210	30	22	CC	ex Esther Schulte-02
Tycho Brahe		Nis	1982	12,183	16,225	159	21	14	Lpg	

managed by Navigo Management Co., Cyprus or † by BUS Shipmanagement, Germany.

Eurasia International (China) Ltd./Hong Kong (China)

Name	Eng	Flag	Year	GRT	DWT	Loa	Bm	Kts	Type	Former names
Asta Samudra		Pan	1994	12,873	18,331	160	26	-	T	
Azul Glory		Hkg	1998	90,267	178,632	289	47	15	B	ex Dyna Aquarius-03
Century River		Pan	1999	57,944	107,212	247	42	-	T	
City of Hamburg		Hkg	1990	24,495	31,627	182	31	18	CC	ex Astrid Schulte-03, Ibn Al Kadi-98, American Senator-97, Choyang Green-97, American Senator 95
Elisabeth Schulte		Hkg	2001	26,718	34,717	210	30	21	CC	
Emerald Queen		Pan	1997	57,943	107,176	247	42	14	T	
Everhard Schulte		Cyp	2004	40,000	75,000	225	32	-	T	
Libra Houston		Hkg	2001	26,582	34,662	210	30	21	CC	ex Caroline Schulte-02, Thekla Schulte-01
Pacific Prosperity		Pan	1998	90,876	179,385	290	47	14	B	ex Dyna Mercury-02
Rudolf Schulte		Cyp	2004	40,000	75,000	225	32	-	T	

Seatrade Groningen B.V.   Netherlands

Funnel: Blue with white 'S' and blue 'G' merged symbol on orange square.
Hull: White with blue 'Seatrade', red boot-topping.

Name	Eng	Flag	Year	GRT	DWT	Loa	Bm	Kts	Type	Former names
Agulhas Stream §		Ant	1998	9,298	11,048	150	22	20	R	
Atlantic Hope *		Pan	1984	7,777	8,494	142	20	18	R	ex Magellan Rex-96
Barents Bay *		Vct	1984	7,726	8,549	139	21	17	R	ex Chiricana-00, Juvante-87
Benguela Stream		Nld	1998	9,298	11,016	150	22	20	R	
Cloudy Bay		Mlt	1984	10,325	11,779	152	22	21	R	ex Astro Bright-01, Nordenham-97
Cold Stream **		Ant	1994	8,414	10,066	140	22	19	R	I/a Prince of Streams
Comoros Stream		Nld	2000	11,382	12,906	155	24	21	R	
Condor Bay		Pan	1990	10,405	10,742	150	23	20	R	ex Ivory Nina-03, Ivory Cape-01
Cooler Bay *		Vct	1979	7,629	7,639	141	20	20	R	ex Anakan-97, Akragas-95, Princesa-94, Crown Cooler-91, Khalij Cooler-90
Crystal Primadonna †		Bhs	1992	7,743	7,726	131	20	19	R	
Crystal Prince †		Atg	1992	7,743	7,726	131	20	19	R	
Discovery Bay		Bhs	1997	8,924	10,100	142	22	21	R	
Disko Bay *		Vct	1978	8,833	9,321	150	21	20	R	ex Thistle-93, Paracale-93, Astoria-92, Asama-89, Asama Maru-86
Eagle Bay		Ant	1992	10,402	10,621	150	23	20	R	ex Ivory Eagle-03
Elsebeth *		Nld	1998	10,519	10,327	152	23	21	R	
Elvira *		Nld	2000	10,532	10,309	152	23	21	R	
Emerald *		Nld	2000	10,532	10,346	152	23	21	R	
Esmeralda *		Nld	1999	10,532	10,358	152	23	21	R	
Falcon Bay		Ant	1993	10,374	10,532	150	23	20	R	ex Ivory Falcon-02
Fortuna Bay		Ant	1993	10,203	11,585	145	22	19	R	ex Fortune Bay-03, Uruguayan Reefer-99
French Bay *		Hkg	1992	10,381	10,621	150	23	20	R	ex Royal Star-99, Chiquita Honshu-94, Royal Star-92
Glacier Bay †		Atg	1985	8,739	9,746	144	22	17	R	ex Cap Verde-95, Causewaybay-89, Cap Delgado-89
Hope Bay §		Ant	1996	8,396	9,639	143	22	20	R	
Hudson Bay †		Atg	1983	8,052	8,945	140	21	17	R	ex Kiwi-99, Central Reefer-95, Southern Laurel-90, Southern Universal-88
Izumo Bay *		Vct	1984	9,273	10,644	150	21	19	R	ex UB Libra-02, Libra-96, Izumo Reefer-95
Kashima Bay #		Cym	1984	9,273	10,647	150	21	19	R	ex UB Gemini-02, Gemini-96, Kashima Reefer-95
Kasuga Bay		Cym	1984	9,274	10,647	150	21	19	R	ex Arimao Universal-02, Kasuga Bay-95
Klipper Stream ‡		Nld	1998	9,305	10,936	150	22	21	R	
Lombok Strait		Nld	2002	13,700	13,512	167	25	22	R	ex Leopard Max-02
Luzon Strait		Nld	2002	13,700	14,413	167	25	22	R	ex Tiger Max-02
Magic		Nld	1989	5,103	6,116	136	16	20	R	
Magnific		Nld	1992	5,103	6,116	136	16	20	R	
Mahone Bay †		Atg	1981	10,651	9,835	151	22	20	R	ex Avocado-99, Racisce-97
Majestic		Nld	1988	5,089	6,105	136	16	20	R	
Maud *		Lbr	1992	9,829	10,461	142	23	19	R	ex Coral Mermaid-01
Maveric		Nld	1993	5,103	6,105	136	16	20	R	
Music		Nld	1990	5,103	6,116	136	16	20	R	
Mystic §		Ant	1988	5,089	6,105	136	16	20	R	

Name	Eng	Flag	Year	GRT	DWT	Loa	Bm	Kts	Type	Former names
Nagoya Bay *		Vct	1983	9,755	12,181	150	22	18	R	ex Actic Dawn-00, Cap Frio-95, Oceanic Trader-93, Ocean Pride-92, I/a Ocean Bride
Northern Mermaid		Bhs	1993	9,829	10,464	142	23	19	R	ex Caribbean Mermaid-02
Pacific		Nld	1996	5,918	8,500	134	16	16	R	
Polarlicht *		Pan	1998	11,417	10,447	154	24	21	R	ex Polarlight-04
Polarsteam		Nld	1999	11,417	10,449	154	24	21	R	ex Polarstern-03
Prince of Seas		Nld	1993	6,363	7,387	120	19	17	R	
Prince of Streams		Ant	1993	7,533	8,384	137	20	18	R	ex Wilmington-02
Prince of Tides **		Bhs	1993	7,329	5,360	134	21	19	R	
Prince of Waves **		Bhs	1993	7,329	8,039	134	21	19	R	
Roman Bay *		Hkg	1992	10,381	10,603	150	23	20	R	ex Roman Star-99, Chiquita Sulu-94
Royal Bay *		Vct	1979	9,038	9,118	151	21	20	R	ex Royal Reefer-96, Barrios-84
Royal Cooler *		Vct	1979	9,020	9,101	151	21	20	R	ex African Queen-96, Turbo-89
Royal Klipper ‡		Nld	2000	11,382	12,906	155	24	21	R	ex Equator Stream-00
Royal Reefer *		Vct	1979	9,018	9,125	151	21	20	R	ex African Princess-96, Hawaii-89
Sable Bay †		Ant	1983	8,739	9,746	144	22	17	R	ex Santorini Rex-96, Cap Valiente-91, Cap Domingo-89
Santa Catharina		Bhs	2000	8,597	9,259	143	22	19	R	
Santa Lucia		Nld	1999	8,507	9,566	143	22	20	R	I/a Santa Lucia II
Santa Maria		Ant	1999	8,507	9,566	143	22	20	R	I/a Santa Maria III
Santiago I *		Pan	1993	7,534	8,053	136	20	19	R	ex Santiago-01
Skausund *		Lbr	1993	9,829	10,457	142	23	19	R	ex Tasman Marmaid-01
Spring Bear *		Bhs	1984	12,615	9,472	152	24	19	R	ex Spring Dream-85
Spring Bob		Nld	1984	12,111	10,098	151	24	19	R	ex Spring Blossom-85
Spring Bok		Nld	1984	12,113	10,113	151	24	18	R	ex Spring Bee-02, Spring Bird-84
Spring Deli		Ant	1984	12,783	9,891	152	24	18	R	ex Spring Delight-03
Spring Dragon *		Vct	1984	12,783	9,906	152	24	18	R	ex Spring Dream-98, Spring Desire-89
Spring Panda		Nld	1984	12,111	10,140	151	24	19	R	ex Spring Ballad-85, Spring Blossom-84
Spring Tiger		Nld	1984	12,340	10,110	148	24	19	R	ex Spring Breeze-90
Storm Bay *		Vct	1983	10,325	11,720	152	22	21	R	ex Atlantic Dawn-01, Nienburg-95
Tama Hope		Bhs	1986	6,579	7,690	146	19	18	R	ex Lamitan-93, Tama Hope-92
Tama Star		Bhs	1987	6,579	7,685	146	19	18	R	ex Bulan-93, Tama Star-92
Tokyo Bay #		Mlt	1978	7,111	8,078	145	19	19	R	ex Tokyo Reefer-94
Vermont Universal *		Bhs	1987	7,286	7,337	145	20	19	R	ex Fortune Reefer-96
Virginia Universal *		Bhs	1988	7,286	7,348	145	20	19	R	ex Wealth Reefer-96
Yasaka Bay #		Cym	1983	9,273	10,647	150	21	19	R	ex Pasadena Universal-02, Yasaka Bay-95

In addition to the above, the company owns or charters about 36 smaller refrigerated vessels.
** owned or managed by subsidiary Dammers Shipmanagement NV, Netherlands Antilles
Various chartered vessels, including † owned by Thein & Heyenga GmbH or § Triton Schiffahrts GmbH, both Germany or ‡ Jaczon BV, Netherlands or # by London Ship Managers Ltd., UK. or * various other owners.
See also F. Laeisz Schiffahrts GmbH.

Shell-Royal Dutch Group

UK

Shell International Trading & Shipping Co. Ltd./UK

Funnel: Red with yellow sea-shell (scallop) or white with narrow red band on lower part of broad yellow band, narrow black top.
Hull: Red with yellow sea-shell, black or grey with red or blue boot-topping.

Name	Eng	Flag	Year	GRT	DWT	Loa	Bm	Kts	Type	Former names
Cardissa **		Iom	1983	15,076	19,999	170	23	15	T	
Estrella Atlantica ‡		Lbr	1982	13,826	28,750	183	29	15	T	ex Humberto Beghin-95
Estrella Austral ‡		Lbr	1984	28,259	45,718	197	32	14	T	ex Feosa Ambassador 2-88
Estrella Pampeana ‡		Lbr	1981	37,685	57,741	229	32	14	T	ex Zenatia-96, Oak River-88, Salena-81
Ficus §		Iom	2001	27,539	44,881	183	32	16	T	I/a Elka Angelique
Fulgur §		Iom	2001	27,539	44,787	183	32	16	T	I/a Elka Eleftheria
Fusus		Iom	2001	27,542	44,788	183	32	16	T	ex Elka Nikolas-01
Hadra ***		Iom	1994	28,277	40,549	183	32	14	T	
Halia ***		Iom	1993	28,277	40,549	183	32	14	T	
Haminea ***		Iom	1994	28,277	46,878	183	32	14	T	
Hastula ***		Iom	1993	28,277	46,842	183	32	14	T	
Hatasia ***		Iom	1994	28,277	46,851	183	32	14	T	
Haustrum ***		Iom	1994	28,277	46,801	183	32	14	T	
Isomeria		Iom	1982	39,932	47,594	210	31	17	Lpg	
Helix †		Aus	1997	28,810	46,186	183	32	14	T	
Nivosa †		Aus	1997	72,609	136,115	265	46	14	T	
Simunye †		Gbr	1997	28,027	44,640	183	32	14	T	ex Engen Simunye-00
Solaris **		Iom	1985	56,456	83,701	244	43	15	T	

Seatrade Groningen. LUZON STRAIT. *Hans Kraijenbosch.*

Seatrade Groningen. ROYAL COOLER. *Hans Kraijenbosch.*

Soc. Portuguesa de Nav. Tanques. ERATI. *M. D. J. Lennon.*

Name	Eng	Flag	Year	GRT	DWT	Loa	Bm	Kts	Type	Former names
Spectrum **		Iom	1985	56,456	83,651	244	43	15	T	
Sponsalis **		Iom	1986	56,613	83,729	245	43	15	T	

newbuilding : one 67,300 dwt tanker on order.
* owned by Shell UK Ltd., UK ** by Shell Tankers BV, Netherlands or *** by Premier Product Tankers Group, Norway
† owned by Shell Co. of Australia Ltd., Australia or ‡ by Shell Compania Argentina de Petroleo SA, Argentina
§ managed for European Navigation Inc., Greece
The Company also has interests in over 20 Lng tankers operated by Australian LNG Ship Operating Co. Pty. Ltd., (formed jointly with BHP Petroleum Pty. Ltd.), by Brunei Shell Tankers Sendirian Berhad (formed jointly with Government of The State of Brunei) and by Nigeria LNG Ltd., Nigeria (formed jointly with Nigerian National Petroleum, Corp. (60%), Agip International BV (10%) and TotalFinaElf (10%)).

Sinotrans Shipping Ltd.   Hong Kong (China)

Funnel: *Dark blue or lattice with dark blue disc with white edged red 'SM' symbol, narrow black top.*
Hull: *Black with red boot-topping.*

Name	Eng	Flag	Year	GRT	DWT	Loa	Bm	Kts	Type	Former names
Cielo di B. Columbia		Hkg	1999	23,259	32,509	174	28	14	BC	ex Vanessa Oldendorff-03, Great Immensity-02
Great Ambition		Hkg	1999	38,426	73,725	225	32	14	B	
Great Bless		Hkg	1997	39,005	73,251	225	32	14	B	
Great Blossom		Hkg	1999	23,259	32,509	174	28	14	B	
Great Bright		Hkg	1997	38,005	73,242	225	32	14	B	
Great Calm		Hkg	1996	26,094	45,215	186	30	14	B	
Great Century		Hkg	1999	38,426	73,747	225	32	14	B	
Great Concord		Hkg	1999	15,983	24,159	160	26	14	B	
Great Creation		Hkg	1998	18,179	27,383	175	26	14	B	
Great Fortune		Hkg	1998	25,889	39,042	187	29	15	B	
Great Gain		Hkg	1998	16,651	27,172	169	26	14	B	
Great Glory		Hkg	1997	39,005	73,251	225	32	14	B	
Great Happy		Hkg	1997	26,094	45,248	186	30	14	B	
Great Harmony		Hkg	1999	15,983	24,159	160	26	14	B	
Great Jade		Hkg	1997	39,005	73,251	225	32	14	B	
Great Loyalty		Hkg	1999	38,426	73,659	225	32	14	B	
Great Luck		Hkg	1998	37,663	71,399	225	32	14	B	
Great Motion		Hkg	1998	18,179	27,338	175	26	14	B	
Great Ocean		Hkg	1991	25,905	43,473	186	30	14	B	
Great Olympia		Hkg	2002	27,176	47,777	188	31	-	B	
Great Peace		Hkg	1996	26,094	45,259	186	30	14	B	
Great Prosperity		Hkg	1999	38,426	73,679	225	32	14	B	
Great Rainbow		Hkg	1998	25,889	39,042	187	29	15	B	
Great Scenery		Hkg	2002	27,176	47,760	188	31	-	B	
Great Success		Hkg	1998	16,651	27,172	169	26	14	B	
MSC Algerie		Cyp	1991	9,870	13,453	148	22	-	Co	ex Trade Fast-02, l/a Kota Cantik
MSC Amsterdam *		Hkg	1995	28,892	41,624	203	31	20	CC	ex Trade Selene-03, MSC Amsterdam-02, Trade Selene-01
MSC Belem *		Hkg	1995	29,195	35,534	196	32	20	CC	ex Trade Harvest-02
MSC Greece *		Hkg	1995	29,195	35,534	196	32	20	CC	ex Trade Maple-02, MSC Hamburg-01, Trade Maple-01
Trade Eternity		Hkg	1995	28,892	41,553	203	31	20	CC	ex MSC London-02, Trade Eternity-01
Trans Friendship		Hkg	1999	14,397	24,021	154	26	13	B	

* managed by Univan Ship Management Ltd., Hong Kong (China)

Solvang ASA   Norway

Funnel: *Brown with blue 'CS' on broad white band.*
Hull: *Brown with red boot-topping.*

Name	Eng	Flag	Year	GRT	DWT	Loa	Bm	Kts	Type	Former names
Clipper Lady		Nis	1978	32,853	40,605	217	32	17	Lpg	ex Reynosa-99
Clipper Moon		Nis	2003	35,012	44,872	205	32	16	Lpg	
Clipper Slagen		Nis	1989	11,822	16,137	158	21	15	Lpg	ex Havkatt-97, Gaz Horizon-94, Sigulda-93
Clipper Star		Nis	2003	34,970	44,807	205	32	16	Lpg	
Clipper Sun		Nis	1978	16,340	16,663	170	24	17	Lpg	ex Nuevo Laredo-00, Sydfonn-79
Cypress Trail *		Nis	1988	42,447	12,763	184	31	18	V	

newbuilding : one 45,000 dwt tanker on order from Japanese builder for 2004 delivery.
* on charter to Eukor Car Carriers Inc. (see under Wallanius-Wilhelmsen)

Soc. Portuguesa de Navios Tanques SA (Soponata)   Portugal

Funnel: Dark green with white band, black top.
Hull: Black with red boot-topping.

Name	Eng	Flag	Year	GRT	DWT	Loa	Bm	Kts	Type	Former names
Bornes		Lbr	1990	52,530	88,950	244	42	13	T	
Erati		Lbr	1992	84,488	140,059	271	49	14	T	
Inago *		Lbr	1993	84,488	159,878	271	49	14	T	
Peneda		Lbr	2002	56,225	105,538	239	42	15	T	
Portel		Lbr	2003	56,225	105,674	239	42	15	T	
Sintra		Lbr	1994	53,773	96,755	244	42	14	T	ex Astro Perseus-00, Yuhsei Maru-99

newbuildings : two 79,200 grt 141,700 dwt tankers on order from Japanese builder for 2006 delivery.
Owned by subsidiary Marenostrum, Portugal, apart from * jointly owned by Bona Shipholding Ltd. (Teekay Shipping Corp.) q.v.

OAO 'Sovcomflot'   Russia

Funnel: Light grey or white with blue 'S' symbol onwhite above pale blue over red horizontal banded rectangle (some variations)
Hull: Black or red with red boot-topping.

Name	Eng	Flag	Year	GRT	DWT	Loa	Bm	Kts	Type	Former names
Anichkov Bridge		Lbr	2003	27,829	47,843	183	32	14	T	
Arbat *		Lbr	1991	28,223	47,083	183	32	14	T	
Azov Sea *		Lbr	1998	27,526	47,363	182	32	15	T	
Barents Sea *		Lbr	1997	27,526	47,431	182	32	15	T	
Bering Sea *		Lbr	1998	27,526	47,431	182	32	15	T	
East Siberian Sea *		Lbr	1998	27,526	47,358	182	32	15	T	
Fili *		Cyp	1991	27,829	47,083	183	32	14	T	
Hermitage Bridge		Lbr	2003	28,000	47,842	183	32	14	T	
Izmaylovo *		Lbr	1991	28,223	47,083	183	32	14	T	
Kara Sea *		Lbr	1998	27,526	47,343	182	32	15	T	
Langepas *		Cyp	1998	21,609	33,425	182	25	-	T	ex Nordamerika-98
Laptev Sea *		Lbr	1998	27,526	47,314	182	32	15	T	
Ligovsky Prospect *		Lbr	2003	62,586	115,000	250	44	-	T	
Moscow Sea *		Lbr	1998	27,526	47,363	182	32	15	T	
Nagatino *		Lbr	1991	28,223	47,083	183	32	14	T	
Narodny Bridge		Lbr	2003	27,829	47,791	183	32	14	T	
Nevskiy Prospect		Lbr	2003	62,300	114,598	250	44	-	T	
Okhotsk Sea *		Lbr	1999	27,526	47,363	182	32	15	T	
Okhta Bridge		Lbr	2004	28,000	47,000	182	32	14	T	
Ostankino *		Cyp	1992	28,223	47,059	183	32	14	T	
Petrodvorets *		Lbr	1999	59,731	105,692	248	43	15	T	ex Astro Saturn-01
Petrokrepost *		Lbr	1999	59,731	98,039	248	43	15	T	ex Astro Maria-01
Petropavlovsk *		Lbr	2002	57,683	106,532	241	42	15	T	
Petrovsk		Lbr	2004	57,700	105,900	241	42	15	T	
Petrozavodsk *		Lbr	2003	57,683	106,449	241	42	15	T	
Polyanka *		Cyp	1992	28,223	47,083	183	32	14	T	
Presnya *		Cyp	1992	28,223	47,083	183	32	14	T	
Romea Champion *		Lbr	1992	79,718	154,970	274	44	14	T	ex Tromso Champion-92
SCF Altai		Lbr	2001	81,085	159,169	274	48	15	T	
SCF Caucasus		Lbr	2002	81,085	159,173	274	48	15	T	
SCF Khibiny		Lbr	2002	81,085	159,156	274	48	15	T	
SCF Sayan *		Lbr	2002	81,085	159,184	274	48	15	T	
SCF Ural *		Lbr	2002	81,085	159,169	274	48	15	T	
SCF Valdai		Lbr	2003	81,085	159,313	274	48	15	T	
SCI Vaibhav		Pan	2003	37,071	47,120	237	32	21	CC	ex Bremen Senator-03
Sokolniki *		Cyp	1992	28,223	47,083	183	32	14	T	
Stena Contender *		Lbr	2003	62,300	115,000	250	44	-	T	ex Liteyny Prospect-04
Troitskiy Bridge		Lbr	2003	27,725	41,158	183	32	14	T	
Tromso Confidence *		Lbr	1991	79,718	154,970	274	44	14	T	
Tromso Fidelity *		Lbr	1991	79,718	154,970	274	44	14	T	
Tromso Reliance *		Lbr	1991	79,718	154,970	274	44	14	T	
Tromso Trust *		Lbr	1991	79,718	154,970	274	44	14	T	
Tropic Brilliance *		Lbr	1992	79,718	154,970	274	44	14	T	ex Tromso Brilliance-92
Tuchkov Bridge *		Lbr	2004	27,500	47,000	183	32	14	T	

newbuildings : two 106,000 dwt, one 47,000 dwt and five 41,000 dwt tankers, plus some smaller vessels.
Controlled by Government of The Republic of Russia (first Soviet maritime enterprise with independent capital)
* owned by Unicom Management Services (Cyprus) Ltd. formed jointly with V.Ships Switzerland SA.
See also Hanjin Shipping Co. Ltd. (Senator Line)

Name	Eng	Flag	Year	GRT	DWT	Loa	Bm	Kts	Type	Former names

Spar Shipping AS

Norway

Funnel: White.
Hull: Black with red boot-topping.

Name	Eng	Flag	Year	GRT	DWT	Loa	Bm	Kts	Type	Former names
Spar Capella		Nis	1990	38,337	70,424	230	32	15	B	ex Maersk Tukang-00
Spar Carina		Nis	1990	38,337	70,424	230	32	15	B	ex Maersk Taikung-01
Spar Cetus		Nis	1998	25,982	45,725	186	30	15	B	ex Golden Protea-02
Spar Corona		Nis	1990	38,337	70,424	230	32	15	B	ex Maersk Tanjong-02
Spar Eight		Nis	1982	22,300	36,227	190	28	14	B	ex Negros Victory-95, Orchid II-91
Spar Emerald		Nis	1987	20,766	34,970	177	30	14	B	ex Mockingbird-97
Spar Garnet *		Nis	1985	18,011	30,674	180	23	14	B	ex Federal Vigra-97, Mary Anne-93
Spar Jade *		Nis	1985	18,011	30,674	180	23	14	B	ex Federal Aalesund-97, Fiona Mary-93
Spar Lupus		Nis	1998	26,400	45,146	186	30	15	B	ex Golden Aloe-02
Spar Opal *		Nis	1984	16,861	28,214	178	23	14	B	ex Matane-97, Federal Matane-97, Consensus Atlantic-92, Lake Shidaka-91
Spar Orion		Nis	1996	26,449	47,639	190	31	14	B	ex Western Orion-01
Spar Ruby *		Nis	1985	16,775	28,259	178	23	14	B	ex Solveig-00, Manila Bellona-98, Liberty Sky-96, Astral Neptune-90
Spar Sirius		Nis	1996	25,968	45,402	186	30	14	B	ex Western Transporter-01
Spar Three		Nis	1982	22,235	35,941	190	28	14	B	ex Diwata-90, Berta-87, Mino Maru-85
Spar Topaz		Nis	1987	22,155	38,455	181	31	14	B	ex Azteca 1-96
Spar Two		Pan	1982	22,258	35,971	180	28	14	B	ex Menina Barbara-93

newbuildings :six 53,000 dwt bulk carriers for 2005/6 delivery from Chinese builder.
* chartered-out to Fednav Ltd. q.v.

Spliethhoff's Bevrachtingskantoor BV

Netherlands

Funnel: Orange with black 'S' on diagonally quartered white/red/orange/blue flag
Hull: Brown with white line above green boot-topping

Name	Eng	Flag	Year	GRT	DWT	Loa	Bm	Kts	Type	Former names
Saimagracht		Nld	2004	16,639	21,250	168	25	19	Co	
Sampogracht		Nld	2004	16,639	21,250	168	25	19	Co	
Scheldegracht		Nld	2000	16,639	21,250	168	25	19	Co	
Schippersgracht		Ant	2000	16,641	21,402	168	25	19	Co	
Singelgracht		Nld	2000	16,641	21,402	168	25	19	Co	
Slotergracht		Nld	2000	16,641	21,402	168	25	19	Co	
Sluisgracht		Nld	2001	16,639	21,250	170	25	19	Co	
Snoekgracht		Nld	2000	16,641	21,400	168	25	19	Co	
Spaarnegracht		Nld	2000	16,641	21,402	168	25	19	Co	
Spiegelgracht		Nld	2000	16,641	21,400	168	25	19	Co	
Spuigracht		Nld	2001	16,639	21,349	172	25	19	Co	
Stadiongracht		Nld	2000	15,500	21,250	168	25	19	Co	
Suomigracht		Nld	2004	16,639	21,250	168	25	19	Co	

newbuildings : two further 21,250 dwt multi-purpose cargo vessels for 2004/5 delivery from Polish builder.
Also own numerous smaller vessels

BigLift Shipping BV

Funnel: Orange with black 'BigLift' or blue mammoth design.
Hull: Yellow with black 'BigLift' or blue mammoth design and 'MAMMOET', red boot-topping.

Name	Eng	Flag	Year	GRT	DWT	Loa	Bm	Kts	Type	Former names
Da Fu **		Pan	1998	14,021	16,957	153	23	15	HL	
Da Hua **		Pan	1998	14,021	16,957	153	23	15	HL	
Da Qiang **		Pan	1998	14,021	16,957	153	23	15	HL	
Da Zhong **		Pan	1998	14,021	16,957	153	23	15	HL	
Enchanter *		Pan	1998	10,990	16,069	138	23	15	HLC	ex Sailer Jupiter-98
Envoyager *		Sgp	1985	15,350	21,183	153	27	15	HL	ex Alps Maru-91
Happy Buccaneer	(2)	Nld	1984	16,341	13,740	146	28	15	HL	
Happy Ranger		Nld	1997	10,990	15,065	138	23	16	HL	
Happy River		Nld	1997	10,990	16,516	138	23	16	HL	
Happy Rover		Nld	1997	10,990	15,593	138	23	16	HL	

* owned by Pool member Mitsui OSK Lines Ltd (managed by New Asian Shipping Co. Ltd, Hong Kong) q.v. or ** by Guangzhou Ocean Shipping (COSCO), China.

Spar Shipping. SPAR ORION. *Hans Kraijenbosch.*

Spliethoff's Bevrachtingskantor. SPIEGELGRACHT. *N. Kemps.*

Spliethoff's (BigLift Shipping). HAPPY RANGER. *F. de Vries.*

Name	Eng	Flag	Year	GRT	DWT	Loa	Bm	Kts	Type	Former names

Star Reefers AS Norway

Funnel: White with red edged blue 5-pointed star, narrow blue band beneath red top.
Hull: Lilac grey, corn or blue with blue waterline over red boot-topping.

Name	Eng	Flag	Year	GRT	DWT	Loa	Bm	Kts	Type	Former names
Auckland Star		Bhs	1985	10,691	11,434	151	22	19	R	ex Horncliff-89, Auckland Star-87
Baltic Mariner †		Lbr	1979	10,424	9,852	151	22	22	R	ex Swan Stream-03, Pocantico-93, Isla Pongal-86, Pocantico-84
Baltic Melody †		Lbr	1980	10,424	9,852	151	22	22	R	ex Swan Ocean-03, Swan Lake-98, Potomac-93, Isla Payana-86, Potomac-84
Baltic Meridian †		Lbr	1980	10,424	9,852	151	22	22	R	ex Swan Lagoon-03, Pocahontas-93, Isla Plaza-86, Pocahontas-84
Belgian Reefer †		Cym	1983	12,383	14,786	145	24	18	R	ex Anne B-92
Brazilian Reefer †		Bhs	1984	12,383	14,786	145	24	16	R	ex Betty B-92
Canterbury Star		Bhs	1986	10,291	11,434	151	22	19	R	
Cape Town Star		Bhs	1993	10,614	10,629	150	23	21	R	ex Caribbean Reef-03, Hornbreeze-98, Geestcrest-95, Hornbreeze-95, Caribbean Universal-94
Caribbean Star *		Pan	1997	11,435	10,362	154	24	20	R	ex Hornsea-00, Caribbean Star-98
Chaiten		Lbr	1988	13,312	12,838	152	24	18	R	
Chiquita Brenda		Bmu	1993	8,665	11,973	151	20	20	R	ex Brenda-00, Chiquita Brenda-97, Chiquita Joy-93
Chiquita Joy		Bmu	1994	8,665	11,793	151	20	22	R	ex Joy-00, Chiquita Joy-97
Colombian Star †		Pan	1998	11,733	10,371	154	24	21	R	
Costa Rica Star *		Pan	1998	11,435	10,350	154	24	21	R	ex Hornwind-02, Costa Rican Star-98
Cote d'Ivoirian Star †		Pan	1998	11,733	11,000	154	24	21	R	
Durban Star		Bhs	1993	10,614	10,629	150	23	20	R	ex Coral Reef-03, Horncloud-98, Geesttide-95, Horncloud-94, Coral Universal-94
English Star		Bhs	1986	10,291	11,434	151	22	19	R	ex Hornsea-89, English Star-87
Harvester		Bhs	1989	8,945	9,867	141	22	20	R	ex Del Monte Harvester-99
Napier Star		Bmu	1994	8,665	11,822	151	20	19	R	ex Chiquita Elke-03, Elke-00, Chiquita Elke-97
Nelson Star		Bmu	1993	8,665	11,830	151	20	22	R	ex Chiquita Jean-03, Jean-00, Chiquita Jean-97
Polar Argentina ‡		Lbr	1992	12,629	10,588	150	23	21	R	ex Horntide-98, Polar Argentina-98, Gordian-95
Polar Brazil ‡		Lbr	1992	12,629	10,588	150	23	21	R	ex Hornstream-98, Polar Brazil-98, Numerian-95
Regal Star *		Pan	1993	10,375	10,520	150	23	20	R	ex Tauu-96, Hornstrait-95, Chiquita Tauu-94
Regent Star		Pan	1993	10,374	10,545	150	23	20	R	ex Nauru-00, Hornsound-95, Chiquita Nauru-94
Scottish Star		Bhs	1985	10,291	13,058	151	22	19	R	
Solent Star †		Pan	2001	10,804	9,709	150	23	21	R	
Southampton Star †		Pan	1999	10,804	9,709	150	23	21	R	
Swan Bay		Lbr	1979	10,853	10,988	161	23	19	R	ex Caribbean Maru-89
Swan Chacabuco		Lbr	1990	13,099	12,974	152	24	18	R	ex Chacabuco-97
Swan River		Lbr	1978	10 853	10,988	161	23	19	R	ex R.P.Jamaica-88, California Maru-87
Tauranga Star		Bmu	1992	7,944	10,963	141	20	20	R	ex Chiquita Frances-02, France-00, Chiquita Frances-98
Trojan Star		Bhs	1984	9,417	11,660	146	21	22	R	ex Walter Jacob-96, Cap Palmas-94, Walter Jacob-93, Bremerhaven-89, Walter Jacob-84
Tudor Star		Bhs	1983	9,417	11,805	146	21	22	R	ex Helene Jacob-96, Saxon Star-94, Helene Jacob-93, Blumenthal-88, Helene Jacob-84
Tundra Consumer		Lbr	1990	11,590	12,683	159	24	18	R	ex Del Monte Consumer-00
Tundra King		Bhs	1990	11,658	12,714	159	24	20	R	ex Del Monte Pride-91
Tundra Princess		Bhs	1991	11,658	12,714	159	24	20	R	ex Del Monte Spirit-91
Tundra Queen		Lbr	1991	11,658	12,714	159	24	20	R	ex Del Monte Quality-91
Tundra Trader		Lbr	1990	11,590	12,519	159	24	18	R	ex Del Monte Trader-99
Wellington Star **		Bhs	1992	7,944	11,103	141	20	21	R	ex Bothnian Reefer-03

Company jointly owned by Swan Shipping and Actinor (40%) with 10 vessels being managed by IUM Shipmanagement AS and others by * by Fleet Management, Hong Kong (China) or ** Dobson Fleet Management, Cyprus.
‡ chartered from Hamburg-Sudamerikanische Dampfschiffahrts-ges (Rudolf A. Oetker), Germany or † from various other owners.

Stelmar Tankers (Management) Ltd. Greece

Funnel: Cream with grey outline of bird in flight, black top.
Hull: Black with white 'Stelmar', red boot-topping.

Name	Eng	Flag	Year	GRT	DWT	Loa	Bm	Kts	Type	Former names
Alcesmar		Cyp	2004	30,058	45,965	183	32	14	T	
Alcmar		Cyp	2004	30,058	45,965	183	32	14	T	
Allenmar		Pan	1988	25,740	41,750	182	30	14	T	ex Petrobulk Challenger-01, Osprey Challenger-96, Pacific Challenger-94
Almar		Pan	1996	28,357	46,162	183	32	14	T	ex Osprey Altair-01

Star Reefers. CARIBBEAN STAR. *Hans Kraijenbosch.*

Star Reefers. CHAITEN. *J. M. Kakebeeke.*

Name	Eng	Flag	Year	GRT	DWT	Loa	Bm	Kts	Type	Former names
Ambermar		Cyp	2002	23,843	35,700	183	27	14	T	
Andromar		Cyp	2004	30,058	45,965	183	32	14	T	
Antigmar		Cyp	2004	30,100	45,800	183	32	14	T	
Aquamar		Cyp	1998	28,400	47,236	183	32	15	T	ex Alam Berkat-02
Ariadmar		Cyp	2004	30,058	45,800	183	32	14	T	
Atalmar		Cyp	2004	30,058	45,800	183	32	15	T	
Cabo Hellas		Cyp	2003	38,900	69,250	228	32	14	T	
Cabo Sounion		Cyp	2004	40,038	69,636	228	32	14	T	
Camar		Pan	1988	26,113	45,372	172	32	14	T	ex Petrobulk Cougar-01
Capemar		Pan	1988	23,127	37,615	175	30	15	T	ex Petrobulk Cape-01, Osprey Cape-96, Telaga Ayu-93, Creation-91, l/a Atlantic Chivalry
City University		Cyp	1987	24,584	39,729	193	32	14	T	ex Ocean Challenger-93
Cleliamar		Cyp	1993	38,653	68,600	226	32	13	T	ex Double Pride-98, l/a Chemoil Pride
Colmar		Cyp	1987	24,584	39,729	193	32	14	T	ex Ocean Conqueror-93
Ermar		Pan	1989	22,838	34,999	186	27	14	T	ex Petrobulk Power-01, Torm Helene-90
Fulmar		Cyp	1989	25,368	39,521	182	31	15	T	ex Kobe Spirit-93
Goldmar		Cyp	2002	40,343	69,684	228	32	14	T	l/a LMZ Mandi
Jacamar		Pan	1999	60,804	104,901	247	42	15	T	
Jademar		Lbr	2002	38,900	69,250	228	32	14	T	
Jamar		Lbr	1988	26,113	46,100	172	32	14	T	ex Petrobulk Jaguar-01
Keymar		Cyp	1993	54,953	95,822	242	42	14	T	ex Takamane Maru-98
Kliomar		Cyp	1989	54,980	96,088	242	42	14	T	ex Sanko Phoenix-97
Limar		Pan	1996	28,357	46,170	183	32	14	T	ex Osprey Lyra-01
Luxmar		Pan	1997	28,357	46,162	183	32	14	T	ex Petrobulk Pollux-01
Maremar		Cyp	1998	28,400	47,225	183	32	15	T	ex Alam Belia-02
Nedimar		Cyp	1996	28,326	43,999	183	32	14	T	
Pearlmar		Lbr	2002	38,900	69,250	228	32	14	T	
Petromar		Pan	2001	23,740	35,000	183	27	14	T	l/a Nordafrika
Polys		Cyp	1993	38,653	68,623	226	32	14	T	ex Double Glory-97
Primar		Cyp	1988	25,368	39,538	182	31	14	T	ex BP Advocate-93, l/a Onomichi Spirit
Reginamar		Lbr	2004	38,900	69,250	228	32	14	T	
Reinemar		Lbr	2004	38,900	69,250	228	32	14	T	
Reymar		Lbr	2004	38,900	69,250	228	32	14	T	
Himar		Pan	1998	28,357	46,162	183	32	14	T	ex Petrobulk Sirius-01
Rosemar		Cyp	2002	40,343	69,697	228	32	14	T	
Rubymar		Cyp	2002	40,343	69,697	228	32	14	T	
Silvermar		Pan	2002	40,343	69,609	228	32	14	T	l/a LMZ Zacvi
Takamar		Pan	1998	60,504	103,244	247	42	15	T	ex P. Alliance-01

newbuildings : eight 45,500 dwt and three 69,250 dwt tankers for 2004/5 delivery.

Polyar Tankers AS/Norway

Funnel: Black with broad yellow band or yellow with white 'S' on broad blue band edged with narrow white and brown bands.
Hull: Black with red boot-topping.

Name	Eng	Flag	Year	GRT	DWT	Loa	Bm	Kts	Type	Former names
Arendal		Nis	1986	60,339	106,722	235	43	14	T	ex Sentinel-99, Golar Nikko-89, Pacific Energy-86
Geilo		Nis	1990	135,546	243,272	320	55	14	T	ex Dione-00, Cosmo Dione-99
Halden		Bhs	1989	142,488	277,020	322	56	14	T	ex Maersk Neptune-01, Maersk Navigator-93
Kition		Bhs	1994	53,829	96,315	243	42	13	T	ex Irene-03
Lania		Pan	1990	137,712	248,050	316	58	14	T	ex Diamond Dream-00
Lofoten		Pan	1991	52,552	97,078	247	42	14	T	ex Isabella-02, Angel River-99
Lysaker		Pan	1989	143,941	276,210	322	56	14	T	ex World Prime-01
Magnitude		Nis	1992	54,962	96,136	242	42	14	T	ex Sanko Paragon-99
Moss		Nis	1992	52,048	96,833	232	42	13	T	ex Diana-02
Myre		Nis	1981	55,924	91,252	247	40	14	T	ex Showa Maru-96
Protaras		Sgp	1989	142,488	255,028	322	56	14	T	ex Maersk Nautilus-02
Stena Episkopi		Pan	1989	142,639	265,316	322	56	14	T	ex World Pendant-01

Controlled by Poly Haji-Ioannou with 25% minority held by P.F.Bassoe & Partners and managed by Cyclops Ships Ltd., Greece.

Stena AB   Sweden

Funnel: White 'S' on wide red band separated from black top and base by narrow white bands.
Hull: Black, grey or blue with 'Stena Bulk', red boot-topping.

Name	Eng	Flag	Year	GRT	DWT	Loa	Bm	Kts	Type	Former names
Stena Alexita **	(2)	Nor	1998	76,836	127,466	263	46	15	T	
Stena Commander †		Ita	2003	41,000	72,365	229	32	-	T	ex Blue Dolphin-03, Stena Comanche-03, Blue Dolphin-03

Stelmar Tankers. KEYMAR. *Hans Kraijenbosch.*

Stena AB. STENA CONFIDENCE. *Hans Kraijenbosch.*

Name	Eng	Flag	Year	GRT	DWT	Loa	Bm	Kts	Type	Former names
Stena Companion		Lbr	2004	43,000	72,637	229	32	-	T	
Stena Compatriot		Lbr	2004	43,000	72,000	229	32	-	T	
Stena Conductor †		Pan	2003	58,100	107,198	247	42	-	T	
Stena Confidence		Bhs	2003	58,118	107,215	247	42	-	T	
Stena Conqueror †		Ita	2003	27,335	47,323	183	32	14	T	ex Hellenica-03
Stena Conquest †		Ita	2003	27,335	47,136	183	32	14	T	ex Hispanica-03
Stena Paris		Swe	2004	35,000	49,000	290	40	-	T	
Stena Provence		Swe	2004	35,000	49,000	290	40	-	T	
Stena Sirita **	(2)	Nor	1999	76,836	127,466	263	46	15	T	
Stena Venture ‡		Hkg	2002	39,272	70,392	229	32	15	T	l/a Sanko Venture
Stena Victory *		Bmu	2001	163,761	312,679	335	70	16	T	
Stena Vision *		Bmu	2001	163,761	312,679	335	70	16	T	

newbuildings : two 113,600 dwt, four 72,000 dwt and two further 49,000 dwt shallow draft tankers on order.
* owned by associated Concordia Maritime AB, subsidiary Universe Tankships (Delaware) LLC which has six 49,000 dwt tankers on order.
** jointly owned with Ugland Marine Services AS and operated by Ugland Nordic Nordic Shipping ASA (see under Teekay)
† chartered from other owners ‡ owned by Dr. Peters KG fund, Germany.

Stolt-Nielsen Transportation Group B.V.   Netherlands

Funnel: White with large white 'S' on red square, narrow black top.
Hull: Yellow with black 'STOLT TANKERS', red or pink boot-topping.

Name	Eng	Flag	Year	GRT	DWT	Loa	Bm	Kts	Type	Former names
Stolt Achievement	(me)	Cym	1999	25,427	37,000	177	31	16	T	
Stolt Aquamarine		Cym	1986	23,964	38,746	177	32	15	T	
Stolt Avance		Lbr	1977	14,857	23,648	171	24	16	T	
Stolt Avenir		Lbr	1978	14,857	23,275	171	24	16	T	
Stolt Capability	(me)	Lbr	1998	24,625	37,042	177	31	16	T	
Stolt Concept	(me)	Cym	1999	24,495	37,236	177	31	16	T	
Stolt Condor		Lbr	1979	21,043	37,200	177	30	16	T	ex Stolt Okpo-79
Stolt Confidence	(me)	Cym	1996	24,625	37,015	177	31	16	T	
Stolt Creativity	(me)	Lbr	1997	24,625	37,271	177	31	16	T	
Stolt Eagle		Lbr	1980	21,043	37,067	177	30	16	T	ex Stolt Ulsan-80
Stolt Efficiency	(me)	Cym	1998	24,625	37,271	177	31	16	T	
Stolt Effort	(me)	Cym	1999	24,495	37,155	177	31	16	T	
Stolt Emerald		Cym	1986	23,964	38,719	177	32	15	T	
Stolt Excellence		Lbr	1979	20,157	31,379	177	27	16	T	
Stolt Falcon		Lbr	1978	21,043	37,201	174	30	15	T	ex Stolt Seoul-79
Stolt Guardian		Lbr	1983	22,904	39,723	175	32	13	T	ex Stolt Uskok-92, Maasuskok-89, Uskok-86, Iver Swift-85, Jo Swift-84, Iver Swift-84
Stolt Hawk		Lbr	1978	21,043	37,080	177	30	16	T	ex Stolt Inchon-79
Stolt Helluland		Cym	1990	18,994	31,454	175	30	15	T	
Stolt Heron		Lbr	1979	21,287	37,200	177	30	16	T	ex Stolt Yosu-79
Stolt Innovation	(me)	Cym	1996	24,625	37,015	177	31	16	T	
Stolt Inspiration	(me)	Cym	1997	24,625	37,205	177	31	16	T	
Stolt Integrity		Lbr	1977	20,157	32,057	177	27	18	T	
Stolt Invention †	(me)	Lbr	1998	24,625	37,271	177	31	16	T	
Stolt Jade		Cym	1986	23,964	38,746	177	32	15	T	
Stolt Loyalty		Lbr	1978	20,157	32,091	177	27	17	T	
Stolt Markland		Cym	1991	18,994	31,433	175	30	15	T	
Stolt Nanami *		Pan	2003	11,549	19,932	143	24	-	T	
Stolt Osprey		Lbr	1978	21,287	37,080	177	30	15	T	ex Stolt Busan-80
Stolt Perseverance	(me)	Cym	2000	25,196	37,059	177	31	16	T	
Stolt Pride		Lbr	1976	20,013	31,942	177	27	17	T	
Stolt Protector		Lbr	1983	22,587	39,782	174	32	14	T	ex Stolt Exporter-92, Exporter-88, Atlas Exporter-83
Stolt Sapphire		Lbr	1986	23,964	38,746	177	32	15	T	
Stolt Sea	(me)	Cym	1999	14,742	22,198	163	24	15	T	
Stolt Sincerity		Lbr	1976	20,013	31,943	177	27	17	T	
Stolt Span	(me)	Lbr	1998	14,775	22,273	163	24	15	T	
Stolt Spray	(me)	Cym	2000	14,180	22,460	163	24	15	T	
Stolt Stream	(me)	Cym	2000	14,180	22,199	163	24	15	T	
Stolt Sun	(me)	Cym	2000	14,152	22,460	163	24	15	T	
Stolt Surf	(me)	Cym	2000	14,180	22,460	163	24	15	T	
Stolt Tenacity		Lbr	1978	20,157	32,093	177	27	17	T	
Stolt Topaz		Cym	1986	23,964	38,818	177	32	15	T	
Stolt Valor **		Hkg	2004	15,600	25,100	159	26	-	T	
Stolt Vestland		Cym	1992	19,034	31,494	175	30	15	T	

Stolt-Nielsen Group. STOLT HELLULAND. *N. Kemps.*

Suisse-Atlantique. ENGIADINA. *Hans Kraijenbosch.*

T&E Ship Management. SIBOHELLE. *N. Kemps.*

Name	Eng	Flag	Year	GRT	DWT	Loa	Bm	Kts	Type	Former names
Stolt Vinland		Cym	1992	19,034	31,434	175	30	15	T	

newbuildings - four 25,000 dwt and two 32,500 dwt tankers for 2004/5 delivery.
* owned by V. Ships (Asia) Pte. Ltd. or ** by Central Marine Co. Ltd., Japan

Suisse-Atlantique Soc. de Navigation Maritime   Switzerland

Funnel: Black with red diagonal cross and two stars on yellow houseflag interrupting two yellow bands.
Hull: Grey with red boot-topping.

Name	Eng	Flag	Year	GRT	DWT	Loa	Bm	Kts	Type	Former names
Bariloche		Che	1999	38,289	73,018	225	32	14	B	
Celerina		Bhs	1999	39,161	73,035	225	32	14	B	
Corviglia		Che	1999	39,161	73,035	225	32	14	B	
Engiadina		Che	2002	27,779	40,878	222	30	22	CC	ex Norasia Engiadina-03, Engiadina-02
General Guisan		Che	1999	39,161	73,035	225	32	14	B	
Lausanne		Che	2003	27,779	40,878	222	30	22	CC	
Moleson		Che	1998	38,289	73,018	225	32	14	B	
Norasia Sils		Che	2003	27,779	40,878	221	30	22	CC	ex Sils-03
Nyon		Bhs	1999	39,161	73,035	225	32	14	B	
Silvretta		Che	1995	39,422	75,132	225	32	14	B	

newbuildings : two 25,000 grt 28,200 dwt container ships on order from South Korean builder for 2005 delivery.

John Swire & Sons Ltd.   UK

The China Navigation Co. Ltd./Hong Kong (China)

Funnel: Black with houseflag.
Hull: Black with red, grey or pink boot-topping.

Name	Eng	Flag	Year	GRT	DWT	Loa	Bm	Kts	Type	Former names
Changsha		Hkg	1991	18,391	23,737	185	28	18	Co	ex Pacific Challenger-99
Chekiang		Hkg	1991	18,391	23,271	185	28	18	Co	ex Atlantic Challenger-99
Erawan		Iom	1982	35,716	64,643	225	32	13	B	ex Camarina-99, Starfest-95, Yamashiro Maru-90
Erradale		Hkg	1994	82,701	163,554	284	44	15	B	
Kwangtung		Hkg	1985	17,527	21,725	182	27	17	Co	ex CGM Kwangtung-95, Kwangtung-94, Woermann Africa-92, Kwangtung-92, Presidente Jose Pardo-89

Bank Line/UK

Funnel: Buff with black top
Hull: Black with red boot-topping.

Name	Eng	Flag	Year	GRT	DWT	Loa	Bm	Kts	Type	Former names
Arunbank		Iom	1983	18,663	22,911	174	25	17	Ro	ex Bratsk-95
Foylebank		Iom	1983	18,663	22,911	174	25	17	Ro	ex Tiksi-95
Speybank		Iom	1983	18,663	22,911	174	25	17	Ro	ex Okha-95
Teignbank		Iom	1984	18,663	22,911	174	25	17	Ro	ex Nikel-95

Chartered from Andrew Weir Shipping Ltd., UK.

T&E Ship Management Alliance (TESMA)   Norway

Funnel: Black with blue and white diagonally divided shield on broad red band or owners colours.
Hull: Grey or brown with red boot-topping.

Name	Eng	Flag	Year	GRT	DWT	Loa	Bm	Kts	Type	Former names
Difko Birtha **		Nis	1987	43,733	83,870	229	32	14	T	ex Sitalouise-01, Burwain Baltic-95, Nordfarer-92
Difko Chaser **		Nis	1990	43,398	84,040	223	32	15	T	ex Northsea Chaser-01, Burwain Adriatic-95, Zafra-95
Difko Hanne **		Nis	1987	43,733	83,970	229	32	14	T	ex Sitalene-01, Burwain Nordic-95, Nordkap-92
Difko Susanne **		Nis	1989	43,398	84,040	229	32	15	T	ex Northsea Bellows-01, Burwain Arctic-95, Zidona-94
Northsea Anvil *‡		Dis	1990	43,733	83,790	229	32	15	T	ex Zaphon-95
Northsea Dowel *		Dis	1989	43,398	84,040	229	32	15	T	ex Burwain Torm-95, Zaria-94
Samco †		Bhs	1989	142,647	255,087	322	56	14	T	ex Fina Samco-91
Samco America †		Fra	2003	160,889	318,778	333	60	-	T	
Samco Asia †		Mhl	2003	160,889	318,000	333	60	-	T	
Samco Scandinavia †		Mhl	2004	160,000	305,000	333	60	-	T	
Sara Viking *		Nis	1990	43,398	84,040	229	32	14	T	ex Torm Sita-01, Bona Bay-96, Golar Perth-93
Selandia		Dis	1996	30,928	48,800	200	31	14	B	ex Star Selandia -98, Selandia-96
Sigana **		Pan	1985	24,943	42,842	190	30	14	B	ex Spring Gannet-98, Sanko Gannet-86

Name	Eng	Flag	Year	GRT	DWT	Loa	Bm	Kts	Type	Former names
Sitria **		Bhs	1985	25,221	41,876	187	29	15	B	ex Falstria-97, Star Falstria-96, Falstria-94, FP Clipper-94
Sivega **		Lbr	1985	24,111	41,081	185	30	14	B	ex Spring Vega-98, Sanko Vega-86
Sitacamilla *		Nis	1987	43,406	59,999	229	32	14	T	ex Burwain Pacific-95, Chrisholm-92
Sitakathrine *		Lbr	1986	43,733	83,970	229	32	14	T	ex Burwain Atlantic-95, Nordflex-91
Sitamarie *		Nor	1988	43,406	59,999	229	32	14	T	ex Burwain Scandic-96, Fredholm-91
Sitamia *		Nis	1988	43,414	84,040	229	32	13	T	ex Petrobulk Mars-97
Sitavera *		Lbr	1989	43,414	84,040	229	32	13	T	ex Petrobulk Jupiter-97

newbuildings : five 55,000 dwt bulk carriers for 2004/5 delivery from Japanese builder.
Joint management company following ending of joint ownership company by two families.
*Managed for various owners including * Waterfront Shipping, ** Fifko or † Saudi Maritime Holding Co., Saudi Arabia.*

Tschudi Shipping Co. AS

Funnel: As 'TESMA' or blue with eight-pointed white snowflake.
Hull: Grey or brown with red boot-topping.

Name	Eng	Flag	Year	GRT	DWT	Loa	Bm	Kts	Type	Former names
Frea		Irl	2003	11,360	16,484	159	23	-	T	ex Julia-03, I/a Julia
Nina		Irl	2004	11,400	16,500	159	23	-	T	
Safmarine Houston *		Est	1999	10,069	12,126	137	22	16	Co	ex Harjumaa-03, Didon-02, Harjumaa-99
Safmarine Onne *		Est	1995	10,069	12,126	137	22	16	Co	ex Sakala-03
Sibohelle ‡		Nis	1993	45,593	83,155	247	32	13	Obo	
Sibotessa ‡‡		Nis	1992	41,189	75,075	229	32	14	Obo	ex Vitessa-95

* owned by 100% controlled Estonian Shipping Co. (ESCO).
‡ on long-term bareboat charter from Dansk Investeringsfond or DMK Leasing A/S, Denmark and ‡‡ jointly operated.

Camillo Eitzen & Co. AS

Funnel: Red with white 'E' inside blue 'C' or * white with broad blue band beneath broad black top, some with 'ESO' below band.
Hull: Red with white 'EITZEN' or black, red boot-topping.

Name	Eng	Flag	Year	GRT	DWT	Loa	Bm	Kts	Type	Former names
Sibeia		Nis	1981	50,764	88,726	229	42	15	T	ex Gorbeia-95, Ambra Grey-93, Viking Osprey-89
Siboelf ‡		Nis	1993	41,189	75,075	229	32	14	Obo	
Sibonina ‡		Nis	1993	45,593	83,155	247	32	14	Obo	
Siboti ‡		Nis	1992	41,189	74,868	229	32	13	Obo	

‡ on long-term bareboat charter from Dansk Investeringsfond or DMK Leasing A/S, Denmark.

Teekay Shipping Corporation   Bahamas

Funnel: White with blue edged red 'TK' symbol, narrow black top.
Hull: Black with red boot-topping.

Name	Eng	Flag	Year	GRT	DWT	Loa	Bm	Kts	Type	Former names
Aegean Leader Ø		Pan	1993	47,171	13,157	180	32	18	V	ex Ocean Beluga-99, Mercury Diamond-96
Aegean Spirit †		Bhs	2002	62,247	112,668	250	44	15	T	
African Spirit		Bhs	2003	79,668	151,736	269	-	-	T	
American Spirit		Bhs	2003	63,213	111,920	244	-	-	T	
Asian Spirit		Bhs	2004	85,000	152,000	-	-	-	T	
Australian Spirit		Bhs	2004	62,000	111,942	244	-	-	T	
Avalon Spirit		Can	1998	57,925	107,181	236	42	-	T	ex Nassau Spirit-02
Bahamas Spirit ††		Bhs	1996	57,947	107,261	247	42	17	T	ex Sanko Trader-01
Barrington **		Aus	1989	21,718	33;239	181	27	14	T	ex Australia Sky-96
Broadwater **		Aus	1986	54,656	94,783	230	46	-	T	ex Australia Star-96
Chios Spirit †		Bhs	2002	62,247	112,679	250	44	-	T	ex Golden Star-02
Columbia Spirit		Bhs	1988	49,279	84,841	234	44	15	T	ex Bona Skipper-99, Ocean Explorer-94
Esther Spirit		Bhs	2004	63,500	113,000	-	-	-	T	
Falster Spirit		Bhs	1995	52,875	95,317	244	42	14	T	ex Bona Rover-99, Vendonna-96
Fountain Spirit		Nis	1982	44,834	78,488	243	32	14	Obo	ex Teekay Fountain-03, Bona Fountain-99, Hoegh Fountain-92
Gotland Spirit		Bhs	1995	52,875	95,370	244	42	14	T	ex Bona Rider-99, Venessa-96
Hamane Spirit		Bhs	1997	57,463	105,203	245	41	14	T	
Hudson Spirit		Bhs	1988	49,279	84,841	234	44	15	T	ex Bona Spinner-99, Ocean Navigator-94
Ionian Spirit †		Bhs	2002	62,247	112,664	250	44	15	T	
Kanata Spirit		Bhs	1999	62,685	113,021	249	44	14	T	
Kareela Spirit		Bhs	1999	62,685	113,021	249	44	14	T	
Karratha Spirit **		Aus	1988	59,289	106,671	257	43	14	T	ex Pioneer Spirit-02
Kiowa Spirit ††		Bhs	1999	62,619	113,334	253	44	14	T	ex Bona Valiant-99
Koa Spirit ††		Bhs	1999	62,619	113,334	253	44	14	T	ex Bona Verity-99
Koyagi Spirit		Bhs	1989	52,787	95,983	232	42	15	T	
Kyeema Spirit		Bhs	1999	62,619	113,357	253	44	14	T	I/a Bona Vigour

Name	Eng	Flag	Year	GRT	DWT	Loa	Bm	Kts	Type	Former names
Kyushu Spirit		Bhs	1991	53,988	95,562	233	42	14	T	
Leyte Spirit		Bhs	1992	57,448	98,744	245	41	14	T	
Luzon Spirit		Bhs	1992	57,448	98,629	245	41	14	T	
Mayon Spirit		Bhs	1992	57,448	98,507	245	41	14	T	
Musashi Spirit		Bhs	1993	153,642	280,654	330	56	16	T	
Nobel Foam		Bhs	1981	45,777	78,532	243	32	14	Obo	ex Foam Spirit-04, Teekay Foam-03, Bona Foam-99, Hoegh Foam-92
Nobel Fortuna		Nis	1982	45,777	78,532	243	32	14	Obo	ex Fortuna Spirit-04, Teekay Fortuna-03, Bona Fortuna-99, Hoegh Fortuna-92, Ambia Fortuna-89, Hoegh Fortuna-86
Nobel Forum		Bhs	1983	45,777	78,394	243	32	14	Obo	ex Forum Spirit-04, Teekay Forum-03, Bona Forum-99, Hoegh Forum-92
Nordic Spirit §		Bhs	2001	83,120	152,292	274	48	15	T	ex Storviken-02
Ocean Princess ‡		Bhs	1981	46,801	82,462	247	32	15	Obo	ex Bona Falcon-97, Hoegh Falcon-92
Oinoussian Spirit †		Bhs	2002	62,247	112,661	250	44	15	T	I/a Golden Sea
Onozo Spirit		Bhs	1990	57,450	100,020	245	41	14	T	
Orkney Spirit		Bhs	1993	55,864	106,233	244	42	14	T	ex Bona Spray-99
Pacific Spirit		Bhs	1988	59,289	106,661	244	43	14	T	
Palmerston **		Aus	1990	26,162	36,701	179	32	14	T	ex Ampol TVA-96
Palmstar Cherry		Bhs	1990	57,450	100,024	245	41	14	T	
Palmstar Lotus		Bhs	1991	57,450	100,314	245	41	14	T	
Palmstar Orchid		Bhs	1989	57,450	100,047	245	41	14	T	
Palmstar Poppy		Bhs	1990	57,450	100,031	245	41	14	T	
Palmstar Rose		Bhs	1990	57,450	100,202	245	41	14	T	
Palmstar Thistle		Bhs	1991	57,450	100,047	245	41	14	T	
Poul Spirit		Bhs	1995	57,463	105,351	245	41	14	T	
Sabine Spirit		Bhs	1989	49,279	84,841	234	44	15	T	ex Bona Shimmer-99, Ocean Leader-94
Samar Spirit **		Bhs	1992	57,448	98,640	245	41	14	Obo	
Seahawk Freighter ‡		Mhl	1982	45,067	75,395	243	32	15	Obo	ex Freighter Spirit-04, Teekay Freighter-03, Bona Freighter-99, Hoegh Freighter-92, Siboseven-89
Sebarok Spirit		Bhs	1993	52,508	95,649	247	42	14	T	
Seletar Spirit		Bhs	1988	57,764	94,998	247	42	14	T	ex Pacific Mercury-98
Semakau Spirit		Bhs	1988	52,484	97,172	247	42	14	T	ex Nissos Amorgos-96, Seto Breeze-95
Senang Spirit		Bhs	1994	52,508	95,649	247	42	14	T	
Sentosa Spirit		Bhs	1989	52,500	97,159	247	42	14	T	
Seraya Spirit		Bhs	1992	52,507	97,119	247	42	14	T	
Shetland Spirit		Bhs	1994	55,864	106,263	244	42	14	T	ex Bona Sailor-99
Shilla Spirit		Bhs	1990	59,289	106,679	244	43	14	T	
Sotra Spirit		Bhs	1995	52,875	95,370	244	42	14	T	ex Bona Robin-99, Ventina-96
Stena Spirit		Bhs	2001	83,120	152,244	274	48	15	T	ex Erviken-01
Teekay Spirit ††		Bhs	1991	57,450	100,336	245	41	14	T	
Torben Spirit		Bhs	1994	57,486	98,622	245	41	14	T	
Torres Spirit		Bhs	1990	54,963	96,144	242	42	14	T	ex Sanko Pioneer-97
Ulsan Spirit		Bhs	1990	59,289	106,679	244	43	14	T	
Vancouver Spirit		Bhs	1992	63,709	103,203	244	42	-	Obo	
Victoria Spirit		Bhs	1993	63,709	103,153	244	42	-	Obo	

newbuildings - eight 115,000 dwt, four 112,000 dwt and two 105,000 dwt tankers from S. Korean and Japanese builders (2004-7)
* owned by Teekay Shipping Ltd., Bahamas, ** by Teekay Shipping (Australia) Pty. Ltd, Australia or *** by Teekay Shipping (Japan) Ltd, Japan.
† owned by Chartworld Shipping Corp., Greece or ‡ managed by V.Ships Norway A/S.
§ managed by Viken Ship Management AS, Norway or †† owned by Dr. Peters KG fund, Germany Ø on charter to NYK q.v.

Navion ASA/Norway

Funnel: White with blue and red coloured/striped rectangle, black top.
Hull: Orange or dark blue with 'Navion' towards stern, red boot-topping.

Name	Eng	Flag	Year	GRT	DWT	Loa	Bm	Kts	Type	Former names
Navion Anglia	(2)	Nor	1999	72,449	126,749	265	43	15	T	
Navion Britannia	(2)	Nor	1998	72,110	124,821	265	43	15	T	
Navion Clipper *		Bhs	1993	42,159	78,228	221	38	14	T	ex Polyclipper-98
Navion Fennia		Bhs	1992	50,907	96,058	241	40	14	T	ex Futura-03
Navion Hispania	(2)	Nor	1999	72,132	126,749	265	43	14	T	
Navion Oceania	(2)	Nor	1999	72,132	126,749	265	43	14	T	
Navion Saga *		Bhs	1991	79,918	149,000	269	46	14	T	ex Polysaga-00
Navion Scandia	(2)	Nor	1998	72,132	126,749	265	43	14	T	
Navion Scotia		Nis	1993	52,348	95,029	238	42	14	T	ex Vinga-98

Teekay Shipping. SENTOSA SPIRIT. *Hans Kraijenbosch.*

Teekay Shipping (Ugland Nordic Shipping). NORDIC SARITA. *M. D. J. Lennon.*

Teekay Shipping (Ugland Nordic Shipping). STENA NATALITA. *Hans Kraijenbosch.*

Name	Eng	Flag	Year	GRT	DWT	Loa	Bm	Kts	Type	Former names
Venture Spirit **		Hkg	2003	159,456	298,287	333	-	-	T	

Vessels managed by Rasmussen Shipmanagement, Norway (controlled by Overseas ShipholdingCorp,)
* Part owned by Overseas ShipholdingCorp , and ** operated for Wah Kwong, Hong Kong.

Ugland Nordic Shipping ASA/Norway

Funnel: White with blue and red coloured/striped rectangle, black top.
Hull: Orange with red boot-topping.

Name	Eng	Flag	Year	GRT	DWT	Loa	Bm	Kts	Type	Former names
Nordic Akarita *		Bhs	1991	58,928	107,223	244	42	14	T	ex Stena Akarita-02, Akarita-96
Nordic Laurita		Nis	1981	42,575	68,139	244	32	15	T	ex Nordic Challenger-97, Houston Accord-89
Nordic Marita *		Cym	1999	58,117	103,894	246	42	14	T	
Nordic Sarita	(2)	Nor	1986	70,434	124,472	252	46	14	T	ex Sarita-98
Nordic Savonita		Nis	1992	58,959	108,153	244	42	15	T	ex Stena Savonita-97, Savonita-94
Nordic Stavanger		Bhs	2003	80,691	148,729	277	46	-	T	
Nordic Svenita *		Bhs	1997	58,269	106,506	250	42	14	T	ex Svenner-98
Nordic Torinita *		Cym	1992	58,959	108,683	244	42	14	T	ex Torinita-96
Nordic Troll *		Nis	1981	38,406	67,436	228	32	14	T	ex Petrotroll-03, Skaustream-93, Jaguar-91
Nordic Trym *		Nis	1987	45,104	80,745	229	32	14	T	ex Petrotrym-03, Primo-95, Osco Beduin-89
Nordic Yukon *		Nis	1992	56,020	97,069	241	41	14	T	ex Wilma Yukon-01, Wilomi Yukon-96
Petroatlantic		Bhs	2003	54,865	92,968	235	42	-	T	
Petronordic *		Bhs	2002	54,885	92,995	234	42	-	T	
Petroskald *		Lbr	1982	23,174	39,750	174	32	14	T	ex Oktelia-86
Stena Natalita	(2)	Cym	2001	62,393	108,073	250	43	14	T	

98% owned except three jointly owned with Stena. * managed by IUM Shipmanagement AS, Norway (see under Ugland)
See also Nordic American Tanker Shipping vessels under BP Shipping Ltd.

Alfred C. Toepfer KG Schiffahrts. GmbH.   Germany

Funnel: White with two narrow green bands above and below large green 'T' beneath black top, or charterers colours.
Hull: Black or green with red boot-topping.

Name	Eng	Flag	Year	GRT	DWT	Loa	Bm	Kts	Type	Former names
MSC Canberra		Lbr	1995	29,181	41,583	203	31	19	CC	ex Joseph-01, TMM Puebla-01, Joseph-00, Zim Venezia I-98, Med Fos-97, Joseph Lykes-96
Nautic II		Lbr	1995	29,181	41,583	203	31	19	CC	ex CMA CGM Monet-02, James-00, James Lykes-96

A/S Dampskibsselskabet Torm   Denmark

Funnel: Black with blue 'T' on broad white band between two broad red bands.
Hull: Black or grey with red boot-topping.

Name	Eng	Flag	Year	GRT	DWT	Loa	Bm	Kts	Type	Former names
Torm Alice		Dis	1995	28,628	47,629	183	32	14	T	
Torm Ann-Marie		Dis	1997	57,031	99,990	244	42	15	T	
Torm Anna		Dis	2004	40,000	75,000	225	32	14	T	
Torm Anne		Sgp	1999	28,932	45,507	180	32	14	T	
Torm Arawa ††		Lbr	1997	18,108	29,096	175	26	14	B	
Torm Asia		Hkg	1994	25,190	44,372	180	30	14	T	
Torm Baltic ¶		Pan	1997	36,592	69,614	225	32	14	B	ex Navios Minerva-02
Torm Estrid		Dis	2004	40,000	75,000	225	32	14	T	
Torm Freya		Dis	2003	30,058	46,342	183	32	14	T	
Torm Gerd		Dis	2002	30,058	46,300	183	32	14	T	
Torm Gertrud		Dis	2002	30,058	46,362	183	32	14	T	
Torm Gotland		Dis	1995	28,628	47,629	183	32	14	T	
Torm Gudrun *		Lbr	2000	57,031	99,965	244	42	15	T	
Torm Gunhild		Dis	1999	28,909	45,457	181	32	14	T	
Torm Helene		Dis	1997	57,031	99,900	244	42	14	T	
Torm Herdis		Nis	1992	36,540	69,618	225	32	14	B	ex Santa Teresa-03, Navios Mariner-02
Torm Hilde		Nis	1990	43,398	84,040	229	32	14	T	ex Sitamona Bona-03, Brave-96, Golar Aberdeen-93
Torm Ingeborg		Nis	2003	57,095	99,900	244	42	14	T	
Torm Kristina *		Lbr	1999	57,080	105,002	244	42	15	T	
Torm Margrethe		Dis	1988	43,530	84,000	229	32	14	T	
Torm Marina		Nis	1990	36,573	69,637	225	32	14	B	
Torm Marlene ¶		Pan	1997	36,592	69,548	225	32	14	B	
Torm Marta		Pan	1997	36,592	69,638	225	32	14	B	
Torm Mary		Dis	2002	30,058	46,634	183	32	14	T	
Torm Pacific †		Lbr	1997	18,108	29,071	175	26	14	B	
Torm Ragnhild		Lbr	2004	40,000	75,000	225	32	14	T	
Torm Rotna ¶		Pan	2001	40,072	75,971	225	32	14	B	

A/S Dampskib. Torm. TORM MARLENE. *N. Kemps.*

A/S Dampskib. Torm. TORM VITA. *Hans Kraijenbosch.*

Name	Eng	Flag	Year	GRT	DWT	Loa	Bm	Kts	Type	Former names
Torm Tekla		Nis	1993	36,952	69,268	225	32	13	B	
Torm Thyra		Dis	2003	30,058	46,308	183	32	14	T	
Torm Tina ¶		Pan	2001	40,030	75,966	225	32	14	B	
Torm Valborg		Nis	2003	57,095	99,900	244	42	14	T	
Torm Vita		Dis	2002	30,058	46,308	183	32	14	T	

newbuildings - four 40,000 grt and six 61,000 grt tankers due for 2004 and 2006/7 delivery respectively from South Korean and Chinese builders
Torm Pool of product tankers comprises nearly 100 vessels.
† owned by Torm Asia Ltd, Hong Kong or †† by Torm Singapore (Pte.) Ltd. (managed by Wah Kwong Ship Management (Hong Kong) Ltd.)
* on charter from Dr. Peters KG fund, Germany or § from various other owners.
¶ owned by subsidiary of Nippon Yusen Kaisha (NYK Line), Japan.

Transeste Schiffahrt GmbH
Germany

Funnel: *Mainly in charterers colours.*
Hull: *Black or dark grey with red boot-topping.*

Name	Eng	Flag	Year	GRT	DWT	Loa	Bm	Kts	Type	Former names
Birte Ritscher **		Atg	1995	14,862	20,346	167	25	19	CC	ex Cala Piedad-02, Kaduna-00, TNX Express-98, Zim Argentina 2-98, CCNI Anakena-96, Birte Ritscher-95
Estestar **		Atg	1990	10,868	15,174	158	23	18	CC	ex Safmarine Shebeli-03, Estestar-02, P&O Nedlloyd Kowie-01, Estestar-00, Kent Scout-00, Ulf Ritscher-98
Estetrader *		Atg	1993	14,953	20,140	167	25	18	CC	ex City of Oxford-03, Kent Courier-01, Seaboard Toronto-00, Keta-00, Wieland-98, Exporter-97, Red Sea Exporter-95, Wieland-94
Sea Tiger		Deu	2001	25,705	33,795	208	30	22	CC	I/a Ulf Ritscher
Trade Bravery *		Atg	1999	25,705	33,843	208	30	22	CC	ex TPL Merchant-02, Lykes Crusader-01
Trade Zale **		Atg	1999	25,705	33,750	208	30	22	CC	ex TPL Eagle-02, TMM San Antonio-01, Jan Ritscher-99
Wieland		Lbr	2004	35,645	42,000	221	32	22	CC	
Wiking *		Atg	1996	16,803	22,878	184	25	19	CC	ex CSAVTianjin-01, Pacific Champion-01, Capricorn Challenger-99, Wiking-97
Wotan		Deu	2001	25,703	33,795	208	30	22	CC	ex MSC Venezuela-03, I/a Wotan

newbuildings : one further 34,300 grt container ship for 2004 delivery.
* managed for Dietrich Tamke K.G. or ** for Gerd Ritscher K.G., both Germany

TransPetrol Services N.V.
Belgium

Funnel: *Black with white 'tp' above white vertical lines.*
Hull: *Black with grey or blue boot-topping.*

Name	Eng	Flag	Year	GRT	DWT	Loa	Bm	Kts	Type	Former names
Advance *		Sgp	1983	30,045	55,337	207	32	15	T	ex Toronto-90, Toro-86, Toro Horten-85
Endurance		Sgp	1988	19,063	39,988	182	27	-	T	
Eternity		Sgp	1988	22,847	39,834	182	27	15	T	
Faith IV *		Sgp	1987	39,131	63,765	229	32	14	T	ex Argo Asia-93
Fidelity		Sgp	1981	30,045	54,626	207	32	15	T	ex Beatrice-88, Vivita-86, Morning Light-84, Viking Lady-83
Loyalty *		Pan	1985	43,363	75,992	229	32	15	T	ex A.C. Atom-93, Toluma-89
Progress *		Nis	1991	58,078	111,777	247	43	14	T	ex Nyhval-96
Promise *		Sgp	1991	58,078	111,587	247	43	14	T	ex Gammatank-00, Apache Spirit-93
Prospect *		Nis	1992	58,078	111,689	247	43	14	T	ex Nyhaap-96
Reliance *		Sgp	1984	29,919	55,289	207	32	14	T	ex Torino-87, Taurus-86, Taurus Horten-85
Respect *		Sgp	1992	22,607	40,374	176	32	15	T	
Rowan *		Bhs	1991	24,731	44,646	182	30	14	T	
Tenacity *		Sgp	1996	53,371	87,240	228	42	15	T	
Trader		Sgp	1987	39,212	63,765	229	32	14	T	ex Ace Trader-97
Tribute *		Lbr	1996	79,643	149,258	276	45	14	T	
Turmoil **		Sgp	1988	22,487	39,872	186	27	14	T	
Venture *		Sgp	1985	43,368	76,000	229	32	14	T	ex Wilanna-90

newbuildings : two 41,000 grt 74,100 dwt and four 30,600 grt 45,800 dwt tankers due 2004/5 from South Korean builder.
* managed by International Tanker Management Holding Ltd., UAE or ** by Wallem Ltd., UK

Name	Eng	Flag	Year	GRT	DWT	Loa	Bm	Kts	Type	Former names

Trireme Vessel Management NV Belgium

Funnel: Dark blue with yellow 'EL' on red disc.
Hull: Orange with red boot-topping.

Name	Eng	Flag	Year	GRT	DWT	Loa	Bm	Kts	Type	Former names
Albemarle Island *		Bhs	1993	14,061	14,160	179	25	21	R	
Arctic Ocean		Bhs	1989	10,829	10,303	151	22	22	R	
Atlantic Ocean		Bhs	1989	10,829	10,285	151	22	22	R	
Baltic Sea		Bhs	1973	6,892	9,072	141	18	22	R	ex Provincia del Guayas-95, Ciudad de Guayaquil-88, Lucky I-84, Lucky-84, Timur Girl-83, Hilco Girl-81, Golar Girl-77
Barrington Island *		Bhs	1993	14,061	14,140	179	25	21	R	
Bering Sea		Bhs	1975	9,618	9,744	153	21	-	R	ex Punta Bianca-94
Celtic Sea		Bhs	1970	9,869	11,902	166	21	22	R	ex Provincia de los Rios-95, Indian Ocean-84, Nippon Reefer-78
Charles Island *		Bhs	1993	14,061	14,140	179	25	21	R	
Coral Sea		Bhs	1976	9,618	9,748	153	21	-	R	ex Punta Verde-94
Duncan Island *		Bhs	1993	14,061	14,140	179	25	21	R	
Hood Island *		Bhs	1994	14,601	14,140	179	25	21	R	
Indian Ocean		Bhs	1989	10,829	10,313	151	22	22	R	

* on long-term bareboat charter from Dansk Investeringsfond or DMK Leasing A/S, Denmark.

Tsakos Shipping & Trading S.A. Greece

Funnel: Yellow with red 'T' on broadwhite band edged with narrow blue bands.
Hull: Black with red boot-topping.

Name	Eng	Flag	Year	GRT	DWT	Loa	Bm	Kts	Type	Former names
Andes *		Grc	2003	39,085	68,467	229	32	14	T	
Aramis		Cyp	1983	37,895	60,906	228	32	15	T	ex Hydra Mar-98, Caribbean Shoot II-90
Argosea		Mlt	1980	74,849	155,213	285	44	16	T	ex Argonaftis-99, Don Humberto-89, I/a Caledonia Team
Athens 2004 *		Grc	1998	57,925	107,181	247	42	14	T	
Athos I		Cyp	1983	37,895	60,880	228	32	15	T	ex Stella Mar-98, Bright Oak-90, Charter Oak-89, I/a Caribbean Sprout II
Atlantida		Cyp	1980	53,944	87,542	243	42	14	T	ex Canadian Liberty-97, Columbia Liberty-85
Australia Bridge		Lbr	1991	37,410	47,273	236	32	18	CC	ex Australian Endurance-96
Aztec		Grc	2003	39,085	68,467	229	32	14	T	
Bregen *		Mlt	1989	38,792	68,157	243	32	15	T	
Commo JC Jimenez		Cyp	1979	54,577	99,244	250	41	15	T	ex Nissos Therassia-96, Kiho-92, Kiho Maru-89
Crux *		Grc	1987	23,926	41,161	172	32	14	T	ex Neptune Crux-99
Dartagnan		Cyp	1984	36,706	61,762	229	32	14	T	ex Centaurus Mar-98, Fumi-90
Delos *		Grc	2004	23,500	37,000	183	27	-	T	
Delphi *		Grc	2004	23,500	37,000	183	27	-	T	
Dion *		Cyp	1984	22,102	40,302	176	32	14	T	ex Mekhanik Yakovenko-93, Aniara-88, Black Marlin-88
El Greco		Pan	1985	133,940	239,781	318	54	14	T	ex Tagawa Maru-01
El Junior		Pan	1995	149,896	260,870	335	58	15	T	ex Tohzan-03
Hesnes *		Mlt	1990	38,792	68,157	243	32	14	T	
Inca *		Grc	2003	39,085	68,467	229	32	14	T	
Irenes Logos		Pan	1995	18,716	24,370	194	28	20	CC	ex Ise-02
Irenes Myth		Cyp	1983	31,356	30,941	220	32	22	CC	ex Global Myth-02, Irenes Myth-97, California Triton-97, Japan Alliance-91
Irenes Power		Cyp	1984	38,155	69,841	237	32	13	B	ex Global Power-02, Irenes Power-97, Ramona-97, Yamato-87
Irenes Vigor		Cyp	1983	35,603	65,224	224	32	16	B	ex Global Vigor-02, Irenes Vigor-97, Oakby-97, Continental Reliance-92
Irenes Vision		Cyp	1982	76,055	145,177	273	43	13	B	ex Sabina-94, Shiraishi Maru-89
La Esperanza *		Pan	1993	158,475	299,700	344	56	14	T	ex Ehm Maersk-03, British Valour-02, Elisabeth Maersk-97
La Madrina *		Grc	1993	158,475	299,700	344	56	14	T	ex Maersk Estelle-04, Estelle Maersk-98
La Paz *		Pan	1995	158,475	299,700	344	56	14	T	ex Evelyn Maersk-03
La Prudencia		Grc	1992	158,475	298,900	344	56	14	T	ex Maersk Eleo-04, Eleo Maersk-98
Liberty *		Cyp	1981	36,657	61,375	225	32	15	T	ex Liberty Bell Venture-94
Libra *		Grc	1988	23,926	41,161	172	32	14	T	ex NOL Libra-99, Neptune Libra-96
Marathon *		Grc	2003	58,127	107,181	247	42	14	T	
Maria Tsakos *		Grc	1998	57,925	107,181	247	42	14	T	
Maya *		Grc	2003	39,085	68,467	229	32	14	T	

Name	Eng	Flag	Year	GRT	DWT	Loa	Bm	Kts	Type	Former names
Millenium *		Pan	1998	156,692	301,178	331	58	15	T	
MSC Brasilia		Grc	1986	35,598	43,270	241	32	21	CC	ex Kobe-02, Hanjin Kobe-02
MSC London		Cyp	1986	36,266	43,270	241	32	21	CC	ex Keelung-03, Hanjin Keelung-02
MSC Sardinia		Cyp	1986	36,270	42,880	241	32	22	CC	ex Hong Kong-03, Hanjin Hongkong-03
Naga		Bhs	1979	52,716	88,251	248	42	15	T	ex Honshu Spirit-98, Tango Maru-89
Oceanida		Cyp	1980	53,917	87,307	243	42	14	T	ex Rosby-99, Crosby-99, Mega Pilot-91, Bergen Pilot-89, Mega Pilot-88, Glorie-88
Opal Queen		Pan	2001	57,920	107,181	247	42	14	T	
P&O Nedlloyd Kilindini		Mlt	1982	19,872	25,214	184	27	19	CC	ex Irenes Horizon-03, MSC Australia-02, Global Horizon-99, Irenes Horizon-97, Sea Fortune I-95, Al Khaimah-94, TSK Chorus-91, Prosper-89, Almudena-88
Panos G *		Cyp	1981	49,101	86,843	244	39	-	T	ex Tomis Liberty-95, Thorstar-93, Jarmona-89, Eva-89
Parthenon		Grc	2003	58,157	107,018	247	42	-	T	
Pella *		Cyp	1985	22,102	40,231	176	32	13	T	ex Mekhanik Kharchenko-93, Riaki-88
Porthos		Cyp	1981	37,758	65,779	228	32	14	T	ex Pegasus Erre-98, Loire-89, Fairfield Phoenix-86, Fairfield Venture-86
Silia T *		Grc	2002	84,586	164,286	274	50	15	T	
Sina		Grc	1992	137,746	254,991	316	58	14	T	ex Diamond Echo-02
Tamyra *		Cyp	1983	49,335	86,843	244	39	15	T	ex Dido-93, Marine Renaissance-89
Toula Z		Grc	1997	57,949	107,222	247	42	14	T	
Triathlon *		Grc	2002	84,586	164,445	274	50	14	T	
Vergina II		Cyp	1991	53,569	96,709	247	42	14	T	ex Lark Lake-95
Victory III *		Ven	1990	38,798	68,160	243	32	15	T	ex Ryvingen-95
WEC Rotterdam		Cyp	1982	19,872	25,214	184	27	20	CC	ex Irenes Synthesis-03, MSC Spain-02, Global Synthesis-99, ACX Clover-98, Irenes Synthesis-95, Maersk Kyoto-95, Sea Dragon-94, Al Khakji-94, Pilaro-91, CGM Champagne-91, Pilar-89

newbuildings : four 164,250 dwt and four 37,000 dwt tankers plus four 39,000 dwt container ships due for 2005/6 delivery
* managed by Tsakos Enegry Management Ltd., Greece.

Ugland International Holdings PLC   Cayman Islands
IUM Shipmanagement AS/Norway

Funnel: Yellow with white 'U' on broad red band below black top.
Hull: Grey, black or orange with black or white 'UGLAND', green or red boot-topping.

Name	Eng	Flag	Year	GRT	DWT	Loa	Bm	Kts	Type	Former names
Benarita *		Nis	1984	23,594	40,688	183	30	14	B	ex Yuming-91, Sanko Elegance-91
Campos Transporter		Nis	1988	22,838	39,777	186	27	14	T	ex Nordholt-99, Torm Herdis-95
Ellenita **		Pan	1984	24,942	42,836	190	30	14	B	ex Golden Topaz-97, Samar Sampaguita-90, Diamond Azalea-89, New Azalea-87, Sanko Azalea-85
Evita **		Nor	1989	72,120	126,352	260	46	14	T	
Fermita **		Pan	2001	30,053	52,380	190	32	14	B	
Gerrita **		Nis	1990	60,866	112,046	243	43	14	T	ex Dicto-97, Dicto Knutsen-94
Jorita *		Nis	1985	23,981	36,726	179	31	14	B	
Juanita **	(2)	Nor	1988	72,129	126,491	260	46	14	T	ex Lisita-89
Livanita *		Pan	1997	26,044	45,426	186	30	15	B	
Lunita **		Pan	1984	24,942	42,838	190	30	14	B	ex Cypress Point-97, Palawan Sampaguita-94, Diamond Camelia-89, New Camelia-87, Sanko Camelia-86
Mattea † (2)		Can	1997	76,216	126,380	272	46	15	T	
Norita *		Nis	1984	22,135	38,891	181	31	14	B	ex Anita-91, Neo Campanula-90, Sanko Campanula-90
Norwave		Mlt	1982	18,477	29,994	171	26	-	T	ex Scarlet Star-03, Julie N-99
Senorita **		Nis	1985	25,982	43,648	186	30	14	B	ex Solar Eterna-89, Eastern Gloria-87, Tsukubasan Maru-87
Tamarita **		Pan	2001	30,053	52,292	190	32	14	B	
Tjore Fremgang		Nis	1992	57,082	96,027	243	38	14	Obo	ex SKS Banner-04, Scanobo Banner-92
Vinland †		Can	2000	76,567	125,827	272	46	14	T	

newbuildings : two 52,000 dwt bulk carriers from Japanese builder fro 2004/5 delivery.
* owned by Ugland Shipping Co. A/S or ** by Ugland Marine Services AS
† owned by Canship Ugland Ltd formed jointly with Canship Ltd or ‡ managed by Canship Ugland Ltd for Mobil Oil Corp., Chevron Corp. and Murphy Oil Corp.
See also Hual under Leif Hoegh and Stena AB.

Tsakos Shipping & Trading. AUSTRALIA BRIDGE (on charter to Kawasaki). *Hans Kraijenbosch.*

Tsakos Shipping & Trading. BREGEN. *Hans Kraijenbosch.*

United Arab Shipping Co. AL-SABAHIA. *Hans Kraijenbosch.*

Name	Eng Flag	Year	GRT	DWT	Loa	Bm	Kts	Type	Former names

United Arab Shipping Co. (S.A.G.) — Kuwait

Funnel: Black, broad white band with red/purple bands above and black/green bands below black 6-spoked wheel containing black crossed anchors on blue centre disc.

Hull: Light grey with black 'UASC', green band over red boot-topping.

Name	Flag	Year	GRT	DWT	Loa	Bm	Kts	Type	Former names
Abu Dhabi	Are	1998	48,154	49,844	277	32	24	CC	
Addiriyah	Sau	1979	20,526	24,272	183	27	17	CC	
Al Ihsa'a	Sau	1983	32,534	35,615	211	32	19	CC	
Al Manakh	Kwt	1983	32,534	35,615	211	32	19	CC	
Al Mariyah	Are	1983	32,534	35,615	211	32	19	CC	
Al Mirqab	Kwt	1983	32,534	35,615	211	32	19	CC	
Al Wajba	Qat	1983	32,534	35,615	211	32	19	CC	
Al-Abdali	Kwt	1998	48,154	49,844	277	32	24	CC	
Al-Farahidi	Bhr	1998	48,154	50,004	277	32	24	CC	
Al-Mutanabbi	Bhr	1998	48,154	49,844	277	32	24	CC	
Al-Sabahia	Kwt	1998	48,154	49,848	277	32	24	CC	
Al-Wattyah	Kwt	1979	20,526	24,302	183	27	17	CC	
Alnoof	Qat	1998	48,154	49,993	277	32	24	CC	
Asir	Sau	1998	48,154	49,856	277	32	24	CC	
Deira	Are	1998	48,154	49,993	277	32	24	CC	
Dubai	Are	1982	32,534	35,615	211	32	19	CC	
Fowairet	Qat	1998	48,154	49,993	277	32	24	CC	
Hammurabi	Kwt	1983	32,534	35,615	211	32	19	CC	ex Australian Advance-98, Hammurabi-86
Ibn Al Moataz	Sau	1977	15,455	23,618	175	24	16	C	
Ibn Bassam	Qat	1977	15,125	23,618	175	24	16	C	
Ibn Younus	Qat	1977	15,455	23,828	175	24	16	C	ex Trident Delta-90, Rickmers Shanghai-88, Ibn Younus-86
Jebel Ali	Are	1979	20,526	24,349	183	27	17	CC	
Khaled Ibn Al Waleed	Are	1983	32,534	35,615	211	32	19	CC	
Najran	Sau	1998	48,154	49,993	277	32	24	CC	
Qatari Ibn Al Fuja'a	Qat	1983	32,534	35,615	211	32	19	CC	ex Kota Selamat-02, Qatari Ibn Al Fuja'a-00

Formed jointly by The Government of The United Arab Emirates, The States of Bahrain, Kuwait and Qatar, The Kingdom of Saudi Arabia and The Republic of Iraq. See also The National Shipping Company of Saudi Arabia .

United Thai Shipping Corp. Ltd. — Thailand

Unithai Shipping Pte. Ltd.

Funnel: Blue with broad white band containing separated red, blue and red shaped vertical bands.

Hull: Black with red boot-topping.

Name	Flag	Year	GRT	DWT	Loa	Bm	Kts	Type	Former names
Chainat Navee	Tha	1978	15,938	20,258	157	25	15	HL	ex Dorinco-94, Malacca Maru-84
Korat Navee	Tha	1978	15,514	23,618	175	24	16	C	ex Trade Ever-94, Hickory-89, Christoffer Oldendorff-88, Theekar-87
Krabi Navee	Tha	1979	13,442	20,850	159	23	14	C	ex Caledonian Express-96, Crystal King-93, Twin Emerald-83
Pattaya Navee	Tha	1978	14,991	22,329	168	23	17	C	ex MC Jade-96, Vincenzia-89
Phayao Navee	Tha	1978	15,296	22,120	163	24	16	C	ex Far East Navee-95, Wakamizu Maru-87
Thai Bright *	Lbr	1984	18,723	26,140	169	26	16	BC	ex Candia-03, Cape York-01, Candia-99, Red Sea Encounter-92, Candia-91, Hanjin Candia-90, Candia-90, Red Sea Encounter-90, Lyme Bay-89, Candia-88
Thai Dawn *	Lbr	1985	18,722	26,140	169	26	16	BC	ex Caria-03, Victoria Bay-98, Caria-95, Santa Fe de Bogota-94, Caria-93, Lanka Abhaya-90, Norasia Caria-87, I/a Caria
Ubon Navee	Tha	1977	13,466	18,257	156	23	14	Ro	ex Fremo Sirius-94, Lagos Venture-87
Uthai Navee	Tha	1978	15,778	24,268	163	25	15	HL	ex Bosco VI-94, Trade Concord-92, Wakagiku Maru-87

* owned by parent IMC Shipping Co. Pte. Ltd. and company 27% owned by Thailand government.

United Thai Shipping. KRABI NAVEE. *J. M. Kakebeeke.*

V. Ships Group. YEOMAN BANK. *M. D. J. Lennon.*

V. Ships Group

Monaco

V. Ships Monaco S.A.M.

Funnel: *Yellow with blue 'V'.*
Hull: *Black or blue with green or red boot-topping.*

Name		Eng	Flag	Year	GRT	DWT	Loa	Bm	Kts	Type	Former names
African Sea			Bhs	1985	15,893	17,850	174	23	15	Ro	ex Halifax-02, PCC Argos-99, Halifax-98, CSAV Rovno-96, Rovno-95
African Sky			Bhs	1986	15,893	17,850	172	23	17	Ro	ex Houston-02, Andrea S-97, Houston-97, Korsun-Shevchenkovskiy-96
African Sun			Bhs	1985	15,893	17,850	174	23	15	Ro	ex Sunderland-02, PCC Buenos Aires-99, Sunderland-99, Global Atlantic-97, Brest-96
Alva Star *			Bhs	1994	38,395	41,722	236	32	21	CC	ex Norasia Malta-01, MSC Jasmine-98, Norasia Malta-96
Azteca †			Bhs	1993	13,237	17,546	155	23	16	Co	ex ANL Progress-03, Melanesian Chief-02, Barnes Bridge-01, Island Chief-00, Chengtu-99, Barnes Bridge-98, SEAL Mauritius-97, Santander-94, Kapitan E. Freyman-93
Battersea Bridge *			Bhs	1992	13,237	17,493	155	24	16	Co	ex Nordana Benefactor-99, Battersea Bridge-98, Zim Houston-97, Zim New York-96, Kapitan A.Krivobokov-92
Bebedouro			Lbr	1986	11,150	14,873	149	23	17	Tfj	
Buckinghamshire *			Bhs	1999	25,219	14,310	216	27	25	CC	ex ADCL Scarlet-01, Norasia Scarlet-00
Cap Vilano			Nis	1992	21,053	30,078	182	28	19	CC	ex Libra Brasil-03, P&O Nedlloyd Pinta-02, P&O Nedlloyd Tema-00, Santa Rosa-99, Panatlantic-97, Santa Rosa-97, Nedlloyd van Rees-96, Santa Rosa 95
Cheshire *			Bhs	1998	25,218	14,310	216	27	25	CC	ex ADCL Savannah-01, Norasia Savannah-00
Euro Ace ‡			Pan	1999	38,530	73,976	225	32	-	B	ex Euro Trader-03
Euro Sea ‡			Mhl	2003	81,310	159,600	274	48	-	T	
G&C Parana †††			Nis	1979	41,905	42,424	183	32	14	Ro	ex G&C Forest-01, Nosac Forest-94, Troll Forest-92, Skaubord-91
Halifax			Mlt	1992	16,515	29,753	164	26	-	T	ex Stardust-99, Hawk-97, Maritime Prudence-94
Hertford			Bhs	1999	15,698	14,169	217	27	25	CC	ex ADCL Selina-01, Norasia Selina-00
Lancashire			Bhs	2000	24,836	11,000	217	27	25	CC	ex ADCL Shereen-01, Norasia Shereen-00
Lincoln			Bhs	2000	15,675	14,150	217	27	25	CC	ex ADCL Salwa-01, Norasia Salwa-00
Lion			Lbr	1985	26,113	46,100	172	32	14	T	ex Petrobulk Lion-96, Jahre Lion-86
Maersk Valletta			Gib	2002	17,189	22,308	179	28	21	CC	I/a Amadeus I
Maersk Vancouver			Gib	2001	17,189	22,200	179	28	21	CC	ex Aquarius-02
Maersk Venice			Gib	2002	17,189	22,308	179	28	21	CC	
Maersk Vigo			Gib	2002	17,189	22,308	179	28	21	CC	
MSC Malaysia			Bhs	1998	25,219	14,310	216	27	25	CC	ex Warwick-03, ADCL Sheba-02, Norasia Sheba-00
Muirfield *			Bhs	1985	22,053	37,568	188	28	14	B	ex Prospero-02, Nan An-01, Mei Kha Lar-94, Trans Pioneer-89, Ocean Diplomat-88
NDS Promoter *			Bhs	1994	13,237	17,493	155	23	16	Co	ex Blackfriars Bridge-02, Libra Callao-99, Blackfriars Bridge-97, SEAL Madagascar-97, Kapitan A. Dotsenko-94
NDS Prosperity †			Bhs	1992	13,237	17,493	155	23	16	Co	ex Richmond Bridge-02, Lykes Victor-01, Richmond Bridge-00, Zim Mexico II-98, Libra Valparaiso-98, Kapitan V. Kiris-96, Zim Itajai-96, Kapitan V. Kiris-94, CMB Kiris-93, Kapitan V. Kiris-92
NDS Proteus *			Bhs	1993	13,237	17,493	155	23	16	Co	ex Westminster Bridge-03, Jolly Giada-03, Westminster Bridge-02, Zim Mexico 1-99, Westminster Bridge-97, Kapitan L. Golubev-97, Nedlloyd Cartagena-95, Kapitan L. Golubev-94
Oxford *			Bhs	1998	25,219	14,310	216	27	25	CC	ex ADCL Shamsaa-01, Norasia Shamsaa-00, Norasia Salome-99
Perth			Bhs	1999	24,836	11,000	217	27	25	CC	ex ADCL Sultana-01, Norasia Sultana-00
Puerto Cortes **	(2)		Bhs	1981	22,131	17,993	173	30	19	Ro	ex Kota Eagle-89, Contender Argent-87, Cavara-86, Contender Argent-84
Safmarine Prime *			Bhs	1998	25,219	14,310	216	27	25	CC	ex Ayrshire-03, ADCL Samantha-01, Norasia Samantha-00
Shropshire			Bhs	2000	15,675	14,150	217	27	25	CC	ex ADCL Sabrina-01, I/a Norasia Sabrina
Siboeva			Nis	1993	45,593	81,785	247	32	13	Obo	
Sibonancy			Nis	1994	45,593	83,155	247	32	14	Obo	

Name	Eng	Flag	Year	GRT	DWT	Loa	Bm	Kts	Type	Former names
Sibonata		Nis	1994	45,493	83,155	247	32	14	Obo	
Sibotura		Lbr	1992	41,189	74,928	229	32	14	Obo	ex Futura-96
Tolteca †		Cyp	1992	13,231	17,300	155	23	16	Co	ex NDS Kuito-03, Tower Bridge-02, Lykes Leader-01, Tower Bridge-00, Nordana Challenger-99, Tower Bridge-98, Maersk Abidjan-98, Kapitan Mochchinskiy-97, Isla Pinzon-96, Kapitan Moshchinskiy-96, Nedlloyd Cristobal-95, Kapitan Moshchinskiy-94, Zim Jamaica-94, Kapitan Moshchinskiy-92
Tula †		Cyp	1994	13,258	17,493	155	23	16	Co	ex Kew Bridge-03, Jolly Ambra-03, Kew Bridge-02, Seaboard Houston-02, Lykes Striker-01, Kew Bridge-00, Zim Houston 1-99, Kew Bridge-98, SEAL Reunion-97, Kapitan N. Petrosyan-94
Universal Challenger *		Bhs	1983	35,809	63,800	225	32	15	B	ex Souillac-95, Maersk Semakau-93, Quorn-88, Malvern-87, Sealock-85
Yeoman Bank		Lbr	1982	24,870	38,997	205	27	15	Bu	ex Salmonpool-90
Yeoman Bontrup		Bhs	1991	55,695	96,725	250	38	15	Bu	ex Western Bridge-02
Yeoman Bridge		Bhs	1991	55,695	96,772	250	38	15	Bu	ex Eastern Bridge-00
Zapoteca *		Bhs	1992	13,237	17,491	155	24	16	Co	ex NDS Bengela-03, Waterloo Bridge-03, Nordana Defender-99, Waterloo Bridge-98, Zim Mexico-97, Zim Santos-96, Kapitan N. Kladko-92

* managed by V.Ships Cyprus Ltd., ‡ by V.Ships Switzerland SA or ‡‡ V.Ships Greece Ltd (formed jointly with LPL Shipping SA).
# owned by PLM International Inc., USA and managed by V.Ships Marine Ltd., USA.
† managed by subsidiary Silver Line Ltd., UK for Sovcomflot, Russia q.v.
** managed for Sea Containers Services Ltd., UK, § for Gestion Maritime S.A.M., Monaco or ††† for Morten Werring's Rederi, Norway

Massoel Gestion SA/Switzerland

Name	Eng	Flag	Year	GRT	DWT	Loa	Bm	Kts	Type	Former names
Appenzell		Che	2001	27,011	46,492	190	31	14	B	
Glarus		Che	2001	27,011	46,513	190	31	14	B	
Luzern		Che	1997	27,552	45,269	190	31	14	B	ex Skaugum-97
Unterwalden		Che	1996	27,552	45,300	190	31	14	B	
Uri		Che	2001	27,011	46,509	190	31	14	B	

MC Shipping Inc./Bermuda

Funnel: White with red 'MC', narrow black top or charterers colours.
Hull: Grey with red boot-topping.

Name	Eng	Flag	Year	GRT	DWT	Loa	Bm	Kts	Type	Former names
La Forge		Bhs	1981	42,501	45,587	225	32	15	Lpg	ex Benny Queen-96
Maersk Bahrain		Bhs	1975	33,401	37,129	239	31	24	CC	ex Anna Maersk-98, pt ex Anders Maersk-84
Maersk Barcelona		Bhs	1975	33,400	37,115	239	31	24	CC	ex Axel Maersk-98, pt ex Anna Maersk-84
Maersk Belawan		Bhs	1976	33,401	37,212	239	31	24	CC	ex Arthur Maersk-98
Maersk Brisbane		Bhs	1976	33,401	37,129	239	31	24	CC	ex Anders Maersk-98, pt ex Arthur Maersk-83

48% owned by V. Ships.

F. A. Vinnen & Co. (GmbH & Co.)   Germany

Funnel: Black with black 'M' on broad white band, white with blue 'V' or charterers colours.
Hull: Black with red boot-topping.

Name	Eng	Flag	Year	GRT	DWT	Loa	Bm	Kts	Type	Former names
EWL Suriname		Lbr	1994	9,600	12,574	150	23	18	CC	ex Merkur Lake-96, Libra Genova-95, Merkur Lake-95
Merkur Bay		Lbr	2002	30,047	35,770	208	32	-	CC	
Merkur Beach		Lbr	1996	16,800	22,900	185	26	19	CC	ex Delmas Charcot-03, Merkur Beach-02, MSC Quito-02, Merkur Beach-99, CSAV Rahue-98, I/a Merkur Beach
Merkur Bridge		Lbr	1993	9,597	12,575	150	22	17	CC	ex Sinar Banda-02, Kota Seri-01, Merkur Bridge-99, New Orient-99, Merkur Bridge-98, Ratana Ganya-97, TSL Bravo-96, Merkur Bridge-93
Merkur Cloud		Lbr	1996	15,929	22,026	168	27	21	CC	ex Calapolos-02, I/a Merkur Cloud
Merkur Delta		Lbr	1995	16,800	22,900	185	25	19	CC	ex CSAV Salerno-01, Jolly Orca-00, CSAV Romeral-99, Merkur Delta-95
Merkur Sea		Cyp	1984	16,430	21,888	166	27	18	CC	ex MSC Santiago-00, Merkur Sea-99, CSAV Ranco-98, City of Glasgow-97, Merkur Sea-93, CMB Merkur-91, Nedlloyd Himalaya-90, Merkur Sea-89, Dutch Senator-89, Ville d'Uranus-87, Merkur Sea-86

Name	Eng	Flag	Year	GRT	DWT	Loa	Bm	Kts	Type	Former names
Merkur Star		Lbr	1996	29,181	39,528	203	31	19	CC	ex MSC Oman-03, Merkur Star-02, CMA CGM Seurat-02, Merkur Star-00, Houston Express-98, Merkur Star-96, I/a John Lykes
Merkur Tide		Lbr	1998	15,929	22,026	168	27	21	CC	ex Calaparana-03, Merkur Tide-01, Atlantico-01, I/a Merkur Tide
MSC California		Lbr	1997	28,662	39,927	202	31	20	CC	ex MSC Gauteng-02, Merkur Sky-02, MSC Sicily-01, Merkur Sky-99, Zim Piraeus-98, Merkur Sky-98

Vroon B.V. Netherlands

Funnel: White with three wavy blue lines at base of blue 'V', narrow blue or black top or † white with blue 'LE', blue top
Hull: White, grey, black or red with red boot-topping.

Name		Flag	Year	GRT	DWT	Loa	Bm	Kts	Type	Former names
Aegean Express		Pan	1997	15,095	18,581	169	27	18	CC	ex YM Bangkok-02, Kuo Ting-01
Andalusian Express		Pan	1995	15,095	18,585	169	27	17	CC	ex Young Chance-03, Choyang Challenger-01
Arabian Express		Pan	1997	15,095	18,300	169	27	18	CC	ex Kuo Yang-03
Australian Express **		Pan	1989	9,949	14,867	150	23	18	CC	ex Premier-98
Bahamian Express		Mhl	2000	17,167	21,614	169	27	20	CC	
Belgian Express		Mhl	2000	16,960	21,373	169	27	20	CC	
Bermudian Express		Mhl	2000	16,850	21,548	169	27	20	CC	
Brazilian Express		Mhl	2001	16,850	21,579	169	27	20	CC	
Canadian Express		Lbr	1986	12,963	20,482	147	25	14	Co	ex Cape York-98, Canadian Express-97, ALS Express-96, Rickmers Dalian-91, Canadian Express-90, Waterfort-90, Canadian Express-90, Bavaria 89, Kriti Gold-88
Chilean Express		Pan	1986	12,963	20,482	147	25	14	C	ex ALS Express-01, Chilean Express-98, T.A. Pathfinder-96, Chilean Express-95, Rickmers Tianjin-95, Kriti Silver-88
Columbian Express		Pan	1986	12,963	20,479	147	25	14	Co	ex ALS Endeavour-01, Columbian Express-98, ALS Strength-97, Kriti Amber-88, ALS Strength-88, Kriti Amber-87
Cormo Express		Nld	1978	25,756	12,711	176	27	17	L	ex Mediterranean Highway-89
Cumbrian Express		Pan	1987	12,963	20,475	147	25	14	Co	ex T.A.Pioneer-99, Cumbrian Express-95, Waterdam-89, Thuringin-89, Kriti Platinum-88
Eurasian Brilliance *		Phl	1985	26,746	9,763	159	28	17	V	ex Rubin Crest-94, Dairyu Maru-92
Libra Leader ‡		Pan	1998	57,674	22,734	200	32	19	V	
MSC Paraguay **		Pan	1985	22,667	33,857	188	28	18	BC	ex Contship America-98, Buxsea-96, Contship America-96, CanMar Intrepid-95, Arabian Sea-94, New York Senator-93, ScanDutch Luzon-88, Andra I-87, Arosia-86, World Peace-85
Pioneer Express		Phl	1982	7,748	8,676	142	20	17	R	ex Pioneer Reefer-93, Rehmannia-88, Raffia Universal-86
United Cold		Phl	1989	8,739	9,692	141	21	12	R	ex E.W. Everest-02
United Cool		Phl	1990	8,739	9,692	141	21	21	R	ex E.W. Whitney-02
United Ice		Pan	1992	9,074	11,581	149	21	19	R	ex Aconcagua-02
Young Liberty		Pan	1995	15,095	18,294	169	27	17	CC	ex Choyang Leader-01, Kuo Fah-95

newbuildings : two 47,000 dwt and four 37,000 dwt tankers for 2005/6 delivery from South Korean builder.
* managed by Univan Ship Management Ltd., Hong Kong (China) or ** by Fleet Management Ltd., Hong Kong (China) ‡ chartered to NYK.
See also Iver Ships, Norway (Brostrom Van Ommeren Shipping AB, Sweden) and Eukor Car Carriers (Wallenius Wilhelmsen).

Wagenborg Shipping BV Netherlands

Funnel: Black with two narrow white bands.
Hull: Light grey with broad red band interrupted by white 'WAGENBORG' and diagonal white stripes, red or black boot-topping.

Name		Flag	Year	GRT	DWT	Loa	Bm	Kts	Type	Former names
Prinsenborg		Nld	2003	13,340	16,615	143	22	16	Co	
Rhoneborg		Nld	1993	18,144	20,027	174	29	18	CC	ex MSC Java-03, European Express-02, Zim Australia-00, European Express-99, Freshwater Bay-96, European Express-94

newbuilding : one 17,600 dwt bulk carrier for 2004 delivery, plus numerous smaller vessels on order.

F. A. Vinnen & Co. MERKUR DELTA. *Hans Kraijenbosch.*

Wagenborg Shipping. PRINSENBORG. *Hans Kraijenbosch.*

Wallenius Wilhelmsen. TAMESIS. *Hans Kraijenbosch.*

Wallenius Wilhelmsen A/S

Norway/Sweden

Funnel: Yellow with yellow 'OW' on broad green band (Wallenius); black with two narrow light blue bands (Wilhelmsen); †† white with USA national flag and 'ARC' houseflag either side of black anchor, narrow black top.

Hull: Green with green 'Wallenius' or 'Wallenius Wilhelmsen' on white upperworks, green or red boot-topping; red, blue or black with red boot-topping (Wilhelmsen); †† blue with blue 'ARC' on white upperworks, red boot-topping.

Name	Eng	Flag	Year	GRT	DWT	Loa	Bm	Kts	Type	Former names
Aegean Breeze †		Sgp	1983	27,876	12,527	164	28	18	V	
Aida		Swe	1991	52,288	29,213	203	32	19	V	
Aniara †		Sgp	1978	45,037	15,406	196	32	20	V	ex Avesta-83
Arabian Breeze †		Sgp	1983	28,116	12,577	164	28	18	V	
Asian Breeze †		Sgp	1983	27,876	12,562	164	28	18	V	
Atlantic Breeze †		Sgp	1986	41,891	17,176	196	29	18	V	ex Bujin-91
Baltic Breeze †		Sgp	1983	28,116	12,466	164	28	18	V	
Boheme		Swe	1999	57,018	22,619	199	32	20	V	
Carmen †		Sgp	1982	50,681	28,566	200	32	19	V	
Don Carlos		Swe	1997	56,893	22,590	199	32	20	V	
Don Juan		Swe	1995	55,598	22,514	199	32	20	V	
Don Pasquale		Swe	1997	55,598	22,590	199	32	20	V	
Don Quijote		Swe	1998	56,893	14,927	199	32	20	V	
Elektra		Swe	1999	57,018	22,588	199	32	20	V	
Falstaff		Swe	1985	51,858	28,529	200	32	20	V	
Figaro †		Sgp	1981	50,681	28,676	200	32	19	V	
Freedom ††		Usa	1997	49,821	19,884	190	32	19	V	ex Takamine-03
Independence ††		Usa	1978	47,089	17,406	195	32	19	V	ex Tellus-03, Nosac Ranger-96, Nosac Mascot-88, Nopal Mascot-84
Isolde		Swe	1985	51,071	28,396	200	32	19	V	
Liberty ††		Usa	1985	51,858	28,509	200	32	20	V	ex Faust-03
Madame Butterfly		Sgp	1981	50,681	28,689	200	32	19	V	
Manon		Swe	1999	57,018	14,863	199	32	20	V	
Medea †		Sgp	1982	50,681	28,566	200	32	19	V	
Mignon		Swe	1999	57,018	14,925	199	32	20	V	
Mosel Ace *		Pan	2000	37,237	12,761	177	31	19	V	
Otello		Swe	1992	52,479	29,152	203	32	20	V	
Pacific Breeze †		Sgp	1986	42,105	17,271	196	29	18	V	
Patriot ††		Usa	1987	47,219	15,680	190	32	18	V	ex Fidelio-03, Skaukar-94, Nosac Skaukar-92
Resolve ††		Usa	1994	49,443	20,082	190	32	19	V	ex Tanabata-03, Nosac Tanabata-96
Rigoletto		Swe	1977	43,487	17,197	192	32	21	V	
Tagus		Nis	1985	48,357	21,900	195	32	19	V	ex Nosac Express-96
Tai Shan **		Nis	1986	48,676	15,577	190	32	18	V	ex Nosac Tai Shan-96
Taiko		Nis	1984	66,532	43,986	262	32	21	Ro	ex Barber Hector-88
Takara **		Nis	1986	48,547	15,546	190	32	18	V	ex Nosac Takara-96
Takasago		Nis	1996	49,821	19,844	190	32	19	V	
Takayama		Nis	1983	27,440	10,599	165	28	18	V	ex Nosac Takayama-96, Takayama-86
Talabot		Nis	1979	39,884	34,605	229	32	22	Ro	ex Barber Perseus-88
Talisman *		Nis	2000	67,140	38,500	241	32	20	Ro	
Tamerlane *		Nis	2001	67,140	38,500	241	32	20	Ro	
Tamesis *		Nis	2000	67,140	39,516	241	32	20	Ro	
Tampa		Nis	1984	66,532	44,013	262	32	21	Ro	ex Barber Tampa-89
Tampere		Nis	1979	40,542	35,098	229	32	22	Ro	ex Barber Nara-89
Tancred **		Nis	1987	48,676	15,577	190	32	18	V	ex Nosac Sea-96, Nosac Tancred-89
Tapiola		Nis	1978	39,535	33,702	229	32	21	Ro	ex Boogabilla-89
Tarago *		Nis	2000	67,140	39,516	241	32	20	Ro	
Taronga		Nis	1996	72,708	48,988	265	32	20	Ro	
Tasco		Nis	1985	48,393	22,067	195	32	19	V	ex Nosac Explorer-96, Nosac Tasco-89
Terrier		Nis	1982	47,947	17,863	194	32	19	V	ex Nosac Rover-96, Nosac Barbro-89, Nopal Barbro-84
Texas		Nis	1984	49,326	44,080	262	32	21	Ro	ex Barber Texas-89
Titus		Swe	1994	55,598	22,862	199	32	20	V	
Toba		Nis	1979	39,535	34,310	229	32	21	Ro	ex Barber Toba-89
Tosca †		Sgp	1978	45,037	15,350	196	32	20	V	
Tourcoing		Nis	1978	39,535	33,719	229	32	21	Ro	
Traviata		Swe	1977	43,487	17,197	190	32	19	V	
Trianon **		Nis	1987	49,792	15,536	190	32	18	V	ex Nosac Star-96
Trinidad **		Nis	1987	49,750	15,528	190	32	18	V	ex Nosac Sky-96
Tristan		Swe	1985	51,071	28,536	200	32	19	V	
Turandot		Swe	1995	55,598	22,815	199	32	20	V	

Name	Eng	Flag	Year	GRT	DWT	Loa	Bm	Kts	Type	Former names
Undine		Swe	2003	57,112	22,616	199	32	20	V	
Verona *		Pan	2000	37,237	12,778	177	31	19	V	

newbuildings - four 62,800 grt 20,000 dwt vehicle carriers on order from Japanese builder.
*† owned by Wallenius Ship Management Pte. Ltd., Singapore or †† by subsidiary American Roll-on Roll-off Carrier (managed by Pacific-Gulf Marine Inc.) both USA. * managed by Barber Shipmanagement Sendirian Berhad, Malaysia, ‡ by Wallenius Lines (Japan) Ltd., ** by Actinor Shipping ASA, Norway.*

Eukor Car Carriers Inc./South Korea

Funnel: Cream with white curved cross on blue globe or owners colours.
Hull: Owners colours, some with 'EUKOR' on superstructure.

Name	Eng	Flag	Year	GRT	DWT	Loa	Bm	Kts	Type	Former names
Asian Beauty **		Pan	1994	44,481	13,308	185	31	18	V	
Asian Captain *		Pan	1998	55,729	21,466	200	32	20	V	
Asian Chorus *		Pan	1997	55,729	21,505	200	32	20	V	
Asian Dynasty ††		Phl	1999	55,719	21,224	200	32	20	V	
Asian Empire *		Pan	1998	55,729	21,485	200	32	20	V	
Asian Glory **		Pan	1994	44,818	13,363	184	31	18	V	
Asian Grace *		Kor	1996	55,680	21,421	200	32	20	V	
Asian King §		Pan	1998	55,729	21,511	200	32	19	V	
Asian Legend *		Pan	1996	55,680	21,421	200	32	20	V	
Asian Majesty *		Pan	1999	55,729	21,483	200	32	20	V	
Asian Parade *		Pan	1996	55,680	21,407	200	32	20	V	
Asian Sun *		Kor	1995	44,891	13,292	185	31	18	V	
Asian Trust *		Pan	2000	55,729	15,800	200	32	20	V	
Asian Venture *		Kor	1995	44,891	13,241	185	31	18	V	
Asian Vision *		Pan	1997	55,680	21,421	200	32	20	V	
Automobile Ace §		Pan	1980	31,587	10,032	176	28	18	V	
Crystal Ray †		Bhs	2000	57,772	21,400	200	32	20	V	
Cypress Pass §		Lbr	1988	42,447	12,763	184	31	18	V	
Diamond Ray †		Mlt	1979	45,571	17,714	190	32	18	V	ex Honshu I-99, Zama-94, Zama Maru-90
Eishun §		Pan	1999	33,854	8,531	173	27	18	V	
Esra §		Pan	1979	22,624	13,086	160	25	15	V	ex Trans Auto-00, Autotrans-87, Kowa Maru-85
Eternal Clipper *		Pan	1980	23,107	10,803	164	25	17	V	ex Hyundai No.1-96
Eternal Mariner *		Pan	1980	23,107	10,758	164	25	17	V	ex Hyundai No.2-96
Eurasian Alliance ††		Phl	1983	27,013	9,358	159	28	17	V	ex Daishun Maru-94
Eurasian Chariot ††		Phl	1985	31,923	12,184	172	30	18	V	ex Eurasian Challenge-95, Ocean Cheer-94
European Emerald ‡		Pan	1984	37,996	13,208	175	29	18	V	ex Nissan Maru-92
Grand Choice ‡		Pan	1999	50,309	16,669	179	32	19	V	
Grand Mark ‡		Pan	2000	50,310	16,681	179	32	19	V	
Grand Pace ‡		Pan	1999	50,309	16,714	179	32	19	V	
Grand Quest ‡		Pan	2000	50,309	16,702	179	32	19	V	
Grand Race ‡		Pan	2000	50,309	16,689	179	32	19	V	
Hyundai No. 103 *		Pan	1986	40,772	12,893	184	31	18	V	
Hyundai No. 105 *		Pan	1986	40,772	12,889	184	31	18	V	
Hyundai No. 106 **		Pan	1987	42,469	12,939	184	31	18	V	
Hyundai No. 107 **		Pan	1987	42,469	12,989	184	31	18	V	
Hyundai No. 108 **		Pan	1987	30,024	9,783	174	28	18	V	
Hyundai No. 109 **		Pan	1987	31,367	9,694	174	28	19	V	ex Toronto-99, Hyundai No.109-97
Hyundai No. 201 *		Pan	1987	31,367	9,694	174	28	18	V	
Hyundai No. 202 *		Pan	1987	31,367	9,694	174	28	18	V	ex Tongala-99, Hyundai No.202-97, Nosac Clipper-93, Hyundai No.202-90
Hyundai No. 203 *		Pan	1988	41,353	12,762	184	31	18	V	ex Atlantic Beauty-92, Hyundai No.203-90
Hyundai No. 205 *		Pan	1987	42,247	12,706	184	31	19	V	ex Eurasian Beauty-93, Hyundai No.205-90
Hyundai No. 206 *		Pan	1987	42,247	12,706	184	31	18	V	ex Oriental Beauty-93, Hyundai No.206-90
Magic Wave ‡		Pan	1980	23,304	7,300	153	26	21	V	ex Maersk Wave-96
Magic Wind ‡		Pan	1981	23,304	7,300	153	26	21	V	ex Maersk Wind-96
Marine Reliance ‡		Mhl	1987	35,750	11,676	174	30	17	V	
Modern Chance ‡		Lbr	1999	33,863	10,834	164	28	18	V	
Modern Drive §		Pan	2000	33,831	10,817	164	28	18	V	
Modern Express ‡		Pan	2001	33,831	10,817	164	28	21	V	
Modern Link ‡		Pan	2000	33,831	10,419	164	28	18	V	
Modern Peak ‡		Pan	1999	33,831	10,817	164	28	18	V	
Morning Breeze ‡		Pan	1977	24,278	8,545	169	26	16	V	ex Morning Grace-99, Puebla-95, Amoroso-93, North Blaze-90, Polar Ace-87
Morning Charm ‡		Pan	1978	21,757	8,045	153	25	18	V	ex Arabian Star-95, Young Soldier-91
Morning Light ‡		Pan	1978	30,070	10,601	180	28	17	V	ex Californian Star-95, Donaire-92, Young Splendour-90

Name	Eng	Flag	Year	GRT	DWT	Loa	Bm	Kts	Type	Former names
Morning Prince ‡		Pan	1979	45,423	13,910	190	32	19	V	ex Prince-95, Prince No.10-94, Prince Maru No.10-86
Morning Queen ‡		Pan	1978	38,974	18,426	199	30	18	V	ex Hamburg Star-95, Golden Ace-91
Morning Saga ‡		Lbr	1981	41,868	13,834	186	32	18	V	ex Viking Star-96, Viking Ace-92, Paramount Ace-90
Pearl Ray †		Lbr	1980	45,376	14,837	190	32	18	V	ex San Marcos-01, Oppama-91, Oppama Maru-90
Platinium Ray †		Bhs	2000	57,772	21,000	200	32	20	V	
Ruby Ray †		Lbr	1978	30,256	10,555	180	28	18	V	ex Lerma-96, Nissan Silvia-84
Sapphire Ray †		Pan	1985	38,874	13,019	184	31	18	V	ex Eternal Sailor-01, Hyundai No. 101-96
Saracen Star §		Pan	1984	26,758	11,554	158	28	17	V	ex Oscar Ace-92
Sea Ahmed §		Lbr	1978	38,266	13,833	176	32	18	V	ex Aya II-01, Pioneer Ace-89
Skaubryn §		Nis	1982	43,312	41,666	183	32	14	Ro	ex Skeena-91
Skaugran §		Nis	1979	41,905	42,424	183	32	14	Ro	
Topaz Ray †		Pan	1985	38,874	12,595	184	31	18	V	ex Eternal Trader-01, Hyundai No. 102-96

Company owned by Wallenius (40%), Wilhelmsen (40%), Hyundai Motor Group (10%) and Kia Motor Corp. (10%)
chartered from various owners including * Hyundai Merchant Marine, ** SAMAMA or Zodiac Maritime Agencies Ltd. (Ofer Bros.) q.v., † Stamco Ship
Management Co. Ltd., Greece, †† Vroon BV, Netherlands, ‡ Cido Shipping Co. Ltd., Japan or Cido Maritime Corp., South Korea or § other owners/managers.

Warwick & Esplen Ltd.   UK
The Hadley Shipping Co. Ltd.
Funnel: Yellow with black 'HSC' inside white diamond, black top.
Hull: Black with red boot-topping.

Name	Eng	Flag	Year	GRT	DWT	Loa	Bm	Kts	Type	Former names
Corato		Iom	1989	36,042	64,293	217	32	14	B	ex Meridian Sky-99
Cumbria		Gbr	1994	35,886	69,043	225	32	14	B	ex Corona Brave-03
Cymbeline		Iom	2001	38,299	73,060	225	32	14	B	

managed by Anglo-Eastern Management (UK) Ltd., UK.

Oskar Wehr KG (GmbH & Co.)   Germany

Funnel: Black with blue 'W' inside blue ring interrupting two blue bands in centre and towards top of broad yellow band or charterers colours.
Hull: Blue or grey with pale blue or red boot-topping.

Name	Eng	Flag	Year	GRT	DWT	Loa	Bm	Kts	Type	Former names
CCNI Arica		Mhl	2002	25,630	33,767	207	30	21	CC	ex Wehr Alster-02
CCNI Aysen		Mhl	2002	25,705	33,795	207	30	21	CC	I/a Wehr Trave
Columbus China		Mhl	2002	25,705	33,793	208	30	21	CC	ex Wehr Warnow-02
CSAV Callao		Mhl	2001	25,703	33,795	203	30	22	CC	I/a Wehr Elbe
CSAV Hong Kong		Mhl	1998	16,801	22,983	184	25	19	CC	ex Wehr Muden-03, TMM Quetzal-01, CSAV Valencia-00, Crowley Express-00, CSAV Rimac-99, I/a Wehr Muden
CSAV Montreal		Mhl	1999	16,177	23,021	184	26	19	CC	ex Norasia Montreal-01. Illapel-00, I/a Wehr Blankensee
Delmas Mascareignes		Lbr	1999	16,802	23,028	185	25	19	CC	ex CMA CGM Bourgainville-04, Wehr Rissen-99
Elqui		Mhl	1999	16,177	23,026	184	26	19	CC	I/a Wehr Schulau
Helga Selmer		Mhl	2004	28,200	50,326	190	32	-	B	
Ida Selmer		Mhl	2003	27,986	50,209	190	32	-	B	
Libra Chile		Mhl	2001	16,802	23,000	185	25	19	CC	I/a Wehr Nienstedten
Libra New York		Mhl	2001	25,703	33,795	203	30	22	CC	I/a Wehr Weser
P&O Nedlloyd Calypso		Mhl	1997	16,801	23,051	184	25	20	CC	ex Costa Rica-02, Wehr Koblenz-01, Panamerican-01, CSAV Rio Amazonas-99, I/a Wehr Koblenz
Sigrid Wehr		Lbr	1995	10,917	13,700	151	24	18	CC	ex Washington Express-01, Sigrid Wehr-00, Independent Venture-98, Sigrid Wehr-96, Cape Scott-95
Wehr Altona *		Deu	1997	16,801	23,051	184	25	19	CC	ex Lykes Pathfinder-02, Norasia Yantian-01, CSAV Ningbo-00, Kota Sejarah-00, CSAV Rio de la Plata-99, I/a Wehr Altona
Wehr Bille		Mhl	2002	25,624	33,739	208	30	21	CC	ex CCNI Antartico-03, Wehr Bille-02
Wehr Flottbek		Lbr	1999	16,802	22,878	184	25	19	CC	ex Alianca Bahia-01, Wehr Flottbek-00
Wehr Havel		Mhl	2002	25,703	33,795	208	30	21	CC	
Wehr Ottensen		Mhl	1997	16,801	23,051	184	25	20	CC	ex Indamex Nhava Sheva-02, Wehr Ottensen-01, CSAV Rio Grande-99, Wehr Ottensen-98

newbuildings : two 55,270 grt 67,470 dwt container ships (named Wehr Hongkong and Wehr Singapore) on order for 2004/6 delivery, also three 55,000 dwt bulk
carriers.
* owned by Dr. Peters KG fund, Germany.

Name	Eng	Flag	Year	GRT	DWT	Loa	Bm	Kts	Type	Former names

Westfal-Larsen Management AS

Norway

Funnel: Yellow with two narrow black bands, narrow black top
Hull: Dark blue or red with red boot-topping.

Name	Eng	Flag	Year	GRT	DWT	Loa	Bm	Kts	Type	Former names
Fossanger *		Nis	1988	22,637	40,264	171	32	14	T	ex Northern Wolf-89, Fort Wolf-88
Mauranger *		Lbr	1995	25,707	41,109	180	31	14	T	ex Bow Tribute-01
Kent Navigator **		Nis	1977	12,804	16,560	164	23	15	BC	ex Star Skoganger-03, Petraia-89, Aldebaran-86, Khalij Enterprise-78, Aldebaran-77
Moldanger *		Lbr	1997	25,707	40,845	180	31	14	T	ex Bow Triton-01
Nordanger		Nis	1992	43,635	59,421	220	34	16	Lpg	ex Baltic Flame-01

* on charter to Team Tankers AS (see under Blystad Shipping) and ** managed by Westfal-Larsen Management AS.

Star Shipping

Funnel: Yellow with two blue stars on white panel with blue top and bottom edges.
Hull: Blue or grey with red boot-topping.

Name	Eng	Flag	Year	GRT	DWT	Loa	Bm	Kts	Type	Former names
Star Alabama †		Nis	1985	20,916	30,204	169	27	15	BC	ex Hawaiian Rainbow-92
Star Altanger *		Sgp	1986	20,125	30,382	169	27	15	BC	ex Northern Dawn-96, Star New York-91, New York Rainbow-89
Star America †		Nis	1985	20,929	30,168	169	27	15	BC	ex Canadian Rainbow-91, Star Canadian-90, Canadian Rainbow-89
Star Atlantic †		Nis	1986	20,125	30,402	165	26	15	BC	ex Hoegh Mistral-03, Star Atlantic-03, Hoegh Mistral-03, Star Texas-90, Texas Rainbow-89
Star Austanger **		Nis	1985	20,915	30,173	169	27	15	BC	ex Anthony Rainbow-92
Star Canopus ‡		Grc	1985	24,943	42,842	190	30	14	B	ex Nordsund-95, Spring Seagull-90, Sanko Seagull-86
Star Davanger **		Sgp	1978	27,125	43,793	183	31	15	BC	ex Star Denver-89, Star Enterprise-85
Star Derby †		Nis	1979	27,104	43,700	183	31	15	BC	ex Star Carrier-85
Star Dieppe †		Nis	1977	27,104	43,082	183	31	15	BC	ex Star Shiraz-79, Star Dieppe-77
Star Djervanger **		Sgp	1978	27,743	43,051	183	31	15	BC	ex Star World-89
Star Dover †		Nis	1977	27,911	43,082	183	31	15	BC	ex Star Estahan-79, Star Dover-77
Star Drivanger *		Sgp	1978	27,735	43,052	183	31	15	BC	ex Star Hong Kong-92
Star Drottanger *		Sgp	1978	27,735	43,051	183	31	15	BC	ex Star Magnate-92
Star Eagle †		Nis	1981	24,479	39,749	180	29	15	BC	
Star Evanger **		Nis	1984	30,163	44,959	211	31	15	BC	ex Celestine-90, Birdie-89, Lily Star-87
Star Evviva †		Nis	1982	24,479	39,718	180	29	15	BC	
Star Florida †		Nis	1985	25,345	40,790	187	29	15	BC	
Star Fraser †		Nis	1985	25,345	40,840	187	29	15	BC	
Star Fuji †		Nis	1985	25,345	40,850	187	29	15	BC	
Star Geiranger		Nis	1986	27,972	43,131	200	29	15	BC	
Star Gran †		Nis	1986	27,192	43,759	198	29	16	BC	ex Triton-86
Star Grindanger		Nis	1986	27,972	43,131	201	29	15	BC	
Star Grip †		Nis	1986	27,192	43,712	198	29	16	BC	
Star Hansa †		Nis	1996	32,749	46,580	198	31	16	BC	
Star Hardanger **		Nis	1995	34,364	44,251	199	31	16	BC	
Star Harmonia †		Nis	1998	32,749	46,604	198	31	16	BC	
Star Heranger **		Nis	1995	34,363	44,251	199	31	16	BC	
Star Herdla †		Nis	1994	32,744	47,942	198	31	16	BC	
Star Hidra †		Nis	1994	32,749	46,547	198	31	16	BC	
Star Hosanger **		Nis	1995	34,363	44,251	199	31	16	BC	
Star Hoyanger **		Nis	1995	34,363	44,251	199	31	16	BC	
Star Ikebana **		Sgp	1999	30,840	39,751	185	31	16	BC	
Star Indiana **		Sgp	2000	30,745	39,760	185	31	16	BC	
Star Inventana *		Sgp	2000	30,745	39,789	185	31	16	BC	
Star Isfjord †		Nis	2000	29,898	41,749	185	31	16	BC	
Star Ismene †		Nis	1999	28,898	41,777	185	31	16	BC	
Star Isoldana *		Sgp	2000	30,745	39,465	185	31	16	BC	
Star Istind †		Nis	1999	29,898	41,749	185	31	16	BC	
Star Langanger *		Sgp	1986	29,275	41,425	195	32	14	BC	ex Hawthorn Hill-89, Geliga-86
Star Leikanger *		Sgp	1986	29,275	41,409	195	32	14	BC	ex Maritime Wisdom-89, Wisteria Hill-87, Gemar-86
Star Okiana *		Sgp	2003	36,324	48,661	199	32	-	BC	
Star Optimana *		Sgp	2003	36,324	48,661	199	32	-	BC	
Star Oshimana *		Sgp	2003	36,324	48,661	199	32	-	BC	
Star Osakana *		Sgp	2004	36,324	48,661	199	32	-	BC	
Star Polaris ‡		Grc	1996	26,897	43,775	190	31	14	B	
Star Pollux ‡		Grc	1996	26,922	43,769	190	31	14	B	

Name	Eng	Flag	Year	GRT	DWT	Loa	Bm	Kts	Type	Former names
Star Siranger *		Sgp	1991	11,878	17,012	149	23	14	BC	ex T.S.Adventure-93
Star Trondanger *		Vgb	1975	19,203	29,438	170	27	15	BC	ex Trondanger-89, Atlantic Rainbow-89, Iran Bandar-79, Atlantic Rainbow-77

newbuildings - one 55,000 dwt and two 36,700 grt 48,000 dwt open-hatch bulk carriers for 2004-6 delivery from Japanese builder
Star Shipping Pools are jointly owned by Westfal-Larsen & Co. A/S and Greig Shipping AS, Norway, also operating some chartered vessels.
* owned by Westfal-Larsen subsidiary Masterbulk Pte. Ltd., Singapore and ** managed by Westfal-Larsen Management AS.
† owned by Greig Shipping A/S or subsidiary A/S Billabong, both Norway.
‡ chartered from Rethymnis & Kulukundis Ltd., UK.

Anders Wilhelmsen & Co. AS   Norway

Funnel: Black with white 'W' on red/black divided diamond between two narrow red bands on broad white band.
Hull: Grey or red with red or grey boot-topping.

Name	Eng	Flag	Year	GRT	DWT	Loa	Bm	Kts	Type	Former names
Wilana		Nis	1997	79,494	149,706	270	45	15	T	
Wilma Yangtze		Nis	1996	79,494	149,591	270	45	15	T	
Wilmina		Nis	1997	79,388	149,775	270	45	15	T	

Managed by Wilhelmsen Marine Services A/S.
See also Royal Caribbean International in Passenger Ship section.

Schiffahrtskantor Reederei Gebruder Winter   Germany

Funnel: Mainly charterers colours
Hull: Grey with red boot-topping.

Name	Eng	Flag	Year	GRT	DWT	Loa	Bm	Kts	Type	Former names
Cala Piedad		Atg	1994	14,968	20,088	167	25	19	CC	ex Concord-03, Mercosul Pintado-03, Safmarine Emonti-02, Egoli Star I-01, Concord-99, Libra Santos-99, DG Concord-97, Concord-97, Victoria Bay-95, Concord-94
Commodore		Atg	2001	30,047	35,770	208	32	22	CC	ex MSC Andes-02, Commodore-01
Courier		Atg	1995	14,860	20,140	167	26	19	CC	ex Indamex Ganges-02, Libra Miami-00, Libra Buenos Aires-97, CSAV Rahue-96, Velma Lykes-95, I/a Courier
Maersk Dakar		Deu	1998	23,897	30,241	188	30	21	CC	ex Classica-02, Libra Buenos Aires-02, Classica-01, CMA Djakarta-00, Jolly Ocra-99, Classica-98
Safmarine Gonubie		Deu	1998	23,897	30,258	188	30	21	CC	ex Libra Houston-02, TMM Veracruz-01, APL Atlantic-00, Columba-99, Maersk Genoa-98, I/a Columba
Shion		Deu	1996	12,029	14,643	157	24	18	CC	ex Caravelle-04, Cala Porlamar-04, Pellini-02, Caravelle-01, UB Puma-97, Caravelle-96
Weisshorn *		Atg	1996	12,029	14,643	157	24	19	CC	ex MSC Ghana-04, Weisshorn-02, DAL East London-01, Weisshorn-00, P&O Nedlloyd Maurttius-99, Weisshorn-98

* owned by Contal Shipping Ltd., Switzerland.

World Wide Shipping Agency (Singapore) Pte. Ltd.   Singapore

Funnel: Blue, white 'W' on broad red band edged with narrow white bands or plain blue with narrow black top.
Hull: Black with red or grey boot-topping.

Name	Eng	Flag	Year	GRT	DWT	Loa	Bm	Kts	Type	Former names
Napa		Sgp	1990	153,347	285,640	328	57	14	T	ex Argo Athena-00
Nile		Pan	1991	153,407	285,739	328	57	15	T	ex Argo Pallas-00
Noto		Pan	1992	153,437	286,006	328	57	14	T	ex Argo Thetis-00
Nuri		Sgp	1992	153,427	285,933	328	58	15	T	ex Argo Daphne-00
Nysa		Sgp	2000	157,814	299,543	332	58	15	T	ex Argo Artemis-00
Sala		Pan	1993	153,506	293,376	328	58	15	T	
Salandi *		Pan	1999	38,852	74,502	225	32	14	B	ex World Rye-04
Sebu		Pan	1993	153,506	293,238	332	57	15	T	ex Seki-94
Siam		Pan	1993	156,539	299,993	332	58	15	T	
Soro		Pan	1993	156,539	299,718	332	58	15	T	
Suva		Pan	1993	153,332	293,371	328	57	15	T	ex Argo Medea-00, Suva-98
Sylt		Pan	1993	153,332	293,297	328	57	15	T	
Taos		Pan	1990	144,567	275,993	326	57	14	T	ex General Monarch-96, Sea Duke-91
Ubud		Pan	1999	149,383	299,990	330	60	16	T	
Ulan		Pan	2000	157,814	277,370	332	58	15	T	
United Peace		Pan	1984	28,822	48,238	168	32	15	T	

Name	Eng	Flag	Year	GRT	DWT	Loa	Bm	Kts	Type	Former names
United Purpose *		Hkg	1995	26,756	43,991	190	31	14	B	
United Resolve *		Pan	1995	77,243	151,049	273	43	14	B	
United Sage		Pan	1998	38,864	74,577	225	32	14	B	
United Support *		Pan	1999	38,852	74,545	225	32	14	B	
United Will		Pan	1992	39,036	68,960	226	32	14	T	
Ural		Pan	2000	149,383	299,990	330	60	16	T	
Utah		Hkg	2001	157,814	299,498	332	58	15	T	
Utik		Hkg	2001	157,814	299,450	332	58	15	T	
World Lake		Hkg	2004	156,500	298,500	332	58	15	T	
World Lion		Hkg	2004	156,500	298,500	332	58	15	T	
World Luck		Pan	2003	158,993	298,555	332	58	15	T	
World Luna		Pan	2003	158,993	298,555	332	58	15	T	
World Phoenix		Pan	1988	143,941	276,052	322	56	14	T	
World Prelude		Pan	1988	142,639	265,243	322	56	14	T	
World Prospect		Pan	1989	143,941	275,984	322	56	14	T	
World Raven		Pan	1996	37,846	72,394	225	32	14	B	ex Toplink-97
World Ribbon *		Pan	1998	38,864	74,522	225	32	15	B	
World Sea		Pan	1989	25,740	41,570	182	30	14	T	
World Spark		Hkg	1996	77,211	150,961	274	45	14	B	
World Spring		Pan	1985	28,822	48,225	168	32	15	T	
World Trumpet		Pan	2000	29,351	49,000	183	32	14	T	
World Trust		Pan	2000	29,351	48,706	183	32	14	T	

newbuildings - one 76,200 dwt bulk carrier from Japanese builder and two 277,000 dwt tankers from South Korean builder.
Controlled by Sohmen family, Hong Kong (China) and * owned by subsidiary International United Shipping Agency Ltd., Hong Kong (China).

Bergesen D.Y. ASA/Norway

Funnel: White with deep black top containing white houseflag with black anchor and diagonal light green stripe.
Igloo Pool vessels blue with narrow white band arced over white disc
Hull: Light green with blue boot-topping or red with light green diagonal stripe and red or grey boot-topping

Name	Eng	Flag	Year	GRT	DWT	Loa	Bm	Kts	Type	Former names
Belokamenka		Rus	1980	188,728	360,700	341	65	16	T	ex Berge Pioneer-03
Berge Arctic		Nis	2001	91,563	174,285	292	48	-	B	
Berge Arrow		Nis	1978	44,502	48,821	229	32	17	Lpg	ex Northern Arrow-84
Berge Athene	(2)	Nis	1979	112,947	225,162	313	50	17	OO	ex Pankar Theodoros-88, Konkar Theodoros-87
Berge Atlantic		Nis	1998	91,962	172,704	292	48	16	B	
Berge Banker	(st)	Nis	1979	153,124	323,100	346	57	16	T	ex BT Banker-90, Nogueira-86
Berge Boston	(st)	Nis	2003	93,844	77,410	277	43	19	Lng	
Berge Captain		Nis	1991	45,032	56,945	224	36	16	Lpg	
Berge Challenger		Nis	1992	45,032	56,885	224	36	16	Lpg	
Berge Clipper		Nis	1992	45,032	56,864	224	36	16	Lpg	
Berge Commander		Nis	1991	45,032	56,875	224	36	16	Lpg	
Berge Danuta		Nis	2000	49,288	50,260	226	36	18	Lpg	
Berge Denise *		Atf	2001	49,292	56,745	226	36	18	Lpg	
Berge Eagle		Nis	1978	44,502	48,986	229	32	17	Lpg	ex Northern Eagle I-84
Berge Enterprise *		Atf	1981	188,728	360,700	341	65	15	T	
Berge Everett	(st)	Nis	2003	93,844	77,410	277	43	19	Lng	
Berge Fjord ***		Nis	1986	159,534	310,698	332	57	13	O	ex Docefjord-00
Berge Flanders		Bhs	1991	42,286	49,345	224	36	16	Lpg	ex Flanders Gloria-03, Gloria-97
Berge Frost		Nis	1983	50,699	56,174	250	36	17	Lpg	ex Floreal-91
Berge Kobe		Nis	1987	47,249	51,466	220	38	16	Lpg	ex Co-op Sunrise-02
Berge Nantes ***		Atf	2003	35,190	44,773	216	32	17	Lpg	
Berge Nice ***		Atf	2003	35,346	44,639	216	32	17	Lpg	
Berge Nisa	(st)	Nis	1983	153,517	322,912	346	57	15	T	ex Nisa-89
Berge Nord		Nis	1997	107,512	218,283	305	53	15	B	
Berge Pacific	(2)	Nis	1986	118,491	231,850	315	56	13	B	ex Iron Pacific-98
Berge Phoenix		Nis	1986	154,098	290,793	334	62	14	Obo	ex Grand Phoenix-00
Berge Rachel		Nis	1984	49,130	63,296	228	36	14	Lpg	
Berge Racine		Nis	1985	49,130	63,254	228	36	14	Lpg	
Berge Ragnhild		Nis	1985	49,130	63,258	228	36	14	Lpg	
Berge Saga		Nis	1979	44,151	55,303	225	34	16	Lpg	
Berge Shan		Nis	1986	100,070	200,692	300	50	13	B	ex Chiribetsu-00, Chiribetsu Maru-95
Berge Sisar		Nis	1979	44,076	55,172	225	34	16	Lpg	
Berge Sisu		Nis	1978	44,076	55,172	225	34	16	Lpg	
Berge Spirit		Nis	1980	44,076	55,173	225	34	16	Lpg	ex Golar Frost-89
Berge Stadt *		Atf	1994	160,467	306,951	332	58	16	T	
Berge Stahl		Nis	1986	175,720	364,767	343	64	13	O	

Name	Eng	Flag	Year	GRT	DWT	Loa	Bm	Kts	Type	Former names
Berge Stavanger		Nis	1993	160,299	306,474	331	58	16	T	
Berge Strand		Nis	1982	43,849	55,361	225	34	16	Lpg	
Berge Sund		Nis	1981	43,849	55,303	225	34	16	Lpg	
Berge Sword		Nis	1979	44,502	48,996	229	32	17	Lpg	ex Excaliber-88, Hoegh Sword-86
Berge Troll		Nis	1977	42,698	54,158	231	35	18	Lpg	ex Extol-88, Monge-87
Berge Vik		Lbr	1987	159,534	310,686	332	57	13	O	ex Tijuca-02
Bergeland		Nis	1992	154,030	322,941	339	55	14	O	
Century		Nis	1974	26,097	22,036	182	29	-	Lgc	ex Lucian-80
Havdrott		Nis	1978	34,577	43,386	220	29	16	Lpg	ex Galpara-87
Havfrost		Nis	1991	34,946	49,513	205	32	15	Lpg	
Havfru		Nis	1973	26,097	22,041	182	29	20	Lgc	ex Vanda-87, Venator-86
Havglimt		Nis	1978	30,950	38,534	206	31	16	Lpg	ex Centum-87
Havis		Nis	1993	34,951	49,513	205	32	15	Lpg	
Havkong		Nis	1978	34,577	43,386	220	29	17	Lpg	ex Galconda-87
Havprins		Nis	1974	33,535	41,256	216	32	17	Lpg	ex Stena Oceanica-88, Mandrill-80, Malmros Multina-79, Dovertown-74
Havrim		Nis	1980	26,207	27,480	197	29	-	Lpg	ex Smolnyy-94
Hebris		Nis	1983	15,397	20,566	158	24	17	Lpg	
Hedda		Nis	1993	22,521	30,815	170	27	18	Lpg	
Hekabe		Nis	1977	34,572	43,386	220	29	16	Lpg	ex Garinda-86
Hektor		Nis	1982	15,405	20,561	158	24	17	Lpg	
Helga		Nis	1994	22,521	30,800	170	27	16	Lpg	
Helice		Nis	1991	34,974	49,513	205	32	16	Lpg	
Helios		Nis	1992	34,974	49,513	205	32	15	Lpg	
Hemina		Nis	1979	34,577	43,386	220	29	16	Lpg	ex Garala-87
Herakles		Nis	1982	20,531	31,485	158	28	15	Lpg	ex Berge Fister-88
Hermion		Nis	1984	15,399	20,567	158	24	17	Lpg	
Hesiod		Bhs	1973	20,684	23,719	178	26	16	Lpg	ex Gambada-86
Hugo N		Nis	1980	34,582	46,486	216	32	-	Lpg	ex Ahkatun-99
Igloo Espoo		Nis	1985	10,105	13,524	136	22	16	Lpg	
Igloo Hav		Nis	1989	11,191	14,520	153	22	16	Lpg	ex Gudrun Maersk-95
Igloo Moss		Nis	1985	10,075	13,774	136	22	16	Lpg	
Igloo Ior		Nis	1989	11,191	12,794	153	22	16	Lpg	ex Gjertrud Maersk-95
Norna §		Pan	1974	20,812	37,797	186	26	15	T	ex Akti A-01, Seafriend-97, Alice G-91, Faith I-91, Faith-97, Varanger-84
Norsea §		Mlt	1977	19,351	33,401	171	26	13	T	ex Sea Elevi-01, Vincenzina-00, Silina-95, Petrobulk Sterling-93, Capri Alfa-90, Fort Kingston-90, Capri Alfa-89, Panama-88
Steven N		Pan	1979	33,807	40,605	217	32	17	Lpg	ex Monterrey-99

newbuildings - six 95,000 grt Lng and two 23,000 grt Lpg tankers for 2004-6 delivery from South Korean builder.
Wholly controlled by Sohmen family's World Nordic ApS and § owned by subsidiary Norchart A/S, Norway.
* managed by The Green Tankers AS, France, ** by Anglo-Eastern Shipmanagement Ltd., Singapore or *** by International Tanker Management Ltd., UAE

Neu Seeschiffahrt GmbH/Germany

Funnel: Blue with'NEU' on blue/white/blue horizontally striped flag on white rectanglr.
Hull: Black, dark grey or brown with red boot-topping.

Name	Eng	Flag	Year	GRT	DWT	Loa	Bm	Kts	Type	Former names
Alfred N		Pan	1991	131,479	260.826	325	54	13	B	ex Lyra-02
Alster N		Pan	1988	171,924	305,893	340	57	13	OO	ex Alster Ore-03
Amy N		Pan	1997	155,051	322,457	332	58	13	B	ex Neckar Ore-01
Arthur N		Pan	1991	131,479	260,823	325	54	13	B	ex Athesis Ore-02
Elbe Ore §		Sgp	1983	113,342	224,222	312	50	13	B	ex Frontier Maru-96
Faith N		Pan	1990	131,479	260,783	325	54	13	B	ex Auriga-02
Harriette N		Sgp	2003	34,582	47,232	216	32	17	Lpg	ex Cantarell-00, I/a Petrogas II
Mosel N		Lbr	1995	63,152	122,311	266	41	14	B	ex Mosel Ore-03
Ruhr Ore		Lbr	1987	171,924	305,863	340	57	13	OO	
Saar N		Lbr	1995	63,152	122,331	266	41	14	B	ex Saar Ore-03
Waterman N		Pan	1985	129,325	259,296	329	54	12	B	ex Hyundai Giant-03

51% interest controlled by Bergesen.
§ owned by John P. Pedersen & Son AS, Norway (managed by Thome Shipmanagement, Singapore)

Name	Eng	Flag	Year	GRT	DWT	Loa	Bm	Kts	Type	Former names

Reederei Hermann Wulff   Germany

Funnel: *Mainly charterers colours*
Hull: *Grey with red boot-yopping.*

Name	Eng	Flag	Year	GRT	DWT	Loa	Bm	Kts	Type	Former names
ACX Primrose	Deu	1996	14,473	18,355	159	24	19	CC	ex Doris Wulff-03, Sakura-01, Norasia Montreal-00, Doris Wulff-99, Direct Jabiru-99, OOCL Amity-98, Doris Wulff-97, Nuova Ionia-96, Doris Wulff-96
Aramac *	Lbr	1999	32,221	39,340	211	32	21	CC	ex Elbwolf-02, Ipex Equality-01, Elbwolf-99
CMA CGM Seagull	Lbr	2002	32,322	39,350	212	32	22	CC	ex P&O Nedlloyd Dammam-03, Antje-Helen Wulff-02
Guatemala	Deu	1996	14,473	18,355	159	24	18	CC	ex P&O Nedlloyd Mobasa-01, Steindeich-98
Hermann	Lbr	1993	16,233	21,540	182	25	20	CC	ex Direct Kea-01, Hermann-99, MSC Cali-99, Hermann-99, Maersk Aarhus-98, Hermann-98, Sea Harmony-97, Hermann-96, CCNI Angol-96, Contship New York-95, Hermann-93, Deppe Europe-93
Ilse Wulff	Lbr	1993	16,233	21,540	182	25	20	CC	ex Direct Kookaburra-01, Isle Wulff-99, Maersk Pretoria-99, Maersk Pireaus-98, TSL Unity-98, Ilse Wulff-95, Contship Rotterdam-94, Ilse-93
NYK Prosperity *	Lbr	1999	32,222	39,128	211	32	22	CC	ex Weserwolf-03, Columbia Bridge-01, Weserwolf-00
P&O Nedlloyd Dubai	Lbr	2002	32,284	39,600	211	32	22	CC	ex Euro Max-02

newbuildings : two 57,000 dwt container ships for 2005 delivery from Polish builder.
* owned by John-Peter Wulff

Yangming Marine Transport Corp .   Taiwan

Funnel: *Black with yellow band on broad red band interupted by white square containing black 'Y' within red outline.*
Hull: *Grey with red 'YANG MING LINE', red boot-topping.*

Name	Eng	Flag	Year	GRT	DWT	Loa	Bm	Kts	Type	Former names
Jupiter Bridge	Lbr	2001	64,005	68,615	275	40	26	CC	ex Ming Bamboo-02
Kota Permas	Lbr	1983	29,872	30,669	210	32	23	CC	ex Med Taichung-03, Maersk Dubai-96, Ming Fortune-94
Med Keelung	Lbr	1983	29,872	30,701	210	32	23	CC	ex Ming Energy-93
Med Taipei	Lbr	1988	40,415	40,845	270	32	20	CC	ex Ville d'Hydra-95, Ming Prosperity-94
Mercury Bridge	Lbr	2001	64,254	68,413	275	40	25	CC	ex Ming Cypress-02
Ming America	Lbr	1992	46,728	46,785	276	32	21	CC	
Ming Asia	Lbr	1991	46,728	46,772	276	32	21	CC	
Ming Champion	Lbr	1997	15,120	19,332	169	27	18	CC	
Ming Container	Twn	1997	15,120	19,353	169	27	18	CC	
Ming Cosmos	Pan	2001	64,254	68,413	275	40	25	CC	
Ming Cultivation	Twn	1996	35,905	69,163	225	32	14	B	ex Bel Best-02
Ming East	Twn	1995	46,697	45,995	276	32	21	CC	ex Maersk Long Beach-96, Ming East-95
Ming Equality	Lbr	1996	36,559	70,252	225	32	14	B	ex Bel Ace-03
Ming Europe	Twn	1992	46,728	46,772	276	32	21	CC	
Ming Green	Lbr	2001	64,254	68,413	275	40	26	CC	
Ming Longevity	Twn	1983	29,872	30,646	210	32	23	CC	ex Gibralter Bridge-98, Ming Longevity-96, Med Hong Kong-95, Maersk Jeddah-93, Ming Longevity-93
Ming North	Lbr	1995	46,697	45,995	276	32	21	CC	
Ming Ocean	Twn	1980	29,872	31,208	210	32	23	CC	ex Dover Bridge-98, Ming Ocean-96
Ming Orchid	Pan	2000	64,254	68,303	275	40	26	CC	
Ming Plum	Pan	2000	64,254	68,413	275	40	26	CC	
Ming Prominence	Lbr	1987	40,436	40,845	270	32	20	CC	
Ming South	Twn	1995	46,697	45,995	276	32	21	CC	
Ming Union	Twn	1997	15,120	19,338	169	27	18	CC	
Ming Victory	Lbr	1997	15,120	19,325	169	27	18	CC	
Ming Virtue	Lbr	2003	39,749	73,840	225	32	14	B	
Ming West	Lbr	1995	46,697	45,995	276	32	21	CC	ex Maersk Singapore-96, Ming West-95
Ming Zenith	Lbr	1996	46,697	45,995	276	32	21	CC	
Ocean Atlantic	Lbr	1980	29,873	31,264	210	32	20	CC	ex Atlantic Bridge-02, Ming Galaxy-98
Ocean Genius	Lbr	1980	29,873	31,265	210	32	20	CC	ex Sun River-01, Ming Sun-98
Ocean Gulf	Lbr	1980	29,873	31,208	210	32	20	CC	ex Gulf Bridge-02, Ming Glory-98
Ocean Luna	Lbr	1980	29,872	31,246	210	32	22	CC	ex Cosco Atlantic-02, Ming Moon-98
Ocean Starlight	Lbr	1980	29,873	31,251	210	32	20	CC	ex Starlight River-02, Ming Star-99

Name	Eng	Flag	Year	GRT	DWT	Loa	Bm	Kts	Type	Former names
Sentosa Bridge		Twn	1982	29,872	30,637	210	32	23	CC	ex Ming Comfort-03, Malacca Bridge-99, Ming Comfort-96
Venus Bridge		Lbr	2001	64,005	68,615	275	40	26	CC	ex Ming Pine-02
YM Hakata *		Sgp	2000	17,167	21,331	169	27	20	CC	ex P&O Nedlloyd Canterbury-03, Mira-02

newbuildings - four 82,340 dwt, five66,000 dwt and two 21,000 dwt container ships, also two 77,000 dwt bulk carriers for 2004/5 delivery .
Controlled by Government of Taiwan, also manages tankers owned by associated Chinese Petroleum Corp.
* on charter from Reederei Horst Zeppenfeld GmbH & Co. KG, Germany. See other ships in index with 'YM' prefix.

World Wide Shipping (Bergesen). BERGE ARCTIC. Hans Kraijenbosch

Yangming Marine Transport. MING ORCHID. *Hans Kraijenbosch.*

INDEX

Name	No.	Name	No.	Name	No.	Name	No.	Name	No.
Avalon Spirit	189	Berge Everett	209	Bow Pioneer	134	Bulk Asia	46	Canelo Arrow	84
Avocet Arrow	84	Berge Fjord	209	Bow Power	134	Bulk Atlanta	46	CanMar Bravery	56
Axel Maersk	113	Berge Flanders	209	Bow Pride	134	Bulk Australia	46	CanMar Dynasty	56
Axios	97	Berge Frost	209	Bow Prima	134	Bulk Europe	46	CanMar Endurance	56
Azalea Ace	110	Berge Kobe	209	Bow Princess	134	Bulk Ispat Leher	46	CanMar Glory	56
Azov Sea	179	Berge Nantes	209	Bow Prosper	134	Bulkazores	46	CanMar Honour	56
Aztec	195	Berge Nice	209	Bow Puma	134	Bunga Anggerik	100	CanMar Pride	56
Azteca	200	Berge Nisa	209	Bow Queen	134	Bunga Bidara	100	Canmar Promise	142
Azul Glory	175	Berge Nord	209	Bow Saturn	134	Bunga Cenderawasih	100	CanMar Spirit	56
		Berge Pacific	209	Bow Sea	134	Bunga Delima	100	CanMar Triumph	58
B. Prus	158	Berge Phoenix	209	Bow Sky	134	Bunga Kasturi	100	CanMar Valour	58
Baco-Liner 1	37	Berge Rachel	209	Bow Spring	134	Bunga Kekaras	100	CanMar Venture	58
Baco-Liner 2	37	Berge Racine	209	Bow Star	134	Bunga Kelana Dua	100	CanMar Victory	58
Baco-Liner 3	37	Berge Ragnhild	209	Bow Sun	134	Bunga Kelana Empat	100	Canterbury Star	182
Bahamas Spirit	189	Berge Saga	209	Bow Transporter	134	Bunga Kelana Enam	100	Cap Aguilar	96
Bahamian Express	202	Berge Shan	209	Bow Viking	134	Bunga Kelana Lima	100	Cap Blanco	138
Bahamian Express	32	Berge Sisar	209	Braemar	18	Bunga Kelana Satu	100	Cap Bonavista	103
Bakra	89	Berge Sisu	209	Bravery	154	Bunga Kelana Tiga	100	Cap Carmel	136
Balao	89	Berge Spirit	209	Bravery Ace	110	Bunga Kelana Tudjuh	100	Cap Castillo	44
Balboa	89	Berge Stadt	209	Brazil Star	140	Bunga Kenanga	100	Cap Cortes	103
Balder	89	Berge Stahl	209	Brazilian Express	202	Bunga Kenari	102	Cap Delgado	103
Balgarka	120	Berge Stavanger	210	Brazilian Reefer	182	Bunga Kerayong	102	Cap Diamant	46
Balgarka	158	Berge Strand	210	Braztrans I	55	Bunga Mawar	102	Cap Domingo	138
Bali Sea	81	Berge Sund	210	Breeze Arrow	40	Bunga Melati Dua	102	Cap Ferrato	131
Balkan	120	Berge Sword	210	Bregen	195	Bunga Melati Empat	102	Cap Finisterre	136
Ballangen	89	Berge Troll	210	Bregen	38	Bunga Melati Enam	102	Cap Frio	126
Balsfjord	89	Berge Vik	210	Bremen	14	Bunga Melati Lima	102	Cap Georges	46
Baltic Breeze	204	Bergeland	210	Bremen Bridge	86	Bunga Melati Satu	102	Cap Jean	46
Baltic Challenger	40	Bergen Arrow	84	Bremen Express	77	Bunga Melati Tiga	102	Cap Laurent	46
Baltic Champion	40	Bergina	38	Bright City	48	Bunga Melati Tudjuh	102	Cap Leon	97
Baltic Commodore	40	Bergitta	38	Bright Days	48	Bunga Melor Dua	102	Cap Lobos	96
Baltic Highway	86	Bering Sea	179	Bright State	48	Bunga Melor Empat	102	Cap Matapan	126
Baltic Leader	122	Bering Sea	195	Brilliance of the Seas	18	Bunga Melor Satu	102	Cap Melville	136
Baltic Mariner	182	Berlin Express	77	Brilliant Ace	110	Bunga Melor Tiga	102	Cap Nelson	136
Baltic Melody	182	Berlin Senator	76	British Adventure	40	Bunga Orkid Dua	102	Cap Norte	63
Baltic Meridian	182	Berlin	12	British Beech	40	Bunga Orkid Empat	102	Cap Ortegal	103
Baltic Sea	195	Bermudian Express	202	British Curlew	40	Bunga Orkid Lima	102	Cap Pasado	96
Baltrum Trader	44	Bernhard Oldendorff	146	British Endeavour	40	Bunga Orkid Satu	102	Cap Pierre	46
Banasol	89	Bernhard Schulte	174	British Endurance	40	Bunga Orkid Tiga	102	Cap Pilar	96
Banastar	89	Berthea	38	British Energy	40	Bunga Pelangi Dua	102	Cap Polonia	136
Banda Sea	81	Bertina	38	British Enterprise	40	Bunga Pelangi	102	Cap Reinga	103
Bandaisan	113	Bertora	38	British Esteem	40	Bunga Raya Dua	102	Cap Roca	136
Bandar Ayu	151	Beryl	154	British Explorer	40	Bunga Raya Satu	102	Cap Romuald	46
Bandar	89	Betty Knutsen	89	British Harrier	40	Bunga Saga Dua	102	Cap San Antonio	136
Bangkok Express	126	Bibi	164	British Hawk	40	Bunga Saga Empat	102	Cap San Augustin	136
Baniyas	89	Big Red Boat II	26	British Hawthorn	40	Bunga Saga Enam	102	Cap San Lorenzo	136
Barachois	51	Bijin	122	British Hazel	40	Bunga Saga Lapan	102	Cap San Marco	136
Barbarossa	103	Bilbao Knutsen	89	British Hunter	40	Bunga Saga Lima	102	Cap San Nicolas	136
Barbet Arrow	84	Bing He	47	British Innovator	40	Bunga Saga Satu	102	Cap San Raphael	136
Barcelona Bridge	126	Birte Ritscher	194	British Laurel	40	Bunga Saga Sembilan	102	Cap Velas	131
Bardu	89	Black Marlin	64	British Loyalty	40	Bunga Saga Sepuloh	102	Cap Vilano	200
Barents Bay	175	Black Prince	18	British Merchant	40	Bunga Saga Tiga	102	Cap Vincent	34
Barents Sea	179	Black Watch	18	British Merlin	40	Bunga Saga Tujuh	102	Cape Ann	170
Bariloche	188	Blandine Delmas	60	British Oak	40	Bunga Semarak	102	Cape Arago	170
Barkald	89	Blue Hawk	122	British Osprey	40	Bunga Siantan	102	Cape Bake	170
Barrington	189	Blue Marlin	64	British Pioneer	40	Bunga Tanjung	102	Cape Balboa	170
Barrington Island	195	Blue Master	100	British Pride	40	Bunga Terasek	102	Cape Banks	170
Bataliony Chlopskie	158	Blue Sky	142	British Progress	40	Bunga Teratai Dua	102	Cape Bata	170
Battersea Bridge	200	Bogdan	120	British Purpose	40	Bunga Teratai Empat	102	Cape Bear	170
Bauta	89	Boheme	204	British Security	40	Bunga Teratai Tiga	102	Cape Benat	170
Bay Bridge	170	Bolero	14	British Swift	40	Bunga Teratai	102	Cape Bille	170
Bay Bridge	86	Bonanza	90	British Tenacity	40	Burgos	117	Cape Bird	170
Baykal Senator	76	Bonn Express	77	British Trader	40	Busan Express	126	Cape Blanc	170
Baynunah	32	Borga	120	British Unity	40	Bussewitz	90	Cape Bon	170
BBC Russia	78	Boris Livanov	128	British Vine	42	Buxcrown	131	Cape Bowen	170
Beatanavis	48	Bornes	179	British Willow	42	Buxfavourite	131	Cape Bruny	170
Beauty River	47	Bosphoros Bridge	86	Bro Albert	42	Buxmaster	131	Cape Charles	122
Bebedouro	200	Bourgogne	54	Bro Alexandre	42	Buxsailor	131	Cape Conway	170
Belgian Express	202	Bow Andes	132	Bro Anton	42	Buxsund	131	Cape Darby	170
Belgian Reefer	182	Bow Cardinal	134	Bro Arthur	42	Buyihe	47	Cape Darnley	170
Belgoroda	92	Bow Cecil	134	Bro Atland	42			Cape Delfaro	170
Belgrace	37	Bow Cedar	134	Bro Axel	42	C. Columbus	14	Cape Delgarde	170
Belgreeting	37	Bow Century	134	Bro Bara	42	Cabo Hellas	184	Cape Denison	170
Belguardian	37	Bow Chain	134	Bro Caroline	42	Cabo Sounion	184	Cape Don	170
Bellatrix Voyager	46	Bow Cheetah	134	Bro Catherine	42	Cadiz Carrier	60	Cape Eagle	140
Bellona	122	Bow Clipper	134	Bro Cecile	42	Cadiz Knutsen	89	Cape Falcon	140
Belmeken	120	Bow Eagle	134	Bro Charlotte	42	Caecilia Schulte	172	Cape Falcon	170
Belnor	37	Bow Fagus	134	Bro Edward	42	Cala Palamos	148	Cape Ferro	170
Belokamenka	209	Bow Faith	134	Bro Elizabeth	42	Cala Palos	148	Cape Frio	170
Benarita	196	Bow Favour	134	Bro Ellen	42	Cala Piedad	208	Cape Hawk	141
Benguela Stream	175	Bow Fighter	134	Bro Etienne	42	Cala Pilar	148	Cape Henry	172
Berana	38	Bow Firda	134	Bro Selma	42	Cala Pinar del Rio	162	Cape Kestrel	141
Berge Arctic	209	Bow Flora	134	Bro Sincero	42	Calanda	170	Cape May	122
Berge Arrow	209	Bow Flower	134	Bro Stella	42	Calaparati	44	Cape North	172
Berge Athene	209	Bow Fortune	134	Bro Tina	42	California Jupiter	122	Cape Norviega	170
Berge Atlantic	209	Bow Heron	134	Broadgate	140	California Mercury	122	Cape Osprey	141
Berge Banker	209	Bow Hunter	134	Broadwater	189	California Senator	76	Cape Preston	170
Berge Boston	209	Bow Lady	134	Brother Glory	140	Californian Highway	86	Cape Sable	172
Berge Captain	209	Bow Lancer	134	Brugge Venture	54	Calliroe Patronicola	152	Cape Santiago	172
Berge Challenger	209	Bow Leopard	134	Bryggen	134	Calypso	14	Cape Serrat	172
Berge Clipper	209	Bow Lion	134	Buccleuch	140	Camar	184	Cape Spear	172
Berge Commander	209	Bow Merkur	134	Buckinghamshire	200	Camellia Ace	110	Cape Town Star	182
Berge Danuta	209	Bow Pacifico	134	Bujin	122	Camilla Rickmers	164	Cape York	170
Berge Denise	209	Bow Panther	134	Bulduri	92	Campos Transporter	196	Capella Voyager	46
Berge Eagle	209	Bow Peace	134	Bulgaria	120	Canada Senator	76	Capemar	184
Berge Enterprise	209	Bow Petros	134	Bulk Africa	46	Canadian Express	202	Capo Noli	46

Name	Pg	Name	Pg	Name	Pg	Name	Pg	Name	Pg
Full Wealth	48	Grand Way	48	Hanjin Colombo	74	Havglimt	210	Hual Seoul	80
Fulmar	184	Grande Africa	73	Hanjin Copenhagen	131	Havis	210	Hual Tokyo	80
Funchal	8	Grande Amburgo	73	Hanjin Dampier	74	Havkong	210	Hual Tracer	80
Fusus	176	Grande America	73	Hanjin Gladstone	74	Havprins	210	Hual Trader	80
		Grande Argentina	74	Hanjin Gothenburg	131	Havrim	210	Hual Trailer	80
G&C Parana	200	Grande Atlantico	73	Hanjin Haypoint	74	Hawk Arrow	84	Hual Tramper	80
Gaby Delmas	60	Grande Brasile	73	Hanjin Helsinki	131	Hawk	68	Hual Transit	80
Gaida	92	Grande Buenos Aires	74	Hanjin Houston	74	Hawtah	120	Hual Transporter	80
Galapagos Explorer II	26	Grande Ellade	73	Hanjin Istanbul	74	Hebridean Princess	26	Hual Trapeze	80
Galaxy Harvest	124	Grande Europa	73	Hanjin Kaohsiung	74	Hebridean Spirit	26	Hual Trapper	80
Galaxy	20	Grande Francia	73	Hanjin Kwangyang	74	Hebris	210	Hual Traveller	80
Gangga Nagara	102	Grande Italia	73	Hanjin Lisbon	131	Hedda	210	Hual Treasure	80
Gannet Arrow	84	Grande Mediterraneo	73	Hanjin London	74	Hedwig Oldendorff	146	Hual Trekker	80
Ganta	124	Grande Napoli	73	Hanjin Los Angeles	74	Heemskerck	155	Hual Tribute	80
Gao He	47	Grande Nigeria	73	Hanjin Madras	74	Heidelburg Express	77	Hual Tricorn	80
Gardno	158	Grande Portogallo	73	Hanjin Madrid	131	Heijin	124	Hual Trident	80
Gas Al Ahmadi	90	Grande Roma	73	Hanjin Malta	74	Heinrich Oldendorff	146	Hual Trinity	80
Gas Al Burgan	90	Grande San Paolo	74	Hanjin Marseilles	74	Heinrich S	169	Hual Triton	80
Gas Al Minagish	90	Grande Scandinavia	74	Hanjin Melbourne	74	Hekabe	210	Hual Triumph	80
Gas Al Mutlaa	90	Grande Spagna	74	Hanjin Nagoya	74	Hektor	210	Hual Trooper	80
Gas Al-Gurain	90	Grandeur of the Seas	18	Hanjin New Orleans	74	Helena Oldendorff	146	Hual Trophy	80
Gas Aries	124	Grasmere Maersk	117	Hanjin Osaka	74	Helene J	86	Hual Tropicana	80
Gas Capricorn	124	Great Ambition	178	Hanjin Oslo	74	Helene Knutsen	89	Hual Trotter	80
Gas Diana	168	Great Bless	178	Hanjin Ottawa	132	Helene Maersk	114	Hual Troubadour	80
Gas Leo	168	Great Blossom	178	Hanjin Paris	74	Helene Rickmers	166	Hual Trove	80
Gas Scorpio	168	Great Bright	178	Hanjin Penang	74	Helga Selmer	206	Hudson Bay	175
Gas Taurus	168	Great Calm	178	Hanjin Pennsylvania	141	Helga	210	Hudson Leader	124
Gebe Oldendorff	146	Great Century	178	Hanjin Philadephia	90	Helice	210	Hudson Spirit	189
Geilo	184	Great Concord	178	Hanjin Phoenix	90	Helios	210	Hudson	151
Gemini Star	169	Great Creation	178	Hanjin Pittsburg	74	Helix	176	Hugo N	210
Gemini Voyager	46	Great Fortune	178	Hanjin Pohang	74	Hellespont Alhambra	156	Hugo Oldendorff	146
General Delgado	32	Great Gain	178	Hanjin Port Kembla	74	Hellespont Fairfax	156	Hui He	47
General Grot-Rowecki	158	Great Glory	178	Hanjin Portland	74	Hellespont Metropolis	156	Humber Bridge	88
General Guisan	188	Great Happy	178	Hanjin Praha	90	Hellespont Tara	156	Humboldt Express	77
General Tyulenev	128	Great Harmony	178	Hanjin Pretoria	90	Helvetia	104	Hume Highway	88
General Villa	32	Great Jade	178	Hanjin Richards Bay	74	Helvetia	64	Huta Zgoda	158
General Vladimir Zaimov	120	Great Loyalty	178	Hanjin Roberts Bank	76	Hemina	210	Hyde Park	141
General Zamora	128	Great Luck	178	Hanjin Rome	76	Henning Maersk	114	Hydra Star	169
Genoa Bridge	88	Great Motion	178	Hanjin San Francisco	76	Henriette Maersk	114	Hyundai Admiral	141
Gent	54	Great Ocean	178	Hanjin Seoul	76	Henriette Schulte	174	Hyundai Advance	80
Genua Express	155	Great Olympia	178	Hanjin Shanghai	76	Henry Hudson Bridge	88	Hyundai Atlas	80
Geo Milev	120	Great Peace	178	Hanjin Sydney	76	Henry Oldendorff	146	Hyundai Banner	80
George Washington Bridge	88	Great Prosperity	178	Hanjin Tacoma	76	Herakles	210	Hyundai Baron	141
Georgi Grigorov	120	Great Rainbow	178	Hanjin Taipei	132	Hercules Highway	88	Hyundai Bridge	80
Georgia Gal	146	Great Scenery	178	Hanjin Tampa	76	Hercules Leader	124	Hyundai Commodore	59
Gerd Knutsen	89	Great Success	178	Hanjin Tokyo	76	Hermann	211	Hyundai Confidence	80
Gerdt Oldendorff	146	Grebe Arrow	84	Hanjin Valencia	76	Hermion	210	Hyundai Continental	80
Geroi Sevastopolya	130	Green Cape	100	Hanjin Vancouver	76	Hermitage Bridge	179	Hyundai Cosmos	80
Gerrita	196	Green Cove	81	Hanjin Vienna	132	Heroic Ace	112	Hyundai Discovery	141
Gertrud Salamon	172	Green Dale	81	Hanjin Washington	76	Hertford	200	Hyundai Dominion	141
Gertrude Oldendorff	146	Green Lake	81	Hanjin Wilmington	76	Hesiod	210	Hyundai Duke	59
Ghana Star I	166	Green Modest	66	Hanne Knutsen	89	Hesnes	195	Hyundai Emperor	141
Ghawar	120	Green Moral	66	Hannover Express	77	Heythrop	140	Hyundai Explorer	83
Gimi	72	Green Mountain	141	Hans Maersk	114	Highgate	141	Hyundai Fortune	80
Gisela Oldendorff	146	Green Point	81	Hans Oldendorff	146	Hilda Knutsen	89	Hyundai Freedom	80
Gitta Oldendorff	146	Green Wave	81	Hansa Africa	96	Hildegaard	100	Hyundai Future	80
Glacier Bay	175	Greenwich Maersk	114	Hansa Bergen	96	Hilli	72	Hyundai General	80
Glarus	201	Grena	120	Hansa Bremen	96	Hinrich Oldendorff	146	Hyundai Glory	80
Glasgow Maersk	114	Greta-C	44	Hansa Centaur	96	Hoechst Express	77	Hyundai Highness	80
Glen Maye	113	Gretke Oldendorff	146	Hansa Challenger	96	Hoegh Galleon	78	Hyundai Highway	80
Glen Roy	113	Grey Fox	100	Hansa Commodore	96	Hoegh Gandria	78	Hyundai Independence	141
Global Harvest	124	Grigoriy Nesterenko	130	Hansa Constitution	96	Hoegh Marlin	78	Hyundai Innovator	83
Global Highway	88	Grouse Arrow	84	Hansa India	96	Hoegh Mascot	78	Hyundai Island	80
Global Victory	80	Guadalupe	151	Hansa Kristiansand	96	Hoegh Merchant	78	Hyundai Kingdom	141
Global Winner	80	Guardian	55	Hansa London	96	Hoegh Merit	78	Hyundai Liberty	141
Glorious Ace	112	Guatemala	211	Hansa Lubeck	96	Hoegh Minerva	78	Hyundai National	141
Glorious Harvest	124	Gull Arrow	84	Hansa Narvik	96	Hoegh Miranda	78	Hyundai No. 103	205
Glory	162			Hansa Rostock	96	Hoegh Monal	78	Hyundai No. 105	205
Gluecksburg	126	H. Kirkenes	96	Hansa Stockholm	96	Hoegh Morus	78	Hyundai No. 106	205
Golar Freeze	72	Hadiyah	90	Hansa Stralsund	96	Hoegh Musketeer	78	Hyundai No. 107	205
Golar Mazo	72	Hadra	176	Hansa Visby	96	Hojin	124	Hyundai No. 108	205
Golar Spirit	72	Hakata	72	Hanseatic	14	Holiday	8	Hyundai No. 109	205
Golar Winter	72	Hakone	124	Happy Buccaneer	180	Hong Kong Express	77	Hyundai No. 201	205
Golden Fountain	72	Halden	184	Happy Ranger	180	Hong Kong Star	172	Hyundai No. 202	205
Golden Gate Bridge	88	Halia	176	Happy River	180	Hong Yun He	47	Hyundai No. 203	205
Golden Isle	170	Halifax	200	Happy Rover	180	Hongkong Senato	76	Hyundai No. 205	205
Golden Princess	12	Hamal Sta	169	Harad	120	Honor River	47	Hyundai No. 206	205
Golden Princess	26	Hamane Spirit	189	Harefield	84	Hood Island	195	Hyundai Oceania	81
Golden Stream	72	Hamburg Express	77	Harmony Ace	112	Hope Bay	175	Hyundai Olympia	81
Goldmar	184	Haminea	176	Harmony	162	Horizon	20	Hyundai Patriot	141
Gosport Maersk	117	Hammurabi	198	Harriette N	210	Hornbay	60	Hyundai Pioneer	83
Gotland Spirit	189	Hanihe	47	Harvester	182	Horncap	60	Hyundai Power	81
Goviken	118	Hanjin Amsterdam	131	Hastula	176	Horncliff	60	Hyundai Progress	81
Grafton	140	Hanjin Antwerp	74	Hatasia	176	Hose Marti	92	Hyundai Prosperity	81
Gran Bretagna	73	Hanjin Barcelona	74	Hatsu Eagle	66	Hotaka Maru	124	Hyundai Republic	141
Grand Benelux	73	Hanjin Basel	131	Hatsu Elite	66	HS Challenger	96	Hyundai Spirit	81
Grand Choice	205	Hanjin Beijing	74	Hatsu Envoy	66	HS Discoverer	96	Hyundai Sprinter	81
Grand Iris	51	Hanjin Berlin	74	Hatsu Ethic	66	Hua Tai He	47	Hyundai Star	81
Grand Lebanon	55	Hanjin Bombay	74	Hatsu Excel	66	Hua Tuo	158	Hyundai Stride	81
Grand Mark	205	Hanjin Brisbane	74	Hatsu Pride	66	Hua Yun He	47	Hyundai Sun	81
Grand Orchid	51	Hanjin Brussels	131	Hatsu Prima	66	Hual Africa	80	Hyundai Universal	81
Grand Pace	205	Hanjin Busan	74	Haustrum	176	Hual America	80	Hyundai Vladivostok	81
Grand Princess	12	Hanjin Cairo	131	Havdrott	210	Hual Asia	80		
Grand Quest	205	Hanjin Calcutta	74	Havelstern	168	Hual Dubai	80	Iason	14
Grand Race	205	Hanjin Capetown	74	Havfrost	210	Hual Durban	80	Ibis Arrow	84
Grand View	48	Hanjin Chicago	131	Havfru	210	Hual Oceania	80	Ibn Al Moataz	198

Name	No.	Name	No.	Name	No.	Name	No.	Name	No.
Libra Houston	175	Lykes Explorer	58	Maersk Rostock	86	Marie Maersk	116	Mikhail Strekalovskiy	98
Libra Leader	202	Lykes Flyer	58	Maersk Rosyth	114	Marie Schulte	63	Milin Kamak	121
Libra New York	206	Lykes Hero	58	Maersk Rotterdam	86	Marielle Bolten	38	Millenium	196
Libra Patagonia	150	Lykes Inspirer	58	Maersk Rouen	118	Marienborg	118	Millennium Explorer	113
Libra Rio	63	Lykes Liberator	58	Maersk Rugen	118	Marine Columbia	154	Millennium Maersk	116
Libra Santos	63	Lykes Motivator	58	Maersk Scotland	118	Marine Hunter	98	Millennium	20
Libra Star	169	Lykes Navigator	58	Maersk Sea	117	Marine Phoenix	141	Milos	38
Lica Maersk	114	Lykes Provider	58	Maersk Sun	117	Marine Reliance	205	Min He	47
Lielupe	92	Lykes Raider	58	Maersk Tacoma	114	Mariner of the Seas	18	Mina Oldendorff	148
Ligovsky Prospect	179	Lykes Ranger	59	Maersk Taiki	117	Marinus Green	37	Mindanao	72
Liguria	55	Lykes Runner	59	Maersk Taiyo	117	Marion Green	37	Mineral Antwerpen	52
Lili Marleen	12	Lykes Voyager	59	Maersk Tampa	83	Marissa Green	38	Mineral Beijing	52
Liliana Dimitrova	121	Lykes Winner	59	Maersk Teal	117	Marit Maersk	116	Mineral Dragon	52
Lily Oldendorff	148	Lysaker	184	Maersk Tide	117	Marivia	60	Mineral Kiwi	52
Lily	136	Lyubov Orlova	30	Maersk Toba	55	Markab Star	169	Mineral Oak	52
Limar	184			Maersk Tokyo	55	Marlene Green	38	Mineral Ordaz	52
Lincoln	200	Maasdam	8	Maersk Toledo	114	Marne	151	Mineral Sines	52
Linda Oldendorff	148	Maasslot L	46	Maersk Trieste	114	Marquisa	102	Mineral Venture	54
Lindavia	60	Maasstad L	46	Maersk Trondheim	55	Mars Glory	169	Mineral Viking	54
Linden Pride	124	Maasstroom L	46	Maersk Vaasa	97	Mars	34	Minerva II	12
Ling Yun He	47	Mabel Rickmers	166	Maersk Valencia	126	Marshal Bagramyan	130	Ming America	211
Linnet Arrow	84	Macau Success	30	Maersk Valletta	200	Marshal Chu(y)kov	130	Ming Asia	211
Lion	200	Maciej Rataj	158	Maersk Valparaiso	34	Marshal Vasilyevskiy	130	Ming Champion	211
Lions Gate Bridge	88	Mackinac Bridge	88	Maersk Vancouver	200	Martorell	112	Ming Container	211
Lita	97	Madame Butterfly	204	Maersk Venice	200	Mary Ann	154	Ming Cosmos	211
Livanita	196	Madeleine Rickmers	166	Maersk Ventspils	97	Mashuk	130	Ming Cultivation	211
Lobivia	60	Madison Maersk	114	Maersk Vigo	200	Masovia	32	Ming East	211
Loch Rannoch	117	Madison	151	Maersk Vilnius	97	Mass Enterprise	48	Ming Equality	211
Lofoten	184	Maersk Aberdeen	117	Maersk Virginia	118	Mass Glory	48	Ming Europe	211
Lofoten	28	Maersk Abidjan	144	Maersk Volos	97	Mass Prosperity	48	Ming Green	211
Logos II	26	Maersk Accra	144	Maersk Wave	117	Mass Success	48	Ming Longevity	211
Loire	151	Maersk Ahram	114	Maersk Wind	117	Mastera	70	Ming North	211
Lombok Strait	175	Maersk Alaska	117	Magas	98	Mate	162	Ming Ocean	211
London Express	77	Maersk Antwerp	117	Magdalena Green	37	Mathilde Maersk	116	Ming Orchid	211
London Senator	76	Maersk Apapa	144	Magic	175	Mathilde Oldendorff	148	Ming Plum	211
London Tower	141	Maersk Arizona	117	Magic Wave	205	Matilde	154	Ming Prominence	211
Long Beach Bridge	88	Maersk Arun	117	Magic Wind	205	Matjam	120	Ming South	211
Lord Hinton	160	Maersk Athens	96	Magleby Maersk	114	Mattea	196	Ming Union	211
Los Angeles Express	128	Maersk Atlantic	117	Magnavia	60	Maud	175	Ming Victory	211
Lowlands Rose	54	Maersk Auckland	96	Magnific	175	Mauranger	207	Ming Virtue	211
Lowlands Saguenay	54	Maersk Avon	117	Magnitude	184	Maveric	175	Ming West	211
Lowlands Yarra	54	Maersk Bahrain	201	Magnolia	68	Max Jacob	83	Ming Zenith	211
Loyalty	194	Maersk Barcelona	201	Magpie	32	Max Oldebdorff	148	Mirfak Star	169
LT Garland	67	Maersk Belawana	201	Mahone Bay	175	Maxim Gorkiy	20	Mistral	14
LT Genova	67	Maersk Bilbao	55	Maikop	98	May Oldendorff	148	Mitrope	160
LT Giant	66	Maersk Brisbanea	201	Majestic	175	Maya	195	Mitsumine	113
LT Glamour	67	Maersk Carolina	117	Majestic Maersk	114	Maya Rickmers	166	Mobil Magnolia	83
LT Gleamy	66	Maersk Cloud	117	Majestic Unity	154	Mayon Spirit	190	Modern Chance	205
LT Going	66	Maersk Constantia	118	Majestic	94	Mayview Maersk	116	Modern Drive	205
LT Grace	67	Maersk Constellation	117	Majesty of the Seas	18	MB Caribe	97	Modern Express	205
LT Greet	67	Maersk Crest	117	Major Hubal	158	Mc-Kinney Maersk	116	Modern Link	205
LT Guard	66	Maersk Curlew	114	Majori	92	MCT Alioth	130	Modern Peak	205
LT Lloydiana	67	Maersk Dakar	208	Makiri Green	37	MCT Almak	130	MOL Advantage	112
LT Peace	66	Maersk Dammam	76	Malaga Carrier	60	MCT Altair	130	MOL Ambition	112
LT Pearl	66	Maersk Darwin	141	Malyovitza	121	MCT Arcturus	130	MOL Brasilia	172
LT Power	66	Maersk Doha	141	Mamry II	158	Meandros	97	MOL Bravery	112
LT Trieste	67	Maersk Dublin	76	Mandarin Arrow	84	Mecta Sea	68	MOL Columbus	112
LT Ulysses	66	Maersk Dundee	141	Manhatten Bridge	88	Med Keelung	211	MOL Discovery	112
LT Unica	67	Maersk Gareloch	118	Manon	204	Med Taipei	211	MOL Efficiency	112
LT Unicorn	66	Maersk Garonne	114	Maple Ace II	112	Medea	204	MOL Elbe	112
LT Unity	66	Maersk Gateshead	114	Mapocho	55	Mediterranean Highway	88	MOL Encore	112
LT Universo	67	Maersk Georgia	118	Mar	92	MegaStar Aries	22	MOL Endeavor	112
LT Ursula	66	Maersk Gironde	114	Maracas Bay	113	MegaStar Taurus	22	MOL Endurance	112
LT Usodimare	67	Maersk Holyhead	114	Marathon	195	Mekhanik Slauta	130	MOL Enterprise	112
LT Utile	67	Maersk Hong Kong	34	Marble Highway	88	Melbourne Highway	88	MOL Excellence	112
Lu Ban	158	Maersk Itajai	34	Marchen Maersk	114	Melfi Canada	44	MOL Expeditor	112
Lu He	47	Maersk Kolkata	55	Marco Polo	22	Melide	32	MOL Express	112
Lu Xun	158	Maersk Kope	114	Mare Adriaticum	77	Melody	16	MOL Fortune	112
Luan He	47	Maersk Malacca	117	Mare Balticum	77	Mercosul Palometa	144	MOL Glory	112
Lucas Oldendorff	148	Maersk Malaga	96	Mare Caspium	77	Mercosul Pescada	168	MOL Golden Wattle	112
Lucie Delmas	62	Maersk Marseille	97	Mare Doricum	77	Mercure	92	MOL Horizon	62
Lucky Transporter	141	Maersk Merlion	117	Mare Gallicum	77	Mercury Ace	112	MOL Ingenuity	112
Lucy Oldendorff	148	Maersk Missouri	118	Mare Hibernum	77	Mercury Bridge	211	MOL Initiative	112
Ludolf Oldendorff	148	Maersk Nassau	169	Mare Ibericum	77	Mercury	20	MOL Integrity	112
Ludwigshafen Express	77	Maersk New Orleans	126	Mare Internum	77	Merida	166	MOL Liberty	112
Luetjenburg	128	Maersk Newark	126	Mare Phoenicium	77	Meridian	154	MOL Maas	112
Luise Oldendorff	90	Maersk Newcastle	126	Mare Thracium	77	Merkur Bay	201	MOL Miracle	112
Luna Maersk	114	Maersk Norfolk	126	Maremar	184	Merkur Beach	201	MOL Performance	112
Lunita	196	Maersk Perth	114	Maren Maersk	114	Merkur Bridge	201	MOL Precision	112
Luo Ba He	47	Maersk Pireaus	97	Marfret Caraibes	90	Merkur Cloud	201	MOL Pride	112
Luo He	47	Maersk Plymouth	114	Marfret Normandie	166	Merkur Delta	201	MOL Priority	112
Luxembourg	54	Maersk Pointer	117	Marfret Provence	166	Merkur Sea	201	MOL Progress	112
Luxmar	184	Maersk Pride	117	Margara	83	Merkur Star	202	MOL Promise	112
Luzern	201	Maersk Prime	117	Margaretha Green	37	Merkur Tide	202	MOL Rainbow	62
Luzon Spirit	190	Maersk Princess	117	Margit Gorthon	72	Merkur	34	MOL Solution	112
Luzon Strait	175	Maersk Rapier	118	Margret Oldendorff	148	Methane Princess	72	MOL Sprinter	150
Lydia Oldendorff	148	Maersk Ravenna	86	Margrethe Maersk	116	Mette Maersk	116	MOL Thames	112
Lykes Achiever	58	Maersk Regent	118	Maria A. Angelicoussi	36	Mexican Reefer	94	MOL Triumph	112
Lykes Ambassador	58	Maersk Rhine	114	Maria A. Angelicoussis	46	Meynell	140	MOL Vigor	122
Lykes Challenger	58	Maersk Rhode Island	118	Maria C	59	Michaela S	169	MOL Vision	122
Lykes Commander	141	Maersk Rhone	174	Maria Gorthon	72	Midjur	121	MOL Wellington	112
Lykes Deliverer	58	Maersk Richmond	118	Maria Green	37	Midnight Sun	113	MOL Wisdom	112
Lykes Discoverer	58	Maersk Riga	114	Maria Knutsen	89	Mighty Servant 1	62	Molda	120
Lykes Eagle	58	Maersk Rio Grande	86	Maria Salamon	172	Mighty Servant 3	62	Moldanger	207
Lykes Energiser	58	Maersk Rochester	118	Maria Tsakos	195	Mignon	204	Moleson	188
Lykes Envoy	150	Maersk Rosario	86	Marie Delmas	62	Mikhail Kutuzov	98		

Name	No.	Name	No.	Name	No.	Name	No.	Name	No.
Mombasa Star	138	MSC Deila	106	MSC Ornella	128	NCC Arar	120	Nord Sea	83
Mona Century	112	MSC Denisse	106	MSC Palermo	92	NCC Asir	120	Nord Stealth	128
Mona Liberty	112	MSC Diego	106	MSC Panama	169	NCC Baha	120	Nordafrika	128
Mona Linden	112	MSC Don Giovanni	106	MSC Paola	108	NCC Jizan	120	Nordamerika	128
Mona Lisa	28	MSC Donata	97	MSC Paraguay	202	NCC Jouf	120	Nordanger	207
Monarch of the Seas	18	MSC Dymphna	106	MSC Parana	83	NCC Jubail	120	Nordasia	128
Monchegorsk	98	MSC Edna	106	MSC Patagonia	108	NCC Madinah *	120	Nordatlantic	128
Moni Rickmers	166	MSC Ela	128	MSC Patricia	108	NCC Mekka	120	Nordbay	150
Moniuszko	158	MSC Eleni	106	MSC Peggy	108	NCC Najran	120	Nordbeach	150
Montania	32	MSC Eleonora	106	MSC Perle	108	NCC Riyad	120	Nordcoast	150
Monte Alban	59	MSC Eliana	106	MSC Perth	172	NCC Tihamah	120	Nordeagle	150
Monte Cervantes	136	MSC Emilia S	106	MSC Peru	83	NCC Yamamah	120	Nordelbe	150
Monte Olivia	136	MSC Emma	106	MSC Pioneer	108	NDS Prodigy	174	Nordems	150
Monte Pascoal	136	MSC Eyra	106	MSC Pretoria	83	NDS Progress	174	Nordenergy	150
Monte Rosa	136	MSC Federica	106	MSC Provence	108	NDS Prominence	174	Nordeuropa	128
Monte Sarmiento	136	MSC Flaminia	132	MSC Rafaela	108	NDS Promoter	200	Nordfalcon	150
Monte Verde	136	MSC Florentina	132	MSC Rebecca	108	NDS Prosperity	200	Nordgulf	150
Montebello	151	MSC Floriana	106	MSC Regina	108	NDS Proteus	200	Nordic Akarita	192
Monterey	16	MSC France	132	MSC Rio Plata	162	NDS Provider	175	Nordic Laurita	192
Monteverde	44	MSC Francesca	106	MSC Romania I	108	Neches	151	Nordic Marita	192
Montreal Senato	76	MSC Gabriella	106	MSC Rosa M	108	Nedimar	184	Nordic Rio	118
Montreux	32	MSC Germany	106	MSC Rossella	108	Nedlloyd Africa	155	Nordic Sarita	192
Moorgate	141	MSC Gianna	106	MSC Sabrina	108	Nedlloyd America	155	Nordic Savonita	192
Morning Breeze	205	MSC Gina	106	MSC Salvador	162	Nedlloyd Asia	155	Nordic Spirit	190
Morning Charm	205	MSC Giorgia	106	MSC Samia	108	Nedlloyd Clarence	155	Nordic Stavanger	192
Morning Cloud	141	MSC Giovanna	106	MSC Sandra	108	Nedlloyd Clement	155	Nordic Svenita	192
Morning Light	205	MSC Giulia	106	MSC Sarah	97	Nedlloyd Europa	155	Nordic Torinita	192
Morning Prince	206	MSC Grace	106	MSC Sardinia	196	Nedlloyd Hongkong	155	Nordic Troll	192
Morning Queen	206	MSC Greece	178	MSC Sariska	108	Nedlloyd Honshu	155	Nordic Trym	192
Morning Saga	206	MSC Himalaya	106	MSC Scandinavia	77	Nedlloyd Oceania	155	Nordic Yukon	192
Morviken	118	MSC Hina	106	MSC Serena	108	Nele Maersk	116	Nordisle	150
Moscow	130	MSC Hudson	122	MSC Sharjah	108	Nelson Star	182	Nordlake	150
Moscow Kremlin	130	MSC Ilaria	107	MSC Shaula	108	Neptune Ace	112	Nordlight	150
Moscow River	130	MSC Ilona	132	MSC Sicily	56	Neptune Voyager	46	Nordmark	150
Moscow Sea	179	MSC Imma	107	MSC Sintra	110	Neptune	154	Nordmars	150
Moscow Stars	130	MSC India	107	MSC Socotra	110	Nevskiy Prospect	179	Nordmax	150
Moscow University	130	MSC Ingrid	107	MSC Sonia	110	New Ace	154	Nordmed	150
Mosel Ace	204	MSC Insa	107	MSC Sophie	110	New Alliance	154	Nordmerkur	150
Mosel N	210	MSC Ipanema	62	MSC Spain	132	New Amber	154	Nordmillennium	150
Moselle	151	MSC Ireland	107	MSC Stefania	110	New Ambition	154	Nordmoritz	150
Moskovskiy Festival	130	MSC Italy	132	MSC Suez	110	New Amity	154	Nordmosel	150
Moss	184	MSC Jade	107	MSC Switzerland	132	New Argosy	154	Nordneptune	150
Mount Fuji	78	MSC Japan	56	MSC Sydney	132	New Assurance	154	Nordocean	150
Mozu Arrow	84	MSC Jasmine	107	MSC Teresa	110	New Circassia	154	Nordpacific	150
MSC Adele	104	MSC Jessica	107	MSC Tina	110	New Confidence	122	Nordpacific	128
MSC Agata	64	MSC Jordan	107	MSC Trinidad	110	New Dynamic	122	Nordpol	150
MSC Alabama	56	MSC Katherine Ann	107	MSC Tuscany	56	New Forest	140	Nordpower	150
MSC Alessia	132	MSC Katie	107	MSC Ulsan	174	New Fortuner	154	Nordrhine	150
MSC Alexa	104	MSC Katrina	107	MSC Uruguay	164	New Nada	124	Nordscot	32
MSC Alexandra	104	MSC Kerry	107	MSC Valeria *	110	New Orient	166	Nordsky	150
MSC Algerie	178	MSC Korea	56	MSC Vanessa	110	New Valor	154	Nordstar	150
MSC Alice	104	MSC Lara	107	MSC Venice	110	New Vanguard	154	Nordstjernen	28
MSC Alpana	104	MSC Laura	107	MSC Veronique	110	New Venture	154	Nordstrand	150
MSC Alyssa	104	MSC Lauren	107	MSC Vietnam	110	New Victory	154	Nordstrength	150
MSC Amsterdam	178	MSC Laurence	107	MSC Viviana	110	New Vista	154	Nordsun	150
MSC Anahita	104	MSC Lausanne	97	MSC Yokohama	56	New Vitality	154	Nordtrave	150
MSC Anastasia	104	MSC Leanne	107	MSC Zrin	110	New York Express	56	Nordvenus	150
MSC Andalucia II	138	MSC Levina	107	MSCMexico	108	New York Highway	88	Nordvind	154
MSC Angela	104	MSC Lieselotte	107	Muirfield	200	Newport Bay	155	Nordweser	150
MSC Aniello	104	MSC Lirica	16	Mulungisi	141	Newport Bridge	88	Norfolk Express	77
MSC Annamaria	104	MSC Lisa	128	Murmansk	98	Nexø Maersk	116	Norilsk	100
MSC Ans	128	MSC London	196	Musashi Spirit	190	Nicolai Maersk	116	Norita	196
MSC Antonia	104	MSC Loretta	107	Music	175	Nicolas Delmas	62	Norman Lady	78
MSC Arabia	104	MSC Ludovica	107	Myre	184	Nicoline Maersk	116	Norna	210
MSC Ariane	104	MSC Luisa	107	Mystic	175	Nida	160	Norsea	210
MSC Arizona	97	MSC Magali	107			Niels Maersk	116	North Sea Producer	118
MSC Atlantic	104	MSC Malaysia	200	Nada V	124	Nike	46	North Star	94
MSC Atlas	162	MSC Malin	107	Naga	196	Nile	151	Northern Devotion	128
MSC Attica	56	MSC Manaus	162	Nagatino	179	Nile	208	Northern Dignity	164
MSC Augusta	104	MSC Maracaibo	148	Nagoya Bay	176	Nina Rickmers	166	Northern Distinction	128
MSC Aurora	104	MSC Maria Laura	107	Najran	198	Nina	189	Northern Fortune	164
MSC Austria	56	MSC Maria	107	Namur	54	Ningbo Star	172	Northern Magnitude	128
MSC Barbara	104	MSC Marianna	107	Nandu Arrow	84	Nippon	124	Northern Mermaid	176
MSC Belem	178	MSC Marina	107	Napa	208	Nippon Highway	88	Northgate	141
MSC Biscay	77	MSC Martina	107	Naparima	113	Nippon Maru	16	Northsea Anvil	188
MSC Boston	55	MSC Matilde	107	Napier Star	182	Nisha	73	Northsea Dowel	188
MSC Brasilia	196	MSC Maureen	132	Nariva	113	Nivosa	176	Northumberland	141
MSC Bremen	162	MSC Maya	107	Narodny Bridge	179	Nkossa II	116	Norviken	118
MSC Brianna	104	MSC Mee May	107	Natalie Bolten	38	Noa	141	Norwave	196
MSC California	202	MSC Melissa	107	Natura	70	Nobel Foam	190	Norway	22
MSC Camille	104	MSC Michaela	108	Nautic	192	Nobel Fortuna	190	Norwegian Crown	22
MSC Canberra	192	MSC Michele	108	Navarino	56	Nobel Forum	190	Norwegian Dawn	22
MSC Carina	104	MSC Mirella	108	Navigator of the Seas	18	Noble	162	Norwegian Dream	22
MSC Carla	104	MSC Monica	108	Navion Anglia	190	Nobleza	124	Norwegian Majesty	22
MSC Carmen	104	MSC Munich	132	Navion Britannia	190	Nogat	160	Norwegian Sea	22
MSC Carole	104	MSC Namibia	56	Navion Clipper	190	Noordam	8, 10	Norwegian Star	22
MSC Chelsea	106	MSC Natalia	108	Navion Europa	89	Nopal Mascot	84	Norwegian Sun	22
MSC Chiara	106	MSC Nederland	108	Navion Fennia	190	Nora Maersk	116	Norwegian Wind	22
MSC Chile	90	MSC Nerissa	108	Navion Hispania	190	Norasia Ayla	63	Norwid	158
MSC China	162	MSC New York	55	Navion Norvegia	89	Norasia Bavaria	166	Noto Gloria	168
MSC Claudia	106	MSC Nicole	108	Navion Oceania	190	Norasia Enterprise	63	Noto	208
MSC Clorinda	106	MSC Nigeria	108	Navion Saga	190	Norasia Malabar	170	Novia	60
MSC Corinna	106	MSC Noa	59	Navion Scandia	190	Norasia Sils	188	Novorossiysk	130
MSC Corsica	106	MSC Normandie	170	Navion Scotia	190	Norasia Sindh	166	Nuevo Leon	141
MSC Cristiana	106	MSC Nuria	108	Naxihe	47	Norasia Valparaiso	166	Nuri	208
MSC Daniela	106	MSC Opera	16			Nord Amalie	128	NYK Andromeda	124

Name	Page		Name	Page		Name	Page
NYK Antares	124		OOCL China	152		P&O Nedlloyd Acapulco	172
NYK Aphrodite	124		OOCL Envoy	152		P&O Nedlloyd Accra	144
NYK Apollo	124		OOCL Exporter	152		P&O Nedlloyd Aconcagua	172
NYK Aquarius	124		OOCL Fair	152		P&O Nedlloyd Adelaide	155
NYK Aretmis	124		OOCL Faith	152		P&O Nedlloyd Adriana	155
NYK Argus	124		OOCL Fidelity	152		P&O Nedlloyd Agulhas	144
NYK Athena	124		OOCL Fortune	152		P&O Nedlloyd Algoa	144
NYK Canopus	124		OOCL France	126		P&O Nedlloyd Altiplano	175
NYK Castor	124		OOCL Freedom	152		P&O Nedlloyd Andes	172
NYK Fantasia	136		OOCL Friendship	152		P&O Nedlloyd Antisana	172
NYK Freesia	128		OOCL Germany	126		P&O Nedlloyd Apapa	144
NYK Kai	124		OOCL Harmony	77		P&O Nedlloyd Atacama	172
NYK Leo	124		OOCL Hong Kong	152		P&O Nedlloyd Auckland	155
NYK Libra	124		OOCL Japan	152		P&O Nedlloyd Bantam	144
NYK Loadstar	124		OOCL Korea	144		P&O Nedlloyd Barentsz	155
NYK Lynx	124		OOCL Long Beach	152		P&O Nedlloyd Barossa Valley	155
NYK Lyra	124		OOCL Los Angeles	126		P&O Nedlloyd Beirut	132
NYK Pasion	169		OOCL Malaysia	126		P&O Nedlloyd Botany	144
NYK Pegasus	124		OOCL Melbourne	152		P&O Nedlloyd Brisbane	156
NYK Phoenix	124		OOCL Montreal	152		P&O Nedlloyd Brunel	162
NYK Pride	83		OOCL Netherlands	152		P&O Nedlloyd Buenos Aires	156
NYK Procyon	124		OOCL New York	126		P&O Nedlloyd Calypso	206
NYK Prosperity	211		OOCL Ningpo	152		P&O Nedlloyd Caracas	59
NYK Sirius	124		OOCL Osaka	152		P&O Nedlloyd Caribbean	59
NYK Springtide	124		OOCL Rotterdam	152		P&O Nedlloyd Chania	162
NYK Starlight	124		OOCL San Francisco	152		P&O Nedlloyd Chicago	77
Nyon	188		OOCL Shanghai	126		P&O Nedlloyd Chusan	144
Nysa	208		OOCL Shenzhen	154		P&O Nedlloyd Cobra	77
Nysted Maersk	116		OOCL Singapore	154		P&O Nedlloyd Coleridge	162
			OOCL Sydney	154		P&O Nedlloyd Cook	156
Obbola	72		OOCL Thailand	144		P&O Nedlloyd Curacao	174
Ocean Atlantic	211		OOCL Xiamen	154		P&O Nedlloyd Damietta	128
Ocean Countess	28		Oosterdam	10		P&O Nedlloyd Dejima	144
Ocean Explorer I	28		Opal Queen	196		P&O Nedlloyd Drake	156
Ocean Genius	211		Opalia	72		P&O Nedlloyd Dubai	211
Ocean Gulf	211		Orange Blossom	37		P&O Nedlloyd Encounter	144
Ocean Highway	88		Orange Sky	37		P&O Nedlloyd Genoa	156
Ocean Luna	211		Orange Star	37		P&O Nedlloyd Houston	156
Ocean Majesty	28		Orange Wave	37		P&O Nedlloyd Houtman	156
Ocean Monarch	28		Oranje	118		P&O Nedlloyd Hudson	156
Ocean Princess	190		Ori A	138		P&O Nedlloyd Hunter Valley	132
Ocean Spirit	112		Oriana	10		P&O Nedlloyd Inca	172
Ocean Starlight	211		Orient Venus	28		P&O Nedlloyd Jakarta	156
Ocean Trader	44		Oriental Bay	155		P&O Nedlloyd Juliana	156
Ocean Village	10		Oriental Green	81		P&O Nedlloyd Kilindini	196
Oceana	10		Oriental Highway	88		P&O Nedlloyd Kobe	155
Oceanic	18		Oriental Phoenix	112		P&O Nedlloyd Kowloon	156
Oceanida	196		Oriental Venture	113		P&O Nedlloyd Los Angeles	156
Oder Trader	44		Orion Diamond	124		P&O Nedlloyd Magellan	126
Odessa	24		Orion Highway	88		P&O Nedlloyd Mahe	166
Odin	154		Orion Leader	124		P&O Nedlloyd Mairangi	144
Odra	160		Orion Reefer	124		P&O Nedlloyd Malindi	86
Odysseus	14		Orion Star	169		P&O Nedlloyd Marita	156
Ohio	151		Orion Trader	113		P&O Nedlloyd Marseille	156
Ohminesan	113		Orion Voyager	46		P&O Nedlloyd Mercator	156
Oinoussian Spirit	190		Orion	34		P&O Nedlloyd Nelson	97
Ojars Vacietis	92		Orkney Spirit	190		P&O Nedlloyd Newark	132
Okhotsk Sea	179		Orla	160		P&O Nedlloyd Nina	156
Okhta Bridge	179		Orleta Lwowskie	160		P&O Nedlloyd Olinda	144
Okoitchitza	121		Ormond	140		P&O Nedlloyd Palliser	144
Oksywie	160		Orontes	151		P&O Nedlloyd Panama	83
Olga	92		Orsula	68		P&O Nedlloyd Pantanal	169
Olga Maersk	116		Ortviken	72		P&O Nedlloyd Pessoa	156
Oliver Jacob	83		Oscilla	72		P&O Nedlloyd Pinta	141
Olivia Maersk	116		Osprey Arrow	84		P&O Nedlloyd Regina	144
Oluf Maersk	116		Osprey	68		P&O Nedlloyd Remuera	144
Olympia	154		Ostankino	179		P&O Nedlloyd Rotterdam	156
Olympia Explorer	14		Ostrand	72		P&O Nedlloyd Salsa	144
Olympia Voyager	16		Otello	204		P&O Nedlloyd Samba	144
Olympian Highway	88		Ottawa	151		P&O Nedlloyd San Francisco	32
Olympic Faith	152		Ouro do Brasil	138		P&O Nedlloyd Seattle	144
Olympic Flair	152		Oval Nova	168		P&O Nedlloyd Shackleton	156
Olympic Galaxy	152		Overseas Ann	154		P&O Nedlloyd Singapore	144
Olympic Legacy	152		Overseas Boston	154		P&O Nedlloyd Southampton	156
Olympic Legend	152		Overseas Cathy	154		P&O Nedlloyd Stuyvesant	156
Olympic Liberty	152		Overseas Chicago	154		P&O Nedlloyd Surat	156
Olympic Loyalty	152		Overseas Chris	154		P&O Nedlloyd Sydney	156
Olympic Melody	152		Overseas Donna	154		P&O Nedlloyd Takoradi	174
Olympic Mentor	152		Overseas Fran	154		P&O Nedlloyd Taranaki	156
Olympic Merit	152		Overseas Harriette	155		P&O Nedlloyd Tasman	156
Olympic Miracle	152		Overseas Josefa Camejo	155		P&O Nedlloyd Tema	144
Olympic Serenity	152		Overseas Joyce	155		P&O Nedlloyd Thekwini	172
Olympic Spirit II	152		Overseas Marilyn	155		P&O Nedlloyd Torres	156
Olympic Sponsor	152		Overseas Mulan	155		P&O Nedlloyd Valentina	156
Olympic Symphony	152		Overseas New Orleans	155		P&O Nedlloyd Veracruz	156
Omar III	24		Overseas New York	155		P&O Nedlloyd Vespucci	126
Onozo Spirit	190		Overseas Philadelphia	155		P&O Nedlloyd Xiamen	141
OOCL Ability	152		Overseas Portland	155		P&O Nedlloyd Yarra Valley	83
OOCL Acclaim	152		Overseas Rosalyn	155		Pacdream	51
OOCL Ambition	152		Overseas Shirley	155		Pacific Aries	124
OOCL America	152		Overseas Sophie	155		Pacific Breeze	204
OOCL Authority	152		Overseas Washington	155		Pacific Bridge	59
OOCL Belgium	152		Oxford	200		Pacific Century	168
OOCL Britain	152		Oxfordshire	38			
OOCL California	152						
OOCL Chicago	152		P&O Nedlloyd Abidjan	144			

Name	Page		Name	Page
Pacific Champ	81		Perth	200
Pacific Courage	81		Peruvian Reefer	94
Pacific Enterprise	154		Peter Maersk	116
Pacific Explorer	55		Petersfield	84
Pacific Highway	88		Petimata OT RMS	121
Pacific Lagoon	72		Petrel Arrow	84
Pacific Leader	124		Petroatlantic	192
Pacific Link	132		Petrodvorets	179
Pacific Navigator	154		Petrokrepost	179
Pacific Princess	12		Petromar	184
Pacific Prosperity	175		Petronordic	192
Pacific Quest	141		Petropavlovsk	179
Pacific Reefer	94		Petroskald	192
Pacific Royal	81		Petrovsk	179
Pacific Ruby	155		Petrozavodsk	179
Pacific Sapphire	155		Peyo Yavorov	121
Pacific Senator	76		Phayao Navee	198
Pacific Sky	12		Pherkad Star	169
Pacific Spirit	190		Philipp Schulte	174
Pacific Success	81		Philippe LD	98
Pacific Trader	44		Philippine Star	138
Pacific Venus	28		Phoenix Diamond	124
Pacific Vitality	154		Phoenix Star	169
Pacific Wave	113		Phoenix Voyager	46
Pacific Winner	55		Pierre LD	98
Pacific	176		Pilgrim	92
Pacific	18		Pilica	160
Paclogger	51		Pine Arrow	84
Pacmonarch	166		Pioneer Express	202
Pacocean	51		Pioneer Leader	125
Pacrose	51		Pioneer	55
Pacsea	51		Pisces Star	169
Pacstar	51		Pittsburg	92
Pacsun	51		Plana	121
Pactimber	51		Planet Ace	112
Pactol River	83		Planter	60
Pactrader	51		Platinium Ray	206
Palmerston	190		Plovdiv	121
Palmstar Cherry	190		Plover Arrow	86
Palmstar Lotus	190		Pluto	34
Palmstar Orchid	190		Pob(y)eda	130
Palmstar Poppy	190		Pochard	78
Palmstar Rose	190		Poetic	94
Palmstar Thistle	190		Pohang Senator	76
Paloma I	26		Pokoj	158
Palva	70		Polar Argentina	136, 182
Pamir	130		Polar Brazil	136, 182
Panama	92		Polar Chile	136
Panatlantic	126		Polar Colombia	136
Panos G	196		Polar Ecuador	136
Papendrecht	51		Polar Uruguay	136
Paradise N	92		Polaris Ace	112
Paradise	8		Polaris Star	169
Paris	92		Polaris	28
Paris Express	77		Polarlicht	176
Paros	38		Polarsteam	176
Parthenon	196		Pole	122
Pascale Knutsen	89		Pollux	34
Patmos Senator	76		Pols Robsons	92
Patricia Delmas	62		Polska Walczaca	160
Patriot	204		Polyanka	179
Patriot	55		Polys	184
Pattaya Navee	198		Polystar	155
Paul Gauguin	18		Pomorze Zachodnie	160
Paul Oldendorff	148		Port Said Senator	76
Paul Rickmers	166		Portel	179
Paula Maersk	116		Porthos	196
Pavel Vavilov	100		Portland Senator	128
Pearl Ace	112		Porto Cervo	46
Pearl Ray	206		Portugal Senator	76
Pearlmar	184		Pos Challenger	81
Pecos	151		Pos Harvester	81
Pegasus Ace	112		Potomac Bridge	128
Pegasus Diamond	124		Potomac	151
Pegasus Highway	88		Poul Spirit	190
Pegasus Leader	124		Powhatan	92
Pegasus	34		Powstaniec Listopadowy	160
Peggy Dow	141		Powstaniec Styczniowy	160
Peking Senator	128		Premium do Brasil	138
Pelat	110		President Adams	122
Pelican Arrow	84		President Grant	122
Pella	196		President Jackson	122
Penang Senator	128		President Polk	122
Pendrecht	51		President Truman	122
Peneda	179		President Wilson	122
Penelope	160		Presnya	179
Penguin Arrow	84		Pretty River	47
Peninsular Bay	156		Pride	92
Peoria	78		Pride of Aloha	22
Pequot	92		Pride of America	22
Perelik	121		Prigipos	83
Perm	98		Primar	184
Pernas Amang	102		Prince of Seas	176
Persenk	121		Prince of Streams	176
Perseus Leader	124		Prince of Tides	176
Perseus Trader	113		Prince of Waves	176

222

Siri Phatra	37	Spring Bear	176	Stolt Avenir	186	Sylt	208	Thies Maersk	117		
Sirius Highway	88	Spring Bob	176	Stolt Capability	186	Synnove Knutsen	89	Thomas Maersk	118		
Sirius Leader	125	Spring Bok	176	Stolt Concept	186	Szare Szeregi	160	Thomson Spirit	22		
Sirius Voyager	47	Spring Deli	176	Stolt Condor	186	Szymanowski	158	Thornbury	100		
Sirius	34	Spring Dragon	176	Stolt Confidence	186			Thurø Maersk	117		
Siskin Arrow	86	Spring Hawk	55	Stolt Creativity	186	Taganrog	130	Tiger Bridge	142		
Sitacamilla	189	Spring Panda	176	Stolt Dorset	38	Tagus	204	Tiger Cloud	90		
Sitakathrine	189	Spring Tiger	176	Stolt Eagle	186	Tahitian Princess	12	Tiger Shark	142		
Sitamarie	189	Springwood	142	Stolt Efficiency	186	Tai He	48	Tiger Sky	128		
Sitamia	189	Spruce Arrow	86	Stolt Effort	186	Tai Shan	204	Tikhoretsk	130		
Sitavera	189	Spuigracht	180	Stolt Emerald	186	Taiko	204	Tikhvin	130		
Sitria	189	St. Katharinen	34	Stolt Excellence	186	Taixing	158	Tim Buck	100		
Sivega	189	St. Lucia	94	Stolt Falcon	186	Taizan	125	Timashevsk	130		
Skagen Maersk	117	Stadiongracht	180	Stolt Guardian	186	Tajima	125	Tineke	142		
Skauboard	83	Stafford	142	Stolt Hawk	186	Takachiho II	125	Tinglev Maersk	118		
Skaubryn	206	Stanislaw Kulczynski	160	Stolt Helluland	186	Takamar	184	Tinos	40		
Skaugran	206	Star Alabama	207	Stolt Heron	186	Takamatsu Maru	125	Titus	204		
Skausund	176	Star Altanger	207	Stolt Innovation	186	Takara	204	Tjore Fremgang	196		
SKS Mersey	84	Star America	207	Stolt Inspiration	186	Takasago Maru	125	TMM Campeche	59		
SKS Mosel	84	Star Atlantic	207	Stolt Integrity	186	Takasago	204	TMM Chiapas	97		
SKS Saluda	84	Star Austanger	207	Stolt Invention	186	Takasuzu	125	TMM Colima	59		
SKS Senne	170	Star Canopus	207	Stolt Jade	186	Takayama	204	TMM Guanajuato	59		
SKS Sinni	170	Star Clipper	20	Stolt Kent	38	Talabot	204	TMM Hermosillo	59		
SKS Sira	170	Star Davanger	207	Stolt Loyalty	186	Talisman	204	TMM Hidalg	90		
SKS Tagus	84	Star Derby	207	Stolt Markland	186	Talty	160	TMM Jalisco	59		
SKS Tana	84	Star Dieppe	207	Stolt Nanami	186	Tama Hope	176	TMM Monterey	138		
SKS Tanaro	84	Star Djervanger	207	Stolt Osprey	186	Tama Star	176	TMM Sinaloa	59		
SKS Tiete	84	Star Dover	207	Stolt Perseverance	186	Taman	130	TMM Sonora	142		
SKS Torrens	84	Star Drivanger	207	Stolt Pride	186	Tamar	151	TMM Tabasco	59		
SKS Trent	84	Star Drottanger	207	Stolt Protector	186	Tamarita	196	TMM Yucatan	59		
SKS Trinity	84	Star Eagle	207	Stolt Sapphire	186	Tambov	130	Toba	204		
SKS Tugela	84	Star Evanger	207	Stolt Sea	186	Tamerlane	204	Tobias Maersk	118		
SKS Tweed	84	Star Evviva	207	Stolt Sincerity	186	Tamesis	204	Togo Star	166		
SKS Tyne	84	Star Florida	207	Stolt Span	186	Tampa	204	Tohdoh	125		
Skulptors Tomskis	92	Star Flyer	20	Stolt Spray	186	Tampere	204	Tokachi	125		
Sky L	36	Star Fraser	207	Stolt Stream	186	Tamyra	196	Toki Arrow	86		
Slavianka	121	Star Fuji	207	Stolt Sun	186	Tanabe	155	Tokyo Bay	176		
Slotergracht	180	Star Geiranger	207	Stolt Surf	186	Tancred	204	Tokyo Express	78		
Sluisgracht	180	Star Gran	207	Stolt Tenacity	186	Tandjung Ayu	151	Tokyo Highway	88		
Snoekgracht	180	Star Grindanger	207	Stolt Topaz	186	Tanja Jacob	83	Tolteca	201		
Snowdon	140	Star Grip	207	Stolt Valor	186	Taos	208	Tolten	55		
Sochi	130	Star Hansa	207	Stolt Vestland	186	Tapiola	204	Tomsk	130		
Sofia	121	Star Hardanger	207	Stolt Vinland	188	Tarago	204	Tonsina	155		
Sofie Maersk	117	Star Harmonia	207	Stonegate	142	Taronga	204	Topaz Ray	206		
Sokolniki	179	Star Heranger	207	Stones	32	Tasco	204	Topaz	94		
Sol do Brasil	138	Star Herdla	207	Storm Bay	176	Tåsinge Maersk	117	Torben Maersk	118		
Solar Wing	113	Star Hidra	207	Stove Campbell	37	Tasman Adventurer	148	Torben Spirit	190		
Solaris	176	Star Hosanger	207	Stove Trader	37	Tasman Discoverer	148	Tordis Knutsen	89		
Solent Star	182	Star Hoyanger	207	Stove Tradition	37	Tasman Endeavour	170	Torill Knutsen	89		
Solidarnosc	160	Star Ikebana	207	Stove Transport	37	Tasman Provider	170	Torm Alice	192		
Solviken	118	Star Indiana	207	Stuttgart Express	78	Tasman Explorer	148	Torm Anna	192		
Somerset	142	Star Inventana	207	Suez Canal Bridge	88	Tasman Mariner	148	Torm Anne	192		
Somjin	151	Star Isfjord	207	Suffolk	142	Tasman Navigator	148	Torm Ann-Marie	192		
Song He	48	Star Ismene	207	Suhail Star	169	Tasman Trader	34	Torm Arawa	192		
Song Yun He	48	Star Isoldana	207	Sulu Warrior	102	Tasman Voyager	148	Torm Asia	192		
Sophia Britannia	56	Star Istind	207	Summer Bay	94	Tateyama	125	Torm Baltic	192		
Sophie Oldendorff	148	Star Langanger	207	Summer Flower	94	Taunton	140	Torm Estrid	192		
Sophie Schulte	174	Star Leikanger	207	Summer Meadow	94	Tauranga Star	182	Torm Freya	192		
Sorø Maersk	117	Star Ohio	47	Summer Phoenix	142	Tausala Samoa	86	Torm Gerd	192		
Soro	208	Star Okiana	207	Summer Wind	94	Tavi	70	Torm Gertrud	192		
Sorokaletiye Pobedy	130	Star Optimana	207	Summit	20	Teal Arrow	86	Torm Gotland	192		
Sotka	70	Star Osakana	207	Sun Ace	113	Teal	62	Torm Gudrun	192		
Sotra Spirit	190	Star Oshimana	207	Sun Princess	12	Team		Torm Gunhild	192		
Southampton Star	182	Star Pisces	22	Sun Suma	86	Team Actinia	38	Torm Helene	192		
Southern Harvest	125	Star Polaris	207	Sun Voyager	47	Team Anemonia	38	Torm Herdis	192		
Southgate	142	Star Pollux	207	Sunbird	16	Team Aniara	38	Torm Hilde	192		
Sovereign Maersk	117	Star Princess	12	Sundream	16	Team Anmaj	38	Torm Ingeborg	192		
Sovereign of the Seas	18	Star Siranger	208	Sungreen	166	Team Jupiter	38	Torm Kristina	192		
Sovereign Unity	155	Star Trondanger	208	Suomigracht	180	Team Mars	38	Torm Margrethe	192		
Spaarnegracht	180	Statendam	10	Super Adventure	37	Team Merkur	38	Torm Marina	192		
Spar Capella	180	Stellar Voyager	47	Super Challenge	37	Team Neptun	38	Torm Marlene	192		
Spar Carina	180	Stena Alexita	184	Super Servant 3	62	Team Saturn	38	Torm Marta	192		
Spar Cetus	180	Stena Commander	184	Super Servant 4	62	Tecam Sea	70	Torm Mary	192		
Spar Corona	180	Stena Companion	186	SuperStar Aries	18	Teekay Spirit	190	Torm Pacific	192		
Spar Eight	180	Stena Compatriot	186	SuperStar Capricorn	22	Teignbank	188	Torm Ragnhild	192		
Spar Emerald	180	Stena Concord	130	SuperStar Gemini	22	Tempera	70	Torm Rotna	192		
Spar Garnet	180	Stena Conductor	186	SuperStar Leo	22	Temryuk	130	Torm Tekla	194		
Spar Jade	180	Stena Confidence	186	SuperStar Virgo	22	Tenacity	194	Torm Thyra	194		
Spar Lupus	180	Stena Conqueror	186	Supreme Harvest	125	Teng He	48	Torm Tina	194		
Spar Opal	180	Stena Conquest	186	Surenes	32	Tenryu	125	Torm Valborg	194		
Spar Orion	180	Stena Consul	130	Surrey	142	Tern Arrow	86	Torm Vita	194		
Spar Ruby	180	Stena Contender	179	Susan Maersk	117	Tern	62	Torres Spirit	190		
Spar Sirius	180	Stena Episkopi	184	Sussex	142	Terrier	204	Tosca	204		
Spar Three	180	Stena Natalita	192	Suva	208	Tervi	70	Toucan Arrow	86		
Spar Topaz	180	Stena Paris	186	Svend Maersk	117	Tete Oldendorff	148	Toula Z	196		
Spar Two	180	Stena Provence	186	Svendborg Maersk	117	Tete Rickmers	166	Touraine	54		
Spectrum	178	Stena Sirita	186	Svilen Russev	121	Texas Highway	88	Tourcoing	204		
Speybank	188	Stena Spirit	190	Swakop	64	Texas	204	Tove Knutsen	89		
Spiegelgracht	180	Stena Venture	186	Swan	62	Thai Bright	198	Tove Maersk	117		
Spirit of Oceanus	24	Stena Victory	186	Swan Arrow	86	Thai Dawn	198	Tower Bridge	88		
Spirit	10	Stena Vision	186	Swan Bay	182	The Azur	14	Trade Bravery	194		
Splendid Ace	113	Stepan Razin	100	Swan Chacabuco	182	The Emerald	14	Trade Eternity	178		
Splendid Harvest	125	Steven N	210	Swan River	182	The Topaz	28	Trade Rainbow	151		
Splendour of the Seas	18	Stolt Achievement	186	Swift	62	The World	30	Trade Zale	194		
Splittnes	32	Stolt Aquamarine	186	Swift Arrow	86	Themsestern	168	Trader	194		
Sponsalis	178	Stolt Avance	186	Sydney Express	146	Theodor Oldendorff	148	Trans Friendship	178